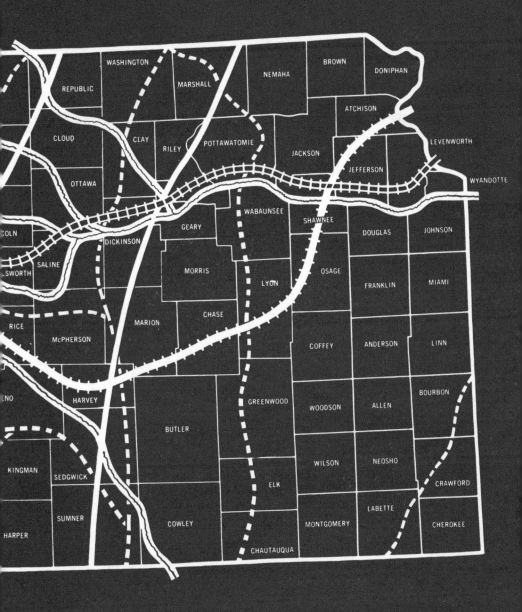

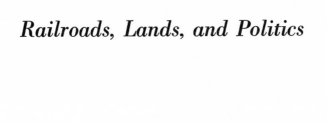

Railroads, Lands, and Politics

RAILROADS, LANDS, AND POLITICS

The Taxation of the Railroad Land Grants, 1864–1897

Leslie E. Decker

AMERICAN HISTORY RESEARCH CENTER

Brown University Press

Providence, Rhode Island

1964

39565

LIBRARY OF CONGRESS CATALOG CARD NUMBER: 64–11940

COPYRIGHT © 1964

BROWN UNIVERSITY

SECOND PRINTING, 1966

MAPS BY AUBREY GREENWALD, JR., AND CLAUDE WESTFALL

PRINTED IN THE UNITED STATES OF AMERICA BY

THE GEORGE BANTA COMPANY, INC., MENASHA, WISCONSIN

to

P W G

who knows

and

E W D

who understands

Acknowledgment

For the gifts of information, insight, skill, patience, or fortitude each supplied somewhere along the way I thank Paul Wallace Gates and James C. Malin, John G. B. Hutchins and George L. Anderson, Edward Whiting Fox and Forrest McDonald; Jane F. Smith and Maurice Moore; Nyle Miller, Robert Richardson, and Lela Barnes; John B. White and Stanley Pargellis; E. C. Schmidt, Arthur Parsons, Jr., Elizabeth O. Cullen, Harry L. Eddy, and Millicent J. Ayton; Robert S. Henry and Carleton Corliss; Edwin C. Shafer, Oscar W. Youngberg, and Keith M. Teague; Frederick W. Crum and F. Roger Dunn; Mayfred Stimming and Edith L. Hary; Mike Glowacki, Connie Newman, Pat McArdle, and Wynne Hollinshead; Helen Ober, Sylvia Coupe, and Ellen Shapiro McDonald; and —finally—Miss Livia Appel, a great editor and a greater lady.

September, 1962, Salem, Maine   LESLIE E. DECKER

Contents

TABLES

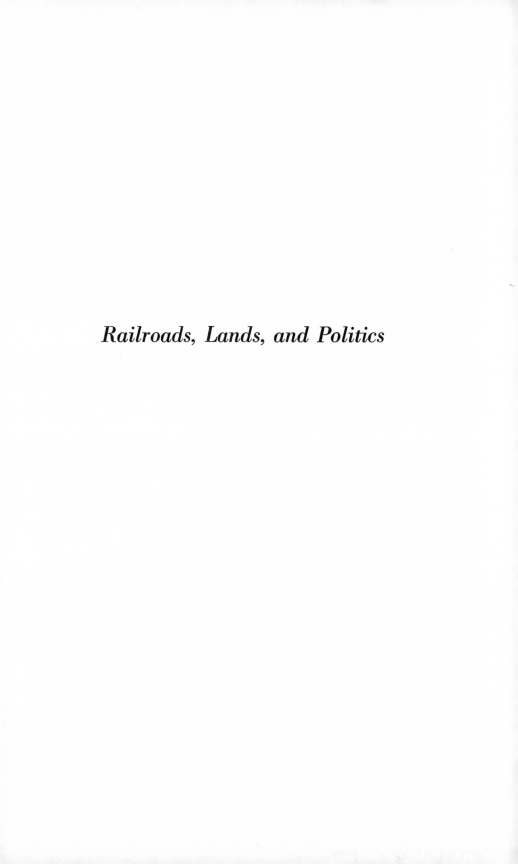

Railroads, Lands, and Politics

One

An Apology

THIS book is not history. Nor is it a history. It is not even a commentary on the study of history. It can be described only as a study in history. It abstracts from the total past a geographically and chronologically delineated segment and from that segment an analytically isolated part. It seeks out, organizes, and analyzes the relics. It reports. Nowhere does it say explicitly—though it does so implicitly in every line—anything about the study of history. It is, in short, a monograph. And, like all but a blessed few such efforts, it leaves to its reader the task of locating the study and the student within the historiographical traditions they follow, and it makes no coherent presentation of its methodological assumptions or of the methodological lessons it teaches.

But if scholars are to avoid relearning old truths with each generation and from scratch, they must tell not only what they found but also how and why they found it; and if they have made mistakes, they must identify them, account for them, and undertake to correct them. These in themselves are old truths, and historians have at various times undertaken to fulfill the obligation. But almost invariably they have done so in after-dinner speeches and potboilers, not in their serious works.

This divorce of theory and practice has evoked a curious duality. On the one hand, most practicing historians—having imbibed the great systems and non-systems of the theoreticians and having watched (or participated in) the classic debates among objectivists, subjectivists, relativists, presentists, and scientists—carry in their baggage a large collection of abstract assumptions and what can only be called revealed truths. On the other hand, these same historians do their research and write as if the only truth was in the record and the only aim the truth. They say that any ideal of reconstruction, even in part, is impossible, yet they strive with remarkable tenacity to attain that ideal. This paradoxical approach does little harm, to most historians. After all, to know what he seeks but not to say he seeks it, or to say that he seeks it not, is as common a characteristic of the prospector as it is of the alchemist.

To most of the "old pros," then, theorizing can be, and usually is, a pleasant exercise in imagination, essentially unrelated to life in the rough. But to the fledgling such seemingly harmless games can be misleading. Just as he begins his struggle with the substantive record, begins learning his way around relics, he is dumped into a morass of theory and counter-theory, of interpretation and counter-interpretation. Always he is confused; often he gets hopelessly lost. Sometimes he never comes out, spending his fruitful years wandering in the wasteland of theory divorced from practice, writing commentaries on the commentaries, and endlessly debating at any provocation all the meaningless issues from other days. More often he does emerge, does do his bit of digging, does add something to the pile. Yet too frequently he comes out marked, his work distorted by a perverted sense of relevance. Either he does his work with direct reference to a great system or hypothesis and sees all he does in its terms (seeking to prove or disprove, alter or amend a preconceived proposition), or he relates all he does to the solution of present problems, to the making of policy (seeking to become a social scientist, a soothsayer and priest). So he studies the Beard thesis or the Turner hypothesis or the class struggle, or he studies one or any combination of *isms*—from capital to constitutional, from urban to agrarian. He does not study the past. He makes Roger Williams and Thomas Jefferson Democrats; he makes the workingmen of the 1830's Proletarians; he makes the Western radicals of the 1890's Fascists. He views the frontier as an Underdeveloped Area and Negro slavery as Racial Segregation. This is not history.

Some fledglings—many more than the Jeremiahs admit—not only hack a way through the morass but become historians as well. That they make it is most emphatically not the result of superior intelligence, greater dedication, or deeper insight. It is the result of a combination of good fortune and avid curiosity. For their salvation is simply this: the substantive record comes to dominate them. Having fallen into or having been directed toward a problem from the past, each ultimately discovers that there are no problems from the past, only past problems; that, in other words, any part of the past is a thing-in-itself to be known and understood, not a riddle to be solved, a lesson for the present, or a map for the future. Then, having discovered the past for what it is, each seeks to know a part of it and to evaluate that part in its own terms. Driven by an insatiable curiosity and an obligation bred from respect, each seeks the only legitimate end of the study of history: from the faint tracings left in the record by its presence to understand a part of the past and to communicate that understanding to others. This is history.

And thereby hangs the tale of the origin, construction, and final decision to publish this monograph, as is, even though it is not history.

In the realm of theory: Two traditions dominate the historiography of the trans-Mississippi West, the Populist and the Positivist. The Populists admitted neither moral nor economic relativity. Their stated view of the origin of the evils that beset them, and therefore their stated remedy for those evils, was precise, uncomplicated, unshadowed. The Positivists held that "scientific" fact is the only basis of knowledge, that the study of phenomena is the only source of truth, that, in other words, all things explicable can be explained in terms of concrete factors with direct and describable connectives. Nothing happens without a cause and all causes have effects. The simplicity and authority of these two points of view captivated Western historians, and for more than half a century they discussed the peopling and the politics of the mid-continent area in Populist-Positivist terms. But the causal webs they spun became their fetters, not because there was anything wrong with seeking causes but because the causes they sought were the unsubtle, unshadowed phenomena of Populist tradition.

The Turnerians showed the way. The simplicity, precision, moralism, and clear causal descriptions of their spatial diagnosis made explication easy and challenge all but impossible. If their dynamic explained the institutional peculiarities and political vagaries of the West, its disappearance explained the revolt of the "agrarians." Given the set of idealized institutions the Turnerians had created, it was but a small step to an explanation of Western institutional weaknesses as part of the same causal structure. If the frontier process had produced the ideal American types, the small agricultural freeholder and the village businessman, it had produced another American type, the capitalist buccaneer. The Western political and institutional arena was the scene of a great conflict, mightily intensified with the approaching end of the frontier, between two groups born of the same soil. Thus the force that produced the "Agrarian Revolt" was the force the Populists said produced it: the struggle between the grasping (and usually victorious) Robber Barons and the anxious and honorable Pioneers.

For more than a generation the Turnerian diagnosis went all but unchallenged as theory; and when it was called to serious account by the theoreticians, in the 1930's and thereafter, the accounting was in the same Populist-Positivist tradition. The inevitable result was a series of simple inversions. For the frontier safety valve was substituted the urban; for the struggle for land, the class struggle; for heterodoxy, orthodoxy; for individualism, cooperation; for American uniqueness, comparative similarity to other parts of the world; for grass-roots democracy, grass-roots fascism; for lines of frontier advance, islands of settlement and influence; for westward migration, simply migration; and so on, ad infinitum. All that happened, with one or two exceptions, was the exchange of one unshadowed and single-factoral causal web for another. Each novel approach found its champions and the battle flared anew with each fresh proposal. Sometimes it seemed that "freshness" had become an end in itself.

In the realm of practice: Historians, while they continued to view the settlement of the trans-Mississippi country as, in Turner's words, "a social process," were not content to leave it at that. They sought to dissect the process and to analyze its components. And dissect and analyze they did. A myriad of avenues was explored. The political, economic, business, social, and many another approach had its day. Segment after segment of Western history was studied. Migration and mortgages, building materials and fencing costs, landlords and tenants, speculation and peculation, railroad rates and money values and elevator practices, ethnic groups and folk traditions, language development, geographic and climatic influences, individual lives and episodes by the score, constitutional practices and changes, political parties and grievances and leadership, federal policy in all its ramifications, and many, many more were carefully scrutinized.

From the study of these special elements there flowed a stream of specialized works and a plethora of widely accepted generalizations: a consensus history of the West—piecemeal and appallingly uneven, but a consensus nonetheless. For practical purposes this is the history that is studied and taught—with varying emphasis and bitter wrangles, to be sure—by most of those who describe themselves as Western historians. It is also, perforce, the substantive starting point for the fledgling's study of Western history. In the realm of theory and interpretation the Robber Barons and the Pioneers still vie, but in the realm of practical historical studies the depth and complexity of the contest is appreciated, and single-factoral causal structures are condemned. For example, hardly a practicing Western historian would take issue with the proposition that the social and political history of the trans-Mississippi West is inseparable from the history of land settlement and utilization on the one hand and the history of railroad development and policy on the other; that the course of frontier development is as expressible in acres privately held, ton miles, numbers of public officeholders, and gross public revenues as it is in changing occupations, social types, and political ideals.

As for this monograph: The specialists have long recognized the interrelationships of politics, lands, and railroads. Political historians, students of Greenbackers and Grangers and Populists, have seen the railroads in a multiple role: as competitors for land, as political overlords, and as economic masters. Land historians have seen railroads functioning as land-sellers as well as transportation agencies. With notable exceptions railroad historians, like most business historians, have written much of management and little of the context of management's actions, but even they have found politics and the politics of landownership common considerations in decisions at the managerial level. Each specialist has been forced to deal, directly or indirectly, in and with the Populist-Positivist tradition, but beyond that common ground specialization has rarely gone. Recognition of these relationships has not normally produced the study of them.

The taxation of the railroad land grants is a specialized subject, but it is also a study in relationships. In all these standard fields of special inquiry—railroads, lands, and politics—taxation is a common theme. In nineteenth-century America, and especially in Western America, land and improvements on the land bore the burden of taxation. And west of the Mississippi, in every state but one, railroads held a substantial portion of that land. Together the several levels of government had legislated more than two hundred and forty million acres to the railroads, most of them west of the river. For various reasons the roads actually received only about a hundred and seventy million acres, yet even this, in the abstract at least, was a princely estate. Thus the Western railroads, both as owners of land and as transportation companies, were ordinarily liable for a share of taxes. What share they paid and the grace with which they paid it was an element in their relations with other landowners, with local businessmen, and with the political climate, an element that could have been as important to their well-being and that of their hinterlands as the rates they charged or the service they gave.

By 1871 the land-granting era was over and the railroads were in trouble. The congressional coffers were closed. Railroad abuses were being publicized. Major controversy in the courts, the Congress, and the press over the settlement of the railroad debts to the government, over the reversal of the granting policy, and over the taxation of the granted lands had its beginnings. At the same time the Grangers were moving west and anti-monopoly politics were becoming popular. The attitude of the public toward railroads was undergoing violent change. In the early years of railroad promotion no praise of them had been too extravagant; railroad development had been eulogized regularly in the speeches of Western public officials and in the editorials of Western newspapers; public aid had been granted willingly, almost eagerly. Now such aid ceased, at least on the federal and state levels (localities continued to vote bond aid throughout the period), and the eulogies gave place to indictments. Railroads became the favorite target of the anti-monopoly press and the reform politicians. Eventually they also became the subjects of restrictive and regulatory legislation.

For more than twenty years the railroads stayed in trouble. And only part of their political troubles stemmed from their allegedly exorbitant and discriminatory rates. For these railroads were more than transportation companies: they were landowning neighbors of many of the "agrarians" who were in revolt against them. If they were good neighbors—if they paid their share of the taxes and treated the buyers of their lands and the settlers on the adjacent public domain well—then the cause for complaint might indeed have been transportation or political policies rather than land policies. If they were bad neighbors—if they avoided or refused to pay their share of taxes, foreclosed on and ejected delinquent land buyers, and interfered in local government— then the cause for complaint might have been land policies and local politics rather than, or in addition to, transportation policies.

Many contemporaries saw and many historians have since seen just such a connection between railroad land and tax policies and the change in popular attitudes. Such practices as high pricing, speculative purchasing of Indian reserves and of neighboring public lands, and large sales to speculators, bonanza farmers, cattlemen, and lumber and mining interests were all condemned. But among the most persistent criticisms was that directed against the land-tax policies of a few of the early federal-through-state-grant roads and against those of nearly all the later direct-federal-grant corporations. The Illinois Central and some of the other federal-through-state-grant roads had been given some degree of statutory tax exemption through state legislation. The direct-grant roads had not received tax exemption directly, but by 1872 judicial interpretation of the granting acts had extended the privilege to a portion of the lands of some of them and, in combination with further legislation, eventually extended it to most other direct-grant roads.

Reformers were especially critical of these direct-grant exemptions, for they saw in them attempts to bilk Western states and counties of much-needed tax revenues and to force the poor settlers on non-grant lands to pay all those that were collectable. Furthermore, because exemptions for these direct-grant lands hinged upon whether the title had legally passed from the government to the railroads and because, in the reform view, the railroads could obtain that legal title as rapidly as they wanted it, the principal fault must lie with the railroad managers. The railroadmen defended themselves against these charges of conspiracy and malintent and pressed countercharges of misrepresentation, political haymaking, breach of contract, and confiscation. For almost fourteen years the debate appeared and reappeared in Congress, in local politics, and in the press until, finally (and after most of the effects of the exemptions had run their course), a law making these lands liable for taxes whether the roads had received legal title or not concluded the contest with an apparently empty victory for the reformers.

Here then, or so it seemed when this study was begun, was a classic example of the injustices suffered by the Pioneers at the hands of the Robber Barons; certainly the reform view set it up that way and certainly the historians, with rare exceptions, have seen it that way. In this view the legal system, the administrative machinery, and the control of political power were all in the hands of the railroadmen and their friends. It followed that they exercised that power in their own best interests. And it followed further that their best interests were not identical with—hardly resembled in fact—the interests of their traditional enemies, the settlers and their friends. It only remained to document by reference to the record the charges of the reformers.

It didn't work. To begin with, there were the countercharges to be explained and they were numerous enough and cogent enough to defy dismissal out of hand. So the documentation of them proceeded apace, and it turned out that they were true, just as true as the charges. There were truth and justice in both positions, but there were also inconsistency, interested testimony, and reams of hearsay evidence in both. The answer had to be sought elsewhere, and the locus of the concrete effects of the exemptions, the local taxing jurisdictions themselves, dictated the next step: the intensive study of land taxability in as many of them as possible. In this way, it seemed, it would be possible to establish the truth of the matter. And it was here that the study of the tax exemption of the railroad land grants as an example of the injustices complained of by the "embattled farmers" of the Populist era and as yet another example of the bilking of the Pioneers by the Robber Barons failed. That was not what it was.

This is not to say that this book reveals what it was, or even exactly how it worked. It doesn't. It does, however, reveal what it was not. The entire result, despite a serious and partly successful attempt to "test" the findings drawn from the national level by the study of the locales, is to prove once again, as has so often been proved before, that the inevitable outcome of starting with a question derived from an interpretive structure—be it the Robber Baron versus the Pioneer or any other—is to dismiss the question and eventually the structure itself. To put it another way: the railroad tax issue was part of a total time and a total place and to isolate it produces not the history it was a part of but the not-history such problem-solving approaches make inevitable.

And so I apologize—to three universities and half a hundred fellow students, to a dozen great teachers, to three score librarians and curators and archivists, to several hundred county officials and newspaper proprietors and railroadmen, to some two thousand authors, to my friend, to my editor, and to Eva. This book is not-history, not history. To make it history would require scrapping it and starting over. The starting over I have done long since, but the scrapping I have decided not to do because, given the morass of theory and interpretation that we fledglings must hack through to become historians and the dangers involved in the process, it is perhaps salutary to publish some of the hackings, complete with the admission that this is what they are. If such publications serve no purpose beyond demonstrating the barrenness of interpretive systems and problem-solving techniques, they will have let some light into the swamp, will have demonstrated the need for some real knowledge and understanding of the past, will have helped open the way to the study of that past without the detours inherent in the study and writing of not-history.

Two

The Judges

TAXATION is a province of government. Who shall pay and how much he shall pay is determined by law. But law is an involved structure, a structure built over a long period of time and from a complex of acts, decisions, and forces. That is to say, law is not made by legislators alone: judges interpret it; legislators amend it; administrators apply it; and those who operate under it obey it, break it, or circumvent it. Thus any study of the taxation of the lands granted to railroads is, first of all, a study of the origins and growth of a multi-faceted and constantly changing legal edifice.

The legal structure that was ultimately to produce widespread tax exemption for railroad land grants had its roots in long-standing local and state practices and precedents. Traditionally American states, counties, and towns had sought to attract industry or transportation facilities by granting tax exemption or tax limitation. In the nineteenth century these practices gradually produced a standard system of statutory tax exemption for railroad property, long before grants of land were added to the enticement. When the federal government began giving land to Western and Southern states to aid local railroads, the states continued the tradition by extending tax exemptions to these lands.

When, in 1862, the central government began to grant lands directly to the railroads themselves, it could not, and the states did not, enact statutory tax exemptions for them. Federal inability to provide such exemptions derived from the tax provisions of the Constitution, which for practical purposes left jurisdiction over the property tax in the province of the states. State unwillingness to do so probably arose from two factors. First, these roads were almost always interstate, not intrastate, lines and thus did not excite the same state and local patriotism that "home-owned" lines had evoked. Second, most of these roads traversed, over at least a part of their route, areas that were not yet states, and by the time these territories did become states the public had grown hostile toward such exemptions.

But federal inability and state unwillingness to grant tax exemptions by statute did not prevent the direct-grant roads from receiving them. As a result of judicial interpretations of the granting acts, complicated by further legislation and by administrative rulings and practices, most of the direct-grant roads did eventually come to enjoy tax exemptions on their granted lands, exemptions that were probably far more valuable to them than those that had been given by statute to the state-grant

10

roads. Taken together, then, the statutory and judicial sources of the privilege produced exemptions for much general railroad property and, by the time it was all over, for many of the lands of most of the land-grant railroads.

Statutory tax exemption usually took one of three forms: outright exemption of all the property of a road for a specified period of time or until a given profit was being earned; exemption on capital stock until a certain rate of dividend was attained; or, what was most common in the Mississippi Valley, the levy of a consolidated state tax, ordinarily on capital stock, in lieu of all or part of local property taxes. Usually a state practiced one or another form of statutory exemption consistently, and normally it extended identical privileges to all roads in the state. Ultimately such exemptions were granted to railroad companies in many states east of the Mississippi and in Louisiana, Missouri, and Texas west of it. At least nineteen states (and three counties) gave some form of statutory exemption to no fewer than fifty-five railroads. Its exact monetary value to the recipients cannot be ascertained, but a conservative estimate places it at thirteen million dollars.[1]

Many Eastern roads received such statutory tax exemptions. By the charter of 1833 Connecticut exempted the Hartford and New Haven from all taxes until profits warranted a five per cent dividend.[2] Between 1867 and 1871 Maine exempted the capital stock of four of its minor roads, each for ten years.[3] Massachusetts never directly exempted its roads, but it early developed a system whereby railroad taxes were centralized in the hands of the state and credit was allowed on local property assessed outside the ten-rod right of way.[4] In New York the Cherry Valley, Sharon and Albany was granted exemption until it paid a semi-annual three per cent dividend, and both the New York and Oswego Midland and the Poughkeepsie and Eastern were exempted until completed, provided they were built within ten years. New York also sold a million and a half acres of land to the Lake Ontario and Hudson River Railroad and made it tax-exempt for twenty-five years, one of the few instances of land exemption in an Eastern state.[5]

Southern and Middle Western states also granted exemptions. Of the many early, and usually short-term, exemptions given in the South

---

[1] Federal Coordinator of Transportation, *Public Aids to Transportation* (4 vols., Government Printing Office, Washington, 1938–1940), 2:61–64, and appendix table 23, pp. 160–162. The Coordinator's study omits some instances. Harry H. Pierce, *Railroads of New York: A Study of Government Aid, 1826–1875* (Harvard University Press, Cambridge, 1953), 18.

[2] Federal Coordinator of Transportation, *Public Aids*, 2:161; Balthasar H. Meyer, *Railway Legislation in the United States* (Macmillan, New York, 1903), 70–71.

[3] Federal Coordinator of Transportation, *Public Aids*, vol. 2, table pp. 160–161.

[4] Charles F. Adams, Jr., to Henry Strong, Boston, September 17, 1872, in the Burlington Archives, Newberry Library, Chicago.

[5] Pierce, *Railroads of New York*, 18.

the most significant were those given by Arkansas and North Carolina. Arkansas exempted the Cairo and Fulton until the road should pay a ten per cent dividend on capital stock, but cancelled it later when the company was reorganized. North Carolina granted three of its most important roads similar privileges, to last until 1891.[6] Ohio's railroad tax policy developed haphazardly through charter provisions in which the legislature restricted both the state and the local right of taxation until the roads should pay dividends. The general property tax was not applied to them until 1852, a year after a tax on dividends over six per cent was levied on all roads in the state.[7] In Missouri not only did the state and numerous municipalities lend their credit abundantly to railroad construction projects, but the legislature also provided, in 1857, for personal property tax exemption for the bonds so pledged and for all bonds issued by the roads as well. This law was subsequently construed, for at least one road, to cover the stock and all the physical property the stock represented. Most of these exemptions were lost by the roads when they defaulted on their bonds during and after the Civil War. The Hannibal and St. Joe, which did not default, retained exemption for the bonds, but eventually did lose its state property tax exemption and retained the privilege only as it applied to county taxes.[8]

The Hannibal and St. Joe exemption in Missouri came to involve some federal-through-state grants, but it was Illinois that first applied the exemption to such lands. The Illinois Central land grant, made in 1850, gave Illinois six alternate sections of land per mile for the benefit of the road to be built under its provisions.[9] The charter of the road, approved by the legislature in February of 1851, exempted from local taxation all property built by or granted to the road for its original seven-hundred-mile line, including the land. In lieu of these taxes the charter imposed a tax of five per cent on gross revenue. This, with a general two per cent state tax, brought the road's total tax to seven per cent of its gross revenues. By 1882 these arrangements had produced $9,087,835 for the state.[10] They also created numerous difficulties on the local level.

[6] Roswell C. McCrea, "Taxation of Transportation Companies," chapter 9 in the *Report of the Industrial Commission* (Government Printing Office, Washington, 1901), 1009.

[7] James C. Dockeray, *Public Utility Taxation in Ohio* (Ohio State University Press, Columbus, 1938), 3-4.

[8] Federal Coordinator of Transportation, *Public Aids*, vol. 2, table pp. 160-161; Frederick N. Judson, *A Treatise upon the Law and Practice of Taxation in Missouri* (E. W. Stephens, Columbia, Missouri, 1900), 31-32, 37, 53, 71, 75, 79, 94-95, 100-102.

[9] 9 *Statutes at Large* 466 (September 20, 1850).

[10] Paul W. Gates, *The Illinois Central Railroad and Its Colonization Work* (Harvard University Press, Cambridge, 1934), 61-65; William K. Ackerman, *Early Illinois Railroads* (Fergus Printing Company, Chicago, 1884), 44-45; Carlton Corliss, *Main Line of Mid-America: The Story of the Illinois Central* (Creative Age Press, New York, 1950), 28.

The local implications of the Illinois Central exemption were far-reaching. When McLean County assessed its right of way, Springfield attorney Abraham Lincoln took the road's case to the State Supreme Court, where its local exemption for land as well as operating property was validated.[11] The railroad land was thus kept off the tax roll as long as the railroad owned it. The reduction in local and county tax revenues inherent in this decision was more serious than it at first appeared. The railroad had adopted, and it retained, long-term credit policies, and it regularly took a lenient attitude toward those who delayed payment. In these circumstances buyers of railroad land were disposed to put off paying for it as long as possible because they could avoid taxation if they did not take title. As late as 1870, twenty years after the grant was made, title to over a million acres of it was still legally in the hands of the railroad company.[12]

Such widespread and long-continuing exemptions would in themselves have produced serious curtailment of local tax revenues and significant local resentment, but their effects were compounded by the application of a provision in the enabling act that Illinois had accepted as a condition of entrance into the Union and in return for specific services, privileges, and gifts given to it by the United States. Under that agreement, which was reached in 1818, long before the railroad grant was made, land sold by the federal government to a private party was exempt from taxation for five years from the date the sale was completed. Consequently government land, like railroad land, was exempt from taxation during the early years of settlement. But there was an important difference. Government land reached the tax rolls within five years of its sale, whereas some railroad land remained untaxable for a much longer time. These conditions, naturally enough, engendered considerable resentment against those who continued to escape taxation and against the railroads as their means of escape, especially among buyers of government land whose five years of grace had elapsed. It is possible that this resentment accounted for some of the anti-railroad sentiment manifest in the Granger movement so popular in Illinois in the 1870's. It is certain that it stimulated recurring efforts of reform groups to secure enforcement of provisions in the railroad's charter which made sale within a specified time mandatory.[13]

[11] Corliss, *Main Line*, 107–109; *Illinois Central vs. McLean County*, 17 *Illinois* 291 (1853).

[12] Gates, *Illinois Central*, 303ff.

[13] *Ibid.*, 303–307; Robert M. Haig, *A History of the General Property Tax in Illinois* (*University of Illinois Studies in the Social Sciences*, vol. 3, nos. 1 and 2, Urbana, 1914), 30–31. That the general government could restrict state tax powers by agreement prior to admitting the state to the Union was not a contravention of constitutional restrictions on the tax power but rather an expression of federal jurisdiction over the public domain. Such agreements—having to do with the assumption of territorial indebtedness, grants to states for public buildings and education, and related matters—were made with every public land state, from Ohio to Arizona.

Lands granted to Michigan, Wisconsin, and Minnesota in 1856 and 1857 for the benefit of numerous railroads[14] received tax treatment similar to that given by Illinois. Michigan passed its land to the companies in "sixty section lots" for each twenty miles of road completed, and gave tax exemption to those on the lower peninsula for seven years and to those on the upper peninsula for ten years. A lieu tax of one per cent on capital stock, to be increased to two per cent after ten years, was levied on the state's southern roads, and the northern roads were given a ten-year exemption from all taxes.[15] In Wisconsin the La Crosse and Milwaukee paid a four per cent lieu tax on capital stock and the Wisconsin and Superior, the Portage and Superior, and the Winnebago and Lake Superior each paid a three per cent lieu tax.[16] The Portage and Superior and the Winnebago and Lake Superior became the Wisconsin Central, which fought consistently, and with some success, to obtain extensions of its exemptions.[17] All Minnesota railroads paid a three per cent capital stock tax to the state in lieu of all other taxes.[18]

Thus until 1862, and in several instances after that time, any railroad's freedom from taxation, whether of operating property or of granted lands, was the outgrowth of a state's legislative policy of statutory tax exemption, a policy designed to encourage promoters to undertake railroad construction. That these exemptions sometimes created anti-railroad sentiment seems clear, but, after all, the exemptions were normally intentional and they applied to a relatively small proportion of the property in most of the communities where they took effect.

Much more important—with respect to the number of communities and individuals affected, the monetary values involved, and the political controversies created—were the apparently inadvertent exemptions that stemmed from the inauguration by Congress of the policy of granting lands directly to railroad corporations. Spawned in the politically explosive decade before the Civil War and brought to legislative fruition at the height of the war, the first of the transcontinentals was constantly in the public eye. So were its successor trans-Missouri railroads. Eventually all figured prominently in national political conflict. Land grants involving well over a hundred million acres of the public domain became the subjects of campaign mud-slinging, legislative maneuver, and administrative manipulation. In this context tax exemption for railroad land-grant lands assumed new significance.

[14] 11 *Statutes at Large* 20, 21 (June 3, 1856) and 195 (March 3, 1857).
[15] John B. Sanborn, *Congressional Grants of Land in Aid of Railways* (*University of Wisconsin Bulletin in Economics, Political Science, and History*, vol. 2, no. 3, Madison, 1899), 96; *Laws of Michigan*, 1855, pp. 153ff.; 1857, pp. 346ff.
[16] Sanborn, *Congressional Grants*, 99–101.
[17] Paul W. Gates, *The Wisconsin Pine Lands of Cornell University: A Study in Land Policy and Absentee Ownership* (Cornell University Press, Ithaca, 1943), 193–206.
[18] Sanborn, *Congressional Grants*, 102.

The legal basis for the exemption from taxation of the lands of the group of lines authorized in 1862 and 1864 as the Pacific Railroad System derived from, but was not directly stated in, provisions ostensibly designed to insure that the railroad companies would fulfill their obligations and that the interests of the United States would be protected. Three provisions were involved. One, the so-called "contingent right of preëmption," appeared in the act of 1862. That act, besides providing for the well-known ten-section-per-mile grant, government first-mortgage bonds, and route, construction, and other operational matters, stipulated that whatever part of the land had not been sold "or disposed of" by the railroads within three years after construction had been completed should be open to settlement and preëmption, at a price not to exceed $1.25 an acre, to be paid to the companies.[19] The act of 1864 doubled the land grant but retained the preëmption stipulation. It also, by amending the law to allow the railroads to sell first-mortgage bonds to private subscribers, relegated the government to the position of the holder of a second mortgage, thereby making the rights of private subscribers paramount in any bankruptcy, forfeiture of contract, or other legal proceeding against the property of the roads.[20] This was the second of the provisions that came to have a bearing on the taxability of the granted lands. The third provision was the most important. It appeared for the first time in the act of 1864 and was enacted almost absent-mindedly, or so it seemed. While the bill was under consideration in the Senate, it was amended at the behest of Senator (soon to be secretary of the interior) James Harlan of Iowa to require that the roads pay the costs of surveying, selecting, and conveying the lands before receiving the government's patents—the actual "deeds" certifying the ownership of specific parcels of land.[21] This feature was retained by the conference committee and was passed over in the House debate on the conference report upon the assurance of Thaddeus Stevens, the House manager, that "all the changes which have been made are in derogation of the rights granted."[22] The section, numbered twenty-one as finally passed, required the roads to pay these costs into a revolving fund "as the titles shall be required" by the railroads, and specified that the fund was to be used by the commissioner of the General Land Office to pay for surveying the lands along the roads.[23]

By these provisions of the granting acts, then, the Congress had attached to the lands granted to the Pacific Railroad System three types of claims or reserved rights—liens they were often called: those of prospective preëmptors, to apply three years after final completion of the

---

[19] 12 *Statutes at Large* 492 (July 1, 1862).
[20] 13 *Statutes at Large* 360 (July 2, 1864).
[21] *Congressional Globe*, 38 Congress, 1 session, 2403 (May 21, 1864).
[22] *Ibid.*, 3481 (July 1, 1864).
[23] 13 *Statutes at Large* 365 (July 2, 1864).

roads; those of mortgagors of the companies, to apply with the sale of the first-mortgage bonds; and those of the government, to apply from the date of the grant. Each lien was in some measure at variance with the others. It was left to the courts to work out their priorities and relationships if they came into conflict, and such conflict was, in the nature of things, inevitable. It was out of that conflict that the decisions making the lands untaxable were to come.

During the next seven years the railroads and the government officials most directly concerned devoted their attention to railroad building. The roads were still considered great national enterprises, and no major conflicts about the ownership and disposal of the land developed. Congress continued to make railroad grants and, following the precedent established by the Pacific Railroad acts, it virtually forsook the old system of using states as intermediaries, electing instead to make grants directly to corporations. Between July 2, 1864, and March 3, 1871, it made grants to the Northern Pacific, the California and Oregon, the Oregon Central, the Atlantic and Pacific, the Santa Fe Pacific, the Southern Pacific, the Texas Pacific, the New Orleans Pacific, and the New Orleans, Baton Rouge and Vicksburg.[24] During the same period it made only three grants to states, one to Minnesota for two roads, the Southern Minnesota and the Hastings and Dakota, one to Kansas for the Kansas and Neosho Valley, and one to Kansas and Nebraska for the St. Joseph and Denver City.[25]

None of these roads received bond aid, and none was limited by the contingent right of preëmption. Nor was any one of them originally required to pay the cost of survey. Instead, they all received land in grants per mile equal to or larger than those that had been made to the roads of the Pacific Railroad System. A further benefit was the reservation of additional strips of land parallel to, but outside of, the primary grant areas, a system that had been used on a much smaller scale in some of the earliest grants to states. From these reservations, usually either equal to or half again as large as the primary area, the roads could select lands as indemnity should it develop that parts of the granted lands had already been homesteaded, preëmpted, or otherwise disposed of. Thus the roads were to be assured of receiving as large a part as possible of the total acreage originally granted to them.

During this grant-making period Congress also began to extend the costs of survey requirement, the provision that eventually, through judi-

[24] Northern Pacific: 13 *Statutes at Large* 365 (July 2, 1864); California and Oregon and Oregon Central: 14 *Statutes at Large* 239 (July 25, 1866); Atlantic and Pacific, Santa Fe Pacific, and Southern Pacific: 14 *Statutes at Large* 292 (July 27, 1866); Southern Pacific Branch, Texas Pacific, New Orleans Pacific, and New Orleans, Baton Rouge and Vicksburg: 16 *Statutes at Large* 573 (March 3, 1871).

[25] 14 *Statutes at Large* 87 (July 4, 1866), 210 (July 23, 1886), 236 (July 25, 1866).

cial construction, was to give most land-grant roads the privilege of tax exemption. In July, 1870, Representative Eugene M. Wilson of Minnesota proposed that the Northern Pacific be made liable for the costs of survey. He introduced the proposal as an amendment to the Sundry Civil Expenses Bill, with the statement that it was in accordance with the recommendation of the commissioner of the General Land Office. Henry Dawes, as chairman, signified the approval of the appropriations committee. William S. Holman of Indiana, long a guardian of the public lands and increasingly a critic of the railroads, said he had no objection if the effect of the provision was to require the company to pay the costs on its own lands, but he wanted the payment made directly by the road and not in the form of a reimbursement to the government. Dawes pointed out that this would create confusion, that the provision had been copied from the act of 1864, and that it had the effect of making the company pay the costs of survey even though control of the speed and location of the surveys remained in the hands of the government. After this explanation the provision was accepted and both houses passed the measure.[26]

Meantime the taxation of the Pacific railroads became a legal issue. The first tax problem to be litigated was inherent in the concept of the Pacific railroads as agents of the federal government. In the state of Kansas the roadbed and rolling stock of the Union Pacific, Eastern Division (later the Kansas Pacific), were assessed and taxes levied. The road obtained an injunction by citing the principles of *McCulloch vs. Maryland* and arguing that it was obliged to perform certain governmental services, to turn part of its earnings over to the government, and to pay the second-mortgage lien that the government held against the road. The case was ultimately carried through the Kansas courts to the United States Supreme Court, which upheld the decision of the higher state courts that the road was taxable.[27]

In Nebraska a similar case was tried with the same result. In February, 1869, the Union Pacific was assessed and taxes were levied. The road sued the treasurer of Lincoln County to restrain collection. The argument of the railroad was almost identical to that of the Eastern Division. The county argued that the principle of *McCulloch vs. Maryland* applied only to necessary instrumentalities of the government, that the federal charter of the road was a fiction, and that it, like any other

[26] *Congressional Globe*, 41 Congress, 2 session, 4876 (June 17, 1870); 16 *Statutes at Large* 305 (July 15, 1870).

[27] *Nebraska Herald* (Plattsmouth), May 12, 1870; 9 *Wallace* 579 (1870); James E. Boyle, *The Financial History of Kansas* (*University of Wisconsin Bulletin in Economics and Political Science*, vol. 5, no. 1, Madison, 1909), 46; a printed document signed by J. P. Usher, attorney for the Union Pacific, Eastern Division, Topeka, dated February 4, 1867, cited in Paul W. Gates, *Fifty Million Acres: Conflicts over Kansas Land Policy, 1854–1890* (Cornell University Press, Ithaca, 1954), 265.

road, was taxable. Judge John F. Dillon of the Omaha District Court held for the county, and the United States Supreme Court, in a decision handed down in December, 1873, upheld the lower court.[28]

The western end of the Pacific Railroad (the Central Pacific) also cited its character as an agent of the government as grounds for tax exemption, but it too lost that part of its case. In January, 1874, Circuit Judge L. S. B. Sawyer ruled, on the basis of the Union Pacific case, that the road and its lands were the property of a private corporation.[29]

Before the final decisions were reached in these cases a new legal controversy arose in Kansas, this time over the taxation of railroad lands rather than of other railroad property. In a case brought against the commissioners of Douglas County in 1870 the Union Pacific, Eastern Division, sought to restrain land taxes assessed for 1866 and 1867 on a hundred thousand acres of the Delaware Tract, a tract that had not been patented to the road until 1868. The county contended that taxable title had passed in 1866, but the court held that the railroad title was contingent on the fulfillment of all obligations leading to the patent, and since it was not until 1868 that all conditions of the purchase had been met, it found no taxable title for the years 1866 and 1867.[30] Though this case concerned purchased lands rather than granted lands, it provided a preview of the attitude of the courts toward unpatented granted lands.

With this precedent, in two concurrent cases the Eastern Division, by now the Kansas Pacific, was able to defeat attempts to levy taxes against its granted lands. These cases involved two quarter sections that had been sold for taxes, one to John H. Prescott and the other to Charles C. Culp, both of whom had paid subsequent taxes. The road sued the tax purchasers to clear its title. It argued (1) that the granting act did not constitute a conveyance of title, since specific conditions (including the payment of the costs of survey) must be met before the patents would be issued, (2) that not all these conditions had been met at the time the tax was levied, since the company had not made its selections nor paid the costs of survey at that time, and (3) that the contingent right of preëmption was a lien that could not be superseded by tax sale and the subsequent issuance of a tax deed. Attorneys for Culp and Prescott countered (1) that the grant itself conveyed title to the land, (2) that the company could compel the issuance of the patent by simply paying the costs, and (3) that, therefore, since the patent was only evidence of the title, it was not a requisite of taxability.[31]

[28] 24 *Federal Cases* 631 (1871). Judge Dillon's decision was also published in the *Nebraska Herald* (Fremont) of May 11, 1871. The Supreme Court case is *Union Pacific Railway Company vs. Penniston,* 18 *Wallace* 5 (1873). See also the *Beatrice Express* (Nebraska), May 3, 1871.

[29] *Huntington vs. Central Pacific,* 12 *Federal Cases* 974 (1874).

[30] 5 *Kansas* 615 (1870).

[31] *Kansas Pacific Railway Company vs. Charles C. Culp and Kansas Pacific Railway Company vs. John H. Prescott,* 9 *Kansas* 38 (1872) ; *In the Supreme Court of*

The Kansas Supreme Court, affirming the decision of the lower court, ruled that since all substantive prerequisites had been fulfilled, the payment of the costs secured conveyance only and did not affect the title. "Where the right to a patent exists," it concluded, "the government holds the legal title only in trust, and the land is subject to taxation."[32] The United States Supreme Court, however, reversed the decision of the lower court when it decided, Justice Miller delivering, that although title itself was not a requisite of taxability, the right to title was, and that since the company had not paid the costs, that the right did not rest with the railroad. Furthermore, Miller held, the contingent right of preëmption provision of the law was an effective stay to the sale of tax title, since such a sale would violate the law by eliminating the right. Incidental to his discussion of the main question, Miller also held that all lands granted under the two Pacific Railroad acts were liable for the costs of survey assessment provided for in the second act.[33]

In Nebraska, as in Kansas, taxation of the granted lands became an issue. The Union Pacific sought an injunction against taxes levied for 1872 on its unpatented lands, and litigation concerning this and related issues plagued Nebraska for the greater part of the decade. In August, 1873, Judge Dundy of the district court granted the injunction sought by the railroad.[34] The following July Circuit Judge Dillon, citing the Prescott decision as precedent, handed down a decision affirming the right to tax patented lands but denying it for unpatented lands. In his decision he cited the payment of costs and issuance of patents as the only criteria of taxability; he denied that the contingent right of preëmption was a factor.[35]

One of these Nebraska cases, *Union Pacific Railway Company vs. Edward C. McShane*, treasurer of Douglas County, was carried to the United States Supreme Court. In his argument Andrew J. Poppleton, for the company, based his plea for tax exemption on grounds of (1) the contingent right of preëmption, (2) the nonpayment of the costs of survey on part of the land, and (3) the withholding by the General Land Office of half the lands from patent to insure completion as a first-class road. Clinton Briggs and J. C. Corwin, for McShane, contended for taxability on the grounds that the company (1) had sold the greater part of the lands in litigation, (2) had received patents to half the lands, and (3) had paid the costs of survey on lands within the limits of the additional grant of the act of 1864 and avowed its willingness to pay costs on the others. Justice Miller, for the court, reversed his own decision in the Prescott case, in so far as it cited the contingent

---

the State of Kansas, Kansas Pacific Railway Company vs. John H. Prescott . . . Brief for the Defendant in Error . . . (Herald Print, Salina, Kansas, n.d.).

[32] 9 *Kansas* 38 (1872).

[33] 16 *Wallace* 603 (1873).

[34] 24 *Federal Cases* 638 (1873) ; *Beatrice Express*, August 14, 28, 1873.

[35] 24 *Federal Cases* 640 (1874) ; *Omaha Bee* (Nebraska), July 8, 1874; *Grand Island Times* (Nebraska), July 8, 1874.

right of preëmption to justify exemption, by denying the sufficiency of such a reservation to keep lands off the tax roll. He held, in part, that such a right would prevent the sale of clear title to railroad land.[36]

The specific reason for Justice Miller's change of position is not clearly indicated in the decision, but it may lie in the opinion of the court, delivered only days before, in the case of *Schulenburg vs. Harriman*, involving a double grant of land in Wisconsin to a road that had never been built. In that case the court declared railroad grants to be *in presenti*, that is, that the granting act itself conveyed title to the land (although, of course, title to specific tracts could be determined only after surveys had been made and the lands located). Therefore, the court continued, there could be no automatic reversion of the land to the government on the ground that conditions of the grant were unfulfilled. Such reversion could be accomplished only by act of Congress.[37] It is obvious that this decision, when applied to railroad land grants in general, raised serious doubt about the validity of the contingent right of preëmption and made inevitable the so-called "forfeiture movement" of the 1870's and 1880's, a movement aimed at recovering by congressional action the lands of railroads that had not fulfilled the conditions of their grants. That the decision was responsible for Justice Miller's change of front also seems likely.

If the Schulenburg decision was the basis of Justice Miller's ruling that the contingent right of preëmption was not a deterrent to taxation, he did not follow out its implications. Instead, he upheld that part of the Prescott decision which declared that the lands could not be taxed until the costs of survey had been paid (because the railroad's title was not established). In fact, in dealing with an exceptional situation, he added a new feature which served to strengthen his earlier decision. He declared that certain lands—those which had been patented under the act of 1862 before the Prescott decision made all lands liable for costs of survey—were taxable whether the costs had been paid or not.[38]

With the McShane decision in its favor the Union Pacific tried to retrieve tax monies paid under protest on the unpatented portion of its lands. Suits were filed against twelve Nebraska counties, and one case, that against Dodge County, was carried through to the highest tribunal. Here the company was unsuccessful. The court held that the payment had been voluntary, since no threats of sale or seizure had been made when payment was proffered and accepted, and was therefore not recoverable.[39] But the loss occasioned by this adverse decision in no way balanced the gain the road could expect from the future application of the nontaxability decision.

[36] 22 *Wallace* 444 (1875).
[37] 21 *Wallace* 44 (1875).
[38] 22 *Wallace* 444 (1875).
[39] 8 *Otto* 541 (1879); *Grand Island Times*, May 17, 1876. The counties involved were Buffalo, Adams, Butler, Dodge, Cuming, Hamilton, Sarpy, Colfax, Hall, York, Platte, and Saunders.

Meantime the Burlington and Missouri River Railroad in Nebraska, one of the branch lines authorized by the act of 1864,[40] was waging a less successful campaign to avoid payment of the taxes assessed against its lands. The South Platte counties, through which the road ran, united in taking action to defeat the injunctions the company had obtained. At a meeting held in Lincoln in August, 1873, the commissioners of eleven counties called attention to the large amounts of local aid given to the company and resolved to unite to collect the taxes. They engaged as their counsel J. C. Corwin of Omaha, who was already fighting the Union Pacific in the McShane case.[41] Eleven months later, at the same time that he rendered his decision in the Union Pacific cases, Judge Dillon held the major portion of the Burlington lands to be taxable. He ruled that the contingent right of preëmption was not applicable to the Burlington, and, inasmuch as the company had already received its patents, he saw the case only as a question of when the patented lands became taxable. He declared that all lands on which the costs of survey had been paid before assessment day, March 17, 1872—which included all those east of the 140th milepost—were taxable for that year, since the costs had been paid on March 7. The remainder of the lands, he held, were not taxable until 1873.[42] One of the cases, *Hunnewell vs. Cass County*, was carried to the United States Supreme Court, which upheld Dillon's pronouncement, Miller again writing the decision.[43] According to one estimate, this decision put two hundred thousand dollars in 1872 taxes into the treasuries of the eastern South Platte counties.[44]

Thus, although the arguments in the taxability cases varied considerably, and though Justice Miller shifted his grounds for ruling in favor of exemption, by early 1875 the highest court had effectively established the general rule that taxable title did not pass to the roads liable for costs of survey until they had paid them. The role of the contingent right of preëmption was not yet clarified, but the lien of the prospective preëmptor was no longer held to be a valid deterrent to taxation. Not yet established were the degree of priority and the effect on taxability of the lien of the mortgagor holding the first-mortgage bonds of the railroad companies.

For four years these questions of ownership and taxability of railroad land produced no new major legal conflict. Then in 1878 Carl Schurz, the new secretary of the interior, declared in a case originating in Kansas that the contingent right of preëmption was valid law, and threw open to preëmptors all the unsold land of the railroads whose grants included such a provision. One Nelson Dudymott, who had preëmpted a quarter section of railroad land in the Kansas Pacific grant

[40] 13 *Statutes at Large* 364 (July 2, 1864).
[41] *Beatrice Express*, August 14, 21, 1873. The counties involved were York, Clay, Hamilton, Gage, Fillmore, Kearney, Lancaster, Adams, Saline, Seward, and Butler.
[42] *Ibid.*, July 9, 1874; *Omaha Bee*, July 8, 1874; 12 *Federal Cases* 893 (1874).
[43] 22 *Wallace* 464 (1875).
[44] *Grand Island Times*, January 27, 1875.

and had fulfilled all the legal requirements, applied to the local register and receiver for patent under the contingent right of preëmption clause of the granting act. The local officers referred the case to the General Land Office, where the commissioner decided for the railroad. Finally, on appeal by Dudymott's attorneys, the case reached the desk of Secretary Schurz. Basing his ruling that the preëmption was a valid one primarily on the decisions of Justice Miller, Schurz held that Miller's ruling in the McShane case—that the contingent right was not sufficient to keep the lands off the tax rolls—was not sufficient to make the law itself invalid. He further stated that the railroads themselves had, in their own literature, considered the provision binding.[45]

The roads appealed for a rehearing and about six weeks later Schurz again decided for Dudymott. This time he was considering not only the Kansas Pacific case but also a similar petition of the Union Pacific. In their petitions the roads had argued for a contrary ruling on the basis of the ruling in *Schulenburg vs. Harriman* and similar cases declaring grants of this sort *in presenti,* and they had contended that the mortgages executed under the act of 1864 were disposals of the grant within the meaning of the law. In answer to these contentions Schurz held, first, that *in presenti* grants or no, the contingent right of preëmption was a condition and part of the contract under which the roads had been constructed and the grants accepted and, second, that Congress, in its requirement for disposal, had contemplated actual sale to bona fide settlers. On this basis he ruled again that all the unsold lands were subject to preëmption.[46]

It was clear that the roads would take legal action to save their lands. When prospective claimants under the Schurz decision rushed to settle on railroad land,[47] the Union Pacific gave notice that it would treat preëmptors as trespassers and would litigate with them to "the court of last resort."[48] Kansas and Nebraska newspapers were of two minds about the wisdom of the decision or the possibility of carrying it out. Many feared that it would upset land titles irreparably.[49] Many feared that the roads would find some method of disposing of the lands that would defeat the secretary.[50] Most held little hope for the settler in conflict with the railroad.[51] A number expressed pleasure that at last the

[45] Commissioner of the General Land Office, *Annual Report,* 1878, pp. 73–77.

[46] *Ibid.,* 77–81.

[47] *Hamilton County News* (Nebraska), August 9, October 4, 1878; *Grand Island Times,* September 22, 1878; *Russell Record* (Kansas), August 1, 1878.

[48] *Topeka Commonwealth* (Kansas), reprinted in the *Russell Record,* August 15, 1878; *Fremont Weekly Herald* (Nebraska), August 8, 1878.

[49] For examples, see the *Junction City Tribune* (Kansas), August 1, 1878, and the *Nebraska State Journal* (Lincoln), April 25, 1879.

[50] For examples, see the *Hamilton County News,* August 16, 1878, and the *Junction City Tribune,* March 2, 1878.

[51] The *Hamilton County News* of August 16, 1878, printed three columns of quotations to this effect from papers published throughout Nebraska.

issue of prior liens was to be settled one way or the other and that either way the lands would at last get on the tax rolls.[52]

The Union Pacific promptly entered a suit of ejectment against one William H. Platt, who had filed a preëmption claim on one of its quarter sections in Hall County, Nebraska, and the action was pushed through the lower courts in time to be considered during the October, 1879, term of the United States Supreme Court. Platt had settled on the property in 1874 and filed for preëmption in September, 1878. The railroad argued that mortgaging the lands constituted a disposition of them because they had been pledged as security for loans with which to construct the road. The preëmptor argued that the mortgage was not a sale and that the contingent right was valid law that had been upheld in the Prescott case. The majority of the court ruled that the mortgage was a disposition within the meaning of the law, that the lien of the prospective preëmptor was superseded by the lien of the mortgageholder. Three justices dissented, among them Justice Miller. The dissenters contended that what the Congress had envisioned was the sale of specific tracts, not the blanket assignment of a lien.[53]

Few newspapers regarded the Platt decision as a blessing to Kansas and Nebraska, but they were relieved that at last the taxation question had been settled. If the companies had disposed of their lands, then someone must have a taxable title.[54] However, the Union Pacific again went to the courts when Buffalo County assessed its lands, and decisions favorable to the road in the lower courts evoked violent protest from many papers. The Kearney, Nebraska, *Press* castigated the company for its tax policy and the courts for upholding the railroads. It protested that the homesteader could not expect relief because "it has been so long since he had anything to do with or say about the government of his father's house."[55] When Judge Dundy granted an injunction in the Buffalo County case, the *Omaha Bee* was similarly resentful; it took him to task for ruling that the McShane case was still applicable and accused him of doing "a great wrong to Nebraska." Both the Platt case and the Buffalo County case, the *Bee* insisted, had been inside jobs: Platt was a railroad employee who had been encouraged by the company's general attorney, Andrew Poppleton, to make the case, and the commissioners of Buffalo County had been induced to refrain from putting up a defense.[56]

Distressing as it was to the "anti-monopoly" newspapers and, they alleged, to the settlers in railroad-grant areas, it was still firmly established that unpatented railroad lands were untaxable. The law, derived

[52] For examples, see the *Russell Record*, August 1, 1878, and the *Farmer's Advocate* of Salina, Kansas, July 24, 1878.

[53] 9 *Otto* 48 (1879).

[54] *Omaha Bee*, April 30, 1879; *Grand Island Times*, April 24, 1879.

[55] Quoted in the *Omaha Bee*, August 31, 1881.

[56] *Omaha Bee*, June 13, 27, 1883. See also the *Fremont Herald*, June 21, 1883.

from the acts of 1862 and 1864 as construed by the courts, had created a situation that enabled the roads to mortgage, sell, and use their land without paying taxes on it. And now, to add the capstone, the amendment to the appropriations bill extending the cost of survey obligation to the Northern Pacific had its turn in the courts. Traill County, Dakota Territory, had assessed the Northern Pacific for taxes on its unpatented lands in that county for the year 1880, and the county treasurer had advertised the lands for sale. The railroad appealed the case from the Supreme Court of the Territory to the October, 1885, term of the Supreme Court of the United States. Attorneys for the county, citing *Schulenburg vs. Harriman*, argued that the grant was *in presenti*, that the right to title was complete, and that therefore the lands were taxable. W. P. Clough, for the road argued nontaxability on the basis of the Prescott and McShane decisions. Again Justice Miller wrote the decision.[57] After holding that the provision for payment of survey costs was a legitimate addition to the appropriations bill, he reiterated his decisions in the two previous tax cases. He went on to assert that, although the court was aware that the railroads were taking advantage of these decisions by "neglecting" to pay the cost of survey "in order to prevent taxation," it could only interpret the law as it existed. "The remedy," he concluded, "lies with Congress and is easy of application."[58]

Again Justice Miller had made the issue clear. Whatever else had been done, it was the actual payment of the costs of survey that was the essential step—without it the land was not taxable. In his statement that the remedy lay with Congress, the Justice was quite correct. In his statement that the application of the remedy was easy, the Justice was quite wrong. More than ten years earlier local agitation had engendered efforts to apply just the remedy he was advising, yet by 1885 no law designed to achieve this end had yet passed both houses in the same Congress. It was not until the next year that a law was enacted to rectify the legislative mistake made in 1864.

[57] 115 *United States Court Reports* 600 (1885).
[58] *Ibid.*, 610–611.

Three

The Legislators

THE first of the Supreme Court decisions exempting from taxation the lands granted to some of the trans-Missouri railroads—the Prescott decision of 1873—made it apparent to all concerned that the simple way to end the practice was to change the law. As judicial precedent after judicial precedent was set it became clear that a legislative remedy for the legislative mistake of 1864 was not just the simple way—it was the only way. But almost fourteen years elapsed before Congress enacted such changes in the law, despite violent agitation by newspapers and politicians in the locales affected and despite sincere and recurring efforts on the part of individual reformers in both houses of Congress. Bill after bill was introduced and a few were passed by ˈne or the other house, but none became law until 1886.

That the obvious remedy for the exemption of the granted lands from taxation was not applied with dispatch is partly attributable to numerous specific causes, but the primary reason lay in a single general cause: confusion. Taxation reform was obstructed by the multiplicity and complexity of other land-reform measures that vied for attention. Often one reform seemed to make another impossible; often equally ardent reformers found themselves on opposite sides of this and other questions; often impinging questions and party loyalty, as well as conflicting testimony and organized opposition, placed the sincere reformer in a quandary.

During the Forty-third and the six succeeding Congresses—that is, between 1872 and 1887—the policy for dealing with the land-grant railroads was more vacillating and uncertain than at any other time. This is not to say that the policy was stable after the Forty-ninth Congress; far from it. But it was in the Congresses of the 1870's and early 1880's that confusion was greatest, that the cross-currents of policies and instrumentalities left the reformers most often at loggerheads, supporting patently inconsistent legislative policies and finding it impossible to develop a program on which the majority of them, or even a few of them, were able to agree at once. Furthermore, throughout the period there were those in Congress and at home who sincerely believed that it was to the advantage of their areas to be lenient with the roads, to give them extensions of construction time and other benefits rather than to force them to meet their obligations promptly. Always there were the so-called "railroad statesmen," paid and unpaid, who worked with great energy to secure or maintain advantages for their roads, even to the disadvantage, if need be, of other roads of the same type. Finally, there were the sectional divisions between the West, which had the roads, the South, which did not have them, and the East, which largely financed and controlled them.

Generally speaking, three major problems were involved in arriving at a policy for dealing with the land-grant railroads. The first of these for which a constructive policy was developed and for which the beginnings of a solution was found was that of settling the debts of the roads that had received loans of government bonds to help finance their construction, namely the companies that constituted the Pacific Railroad System. The second problem for which a solution was finally found was that of vesting a taxable title to their lands in the roads whose granting acts or subsequent legislation had indirectly exempted from the payment of land taxes. The third problem, for which a very late and generally inconsequential provision was made, was that of obtaining by congressional enactment the forfeiture of the lands of those railroads that had not fulfilled the conditions of their grants. The problem of settling the railroad debts to the government received greatest attention in the 1870's; that of providing for the taxation of the land grants in the mid-1870's and again after 1880; and that of declaring forfeit the unearned grants after 1880. But always the three problems in all their aspects vied with one another for attention and divided the interests and energies of all interested parties.

Vehement criticism of both the railroads and the judiciary began while the tax cases were still in the lower courts. In January of 1872 the Nebraska legislature memorialized the state's congressional representatives to seek action compelling all railroads to take title to their lands.[1] When, in August of 1873, Judge Dundy of the Omaha District Court granted injunctions against land taxes levied on the Union Pacific and the Burlington, Nebraska newspapers, conservative and anti-monopoly alike, almost unanimously argued that the roads must pay their taxes if financial ruin was to be prevented. The *Omaha Bee*, under the editorship of Edward Rosewater, a Bohemian immigrant of pronounced anti-monopoly leanings, predicted general bankruptcy if the decision should be adverse to the counties.[2] Rosewater declared that the counties had contracted indebtedness for public improvements, "enhancing the value of these railroad lands as much as any other, under the belief that they were taxable. And now comes the railroad company . . . and refuses to pay taxes, leaving them hopelessly bankrupt."[3] The *Beatrice Express*, a generally conservative paper, called the whole affair "the railroad tax swindle" and, although agreeing that the decisions

[1] *Laws of Nebraska*, 1872, pp. 27–28.
[2] *Omaha Bee*, August 6, 1873.
[3] *Ibid.*, September 3, 1873.

might be good law, suggested that the roads could not afford "to stir up the hostility of the people of the state by persisting in such refusal."[4] The *Grand Island Times,* farther west than the *Bee* and the *Express* and in general an anti-monopoly paper, observed: "Of all the impositions that the railroad monopolies have tried to perpetrate upon the people of this country, the resistence to taxation of the UPRR and B & MRR is by far ahead of anything in that line that has come under our observation."[5] The *Omaha Weekly Republican,* a generally pro-railroad, conservative Republican paper, called for an attack on the roads by means of a mass settlement on their lands under the contingent right of preëmption provision of the granting acts. It also printed a letter signed "John Smith" in which the fears of the most apprehensive were clearly stated. To "Smith" the taxation of the railroad lands was "an absorbing and all important question." He pointed out that many counties had constructed courthouses, jails, schools, bridges, and roads and had issued bonds the payment of which was "predicated on the taxation of the lands." The nonpayment of taxes, he asserted, had ruined the market for these bonds and would ultimately bankrupt the counties. Consequently, he concluded: "Improvements must stop; road, bridges, court houses and local improvements of all kinds must remain dormant."[6]

A few papers, to be sure, viewed the matter in a different light. The *Omaha Weekly Herald,* operated by "Doctor" Miller, a railroad Democrat who was especially partial to the Union Pacific, scolded the complaining papers, the *Bee* in particular, for their tirades against the roads. Citing the example of Dawson County, in western Nebraska, which had just issued bonds to pay for a new courthouse, he hinted that the critics were uninformed or, worse, that they were attempting to shift the burden of taxes to other private citizens. Where, he asked, did these "intelligent" newspaper editors think the railroad tax money would come from? It would come, he insisted, from the pockets of other Nebraskans, for if the railroads were forced to pay more land taxes, they would inevitably pass on the increased costs by raising their freight and passenger rates, and the burden would fall mainly on the people in the more densely populated eastern counties.[7] Miller's old friend, a former territorial official and leading Democrat, J. Sterling Morton, was more blunt. In a letter to the *Herald* he asserted that the noisiest advocates of taxing the railroad lands were the homesteaders, who had themselves, through "a questionable piece of legislation," been given their lands "free" and were exempt from taxes on it for five to seven years. Both the "individual homesteaders and the cor-

[4] *Beatrice Express,* August 21, 1873.
[5] *Grand Island Times,* August 20, 1873.
[6] *Omaha Weekly Republican,* August 23, 1873.
[7] *Omaha Weekly Herald,* September 5, 1873.

porate railroaders," Morton opined, enjoyed a preferred status, whereas both "ought, in justice, to pay taxes equally with the rest of the people of the State."[8]

Furthermore, some possibility of settlement appeared when it was reported that the three government-appointed members of the board of directors of the Union Pacific had declared the road completed and therefore entitled to all its patents, and when rumors were circulated that the roads planned to pay their taxes without waiting for the decision of the highest court.[9]

But in both Kansas and Nebraska there were soon repercussions in political circles. In Kansas, where the Prescott decision and the cases leading to it had produced little commotion in the newspapers,[10] the McShane case evoked from the Farmer's Market Exchange of two counties on the Kansas Pacific a resolution demanding equal assessment and taxation for all and asking Kansas congressional representatives to take action to compel "the several" roads to take title to their lands.[11] But again it was in Nebraska that reaction was most pronounced. The issue was an ideal one for the Grangers and was soon taken up by them. In an address delivered in Gage County in September, 1873, A. Devo, lecturer of the State Grange, provided an excellent illustration of the uses to which tax avoidance on the part of the railroads could be put in political oratory:

With one half of a territory as lovely as any land on the face of God's earth given to them, these cormorants, by extortionate charges for transportation, grab all the profits of the produce raised on the other half of the country, and then with consummate meanness dodge the payment of their part of the taxes and seek to throw a nearly double burden upon the already plundered people. . . .

We want roads, but we want them as co-laborers to work side by side with other interests in building up a commonwealth; and not as vampires, to suck the lifeblood from all other industries. We want the train to go thundering through every county in the State, but wish its shrieking whistle may sound to the citizen as a note of rejoicing and not as a beast of prey.[12]

It was too late in the year for the issue to find its way into the political party platforms of 1873; besides, there were no major state elections that year. But in the counties taxation of the railroad lands became a real issue. County officials had found it expedient to unite in fighting

[8] *Ibid.*, August 27, 1873. The letter was dated August 17.

[9] *Omaha Bee*, December 31, 1873; *Grand Island Times*, September 3, December 31, 1873.

[10] The *Junction City Union*, though not yet violently anti-railroad, did publish a letter, signed "McB," which severely criticized the Kansas Pacific for its tax-evasion policy, January 8, 1870.

[11] Published in the *Manhattan Nationalist*, June 12, 1873. The resolution was equally concerned with "unjust" discrimination in fares and freights.

[12] Published in the *Beatrice Express*, September 18, 1873.

the injunction cases in the lower courts, and now they took up the cry for congressional action, sometimes through formal resolutions forwarded directly to their representatives in Congress.[13]

The Nebraska delegation in the first session of the Forty-third Congress responded by giving the drive for action most of its impetus and a large part of its sustaining force. True, the issue was recognized in other parts of the country: it found its way into Eastern newspapers from the time it became a Supreme Court case,[14] and the first bill introduced on the subject was presented by a Nevada Democrat, Charles W. Kendall.[15] But it was Lorenzo Crounse, Democrat of Fort Calhoun, Nebraska, and William A. Phillips, Republican of Salina, Kansas, who did most of the work and got the credit for the passage of a bill. Between mid-December of 1872 and early February of 1873 five bills designed to achieve taxation were introduced in the House: one each by Phillips, Crounse, and Samuel J. Randall of Pennsylvania, and two by Kendall. All were referred to the Committee on Public Lands.[16]

In his home state Crounse was highly praised for his role in presenting the problem for congressional consideration.[17] The *Omaha Bee,* always suspicious of the "monopolies," expected "serious opposition," but said that if Crounse succeeded he would have rendered the state a great service.[18] On February 6, two days after the publication of this laudatory article on Crounse, Senator Phineas Hitchcock, formerly territorial representative and now senator from Nebraska, introduced a similar bill in the Senate.[19] Within the next two months Senator John J. Ingalls of Kansas introduced one and Senator William B. Allison of Iowa two additional proposals designed to authorize state and local taxation of railroad lands.[20]

Every bill contained in one form or another the provision that the land patents be issued within a year after the completion of surveys of the lands involved. This prompted the Washington correspondent of the *St. Louis Democrat,* commenting on the bills a few days after Hitchcock had added his version to the growing list, to speculate that they might be opposed by the commissioner of the General Land Office on the ground that their passage would destroy his only weapon for pro-

[13] For an example see the Proceedings of the Board of County Commissioners of Adams County, Nebraska, 1:116, in the office of the County Treasurer, Hastings, Nebraska. The resolution was adopted March 10, 1874.

[14] See the *New York* (semi-weekly) *Evening Post,* August 15, 1873.

[15] House Bill 760, *Congressional Record,* 43 Congress, 1 session, 208 (December 15, 1873).

[16] House bills 1028, 1152, 1502, 1926.

[17] *Grand Island Times,* February 4, 1874; *Nebraska Herald* (Fremont), February 12, 1874; *Beatrice Express,* February 5, 1874.

[18] *Omaha Bee,* February 4, 1874.

[19] Senate Bill 453, *Congressional Record,* 43 Congress, 1 session, 1256 (February 6, 1874); *Beatrice Express,* February 26, 1874.

[20] Senate bills 713, 724, 788.

tecting the interests of the United States. If the legislation forced him to issue the patents at once, he could not use the threat to withhold them as a means of making the roads comply with his directives.[21]

The House Committee on Public Lands had early discovered that it faced a knotty problem. As was the practice with land bills, copies of the proposals were sent to the secretary of the interior and referred by him to the commissioner of the General Land Office. The commissioner, Willis Drummond, found much to criticize in each of the bills. To Kendall's first bill, which provided that the patents be issued within a year, his objections were general. He pointed out, just as the *Democrat* had said he might, that unless other means were provided, the threat of withholding the patents was the only weapon the government had for insuring payment of the costs of survey. Thus, he argued, a choice would have to be made between collecting the costs and making the lands taxable. Litigation was pending, he added, which would probably show that some of the roads owed large sums to the United States, and immediate issuance of the patents would remove the only lien the government had on the unpatented lands. But he concluded his evaluation of the bill by expressing his sympathy with the general aim of taxing the railroad lands.[22]

After this cool reception of the proposals Drummond gradually warmed to the task and continually advised the committee in its deliberations. He objected to Phillips' bill because it imposed the penalty of forfeiture of its unpatented lands on any road that failed to pay the costs of survey within six months. He regarded this as neither equitable nor constitutional. He also felt that the mechanism the bill provided for adjusting the grants and expediting the issuance of the patents would disturb administrative arrangements already made by the Land Office. The ground for his objection to the Crounse bill was almost identical. This bill, which made the lands taxable before the costs of survey were paid, included a feature calling for the issuance of patents directly to purchasers of tax titles if they paid the costs of survey. This provision, he felt, would throw so much work on an already overloaded administrative department that proper safeguards would be impossible. Drummond found Kendall's second bill more acceptable. It was a general bill providing a simple and economical method of ascertaining what lands were to be listed as taxable and of getting that information to the state governments. But it too contained the objectionable provision that purchasers of tax title get their patents directly from the General Land Office.[23]

The bill finally approved by the House Committee on Public Lands was in general accordance with Drummond's views. The committee in-

[21] Quoted in the *Omaha Bee*, February 11, 1874.
[22] 44 Congress, 1 session, *Senate Executive Document 20* (1876), pp. 2–3.
[23] This entire series of letters and the texts of the bills are included *ibid.*

troduced its first bill in mid-April of 1874, but it was allowed to lie and three weeks later the committee introduced a substitute measure.[24] The second bill provided (1) that neglect to pay the costs of survey should not preclude the vesting of taxable title, (2) that upon tax sale the buyer was to pay the costs of survey, whereupon the patent would be issued to the railroad, subject to the tax title, (3) that the commissioner of the General Land Office was to deliver without delay all the patents applied for by the companies, and (4) that if any company failed to pay the costs of survey, lists of the lands involved were to be delivered to state authorities, who would meet the expense of preparing them.[25] This arrangement vested the taxable title in the railroad company regardless of who paid the costs of survey and left it to the claimants against the roads to seek redress in the courts.

The committee report on the measure was designed to accompany the first bill. After presenting the legal history of the controversy and citing railroad literature to demonstrate that the companies treated the land as their property, the committee asserted that the taxes on the land of the Union Pacific alone would amount to nearly three hundred thousand dollars a year, and concluded its recommendation in favor of the bill with the assertion that it was designed simply to provide that the roads, "In common with all property-holders, shall bear their just proportions of the burdens of government."[26]

When, on May 11, Representative Crounse called the committee bill up from the calendar and moved that the rules be suspended so that it might be passed, another facet of the possible opposition came to light. William S. Holman of Indiana, an opponent of any concessions to the land-grant roads since the early 1870's, had joined S. A. Hurlbut of Illinois and H. F. Page of California in exploring the possibilities of declaring forfeit by congressional enactment the lands of those roads that had not completed construction within the time limit set in the original granting act.[27] When Crounse presented the bill and Nathan Bradley of Michigan, as spokesman for the Committee on Public Lands, signified the unanimous agreement of the committee, Holman raised the issue of forfeiture. He insisted that any taxation bill must contain a carefully worded provision guaranteeing that the legislation would not be construed to cancel forfeiture liabilities incurred by the roads. After a short discussion Crounse and Bradley agreed to an amendment to

[24] House bills 3026 and 3281 in the *Congressional Record*, 43 Congress, 1 session, 3160 (April 17, 1874) and 3727 (May 8, 1874).

[25] *Ibid.*, 3773 (May 11, 1874).

[26] 43 Congress, 1 session, *House Report 474* (1874). The quotation is from page 5.

[27] Compare Holman's views recorded in the *Congressional Globe*, 42 Congress, 1 session, 1274 (February 28, 1872), and *ibid.*, 38 Congress, 1 session, 3148–3156 (June 21, 1864). Both Hurlbut and Page had forfeiture bills on the docket in this term, House bills 1568 and 2847.

this effect introduced by Holman. The rules were suspended and the bill passed, without a recorded vote.[28]

Immediately after the House taxation bill was passed the *Grand Island Times* prophesied that the Senate would not dare kill it,[29] and the *Nebraska State Journal* confidently predicted a great windfall in back taxes to the counties involved.[30] They were wrong. The bill went to the Senate and died. It was reported from the Committee on Railroads in mid-June with an amendment striking out the entire House bill and substituting for it another which simply repealed section 21 of the act of 1864 and thereby abrogated the lien of the government, but the bill got no farther in the remainder of the session.[31]

Some newspapers in Nebraska, doubtful of its chances from the beginning, had a ready explanation. On June 24 the *Omaha Bee* reported that the bill had been "taken in hand" by the Senate Committee on Railroads, of which Nebraska's Hitchcock was a member, and predicted that the committee would attach an amendment that would defeat the purpose of the bill. On July 1 the *Bee* reprinted the statement of the *Seward Atlas* that Nebraska's senators would be held responsible for the lack of action in the Senate, and published a letter from its Washington correspondent presenting the Senate's substitute measure and predicting that it could not pass either house. Editor Rosewater's comment was that, whatever the final disposal of the bill, it was clear that it had "become a dead letter through the manipulation of the Senate Committee on Pacific Railroads."

Editor Miller of the *Omaha Herald* was not displeased with the turn of events and was much more specific in giving what he considered credit to those responsible. When the bill passed the House, Miller had been critical of its failure to specify, in conjunction with the tax provisions, the title, "So long denied," should be issued to the roads.[32] When defeat of the bill was assured Miller asserted that in "defeating Crounse's bill to tax Union Pacific lands without providing that [Secretary of the Interior] Delano should issue the patents to them, Senator Hitchcock did the right thing at the right time and in the right way."[33] Rosewater objected to Miller's argument that it was bad policy to work hardship on the Union Pacific by such legislation. He agreed that taxation of the lands did work such a hardship, but insisted that nontaxation of them worked a greater hardship on settlers, and he gave his estimate of Senator Hitchcock in the words of the *Sarpy Sentinel:* "Senators will bear in mind that for their action on this bill they will be brought to judgement."[34]

[28] *Congressional Record*, 43 Congress, 1 session, 3773 (May 11, 1874).
[29] *Grand Island Times*, May 20, 1874.
[30] *Nebraska State Journal* (Lincoln), May 22, 1874.
[31] 43 Congress, 1 session, *House Report 474* (1874), p. 10.
[32] *Omaha Weekly Herald*, May 29, 1874.
[33] *Ibid.*, July 3, 1874.
[34] *Omaha Bee*, July 8, 15, 1874.

In the second session of the Forty-third Congress nothing was accomplished with reference to the taxation of the unpatented lands save the ultimate discharge of Allison's two tax bills from the Senate calendar.[35] That this pleased Union Pacific and Kansas Pacific officials is likely. That it did not displease "Doctor" Miller and men with comparable views is clear. That it pleased the government directors of the Union Pacific, charged with protecting the interests of the United States, is also clear. In their report for 1874 they asserted that the whole difficulty stemmed from an order of the secretary of the interior, issued in 1869, that had withheld half the granted lands from patent until the road was accepted as completed in first-class condition, and that now, with the final acceptance of the road as completed, the remaining patents could be issued. Finally, it was their judgment that at least some of the bills introduced into Congress "would have been mischievious in operation if enacted, by bringing into the land system of the government exceptional and unusual principles and rules, and rendering title to vast bodies of land complicated and uncertain."[36]

In December of 1875, when the Forty-fourth Congress convened, Crounse, Phillips, and company were prepared to try again. But they were not the only seekers after reform, nor was theirs the only reform sought. The taxation bills had to compete with a formidable array of proposed railroad legislation. Senator J. R. West of Louisiana introduced one bill to change the rates which the government was to pay for its transportation and another to require that the bond-aided roads begin paying interest on their debts to the government.[37] A substitute for these, reported from the Senate Committee on Pacific Railroads by Allen G. Thurman of Ohio, led to a large amount of debate.[38]

Two other important new bills were also designed to readjust the operational or financial accounts of the land-grant railroads. Senator George B. Wright of Iowa introduced a bill requiring the Union Pacific to carry freight transferred to it at its junction with one of the "feeder" lines (the Central Branch) at the same rate as freight sent all the way on the main line. This would give shippers along the feeder the advantage of the Union Pacific's long-haul rates, which were much lower than the short-haul rates they were now paying. This so-called "prorating system" would also benefit the feeder line by increasing its tonnage from the Far West. Representative George W. McCrary of Iowa introduced a similar bill with reference to the Burlington and the Union Pacific.[39] Neither bill passed, but during the

---

[35] *Congressional Record*, 43 Congress, 2 session, 2070 (March 2, 1875).

[36] Published in Union Pacific, *Annual Report*, 1874, pp. 41–42.

[37] *Congressional Record*, 44 Congress, 1 session, 429 (January 17, 1876), 515–516 (January 20, 1876).

[38] *Ibid.*, 4514 (July 12, 1876); 2 session, 983–1964, *passim* (January 26–February 27, 1877).

[39] Senate Bill 60, *Congressional Record*, 44 Congress, 1 session, 193–194 (December 13, 1875), 573 (January 24, 1876), 1362–1363 (February 29, 1876), 1402–

House debate on the McCrary bill Representative Crounse of Nebraska, the leading exponent of taxation, exemplified the problems of the reformers when he strongly supported the Burlington in its bid for prorating, even though his district spanned Union Pacific territory. To justify his position he referred to his taxation bills as evidence that he believed both prorating and taxation were designed to benefit the people of the whole state.[40] For Crounse purely anti-railroad opinions and actions were not the way to reform.

Land bills, not all of them restrictive, were also numerous in this Congress. Senator Stephen W. Dorsey of Arkansas introduced a bill granting land to Tom Scott's Texas and Pacific.[41] The Senate passed a bill, introduced by S. J. R. MacMillan of Minnesota, extending to 1887 the deadline for completion of the Northern Pacific.[42] That the bill failed in the House was largely owing to the efforts of Holman of Indiana. On three separate occasions, sometimes with help, he blocked its consideration in the Committee of the Whole House.[43] Apparently out of eagerness to protect the settler and the public lands, Holman also objected vigorously to a bill introduced by Senator Ingalls of Kansas which declared forfeit, at the request of the road, the small and troublesome grant of the Kansas and Neosho Valley Railroad Company, until he was assured that the forfeiture worked neither hardship on the settlers nor special advantage to the railroad. The Indiana objector having been pacified, the bill passed, and the forfeiture, insignificant and uncontroversial as it was, was achieved.[44]

Three other land bills of importance besides bills specifically designed to achieve taxation were introduced in this Congress. Senator Booth of California proposed a measure to arrange sale of lands under the contingent right of preëmption, Senator I. P. Christiancy of Michigan one to repeal the costs of survey provision attached in 1870 to the Northern Pacific, and Representative W. S. King of Minnesota one to reduce the minimum price of the even-numbered sections in the Northern Pacific grant area to the usual $1.25 per acre.[45] None passed.

Four bills designed specifically to achieve taxation of the granted lands were introduced in the Forty-fourth Congress. Senator Booth of

---

1403 (March 2, 1876) ; 2 session, 392 (January 2, 1877), 394–396 (January 3, 1877), 397–406 (January 3, 1877), 575 (January 11, 1877) ; House Bill 4075, *ibid.*, 1 session, 5319 (August 8, 1876) ; 2 session, 93–95 (December 7, 1876), 172–177 (December 13, 1876).

[40] *Ibid.*, 2 session, 175 (December 13, 1876).

[41] *Ibid.*, 1549 (February 14, 1877).

[42] *Ibid.*, 1 session, 186–187 (December 8, 1875), 958–959 (February 9, 1876), 993–996 (February 10, 1876).

[43] *Ibid.*, 2 session, 92–93 (December 7, 1876), 922–924 (January 24, 1877), 2131–2132 (March 2, 1877).

[44] *Ibid.*, 1567 (February 14, 1877), 2136 (March 2, 1877).

[45] *Ibid.*, 310 (January 10, 1876), 1450 (March 3, 1876), 2458 (April 13, 1876), 3445 (June 1, 1876), 3671 (June 8, 1876), 3898 (June 20, 1876), 4230 (June 29, 1876), 4677 (July 18, 1876).

California introduced one such bill, but most of the leadership again came from Nebraska's Crounse and from the Kansans in Congress. Phillips was the first to introduce a bill, in December, 1875, and he was promptly seconded in the Senate by James M. Harvey, also of Kansas.[46] This early activity of Kansans was stimulated by pressure from home. The Kansas legislature had earlier called for immediate passage of the Crounse bill, and in January, 1876, shortly after the new session of Congress opened, it urged Kansas congressmen to renew the fight.[47] Crounse's new bill, introduced late,[48] failed as had his earlier one, this time for similar but perhaps more complex reasons.

The debate on the new Crounse bill was almost a reiteration of the discussion of his earlier proposal. Crounse himself reported the bill back from the Committee on Public Lands, and Holman immediately raised the point of order that the bill had the effect of making further appropriations of the public lands. Phillips supported Crounse's assertion that it did not do so, and Holman agreed to withdraw the point if Crounse would explain the bill. This Crounse undertook to do by discussing the legal history of section 21 of the act of 1864 and summarizing the provisions of his own proposal. The bill was identical to that passed by the House in the preceding Congress: it made the lands taxable whether the costs of survey had been paid or not and directed that the purchaser of a tax title might pay the costs of survey, whereupon the patent would be issued to the company but subject to the tax title. The explanation was interrupted by R. P. Bland of Missouri, who objected that the roads might get title to the lands indirectly by buying them at tax sales. Crounse pointed out that such action on the part of the companies would gain them nothing, and he went on to argue the justice of making railroad land subject to taxation as soon as it came into the possession of the road. The bill was then passed, without a recorded vote.[49]

In the Senate Crounse's bill suffered the same fate as had its forerunner in the previous Congress. It went to committee, was reported out with amendments, and died. The Harvey and Booth bills also died in committee. In the middle of the second session Senator Harvey introduced what was essentially the Crounse bill as an amendment to Thurman's debt-funding bill, but dilatory tactics by Saulsbury of Delaware and Morrill of Vermont killed it.[50] Again the reformers had been defeated, apparently for much the same reasons as before. But this time the forces working against the bills were in clearer array.

[46] *Ibid.*, 212 (December 15, 1876), 428 (January 4, 1877), 531 (January 10, 1877).

[47] *Laws of Kansas*, 1875, pp. 240–241; 1876, pp. 331–332.

[48] *Congressional Record*, 44 Congress, 1 session, 592 (January 24, 1876).

[49] *Ibid.*, 1520–1522 (March 7, 1876), 1554 (March 8, 1876).

[50] *Ibid.*, 1547 (March 8, 1876), 2175 (April 4, 1876); 2 session, 1554–1555 (February 14, 1877), 1638–1639 (February 16, 1877), 1962–1964 (February 27, 1877).

In the first place the opposition of the roads themselves, at least that of the West Coast companies, was unequivocally stated and widely publicized. J. H. Storrs, attorney for the Central Pacific, argued in a printed pamphlet (1) that the granting act was a contract which the United States, as one of the parties, could not alter; (2) that the lands in question were unsurveyed and could not be surveyed in the time allotted by the bills; (3) that the act of 1864 stipulated that patenting should take place as the lands were required by the companies; and (4) that the Central Pacific was already paying taxes on 862,719 acres and the Southern Pacific on 354,584 acres of patented but unsold land.[51] He contended that the bill should be entitled "A Bill for the Benefit of Tax-Sale Speculators" and concluded that, since the roads would be unable to pay the taxes that the Western states and counties would levy, the effect of the measure would be to put the granted lands "into the hands of the land sharks in the frontier states and territories."[52]

A second factor in the defeat of the reformers in this Congress was administrative opposition, which had not diminished perceptibly despite changes in the personnel of the Department of the Interior. Secretary Zachary Chandler made this known to the Senate Committee on Public Lands when, in answer to an inquiry, he asserted that it was unwise to make the lands taxable before patent was issued. Since it was impossible to maintain an ejectment action in court without a patent to the land in question, Chandler contended, prior taxation in states like Kansas, where only two years were allowed for bringing such a suit, would permit the tax title to supersede the patent.[53]

Whether despite or because of the large amount of agitation on the one hand and the forces working against legislation on the other, there emerged from this Forty-fourth Congress a provision that was of prime significance for the problem of taxing the lands of the land-grant railroads. In June of 1876 the Senate Committee on Appropriations inserted into the Sundry Civil Appropriations Bill an amendment extending the costs of survey provisions of the act of 1864 to all land-grant railroads that had not been specifically exempted in their granting acts.[54] This provision, as already construed by the Supreme Court of the United States in the Prescott and McShane cases, extended the applicability of the nontaxability feature, allegedly utilized by the

[51] *Argument of James H. Storrs, Counsel of Central Pacific Railroad Company, before the Committee on Public Lands, United States Senate . . . in Relation to the Taxation of Lands Granted to Railroad Companies, March 8, 1876* (John L. Ginck, Washington, 1876).

[52] *Ibid.*, 12–13.

[53] Chandler to Richard J. Oglesby, Chairman of the Senate Committee on Public Lands, August 8, 1876, in the National Archives, Record Group 48 (Records of the Office of the Secretary of the Interior), Lands and Railroads, Letters Sent.

[54] *Congressional Record*, 44 Congress, 1 session, 4281 (June 30, 1876); 19 *Statutes at Large* 121 (July 31, 1876); Thomas Donaldson, *The Public Domain: Its History with Statistics* (2d edition, Government Printing Office, Washington, 1884), 938.

roads to avoid taxation, to virtually all roads that had received direct grants of land. And this was done by a Congress rife with agitation to remove this very feature from earlier grants.

For the most part the role of personalities and interests in the enactment of this provision is undiscoverable. There is no indication which party or parties originally got it into the Senate bill. It was not mentioned in the debates on the report of the committee of conference. The most significant commentary on the treatment the provision received on the one hand and the inconsistent and often indefinable role of the "reformers" on the other, is the personnel of the conference committee that considered the bill without removing or substantially altering the amendment. For the Senate Windom of Minnesota and O. P. Morton of Indiana sat on the committee. Two of the members from the House were S. J. Randall of Pennsylvania and Eugene Hale of Maine. The third was that long-time defender of the public lands, William S. Holman of Indiana.[55]

During the next three sessions of Congress the reform congressmen from Kansas and Nebraska temporarily ceased to be a force. Crounse of Nebraska had lost his seat to Frank Welch, who had little influence during his first term. Phillips of Kansas was still in the House, but he introduced no tax bill in the first session of the Forty-fifth Congress, and the bill he presented in the second session, though favorably reported by the Committee on Public Lands, was recommitted and was not returned to the House calendar.[56] When the Forty-sixth Congress convened in March of 1879, Phillips too had been replaced, and his successor, John A. Anderson of Junction City, had yet to begin a campaign on the issue.

During the period between the fall of 1877 and the spring of 1880 the indebtedness issue was partly settled, the forfeiture problem was thoroughly but fruitlessly agitated, and the taxation question was scarcely agitated at all. The Forty-fifth Congress, after a lengthy debate carried over from the previous Congress, passed the Thurman Act, a funding bill that "settled" the problem of debt arrangements for the Union Pacific and Central Pacific roads for nearly a decade.[57] Thurman's efforts to extend such legislation to the Kansas Pacific failed, as did the efforts of Dorsey of Arkansas and Chalmers of Mississippi to achieve passage of similar bills.[58]

[55] *Congressional Record*, 44 Congress, 1 session, 4721–4729 (July 19, 1876), 4755–4772 (July 20, 1876).

[56] *Ibid.*, 4721–4729 (July 19, 1876), 4755–4772 (July 20, 1876); 45 Congress, 2 session, 195 (October 29, 1877), 3011 (May 1, 1878). The report is *House Report 709* (1878), a shortened version of 43 Congress, 1 session, *House Report 474* (1874).

[57] Senate Bill 15, *Congressional Record*, 45 Congress, 1 session, 58 (October 16, 1877), and 2 session, 1445–2990, *passim* (March 4–April 30, 1878). The law is 20 *Statutes at Large* 56 (May 7, 1878).

[58] Senate bills 512 and 1368 and House Bill 4153.

In this Congress and the first session of the Forty-sixth Congress forfeiture was the most agitated issue. During the Forty-fifth Congress Senators Booth of California and Plumb of Kansas introduced forfeiture bills; in the House H. F. Page of California introduced another and B. S. Fuller of Indiana, in the absence of Holman, introduced three and got one of them out of committee. Booth also introduced a measure closely related to the forfeiture bills, one that would restore to market the lands that had been withdrawn from the public domain to preserve them for fulfilling provisions of land-grant acts. This bill got no further than introduction.[59] In the first session of the Forty-sixth Congress the Booth and Plumb forfeiture bills were introduced again, and in the House a new proponent of forfeiture, John Whiteaker of Oregon, introduced his version. Again they got nowhere.[60]

The confusion was rendered complete when, at the height of the forfeiture agitation in this first session of the Forty-sixth Congress, there appeared on the calendars for the first time in years a series of bills proposing new grants. One proposal, that of Territorial Representative G. G. Bennett of Dakota, came from the West, but most of the agitation came from the South. J. R. Chalmers of Mississippi, E. J. Ellis of Louisiana, and Tennesseans Casey Young and Benton McMillan all introduced bills designed to appropriate land for the building of railroads in the South.[61] That these bills were introduced in such numbers by representatives from the Southern states may bolster the contention that a deal had been made between conservative Southern politicians and Northern capitalists in the so-called "Compromise of 1877."[62] But if this was true, it was one of the occasions when the Northerners did not deliver, for none of the bills ever got out of committee.

The year 1880 opened a new era in the agitation for adjustment and final settlement with the land-grant railroads. Strong campaigns for taxation and forfeiture, launched by a few congressional personalities, gained increasing momentum and eventually became irresistible. Bills declaring forfeit the grants of individual railroads appeared on the legislative calendars in ever-increasing numbers, and several were passed. General bills designed to declare forfeit the lands of all roads that had not been completed within the time specified also became more and more numerous and a general forfeiture bill was finally passed.[63] The taxation campaign was waged differently. Beginning in

[59] Senate bills 147, 407, 627 and House bills, 3010, 1390, 3544, 6389.
[60] Senate bills 90 and 196 and House Bill 2195.
[61] House bills 468, 1602, 1707, 2325. Chalmer's resolution is in the *Congressional Record*, 46 Congress, 1 session, 432 (April 14, 1879).
[62] C. Vann Woodward, in his *Reunion and Reaction: The Compromise of 1877 and the End of Reconstruction* (Little, Brown and Company, Boston, 1951), has analyzed the results of the Hayes-Tilden election in these terms. For the story of internal improvements, see *passim* but especially pages 1–67 and 230–237.
[63] The only scholarly study of forfeiture is that by David M. Ellis, "The Forfeiture of Railroad Land Grants, 1867–1894," in the *Mississippi Valley Historical*

May of 1880, one man led all others as the champion of land-grant taxation. He made the issue his own both in Congress and at home. By 1884 he had been joined by many others, and two years later the champions of taxation were almost as numerous as the champions of forfeiture. Through it all the conflict between the two issues—whether to preserve the public domain by withholding patents to the grantees' land or declaring it forfeit, or to hasten passage of title to the land so that it could be taxed—made the achievement of either reform doubly difficult.

In the first congressional session of the eighties a number of new personalities entered the lists in favor of forfeiture. Most of the new-comers were representatives of the Southern or former Border States. The Southerners, having failed in the preceding session of Congress to win the internal improvements legislation they wanted, were perhaps trying to force the issue in this session. In any event the session had scarcely begun when Senator John T. Morgan of Alabama introduced a general forfeiture resolution. It was promptly squelched by the objection of Pendleton of Ohio and referred to the Committee on the Judiciary.[64] Senator B. F. Jonas of Louisiana also introduced a forfeiture bill, but this was a granting bill as well and closely related to the granting proposals made by Southerners in the first session and still being pushed by Alabama and Mississippi congressmen. Jonas' proposal was to transfer the grant of the Texas Pacific to the New Orleans Pacific. This too died in committee.[65] In the House, representatives from the former Border States were now, for the first time, pushing bills to abrogate grants. R. M. McLane of Maryland, a member of the Committee on the Pacific Railroads, pushed a general forfeiture bill, and B. F. Martin of West Virginia introduced a bill to recover the grant of the Atlantic and Pacific. Northern and Western proponents of forfeiture included holdovers Plumb and Whiteaker and newcomers Henry B. Anthony of Rhode Island, D. W. Voorhees of Indiana, and J. H. Slater of Oregon. Anthony and Voorhees were anxious, as had been their predecessors, to obtain general forfeiture legislation. Slater sought merely to declare forfeit the grant of a "local" road, the Oregon Central.[66] Still, despite all the new proponents of legislation, the move for forfeiture in this session accomplished nothing in the way of remedies for the evils it was designed to cure.

Review, 33:27–60 (June, 1946), a summary of an unpublished master's thesis, Cornell University, 1939. The law is 26 *Statutes at Large* 496 (September 29, 1890).

[64] Senate Resolution 54, *Congressional Record*, 46 Congress, 2 session, 136–137 (December 17, 1879).

[65] Senate Bill 1066 and House Bill 5543, *Congressional Record*, 46 Congress, 2 session, 234 (January 8, 1880).

[66] *Ibid.*, 295 (January 13, 1880), 979, 995 (February 18, 1880), 2343 (April 13, 1880), 2528 (April 19, 1880), 3102 (May 7 1880), 3309 (May 13, 1880), 3505 (May 19, 1880).

It was in this session of Congress that the movement to tax unpatented railroad lands found its prophet: John A. Anderson of Junction City, Kansas, a former Presbyterian minister, former president of Kansas State College at Manhattan, and now successor to William A. Phillips as representative of the first congressional district of Kansas, a district which at that time included nearly all the organized counties in the northern half of the state.[67] For his maiden speech in the House Anderson chose the subject that was to become his rallying cry, the taxation of railroad lands. The occasion for the speech was the consideration of the Post Office Appropriations Bill, to which he offered a taxation amendment. A point of order was immediately raised but was held in abeyance until the speech had been delivered.

In this obviously set speech Anderson carefully outlined the main points of his argument and his aim as he was to repeat them over the next six years, first as a lone agitator and later as the spokesman of a growing group of reformers. He stated that his object was to require the Kansas Pacific to pay the costs of survey and thus to make its lands taxable. The existing situation, he alleged, permitted the railroad to withhold nearly a quarter of a million dollars from the tax rolls annually, and his summary of the situation in thirty-seven counties showed that 2,863,262 acres, valued at $13,593,731 and worth $239,909 in taxes annually, were tax-exempt. Then he summarized in detail the acts of 1862 and 1864, with particular attention to that part of section 21 of the latter act which provided that the roads should pay the costs of survey "as the titles shall be required," hinting strongly that this was included designedly. He quoted the McShane and Prescott decisions at some length. He alleged that the settler on government land had to pay taxes when he received title, normally in five years or sooner, and thus had to support public improvements for the benefit of all, whereas the railroad and the purchaser of railroad land escaped this burden. Finally, Anderson defended his proposal against the point of order by insisting that the amendment was germane to the bill under consideration. When the Speaker ruled it out of order, he accepted the pronouncement with obvious bad grace[68] and said no more on the subject during the remainder of the Forty-sixth Congress. But in this Congress he proposed

---

[67] A laudatory sketch of Anderson by his strongest political supporter is George W. Martin's "John A. Anderson—A Character Sketch," in the *Transactions of the Kansas State Historical Society*, 8:315–323 (1904). Letters documenting the Martin-Anderson political alliance are in the manuscript collections under their respective names at the Kansas State Historical Society, Topeka. See especially a series from Anderson to Martin, all from Washington and all concerned with local political maneuvering, dated from February 21, 1882, to January 17, 1883.

[68] *Congressional Record*, 46 Congress, 2 session, 3020–3023 (May 5, 1880). Anderson enlisted the aid of the General Land Office for gathering information. See Anderson to J. A. Williamson (interdepartmental telegram), June 3, 1880, and reply of the same date, in the National Archives, Record Group 49 (Records of the General Land Office), Railroad Land Grant Records, box 37. Hereafter this collection will be cited as Record Group 49.

three bills to achieve taxation either with or without the issuance of the patents.[69]

In the fall of 1880 Anderson's opponents in his home district denounced his effort as a political trick suggested by a home-town politician, designed not to correct the abuse but to attract votes.[70] But he was re-elected. The Kansas legislature passed a resolution calling for tax legislation,[71] and on his return to Congress Anderson found a number of fellow supporters of tax measures, all from Kansas and Nebraska. The Colorado legislature had also passed a resolution calling for taxation,[72] but this evoked no immediate action on the part of representatives from Colorado.

Anderson himself early introduced a bill to achieve his object. After six months, during which a second bill was introduced by Anderson, the Committee on Pacific Railroads, under the leadership of Benjamin Butterworth of Ohio, introduced a substitute measure calling for payment of the costs of survey by the Kansas Pacific and providing that the road be made subject to the Thurman Act.[73] But Anderson did not wait for the committee; late in January he addressed remarks on his own first bill, taking a position almost identical to the one he had two years before. He was less critical of the legislators who had enacted section 21 of the act of 1864, but he made his first overt accusation that the railroads had suppressed his effort in the previous Congress and would vigorously oppose it in this one.[74] Furthermore, priming himself with information from the General Land Office, he again sought to get the provision attached to an appropriations bill.[75]

This time the debate was a torrid one. In the discussion of the point of order a number of representatives took sides for or against Anderson's proposal. His chief backing came from his fellow Kansas representatives, Thomas Ryan and Dudley Haskell, and he received minor support from George M. Robeson of New Jersey. The opposition in-

[69] House bills 4728, 6413, 7167.

[70] See the *Junction City Union*, August 26, 1880. There may be some justice in the charge; at least Martin may have suggested the issue. See Anderson to Martin, Washington, February 21, 1882, in the George Martin Papers, in the Kansas State Historical Society, Topeka.

[71] *Laws of Kansas*, 1881, p. 331; *Junction City Union*, February 5, 1881.

[72] *Congressional Record*, 47 Congress, 1 session, 53 (December 8, 1881). The resolution was presented by Senator Teller.

[73] *Ibid.*, 100 (December 13, 1881), 2531 (April 3, 1881), 4579 (June 6, 1882); *House Report 1312* (1882). Anderson later expressed the opinion that Butterworth was on his side. See Anderson to Martin, Washington, March 7, 1882, and July 8, 1882, in the George Martin Papers, in the Kansas State Historical Society.

[74] *Congressional Record*, 47 Congress, 1 session, 660–665 (January 26, 1882).

[75] Anderson to Department of the Interior (interdepartmental telegram), July 11, 1882, and reply of the same date, in Record Group 49, Railroad Land Grant Records, box 37. Anderson revealed his plans for the appropriation-bill tactic to Martin, defending them partly on the ground that taxation would be a "living issue" in the congressional elections of 1882 and 1884. See letters dated July 10, 1882, and January 17, 1883, in the George Martin Papers, in the Kansas State Historical Society.

cluded Frank Hiscock of New York, Butterworth of Ohio, and Dunn of Arkansas, all members of the Committee on Pacific Railroads, T. C. Pound of Wisconsin, and, above all, George C. Hazelton, also of Wisconsin, chairman of the Committee on Railroads. Both Anderson and the committee members made it clear that in bringing up the proposal in this way Anderson was motivated by a desire to bypass the committee, which he felt was trying to block him. Hazelton was particularly bitter toward Anderson for questioning the motives of the committee and insisted that the Kansas delegation was trying to get the lands taxed in any way possible, without considering the problem of getting the patents from the Land Office. In any event, on two separate occasions during the debate the chair ruled the amendment out of order and on both occasions Anderson's appeal was overwhelmingly defeated in the Committee of the Whole House.[76]

With this defeat the taxation move in the House was scotched. Nevertheless in the second session Ryan, Anderson's Kansas colleague, offered a resolution incorporating the Anderson bill, only to have it blocked by New York's Hiscock, and, too late in the session to accomplish anything, E. K. Valentine of Nebraska introduced a taxation bill designed to apply to the Union Pacific.[77]

Taxation also found new champions in the Senate. Plumb of Kansas, who had been introducing forfeiture bills ever since his election, returned now to the problem of taxation. Encouraged perhaps by the political success of Anderson, by the resolution of the Kansas legislature, and by citizen memorialists, he introduced a general taxation bill early in the first session of this Congress.[78] A second champion, Charles H. Van Wyck, a prewar representative from New York and now newly elected senator from Nebraska,[79] also introduced a general tax bill.[80] The Plumb bill, like the earlier Crounse bills, provided for taxation of the lands before patents were issued and for the payment of costs of survey by the purchaser of the tax title. It was amended in the Senate Judiciary Committee, of which Ingalls of Kansas was chairman, to apply only to lands "selected" as well as surveyed.[81] Anti-monopoly newspapers in Kansas hastened to point out that this provision effectively

[76] *Congressional Record*, 47 Congress, 1 session, 5904–5910 (July 11, 1882).

[77] *Ibid.*, 2 session, 16 (December 4, 1882), 2747–2748 (February 15, 1883).

[78] *Ibid.*, 1 session, 49 (December 7, 1881), 1629 (March 6, 1882).

[79] Marie U. Harmer and James L. Sellers, "Charles H. Van Wyck—Soldier and Statesman," in *Nebraska History*, 12:81–128, 190–246, 322–373 (1931) and 13:3–36 (1932). The Van Wyck Papers, in the Kansas University Library at Lawrence, are devoid of correspondence bearing directly on the taxation issue.

[80] Senate Bill 1306.

[81] *Congressional Record*, 47 Congress, 2 session, 4702 (June 9, 1882). Anderson viewed Plumb as a friend of reform and Ingalls as its bitter enemy, at least until January 17, 1883. Unfortunately neither the Martin nor the Anderson papers include political correspondence after that date, despite the fact that the two men were in constant personal touch, that Anderson often ran Martin's business for him, and that they were closely identified in political discussions in the local newspapers up to Anderson's death in May of 1893.

pulled the teeth of the bill, since lands "selected" were already subject to taxation, inasmuch as "selection" under the Land Office rules then in operation required payment of the costs of survey.[82] Still, when the bill came before the Senate in mid-June, Plumb made no objection, and after a short debate in which Conger of Michigan sought and received from Ingalls assurances that the bill did not affect forfeiture, it was passed and sent to Hazelton's committee in the House. There it died. The Van Wyck bill, which was designed to quitclaim to the taxing agent the interest of the United States in the costs of survey payments on land sold at tax sale, was reported back from committee in the second session but died on the calendar.[83]

That John Anderson was not wholly nor perhaps even primarily responsible for the new interest in a tax measure is clear. Perhaps a major reason for that interest was the general realization that the Supreme Court decision invalidating the contingent right of preëmption would not place the granted lands on the tax rolls. The bitter accusations of the *Omaha Bee* and the *Nebraska Herald* that collusion had been practiced in this and related decisions[84] were clearly reflected in the report that the Senate Committee on Public Lands submitted on the Van Wyck bill. The committee cited the Platt case as evidence for its implication that the courts had been inconsistent in order to benefit the railroads, by first holding the contingent right sufficient to prevent taxation and later invalidating it to keep settlers off the land.[85]

Still, that Anderson's course was being repeated, though not necessarily as a model, is clearly demonstrated. Each of the Kansas and Nebraska delegates who took up the fight for taxation made political capital from it. In the eyes of the anti-monopoly newspapers Plumb had joined Anderson as a champion of the people, and in the straight Republican papers he was given credit for initiating the move and for presenting the most effective and best-drawn legislative proposal in its behalf.[86] The anti-monopoly papers gave Van Wyck the same sort of credit, but they accused Valentine, the latecomer, of simply imitating Van Wyck and then only when there was no likelihood of success.[87]

With the launching of the Forty-eighth Congress in December of 1883, the movement for railroad-land reform in general and for railroad-land taxation in particular gained new strength. The Nebraska leg-

[82] *Junction City Union*, November 11, 25, 1882; *Manhattan Nationalist*, November 10, 1882.

[83] *Congressional Record*, 47 Congress, 2 session, 257 (December 13, 1882), 548 (December 22, 1882), 4702 (June 9, 1882), 5427 (June 27, 1882); 1 session, 1369 (February 23, 1882).

[84] *Omaha Bee*, June 13, 27, 1883; *Nebraska Herald*, August 31, 1881.

[85] 47 Congress, 3 session, *Senate Report 990* (1883).

[86] *Omaha Bee*, December 21, 1881, February 22, 1882; *Atchison Champion* (Kansas), January 22, 1882; *Topeka Commonwealth* (Kansas), March 21, 1882; *Manhattan Nationalist*, June 15, 1882.

[87] *Omaha Bee*, June 21, December 13, 1882, December 19, 1883; *Fremont Herald*, December 28, 1882.

islature added its voice to that of Kansas by calling for a tax law. The Nebraska resolution accepted the argument used by Crounse in the seventies and repeated in greater detail by Anderson and his compatriots in later debates, namely that the fault lay entirely with the roads and that only Congress could provide the remedy.[88] Furthermore, the executive department of the federal government now reversed itself and joined the campaign. Secretary of the Interior Henry M. Teller of Colorado, in his annual report for 1883, asserted that the roads were avoiding taxation by refraining from patenting their less valuable lands, and he urged that Congress take "prompt and serious action."[89] Teller and William A. J. Sparks, commissioner of the General Land Office under Teller's successor, continued to complain of delay on the part of the railroads and to urge congressional action.[90] Finally, in Congress itself the wave of land reform, particularly as expressed in forfeiture movements, was rising rapidly. This was not entirely advantageous to advocates of taxation, since they had found, and would continue to find, proponents of forfeiture fighting them, but it created an atmosphere of land-grant reform in which the tax proposals could be pushed more effectively.

Congressional supporters of forfeiture, already numerous when Anderson began his campaign for taxation in 1880, had continued to increase, and in 1884 and 1885 they achieved their first major victories. In the Congress convening in 1881 (the Forty-seventh) two Senate bills, one Senate resolution, six House bills, and three House resolutions were introduced, but none was passed.[91] In the Forty-eighth Congress, which convened in 1883, five Senate bills, eleven House bills, and two resolutions were introduced;[92] for the first time some of them got through committee and on the calendars, and some of them were passed. In this Congress three major forfeitures were achieved: the Iron Mountain of Missouri, the Oregon Central, and the Texas Pacific lost portions of or all their grants.[93] In the next Congress, convening in December of 1885, three more bills were passed, declaring forfeit all or parts of the grants of the Atlantic and Pacific, the New Orleans, Baton Rouge and Vicksburg, and a number of minor Southern roads.[94] The advocates of for-

---

[88] *Laws of Nebraska*, 1883, p. 381. A copy of the resolution was presented in Congress by Senator Charles Manderson. *Congressional Record*, 48 Congress, 1 session, 45 (December 5, 1883).

[89] Secretary of the Interior, *Annual Report*, 1883, pp. xxxiv–xxxv.

[90] *Ibid.*, 1884, pp. xviii–xix; Commissioner of the General Land Office, *Annual Report*, 1885, pp. 197–198.

[91] Senate bills 347, 1084; Senate Resolution 27; House bills 2382, 2580, 2878, 3606, 5362, 6390; House resolutions 91, 105, 264.

[92] Senate bills 58, 62, 67, 177, 428; House bills 44, 119, 174, 188, 292, 316, 1309, 1884, 2020, 3520, 4996; House resolutions 4, 5.

[93] 23 *Statutes at Large* 61 (June 28, 1884), 296 (January 31, 1885), 337 (February 28, 1885).

[94] 24 *Statutes at Large* 123 (July 6, 1886), 140 (July 10, 1886), 391 (February 8, 1887).

feiture, although still proposing legislation on other individual roads—especially the Northern Pacific—concentrated increasingly on achieving a general forfeiture act to apply to all roads completed after the expiration of the time limits set in their granting acts. In the end the reformers met what the staunchest supporters of forfeiture considered defeat when the General Forfeiture Act, passed in 1890, reclaimed only those portions of the grants which lay alongside sections of roads still uncompleted on the date of its passage.[95]

It is manifestly impossible to delineate the motives of the advocates of forfeiture, just as it is those of the advocates of taxation. The unchallenged leader of the group demanding forfeiture, the man to whom was applied the sobriquet "grand old man of the forfeiture movement,"[96] was William S. Holman of Indiana. Other leaders whose records were consistently anti-railroad, though somewhat less markedly so than Holman's, were Payson of Illinois, Plumb of Kansas, Booth of California, and Van Wyck of Nebraska.

Another extreme is illustrated by the activities of Representative George W. Cassidy of Nevada, who as a Democratic representative from a town on the Central Pacific Railroad, introduced into the Forty-seventh Congress a bill designed to effect forfeiture of the Northern Pacific's grant, and yet in the forty-eighth Congress consistently opposed taxation legislation. This course is explicable in terms of his allegiance to the home-town railroad, which in the first instance sought to embarrass a serious rival and in the second opposed legislation manifestly detrimental to its own interest.[97]

Senator John Mitchell of Oregon pursued a similar course. First he attempted to effect forfeiture of lands of the Northern Pacific for the benefit of one of its Oregon rivals; then later, when Henry Villard took control of the Northern Pacific, he worked against forfeiture and also fought the Union Pacific's attempts to tap Villard's territory.[98]

These are only the few whose motives can be tentatively established on the basis of documentary evidence or their legislative records. The motives of the Congress as a whole, or of individual members of it who waxed hot and cold on one or the other of the issues, can be the subject of informed guesses, no more. There is perhaps no better illustration

[95] For a concise resumé of this movement see David M. Ellis, "The Forfeiture of Railroad Land Grants, 1867–1894," in the *Mississippi Valley Historical Review*, 33:52–56 (June, 1946). The law is 26 *Statutes at Large* 496 (September 29, 1890).

[96] Ellis, "Forfeiture," in the *Mississippi Valley Historical Review*, 33:52.

[97] This analysis is made in James B. Hedges, *Henry Villard and the Railways of the Northwest* (Yale University Press, New Haven, 1930), 106. For biographical data on Cassidy see the *Biographical Directory of the American Congress, 1774–1949* (Government Printing Office, Washington, 1950), 958.

[98] An example of Mitchell's operations is his letter to J. A. Williamson, Commissioner of the General Land Office, Washington, November 28, 1877, in Record Group 49, Railroad Land Grant Records, Box 66. See also Hedges, *Villard*, 47n, 49–54, 103–104.

of the difficulty inherent in the study of motives than is afforded by the history of the taxation movement in the Forty-eighth and Forty-ninth congresses.

In the Forty-eighth Congress the Senate almost exactly duplicated its treatment of the taxation bills of the preceding sessions. Both Plumb and Van Wyck re-introduced their bills, and again it was Plumb's that was reported from committee. Again the committee bill differed fundamentally from the original proposal in that it substituted for the Plumb provision making all granted lands taxable another one limiting taxability to such lands as had been surveyed and selected.[99] This may explain why on two occasions both Plumb and Van Wyck were willing to allow the bill to be set back on the calendar and why, toward the close of the second session, Plumb himself moved that it be indefinitely postponed. When it was debated Senator Ingalls, perhaps to clear himself of the charge of tooth-pulling, asserted that although he could not consent unreservedly to the amendment requiring selection, he would accept it because he thought it was the best bill that could be passed at the time.[1] But the bill never came to a vote. Furthermore, the bill that the House passed in this session died on the Senate calendar.

Though the House bill failed in the Senate (as usual), consideration of it in the House had produced a number of new developments and brought into focus some of the arguments that divided the legislators. As usual, Anderson introduced his taxation measure in the opening days of the Congress, and he was soon joined by Valentine and James Laird of Nebraska and Dunn of Arkansas. This time it was early in the session when the committee bill, managed by Charles F. Crisp of Georgia, was reported. However, a minority of the committee, led by Lewis Hanback of Kansas, also submitted a report and a fundamentally different bill.[2] The majority report proposed a legal remedy for the failure of the roads to pay their fees and take title: the injured party was considered to be the United States, and that party was to take the problem to the courts for solution. The minority bill required that administrative officers issue patents to all lands to which the companies were legally entitled, irrespective of whether the costs of survey had been paid; call on the companies to pay them; and proceed from there to litigation. In the first instance the patents would not be issued until after the costs of survey had been collected in court. In the second the patents would be issued immediately and the costs of survey collected later by litigation.[3]

[99] Senate bills 59 and 60.
[1] *Congressional Record*, 48 Congress, 2 session, 426 (December 23, 1884), 1492 (February 10, 1885), 1945 (February 20, 1885); 1 session, 1380–1381 (February 26, 1884).
[2] *Ibid.*, 1 session, 75 (December 10, 1883), 95 (December 11, 1883), 532 (January 21, 1884), 1359 (February 25, 1884), 3821 (May 5, 1884).
[3] Copies of both bills appear *ibid.*, 5164 (June 14, 1884).

The bills ran the gamut of difficulties. When Crisp called them up on the afternoon of June 14, Randall of Pennsylvania insisted on a vote to decide whether the measures should be considered. The House, in a recorded vote, decided not to consider, Holman being the only one of the land-reform group to vote with the majority. Cassidy of Nevada moved to set aside the following Wednesday for consideration of the bills and when the House would not agree to that, another vote was taken and this time consideration was agreed upon.[4]

The discussion revolved around the two methods proposed by the two factions of the committee. Crisp, for the majority, argued that the costs of survey constituted a lien of the federal government and that Congress should not abrogate it. He conceded that the real object of the legislation was to achieve the taxation of the lands, but he refused to let this override his determination to guarantee payment to the United States of the amounts due it from the various railroads. Hanback, for the minority, argued that litigation would not solve the problem, that the immediate need was for taxation, and that his object was to tax the lands first and litigate later. In the two-day debate that followed, the majority bill received support from Crisp himself, Bayne of Pennsylvania, Payson of Illinois, Cassidy of Nevada, Millard of New York, and Broadhead of Missouri. The minority bill received its backing from Hanback, Ryan, and Anderson of Kansas and Weaver and Laird of Nebraska. Those in opposition said little and confined themselves almost entirely to questioning the speakers. The only two congressmen who spoke out clearly against both bills were Hiscock of New York and Hepburn of Iowa. In these debates it was Hanback rather than Anderson who led the attack, but Anderson did find the opportunity to hold forth in his characteristic manner. If anything, he was more vehement than ever before in his denunciation of the railroads, calling for the forfeiture of unpatented lands if the roads would not agree to give local government the financial support justly due it.[5]

The companion issues of forfeiture and debt settlement plagued consideration of the bill. At the outset J. H. Budd of California had to be assured that the bill did not apply to unearned grants. Later Payson of Illinois departed from his original support of the majority bill and proposed the penalty of forfeiture for noncompliance, as suggested by Anderson. Holman took no part in the debate. Hiscock, in his fight against the bill, raised the issue of debt settlement when he insisted that all the assets of the bond-aided companies were committed by the Thurman Act, that no more judgments could be levied against the roads.[6]

[4] *Ibid.*, 5163–5164 (June 14, 1884); *House Journal*, 48 Congress, 1 session, 1454–1455 (June 14, 1884).

[5] The entire debate is encompassed in the *Congressional Record*, 48 Congress, 1 session, 5163–5170 (June 14, 1884), 5262–5273 (June 17, 1884).

[6] *Ibid.*, 5165 (June 14, 1884), 5264, 5269–5270 (June 17, 1884).

It was the minority's version of the bill that finally passed the House. On the second day of debate, after much haggling over the priority of previous amendments, Hanback offered his proposal for immediate taxation as an amendment to the majority's bill. Over the protests of Representative Crisp, the House passed the amendment, then the bill.[7]

Analysis of the roll-call vote on the measure leads to no concrete conclusions. The Democrats controlled the House, but it was their bill that was superseded. This may explain why fifty-eight of the sixty-five Republicans voted for the substitute measure and seventy-four of the hundred and three Democrats against it. A sectional breakdown of the vote tends only to bolster the conclusion that it was based largely on party affiliation. In all sections save one, party tended to rule. Even the Republican representatives of the New England and Middle Atlantic states, where the majority of the stock of the affected roads was held, voted with their party. The one group whose vote cannot be said to reflect party affiliation was that representing the public-land states directly affected by the measure. All save one of the congressmen from these areas voted for the Hanback immediate-taxation version, but most of them, too, were Republicans. The one nay vote in this group was cast by a Democrat, Cassidy of Nevada, but his vote is perhaps less accurately attributable to support of his party than to his commitment to the Central Pacific Railroad, as best expressed in his conduct on the forfeiture issue.

By the end of 1885 the long battle on the taxation issue approached a climax. The fourteen-year struggle, though fruitless of tangible reforms, had resulted in strong opposition to further exemption and in the making of at least one political reputation, that of John A. Anderson of Kansas. Furthermore, the label "land reformer" was becoming increasingly popular in some parts of the country. The forfeiture movement was at its height. The incumbent commissioner of the General Land Office, William A. J. Sparks, was the most ardent reformer yet to hold the office.[8] The national administration, the first Democratic presidency since the Civil War, although by no means a radical one, had a record to make and was able to make its best showing in various reform moves. In the West the tide of third-party revolt was rising from indigenous anti-monopoly predilections and was soon to become, with reinforcement from other radical movements, a force too strong to be either ignored or suppressed.

In the atmosphere that produced such reforms as the first independent regulatory commission, a contract-labor law, the Dawes Act, executive prohibition of the fencing of the public domain, and cancellation of land-grant withdrawals of thousands of acres, few politicians would stand openly against taxation. And yet it was in the Forty-ninth Con-

[7] *Ibid.*, 5272 (June 17, 1884).
[8] John B. Rae, "Commissioner Sparks and the Railroad Land Grants," in the *Mississippi Valley Historical Review*, 25:211–230 (September, 1933).

gress, where taxation legislation was finally achieved, that the lines of opposing forces were most sharply drawn, that the arguments for and against taxation were most clearly presented, that arguments over responsibility for the slow pace of the patenting process reduced the issue to a judgment for or against the railroads as opposed to the Land Office, and that judgment was ultimately rendered against the railroads.

In this Congress the House career of the taxation issue was noteworthy in two respects: the unprecedented number of bills introduced and the clarity with which the cross-currents of land reform were manifest in the bills presented. One or another version was proposed by Anderson of Kansas, Dunn of Arkansas, Payson of Illinois, Cobb of Indiana, Laird and Weaver of Nebraska, Campbell of New York, Crisp of Georgia, Springer of Illinois, and Territorial Delegates Toole of Montana and Gifford of Dakota.[9] Laird of Nebraska and Payson of Illinois each presented two contradictory measures—one providing for the forfeiture of unpatented lands and another that would make them taxable.[10] The problem of conflict between forfeiture and taxation was brought out even more clearly in the proposals of Cobb and Springer, who first introduced bills to get lands patented and taxes paid, then introduced resolves that all patenting cease until forfeiture of the grants of uncompleted roads was accomplished.[11] John A. Anderson was guilty of the same contradictory behavior. He introduced, in addition to his perennial taxation bill, an "adjustment bill" calling for the settlement of land-grant questions in Kansas. The adjustment bill grew out of the campaign of former Governor Samuel Crawford, as a paid agent of the state, to achieve an adjustment on the basis of an immediate cessation of patenting in Kansas and the reversion to the public domain of all lands not earned by the roads.[12]

As the taxation bill, including the Hanback provision for immediate taxation,[13] wended its now familiar way through the House, another development complicated the situation. For the first time since the campaign against the Crounse bill a decade earlier, railroads presented their case in published pamphlets. The burden of their argument was (1) that the roads were unable to obtain all the patents they applied for because of the inefficiency of the Land Office; (2) that if they did

[9] House bills 70, 276, 378, 456, 1410, 1611, 2882, 3077, 3752, and 5808.
[10] House bills 1414 and 3279.
[11] House resolutions 10 and 20.
[12] Anderson's bill is House Bill 3076. Crawford's case is summarized in a series of five pamphlets, published 1884–1886, presenting the arguments he used before congressional committees and Land Office officials, all in the Bureau of Railway Economics Library, Washington. The railroad's published reply is John S. Blair, *Before the Secretary of the Interior in the Matter of the Applications of the Union Pacific Railway Company for Patents . . .* (Gibson Brothers, Washington, 1886). Anderson's role in the Crawford campaign is described in a letter from Samuel Crawford to George A. Martin, Washington, March 22, 1905, in the Anderson Papers.
[13] *Congressional Record,* 49 Congress, 1 session, 2200 (May 8, 1886).

choose to delay applying for patents, they were protected by the "as they shall require them" clause of section 21 of the act of 1864; and (3) that the taxation-without-patent program being proposed would complicate titles and accrue to the benefit of speculators.[14] The railroad pamphlets did not figure in the House's consideration of the measure; it remained for the interested senators to use the ammunition thus presented them.

It was in the Senate, the graveyard of the earlier tax measures, that the final battle for taxation was fought. Early in the session Van Wyck of Nebraska introduced his usual tax measure.[15] A month later Hawley of Connecticut presented a similar measure and took occasion to describe the abuse that the bill was designed to eliminate. Van Wyck seconded Hawley and assured the Senate that the Committee on Public Lands, of which he was now a member, would soon present its own bill. On the same occasion Henry M. Teller, now representing Colorado in the Senate, reminded his colleagues that while serving as secretary of the interior he had recommended immediate passage of tax legislation. To complete the presentation Joseph Dolph of Oregon took the opportunity to defend the Northern Pacific against any charge of willfully delaying patents to avoid taxation. After this exchange Hawley's bill was referred to the Committee on Public Lands.[16]

The committee measure, Senate Bill Number 1812, was introduced in early March of 1886.[17] A month later, though Plumb of Kansas actually had charge of it, Van Wyck served notice that he would call the bill up for consideration at the next opportunity. The following Wednesday he called for unanimous consent, but in the face of the objection of Henry W. Blair of New Hampshire, who was to prove himself the most outspoken critic of the tax move, the motion was postponed until the following day. On Thursday, after more dilatory tactics—Blair protesting in vain that he was not ready to undertake consideration, then Cullom of Illinois, Edmunds of Vermont, and Blair occupying time with private bills—consideration of the tax bill was finally undertaken.[18]

This first debate was confined almost exclusively to a presentation of the case by Van Wyck and a rebuttal by Blair. Van Wyck's presentation was short. He pointed out that the bill had been considered and passed by one house or the other in the two preceding Congresses. "The non-action of Congress has been a marvel," he said, "only explainable

---

[14] W. H. Mills, *Payment of Survey Fees upon and Taxation of Granted Lands: . . . Letter Addressed to the Chairman of the Senate Committee on Public Lands* (no imprint, San Francisco, March 2, 1886) ; G. H. Tweed, *In the Matter of the Payment for Surveys and the Taxation of Granted Lands of the Central Pacific Railroad* (no imprint).

[15] Senate Bill 334.

[16] *Congressional Record*, 49 Congress, 1 session, 1428–1429 (February 15, 1886).

[17] The accompanying report is *Senate Report 199* (1886).

[18] *Congressional Record*, 49 Congress, 1 session, 3349 (April 10, 1886), 3692 (April 21, 1886), 3717–3718 (April 22, 1886).

by reason of that subtle and mysterious influence which has so often controlled subjects of this kind."[19] He charged that the roads had delib- erately delayed patenting to avoid taxes, whereas at the same time the adjoining land was subject to taxation. Finally, he indicated that the bill as proposed permitted taxation only in organized counties and would thus protect the roads from fraudulent or excessive assessments.[20]

Blair opened his attack with the statement that although there was "a certain superficial appearance of propriety" in Van Wyck's bill, the proposal was actually confiscatory, broke faith with the roads and in- vestors in them, and was drafted for the benefit of speculators. He con- tended that the roads, as great national enterprises undertaken by pri- vate capital at the instigation of and in response to enticements offered by the government in a time of tribulation, had fulfilled their obliga- tions, and it was now the duty of the country to allow them to enjoy the benefits of the increased value which they themselves had created. When the lands were granted, he said, it was not contemplated that they would be taxed. Private capital had been invested in mortgages secured by the untaxed lands. Taxation imposed now, when the low earnings of the roads would not enable them to pay the levies, would amount to confiscation of the lands for the benefit of tax buyers, who would in- variably be land sharks and speculators. Furthermore, it was the Land Office, not the individual railroad, that was responsible for the slow passage of patents, as was evinced by the fact that the roads always had more selections pending action than the officials of the government could or would process. He prophesied that the organized counties would levy excessive taxes and use the payments to finance expensive public improvements before such expenditures were justified.[21]

Blair concluded by offering a series of amendments designed to fore- stall these evils. These amendments called for (1) the restriction of ownership of public lands acquired in the future to 320 acres of agri- cultural tracts or 640 acres of other types, with the penalty of forfei- ture for violation; (2) the maintenance of the railroad-mortgage lien against any and all purchasers of tax title under the act; (3) the re- striction of local taxation to lands valued in excess of $2.50 an acre and to sections adjacent to sections of public land actually occupied and improved; (4) the reservation by the United States of the right to purchase the lands at tax sale and restore them to the public domain; and (5) the restriction of individual purchases at tax sale to 160 acres. This speech was followed by the presentation of additional amendments by Edmunds of Vermont and Allison of Iowa and Van Wyck's an- nouncement that he would bring the bill up again on the next legisla- tive day.[22] Thus ended the first phase of the verbal duel.

[19] *Ibid.*, 3719 (April 22, 1886).
[20] *Ibid.*
[21] *Ibid.*
[22] *Ibid.*, 3719–3721 (April 22, 1886).

In the second debate, delayed for nearly a month by the insistence of Conger of Michigan that the calendar order be adhered to,[23] the principal participants were Teller of Colorado and Dolph of Oregon, though Van Wyck and Blair continued their verbal fencing. The occasion for Teller's entry into the discussion arose when Blair insisted that the alleged evil of nontaxability was confined to Kansas and Nebraska and went on to offer an amendment requiring the secretary of the interior to value the unpatented lands for tax purposes. This Teller saw as interference with local functions. He denied Blair's allegation that the evil was confined to these two states, insisting that his own state, most of the territories, and many other states had more such land than either of them. He parried the ensuing series of thrusts from Blair, Mitchell of Oregon, and Edmunds of Vermont regarding the dates when title to the grants passed to the roads by asserting that the grants were *in presenti* and that it was evidence of title, rather than the title itself, which the patent represented and which the Supreme Court had decided was necessary for taxation.[24]

Dolph participated a bit in the heckling of Teller, but made his main attack from the quarter of Land Office responsibility for the slow patenting of the past. Citing a report of the secretary of the interior,[25] he showed that no patents had been delivered for about eleven million acres already selected by the Northern Pacific. This backlog of selections he attributed to the government's policy of withholding patents pending congressional action on the forfeiture of the lands. He concluded by insisting that he was not attempting to block the bill, that he merely desired to see justice done, and that above all he did not wish to see the motives of the companies impugned.[26]

From the time of Dolph's entry into the debate in late May until its final passage in early June, the bill was in grave danger of being talked to a standstill by its ardent supporters and its persistent enemies. The interaction of forfeiture, debt settlement, and taxation soon became very clear as senators hurled accusations impugning personal motives and questioned the compatability of proposed policies.

Twice in debate on a bill to forfeit part of the grant of the Northern Pacific in Oregon[27] and once in debate on the tax bill, Senator Van Wyck was both the object of attack and the attacker. Dolph, Mitchell, and Edmunds joined in accusing Van Wyck first of trying to defeat the forfeiture measure and second of trying to use the sinking fund established by the Thurman Act for the benefit of the Union Pacific by introducing a bill authorizing the road to use the fund to build branch lines.[28] Van Wyck responded with an equally virulent counterattack.

---

[23] *Ibid.*, 4305 (May 10, 1886).
[24] *Ibid.*, 4962–4991 (May 26–27, 1886).
[25] 49 Congress, 1 session, *Senate Executive Document 126* (1886).
[26] *Congressional Record*, 49 Congress, 1 session, 4953–4958 (May 26, 1886).
[27] Senate Bill 2152.
[28] Senate Bill 2395.

He defended his course as one designed to benefit the people in the West, not the roads. He implied without subtlety that the Senate was infested by men in the pay of the railroad companies and left no doubt that he considered his three attackers among them. He assured the Senate that he opposed the Northern Pacific forfeiture bill because it was precisely what the railroad wanted: a small forfeiture as a sop to forestall those who sought to declare forfeit all the grant along that portion of the road completed after the expiration of the time limit. In reply to the contention that taxation and forfeiture were mutually exclusive, he held that the lands should be taxable as long as the companies enjoyed the right to use them, just as if they owned them in fee simple. Finally, he defended his branch-lines proposal against charges of inconsistency and pro-railroad leanings. The Thurman Act, he contended, had tied up investment capital in the sinking fund, and that fund should be utilized by the government to insure that branch lines, constructed and operated with proper safeguards, were built in an area where reasonably inexpensive transportation was still a crying need.[29]

On June 2 the debate returned to a specific discussion of the taxation question, but the issues raised in the related debates were repeatedly interjected, particularly the proposition that taxation and forfeiture were incompatible. Dolph opened the day's discussion with a reiteration of his charge that the Land Office was responsible for the delay. Plumb demurred. No matter who was at fault, he said, the question was simply one of removing the United States as a block to taxability. When questioned on the compatibility of forfeiture and tax legislation, Plumb replied that the objection was covered by a clause in the bill stating that it did not preclude future forfeiture legislation.[30]

At this point Evarts of New York proposed an amendment restricting the application of the bill to lands "ascertained and allocated as within the grant." This was precisely the kind of amendment that had been attached to the two previously considered Senate bills. Plumb answered that the survey itself allocated the lands, whereas Evarts' proposal seemed to call for further administrative action. Teller supported Plumb's objection and went on to maintain that this clause would defeat the very purpose of the bill, immediate taxation, because it would require that an entire grant be adjusted before any part of the land could be taxed.[31] When the Evarts amendment came to a vote, it was supported by only nine senators. These were, almost to a man, the outspoken critics of all or a substantial part of the bill: Evarts, Blair, Edmunds, Mitchell of Oregon, Conger of Michigan, Hoar of Massachusetts, Morrill of Vermont, and Leland Stanford and George Hearst of California. Senator Dolph was not in the chamber at the time.[32]

[29] *Congressional Record*, 49 Congress, 1 session, 5019–5028 (May 28, 1886), 5139–5140 (June 2, 1886).

[30] *Ibid.*, 5140–5146 (June 2, 1886).

[31] *Ibid.*, 5146–5148 (June 2, 1886).

[32] *Senate Journal*, 49 Congress, 1 session, 842 (June 2, 1886).

The disposition of the Evarts amendment brought before the Senate the amendment, proposed earlier by Hoar, that the bill limit to 640 acres the amount of land that any one person could purchase. This directed debate toward a side issue, and the remainder of the day was spent in argument over the legality, propriety, and wisdom of such restrictive legislation. Virtually all the debate was carried on by the opponents of the taxation bill. Dolph, Hoar, Evarts, and Conger quibbled with one another for no apparent reason other than to kill time.[33]

On the following day Plumb opened the debate by attempting to show that the Hoar amendment would only serve to embarrass the bill, after which the senators returned to the subject, filling page after page of the record with examples of large citizen and alien landholdings. The debate raged on despite the withdrawal of the amendment and despite Plumb's charge that the long discussion was only blocking consideration of the subject at hand. When Call of Florida charged that the committee bill would forestall future moves for forfeiture, by enabling the railroads themselves to purchase the land at tax sale, the debate returned temporarily to the bill itself. But after an exchange between Call of Florida and George of Mississippi and the rejection of Call's proposal that railroads be excluded from bidding at the sales, Senator Blair again returned to the subject of alien landholding, further burdening the debate with data on the Scully holdings in Illinois.[34]

Only when Van Wyck joined Plumb in calling for final consideration and passage did the senators succeed in getting away from the side issue and back to the bill. Together Plumb and Van Wyck perfected its language through a series of small amendments, substituting the bill as passed for the House bill previously passed, and getting a favorable vote on their measure. Van Wyck then got formal approval of Senate insistence on its substitution and of the immediate appointment of a conference committee. The conferees appointed were Plumb, Van Wyck, and Walthall of Mississippi for the Senate and Crisp, Hanback, and Richardson of Tennessee for the House. The conference report, submitted for consideration on June 26, accepted the Senate bill in its entirety but added a section asserting the right of Congress to alter and amend the act.[35]

At this point a new danger, arising this time in the House, threatened to prevent passage of the bill. Led by Holman of Indiana, the advocates of forfeiture, who had not participated in the earlier debates in the House, expressed the fear that the bill would prevent further forfeiture legislation and enable roads to obtain title to unearned lands at tax sale. Crisp, managing the bill, was subjected to close questioning by Holman, Reagan of Texas, and Oates of Alabama, but they subsided

[33] *Congressional Record*, 49 Congress, 1 session, 5148–5153 (June 2, 1886).
[34] *Ibid.*, 5190–5195 (June 3, 1886).
[35] *Ibid.*, 5195–5196 (June 3, 1886), 5229 (June 4, 1886), 5422 (June 8, 1886), 6165–6166 (June 26, 1886).

after he presented his explanation, which was an almost exact repetition of the arguments used by Plumb and George to meet similar objections in the Senate. A further difficulty arose when Laird of Nebraska objected to the restriction of the application of the bill to organized counties, but his effort to propose an amendment was ruled out of order and the report was accepted, without a recorded vote. Three days later the Senate also concurred in the report. The president signed the bill on July 12,[36] thus bringing to a successful conclusion the fourteen-year campaign to achieve taxation of the unpatented lands of the land-grant railroad companies.

As finally enacted the tax law was designed to eliminate most of the grievances cited to achieve its passage. Its basic provision was, of course, that neither failure to pay the costs of survey nor lack of patent was to be so construed as to exempt railroad land from taxation, provided only that lands alongside uncompleted (thus unearned) sections of a road were still exempt, that lands were not to be taxable until they had been surveyed, and that a county government must be organized before taxes could be levied. If unpatented land was sold for taxes the purchaser of the tax title was to be liable for the costs of survey, but the secretary of the interior was to demand payment from the road, and if it was not forthcoming within thirty days, was to instruct the attorney general to bring recovery suit against the company. The proceeds of these suits were then to be used to reimburse tax-sale buyers for the costs of survey they had paid. Finally, Congress reserved all rights and liens of whatever nature belonging to the United States, the privilege of preferred purchase for the government at tax sales of these lands, if it wished to exercise it, the right to decree forfeiture of the lands of any road completed out of time, and the right to further amend the land-grant acts.[37] By these provisions Congress had finally ended the long-standing patent-forfeiture-taxation impasse by simply detaching the patent problem from the other two. Organized counties in surveyed areas could now tax railroad land regardless of what stage in the patenting process it had reached, even if the land was subject to possible forfeiture.

In Kansas and Nebraska the newspaper reaction was slight. Indeed, most papers seem to have completely ignored the passage of the bill. In Kansas the chief advocate of taxation, John A. Anderson, was doing battle for his political life, and his success in the field of tax legislation had come prior to the Forty-ninth Congress. In Nebraska Van Wyck was engaged in a struggle to retain his seat in the Senate. References to the tax issue were confined almost exclusively to the political arena, as illustrations of the abilities and convictions of the candidates.[38]

[36] *Ibid.*, 6166–6167 (June 26, 1886), 6266 (June 29, 1886), 6810 (July 12, 1886).

[37] 24 *Statutes at Large* 143 (July 10, 1886).

[38] *Omaha Bee*, December 16, 30, 1885, March 24, June 16, 1886; *Junction City Union*, August 14, 1886.

Editor Rosewater of the *Omaha Bee* did pause long enough in his campaign for Van Wyck to observe of the tax legislation itself that it was "better late than never," but upon the passage of the bill he was content to quote the *New York Times*, which assigned credit for the outcome to the "brilliant tactics" of Van Wyck, whose strategy had produced stronger legislation than the advocates of the reform had hoped to obtain.[39]

The passage of the taxation bill did not materially affect the speed with which patents were issued to the railroad companies. What it did do, in the first place, was to clear the congressional arena of one of the problems confusing the issue of land reform. The legislators were now free to consider the less complex questions of debt settlement and forfeiture, and the legislative petitioners were free to concentrate as never before on the remaining issues.[40] In the second place, the act of 1886 rendered judgment in the land-tax case. Congress, as judge of the actions of the railroad companies, had rendered a resounding verdict that the railroads were guilty of utilizing the mechanism of nonpayment of survey fees to avoid the payment of state and local land taxes.

[39] *Omaha Bee*, June 23, 1886.
[40] *Laws of Kansas*, 1887, pp. 347–348; *Laws of Nebraska*, 1891, p. 462.

Four

The Administrators

IN BOTH the legal and the legislative controversy over the taxation of the railroad lands the primary concern was with the admittedly slow rate at which land patents reached the railroad companies. But before a remedy could be found, responsibility for the delays had to be established. The courts had, by 1885, placed the blame squarely on the roads themselves and in later decisions—occasioned by moves of the railroads to test the act of 1886—they maintained this position.[1] The Congress also, by the passage of the taxation bill of 1886, had adjudged the roads responsible, and when congressional concern with the patent issue—deriving from the earlier difficulties and the forfeiture question—continued into the 1890's, this judgment was never substantially modified.

In reaching these conclusions both the courts and the Congress had almost completely ignored a fundamental aspect of the whole question: the administrative. Since the courts deal with specific cases on their own merits, it is understandable that they never attempted a general view of the problem. Congressional behavior is less easily explained. That Western congressmen knew at least something of the administrative difficulties seems likely, since they dealt regularly with the Land Office on behalf of their constituents. But if they did recognize that there were administrative problems surrounding the railroad-patent controversy, such recognition had little effect on their actions. Three interpretations of their actions are possible: (1) they did not know; (2) they knew but did not understand; or (3) they knew and understood but chose to ignore the problem. No direct evidence had been found to support any of these interpretations. The record shows only that for whatever reasons, they failed to take into account the real contributions made by the administrators to the evil they sought to correct. And those contributions were great.

As implementors of the law the administrators were, perforce, interpreters of it. And their interpretations, usually based upon the assumption that the railroads were to get only that land expressly allowed them by the strictest reading of the law and, after 1880, upon the additional

[1] See *Ankenny vs. Clark,* 148 *United States Court Reports* 345 (1892); *Northern Pacific Railroad vs. Patterson,* 154 *United States Court Reports* 130 (1893); *Barden vs. Northern Pacific Railroad,* 154 *United States Court Reports* 288 (1893); *Central Pacific Railroad vs. Nevada,* 162 *United States Court Reports* 512 (1895).

assumption that legislation further restricting these allowances was in the offing, were commonly not consistent with a policy of expeditious patenting. They suspended the patenting process whenever, in their judgment, the occasion demanded it; they asked for what their critics deemed unreasonable proofs; and they changed the rulings of their predecessors whenever their own interpretation of the law dictated such changes. That the administrators played the role they did is neither surprising nor reprehensible. It is, however, fact. And to ignore the fact was to prejudice the case.

The acts of Congress granting lands directly to railroad corporations, like most other economic legislation of the nineteenth century, were loosely drawn.[2] No careful delineation was made of the rights and duties of either the companies or the government. Overlapping grants were made without provision for dividing the lands between the grantees.[3] No special agency was created, no special provision made, for the administration of the grants. Furthermore, during the granting period Congress enacted a homestead law and a college subsidy law and, soon thereafter, a timber-culture law, a desert-land law, and other new methods of alienating the title of the United States. Older laws, most notably the Preëmption Act, also remained on the statute books to complicate the program still further. All in all it was a thoroughly "incongruous land system," the various parts of which seemingly worked at cross-purposes.[4]

In these circumstances the General Land Office, having few precedents on which to draw, was forced to proceed by trial and error. True, it had gained valuable experience during the twelve years it had dealt with railroads under the earlier federal-through-state land-grant program. But at that time the state was made an intermediary and the land was usually patented to the state or to the railroad on evidence presented by a state official, most often the governor, that the conditions of the grant had been fulfilled.[5] Beginning in 1862 the federal government dealt directly with the corporations, did its own inspecting, and sometimes was forced to defend the interests of a corporation against those of a state.

[2] Much of the material included in the following section of this chapter has already appeared in the author's "The Railroads and the Land Office: Administrative Policy and the Land Patent Controversy, 1864–1896," in the *Mississippi Valley Historical Review*, 46:679–699 (March, 1960), and is used by permission.

[3] The map in Willis Drummond, Jr., "Land Grants in Aid of Internal Improvements," Chapter 10 of J. W. Powell's *Report on the Arid Region of the United States* (Government Printing Office, Washington, 1878) illustrates the overlap. See also Robert S. Henry, "The Railroad Land Grant Legend in American History Texts," in the *Mississippi Valley Historical Review*, 32:171–194 (September, 1945).

[4] Paul W. Gates, "The Homestead Law in an Incongruous Land System," in the *American Historical Review*, 41:652–681 (July, 1936).

[5] For information on methods of disposition of the state grants see John B. Sanborn's *Congressional Grants of Land in Aid of Railways* (*University of Wisconsin Bulletin in Economics, Political Science, and History*, vol. 2, no. 1, Madison, 1899), 93–119.

Although the administration of the corporation grants occasioned far-reaching changes in the machinery of the Land Office, it complicated the agency's task of surveying the public lands only in that, by calling for greater speed in completing the surveys, it vastly expanded the magnitude of the operation. The amount of land remaining unsurveyed in the public-lands states in selected years is shown in Table 1. Usually the unsurveyed area was reduced in direct proportion to the size of the congressional appropriation devoted to that purpose. The

TABLE 1.—AREA OF UNSURVEYED LAND, BY STATES AND TERRITORIES, 1872–1890 (IN THOUSANDS OF ACRES)

State or Territory	Total Acreage as Estimated in 1872	Acreage Unsurveyed as of June 30				
		1872	1875	1880	1885	1890
Minnesota	53,460	21,272	16,381	13,510	11,352	10,982
Kansas	52,044	12,464				
Nebraska	48,637	23,403	14,078	7,052	1,648	65
California	120,948	84,796	79,932	48,644	29,225	28,803
Nevada	71,738	65,572	61,667	58,437	38,947	38,512
Oregon	60,975	48,755	33,156	37,908	21,328	20,477
Washington	44,769	37,765	33,506	28,837	23,622	22,973
Colorado	66,880	55,901	49,088	40,658	9,267	7,456
Utah	54,065	49,483	47,418	44,283	41,154	40,328
Arizona	72,906	70,438	69,399	67,098	59,691	57,961
New Mexico	77,569	73,146	71,360	67,025	32,201	28,930
Dakota	96,596	89,154	79,857	71,422	49,204	45,719
Idaho	55,228	52,863	50,308	47,739	44,972	44,548
Montana	92,107	88,486	84,023	80,652	73,884	71,754
Wyoming	62,645	60,791	56,174	53,381	15,666	15,482
Louisiana	26,461	2,771	2,322	1,149	1,663	1,663
Total	936,090	837,058	759,648	667,795	453,825	335,654
Percentage decrease			10.2	13.8	42.7	35.2

Compiled from the annual reports of the commissioners of the General Land Office, 1872, p. 277; 1875, p. 377; 1880, p. 206; 1885, p. 310; and 1890, p. 179.

area was decreased steadily in most states and territories and particularly rapidly in the central plains states. Though the official reports do not indicate the location of the unsurveyed lands within each state, the consistency and growing speed with which reductions were made tends to corroborate the contention that most railroad land grants were surveyed rapidly, well in advance of substantial settlement.[6]

Still, the lack of any surveys in some areas and the need for resurveys in others obstructed the process of final adjustment, which was, at the suggestion of Commissioner W. A. J. Sparks, made mandatory by

[6] Secretary of the Interior, *Annual Report*, 1887, p. 10n; 50 Congress, 1 session, *Senate Executive Document 51* (1888), p. 145.

the Land Grant Adjustment Act of 1887.[7] Repeatedly Sparks and his successors appealed for more funds to carry out the required mapping. These requests make it clear that the lands of the Union Pacific, the Kansas Pacific, and the Central Pacific had been surveyed in large part by 1880, had been almost entirely covered by the mid-eighties, and by the late eighties needed only to be resurveyed in certain areas. But as late as 1890 a large part of the lands of the Northern Pacific, the Oregon and California, the California and Oregon, the Southern Pacific, and the Atlantic and Pacific still lacked original surveys,[8] as is substantiated by the data in Table 1.

This tardiness in completing surveys lends weight to the argument that some of the delays in patenting railroad lands were attributable to delays in surveying. It is clear, however, that in the central plains states no such lack of surveys could have existed after 1875, and that at no time could the failure of the roads to pay the costs of survey have caused any delay, since, with one minor exception, that cost was always arrived at and assessed only after the survey had been made.[9] In 1895 Congress finally responded to the pleas of the General Land Office and passed a law establishing a hundred-thousand-dollar revolving fund for the purpose of expediting surveys and resurveys of lands within the limits of railroad grants and, consequently, the patenting of the lands to the companies.[10] Thereby it finally eliminated the grounds for complaint by either administrative officers or railroadmen.

The process of conveying title to the direct-grant railroads began on November 4, 1864, with the issuance of an order withdrawing lands along the routes of the Pacific Railroad System from the operation of the land laws.[11] Soon thereafter the order was amended to include only odd-numbered sections in the surveyed areas. Within ten days after the issuance of the original order the first of many circulars outlining the procedure for patenting the land was dispatched to the officers of the local land offices. Soon new problems were foreseen, and these instructions, too, were amended by circular letter.[12]

[7] 24 *Statutes at Large* 556 (March 3, 1887).

[8] Commissioner of the General Land Office, *Annual Report*, 1888, p. 28; 1890, pp. 19–20; 1895, p. 264; 51 Congress, 1 session, *House Executive Document 453* (1890), p. 6.

[9] For a short period in the late sixties administrative officers viewed the law as a requirement that deposits be made by the railroads in advance of the survey. Jacob D. Cox to Oscar F. Davis, September 22, 1869, in the National Archives, Record Group 48 (Records of the Office of the Secretary of the Interior), Pacific Railroads, Letters Sent. Hereafter this collection will be cited as Record Group 48.

[10] 28 *Statutes at Large* 937 (March 2, 1895).

[11] John P. Usher, Secretary of the Interior, to the Commissioner of the General Land Office, November 21, 1864, in Record Group 48, Pacific Railroads, Letters Sent.

[12] General Land Office Circular, *Railroad Land Grants*, Washington, November 14, 1864, and Circular Letter to Register and Receiver at Sioux City, Des Moines, Fort Dodge, San Francisco, Marysville, Carson City, Council Bluffs, and Stockton, December 29, 1864, in the National Archives, Record Group 49 (Records of the

The rules as amended required (1) that the grantee company file lists of claimed lands with the register and receiver in the local land office; (2) that these local officers check the lists against the plats and records in their possession, collect the fees allowed them by law, and forward the lists to the General Land Office with evidence that their fees and the assessments for the costs of survey had been paid; (3) that the clerks of the Land Office check these lists against their own records, suspend action on all tracts that were in conflict, and draw up clear lists; (4) that the clear lists be approved by the commissioner of the General Land Office and by the secretary of the interior as the basis for patents; and, finally, (5) that copies of these lists be approved by the president as patented tracts. These procedures constituted the framework within which all further rules were established. For the most part such new rules as were adopted represented only minor modifications, but two major changes were made, one in the selection techniques used at the local offices and the other in the verification methods used in the General Land Office.

Modification of the selection rules came early. The first two secretaries of the interior to deal with the problem, J. P. Usher and James Harlan, both expected that the railroads would select their lands in blocks adjacent to completed twenty- or forty-mile sections of the road, and it was upon this assumption that the machinery they created was predicated.[13] But in October of 1866 Usher, now attorney for the Union Pacific, Eastern Division, urged upon the General Land Office that conflicting claims were likely to be filed and that, for this and "other reasons," the company might not be in a position to apply for all the lands at once. On these grounds he requested that the Land Office allow the road to select and receive patents for whatever smaller number of tracts it saw fit to claim, deferring action on the others until such time as the company made application for them and applied for patents.[14] In its reply the General Land Office did not clearly deny this privilege, but indicated that its officers would decide what lands were to be suspended from the lists.[15] Though no clear permissive ruling was made on the subject until 1869, this was the beginning of the end of the concept of block patenting. In 1869, in response to a request from the land commissioner of the Union Pacific, Eastern Division, the commissioner of

---

General Land Office), Letters Sent. Hereafter this collection will be cited as Record Group 49.

[13] Usher to the Commissioner of the General Land Office, March 2, 1865, and James Harlan to the Commissioner of the General Land Office, November 2, 1865, May 21, 1866, in Record Group 48, Letters Sent. Some account of Usher's connection with the Kansas Pacific is in Elmo R. Richardson and Alan W. Farley, *John Palmer Usher, Lincoln's Secretary of the Interior* (University of Kansas, Lawrence, 1960), 96–108.

[14] Usher to Joseph S. Wilson, Washington, October 10, 1866, in Record Group 49, Railroad Land Grant Records, box 36.

[15] Wilson to Usher, October 12, 1866, in Record Group 49, Letters Sent.

the General Land Office concluded that since the granting acts did not specify block selection, he saw no objection to partial selection. He did, however, require that each list be confined to lands along a single forty-mile section of the road as originally approved.[16] In time this change of policy resulted in a virtual inundation of the General Land Office. Dozens of lists, many enumerating hundreds of isolated 160-acre tracts, were filed for single forty-mile sections of track. This necessitated the cross-checking and cross-referencing of every application for patent, and despite these precautions a railroad often received a second patent on a tract or received no patent for land which it thought it held. Table 2 indicates, for some of the roads, the magnitude of the listing and approving process that grew out of the partial listing policy.

The administrative task involved in transferring tens of millions of acres of land by so complex a method was not to be taken lightly. Infinite care was required in establishing administrative and legal safeguards, rules of procedure, and methods of verification to prevent waste motion, error, and consequent delay. Such careful attention the Land Office could not provide.[17] It was handicapped by clerical shortages, by problems deriving from its dependence on a legislative body for funds and on political spoilsmen for workers, and by a succession of superiors appointed for political reasons rather than for administrative ability.[18] Nonetheless, the General Land Office did develop a logical and reasonably efficient patenting procedure.

Still in force was the original five-step process of inspection and approval by the local register and receiver, the staff of the General Land Office, the commissioner, the secretary, and the president.[19] Some additional changes were made in the methods of verifying lists at the local level—particularly in the form of affidavits attesting that given tracts contained no minerals, in requirements for the designation of lands lost

[16] Commissioner of the General Land Office to Register and Receiver, Junction City, Kansas, March 5, 1869, in Record Group 49, Letters Sent.

[17] See Harold H. Dunham, *Government Handout: A Study of the Administration of the Public Lands, 1875–1891* (the author, New York, 1941), chapter 7.

[18] In their annual reports the commissioners of the General Land Office complained of and asked that many things be remedied, but the most constant cry was for more and better paid and better qualified clerks. Commissioner of the General Land Office, *Annual Report*, 1871, p. 38; 1872, pp. 5–6; 1873, pp. 5–6; 1874, p. 7; 1875, pp. 21–22; 1876, pp. 14–16; 1877, p. 3; 1878, p. 145; 1879, pp. 85, 224; 1880, pp. 2–13; 1881, pp. 14–26; 1882, pp. 15–16; 1883, pp. 31–32; 1886, pp. 45–107; 1887, pp. 181–189; 1888, pp. 101–102, 200, 214; 1889, pp. 63–65; 1891, pp. 61–66; 1895, pp. 55, 87.

[19] General Land Office, *Circular No. 15* (1872) and *Circular of Instructions . . . in Regard to Selections in Satisfaction of Railroads . . .* (1879), both in the Bureau of Railway Economics Library, Washington; Commissioner of the General Land Office to Register and Receiver, Junction City, Kansas, November 9, 1869, and to Henry M. Teller, January 21, 1884, in Record Group 49, Division F, Letters Sent; and William H. Mills to W. A. J. Sparks, San Francisco, August 18, 1885, in Record Group 49, Railroad Land Grant Records, box 16.

THE ADMINISTRATORS | 63

TABLE 2.—LAND SELECTIONS FILED BY CERTAIN RAILROADS, 1865–1897

Railroad	Location of Land Selected	Inclusive Dates of Selections	Number of Lists
Atlantic and Pacific		1865–1897	82
Burlington and Missouri River	Nebraska	1872	12
California and Oregon	California	1871–1897	153
Central Pacific	California	1865–1896	111
	Nevada	1876–1897	41
	Utah	1884–1896	50
(Total for the Central Pacific......................			202)
Northern Pacific	Wisconsin	1882–1891	6
	Minnesota	1872–1897	283
	Dakota	1874–1897	205
	Montana	1882–1897	465
	Idaho	1885–1897	44
	Washington	1876–1897	375
	Oregon	1885–1897	8
(Total for the Northern Pacific.....................			1,386)
Oregon and California	Oregon	1870–1897	285
Oregon Central	Oregon	1877–1897	23
Sioux City and Pacific	Iowa	1868–1876	6
	Nebraska	1869–1896	16
(Total for the Sioux City and Pacific................			22)
Southern Pacific, main line	California	1871–1897	372
branch line	California	1877–1897	219
(Total for the Southern Pacific.....................			591)
Union Pacific	Nebraska	1868–1897	71
	Colorado	1891–1897	16
	Wyoming	1874–1897	37
	Utah	1876–1897	19
(Total for the Union Pacific......................			143)
Union Pacific, Eastern Division			
(Kansas Pacific)	Kansas	1870–1897	105
	Colorado	1874–1897	14
Denver Pacific	Colorado	1874–1897	16
(Total for the Union Pacific, Eastern Division........			135)
Union Pacific, Central Branch	Kansas	1870–1884	17
	Nebraska		1
(Total for the Union Pacific, Central Branch..........			18)
Total Lists...			3,052

Compiled from "Selections Docket," a ledger in which all selections up to December 31, 1897, were supposedly entered, in Record Group 48, Lands and Railroads. Many selections were made after 1897. See also the Commissioner of the General Land Office, *Annual Report*, 1896, pp. 248–250.

to prior claimants within the primary limits of the grants, and in the methods used to arrive at costs of survey charges[20]—but the major modification of procedure was made in the machinery of the General Land Office itself.

The principal change in the organization at Washington was that made in July of 1872 with the establishment of Division F, in which railroad-land business was henceforth to be centered.[21] The new division did not have full jurisdiction: selections in mineral areas, estimates of survey costs, and contested entries involved various other divisions. But with these exceptions Division F was the major participant in the process of patenting lands to railroads. It handled problems involving the dates when lands were withdrawn from the public domain, the dates when the railroads' rights to granted lands took effect, the dates and legitimacy of prior settlement, and questions of rights as between railroads and states and between railroads and railroads. The most important cases eventually found their way to the courts, but a large majority of them were adjudicated by the clerks in the General Land Office, especially by the clerks of Division F.

By June 30, 1876, twenty-four hundred cases had been filed with the division. By 1879 nearly four thousand had been entered and two years later more than a thousand of them were still on the dockets. Unfortunately neither the total number of new cases filed nor the total number adjudicated is available for the critical years between 1880 and 1888. The work of the "judicial branch" of Division F from 1888 through 1896 is summarized in Table 3. Many of 21,673 cases decided were routine, the decisions being based on precedents established by the commissioner, the secretary, or the courts. But each case, whether routine or not, had to be put through the channels either as a contest or as an application. The remainder of the energies of the clerks in the division, when they were not engaged in preparing reports for Congress or for administrative officers in their own or other departments, was expended in compiling clear lists for patent.[22]

Interruptions of the patenting process were frequent and of long duration. Between 1868 and 1895 numerous suspension orders were issued by secretaries of the interior. These suspensions derived from the dual character of the administrative function: the administrator must

[20] Changes in mineral procedure are chronicled in a series of documents filed under Henry Beard to L. Q. C. Lamar, May 2, 1886, in Record Group 48, Lands and Railroads, Letters Received, and in *Circular on Mineral Lands*, July 9, 1884, summarized in Commissioner of the General Land Office, *Annual Report*, 1895, p. 262. For changes in the requirements for the designation of lands lost in place see W. K. Mendenhall to Nathan C. McFarland, Washington, April 2, 1883, and H. M. Teller to the Commissioner of the General Land Office, May 28, 1883, in Record Group 49, Railroad Land Grant Records, box 41; also William Walker, Acting Commissioner, to L. Q. C. Lamar, August 3, 1885, in Record Group 49, Division F, Letters Sent.

[21] Commissioner of the General Land Office, *Annual Report*, 1873, pp. 13–14.

[22] *Ibid.*, 1882, p. 93; 1883, p. 66; 1890, pp. 180–181.

THE ADMINISTRATORS | 65

enforce the law, but he can (and usually does) also anticipate further legislation. Thus the Land Office was not only directly charged with executing the provisions of the granting acts but was also indirectly charged with interpreting the winds of land reform that blew so strongly in the eighties. The patents were the documents that finally alienated particular tracts from the government. Only by refusal to issue them could contested cases be kept alive until Congress might act. Refusal to issue them was also a weapon that could be used to force the railroads to do what the law, or the official interpreting it, required. For the most part it was the only weapon the administrative branch of the government retained.[23] It was for these reasons that the patenting proc-

TABLE 3.—LAND CASES HANDLED BY DIVISION F OF THE GENERAL
LAND OFFICE, 1888–1896

Year	Applications for Entry		Entries Already Made	
	Pending	Decided	Pending	Decided
1888	7,691	2,338	4,337	450
1889	4,438	3,346	3,921	636
1890	4,194	2,435	3,864	1,527
1891	2,975	2,907	3,635	954
1892	2,800	1,186	3,327	1,401
1893	2,454	888	3,160	956
1894	1,150	624	622	125
1895	1,078	738	867	210
1896	1,022	757	781	195
Total Decided		15,219		6,454

Compiled from the annual reports of the commissioners of the General Land Office, 1888–1896· The more important decisions were often printed in the reports.

ess was suspended, with the inevitable result that the railroad companies received their patents only after considerable delay.

The first important application of the suspension policy grew out of an attempt to enforce the requirement imposed in the granting acts that the lines in the Pacific Railroad System be built as "first class railroads." Government inspectors had approved each section of them as built, but in August, 1868, when one of the inspectors reported the use of temporary trestles and other inadequate structures, Secretary Browning suggested a complete reinspection of the Union and Central Pacific roads.[24] Presidential approval was obtained and in October a

[23] A statement of the philosophy underlying suspension practices was made by Columbus Delano, Secretary of the Interior, in a letter to William M. Stewart, Chairman of the Senate Committee on Railroads, June 17, 1874, in Record Group 48, Lands and Railroads, Letters Sent.

[24] Orville H. Browning to William M. Evarts, Attorney General, August 15, 1868, and to the President, August 19, 1868; William T. Otto, Acting Secretary of the

commission was appointed to reinspect them. Later its instructions were extended to include all the bond-aided lines.[25] The commission's report, submitted in mid-December, revealed unsatisfactory conditions, and on December 18, 1868, Browning ordered the commissioner of the General Land Office to suspend the issuance of patents to the Union Pacific, the Union Pacific, Eastern Division, the Sioux City and Pacific, and the Central Branch, Union Pacific.[26] After further inspections the order was extended to the Central Pacific.[27] In mid-1869, pursuant to a joint congressional resolution,[28] a commission of "eminent citizens" was appointed to reinspect the lines. Its report indicated the need for numerous repairs and further structural improvements. Secretary Cox, Browning's successor, though he accepted the report as a basis for adjustment, ordered the commissioner of the General Land Office to issue to the Union and Central Pacific railroads, in alternate odd sections, patents for only half the lands that had been granted to them.[29]

This suspension lasted five years. Both companies intermittently sought revocation of the order. Henry Beard, attorney for the Central Pacific, and O. F. Davis, land commissioner of the Union Pacific, addressed requests to the secretary in 1871. Early in 1872 E. H. Rollins, secretary and treasurer of the Union Pacific, joined these petitioners.[30] In October, 1873, Union Pacific officials argued that of the whole grant only some 1,200,000 acres were involved in the request for revocation and that the remaining 10,000,000 acres should be ample security for the completion of the road as required by law.[31]

The most penetrating discussion of the problems raised by the suspension of patenting was that included in the petition of John Duff, acting president of the Union Pacific, in January, 1874. Duff pointed out that only a tenth of the land due the company had been received, whereas the Burlington and Missouri River road, built under the same

---

Interior, to the President, September 25, 1868, both in Record Group 48, Pacific Railroads, Letters Sent.

[25] Instructions to the Commission of Standards of Equipment, October 7, 9, 15, 1868, in Record Group 48, Pacific Railroads, Letters Sent.

[26] O. H. Browning to Schuyler Colfax, December 18, 1868, and to the Commissioner of the General Land Office, same date, in Record Group 48, Pacific Railroads, Letters Sent.

[27] J. D. Cox, to the Commissioner of the General Land Office, March 22, 1869, 1868, in Record Group 48, Pacific Railroads, Letters Sent.

[28] 16 Statutes at Large 56 (April 10, 1869).

[29] The instructions were dated August 14, 1869, and the partial suspension order is addressed to J. S. Wilson, November 3, 1869. Both are in Record Group 48, Pacific Railroads, Letters Sent.

[30] C. Delano to Henry Beard, March 27, 1871, in Record Group 48, Pacific Railroads, Letters Sent; O. F. Davis to Delano, Washington, October 14, 1871, and Omaha, November 8, 1871, in Record Group 48, Land and Railroads, Letters Received; and E. H. Rollins to Willis Drummond, Boston, January 23, 1872, in Record Group 49, Railroad Land Grant Records, box 85.

[31] W. K. Mendenhall to Delano, Washington, October 2, 1873, in Record Group 48, Lands and Railroads, Letters Received.

act, had already received its patents. In discussing the situation in Nebraska he cited the judicial decisions exempting unpatented lands from taxation and asserted: "No board of directors would be justified in waiving such exemption and paying the taxes levied by the state." He expressed anxiety over the "antagonism thus produced between the state and the company" and over the hardships imposed on buyers of railroad land who, because of the suspension of patenting, could not get their deeds. In conclusion he said: "So long as the present condition of affairs continues the interests of the company will be impaired, the settlements of the public lands in the vicinity of the railroad retarded, and the progress and growth of the state seriously obstructed."[32]

In his reply to Duff the new secretary, Columbus Delano, asserted that, as he had informed other petitioners, the problem was the responsibility of the companies involved, since the two personal inspections made by government directors prior to that time were not sufficient bases for an official judgment. The roads must apply to the president for a full-dress re-examination, for which, in the absence of legislation, the roads must pay.[33] Apparently such a request was made and granted, for in the summer of 1874 the secretary appointed a commission to inspect the Union Pacific. Later he instructed the commissioners to include the Central Pacific in their investigation. The reports were submitted to the president on November 3 and 12, 1874, with the recommendation that he order revocation of the suspension.[34] The letters were endorsed by Grant on the fourteenth, and four days later, just over five years after the issuance of the first important suspension order, the commissioner of the General Land Office was instructed to resume patenting on all Union and Central Pacific lands.[35]

The second major suspension of patenting grew out of administrative efforts to enforce provisions of the act of 1864 requiring payment of costs of survey. Secretaries Usher and Harlan applied the requirement to all the Pacific Railroad lands granted by the 1862 and 1864 acts, and the first directives on patenting procedures ordered such payments and established a system for arriving at estimates of them.[36] But

[32] John Duff to Delano, New York, January 23, 1874, in Record Group 48, Lands and Railroads, Letters Received.
[33] Delano to Duff, February 9, 1874, in Record Group 48, Lands and Railroads, Letters Sent.
[34] Benjamin R. Cowen, Assistant Secretary of the Interior, to Jesse L. Williams, John L. Merriman, and John C. Delano, May 14, 1874, and to James Moore, August 19, 1874; Delano to C. P. Huntington, September 21, 1874, to E. L. Sullivan, Calvin Brown, and John W. Dwyer, same date, and to the President, November 3, 14, 1874, all in Record Group 48, Lands and Railroads, Letters Sent.
[35] Delano to the President, November 12, 1874 (endorsed by U. S. Grant, November 14, 1874), in Record Group 48, Lands and Railroads, Letters Received; Delano to Samuel S. Burdett, Commissioner of the General Land Office, November 18, 1874, in Record Group 48, Lands and Railroads, Letters Sent.
[36] Usher to the Commissioner of the General Land Office, March 2, 1865; Harlan to the Commissioner of the General Land Office, August 24, 1865, and May 21,

in November, 1866, shortly after his appointment, Secretary Browning decided that since the act of 1864 was amendatory to the act of 1862, only the additional lands granted by the later legislation were liable for such costs.[37] Browning's ruling stood for six years. Then in 1872, in the Prescott case, the United States Supreme Court, as a part of its decision that unpatented lands were untaxable, declared that lands granted under both acts were subject to payment of the costs of survey.[38] This decision set off the long controversy over local taxation and established the basis for much of the contention that it was the railroadmen who were responsible for slow patenting. One of its first effects, however, was to produce suspensions by the administrators. In September, 1873, after Willis Drummond, the incumbent commissioner, had brought the Prescott decision to his attention, Acting Secretary B. R. Cowen ruled that henceforth costs of survey were to be paid on all lands.[39] Later the new secretary, Delano, ruled that lands previously patented were also subject to these costs and that no further patents were to issue until they had been paid.[40] All the railroads save one soon paid the arrears, and suspension of their patents was short-lived. Only the Central Branch, Union Pacific, did not do so, and consequently it received no further direct patents until 1886.[41]

When a similar ruling was applied to the largest of all grants, the result was more far-reaching. The Northern Pacific had not originally been required to pay the costs of survey, but in 1870 Congress had extended the provision to it.[42] Apparently the Land Office overlooked this new directive for four years, during which time five patents, totaling 743,906 acres, were issued to the company.[43] When the oversight was discovered, the issuance of patents was suspended and payment demanded.[44] The company refused to comply, argued legal exemption,

1866; and W. T. Otto, Acting Secretary of the Interior, to the Commissioner of the General Land Office, May 24, 1867, all in Record Group 48, Letters Sent. Also Harlan to the Commissioner of the General Land Office, November 2, 1865, in Record Group 49, Railroad Land Grant Records, box 36.

[37] O. H. Browning to the Commissioner of the General Land Office, November 8, 1865, in Record Group 48, Letters Sent; General Land Office, *Circular No. 15,* January 24, 1867.

[38] 16 *Wallace* 603 (1873).

[39] B. R. Cowen to the Commissioner of the General Land Office, September 11, 1873, in Record Group 48, Lands and Railroads, Letters Sent.

[40] S. S. Burdett, Commissioner of the General Land Office, to Delano, December 14, 1874, in Record Group 49, Division F, Letters Sent, and Delano to Burdett, December 17, 1874, in Record Group 48, Lands and Railroads, Letters Sent.

[41] Commissioner of the General Land Office to W. F. Downs, Land Commissioner, Central Branch, Union Pacific, January 5, 1875, and to H. M. Teller, Secretary of the Interior, January 21, 1884, both in Record Group 49, Division F, Letters Sent; see also Commissioner of the General Land Office, *Annual Report,* 1886, p. 297.

[42] 16 *Statutes at Large* 305 (July 15, 1870).

[43] 49 Congress, 1 session, *Senate Executive Document 126* (1886), p. 12.

[44] W. W. Curtiss, Acting Commissioner, to W. K. Mendenhall, May 27, 1874, in Record Group 49, Division F, Letters Sent.

haggled over some costs paid on lands patented to another road, and raised related issues for eight years.[45] Then, in 1882, the company's board of directors resolved to pay the fees, under protest.[46] The motives of the company are not altogether clear. What is clear is that the General Land Office, in executing the duties assigned to it by law, found it necessary because of the company's opposition—to save taxes or for some other reason—to suspend the patenting of the Northern Pacific lands for eight years.

The Northern Pacific case was the most important instance of the application of the "no costs, no patent" principle, and it constituted the most substantial basis for the contention that the railroads used the mechanism for their own ends, but the application of the principle did not stop there. Congress furnished additional grounds for its use by one or another of the parties concerned when in July of 1876 it provided that all roads not exempted by law must pay the costs of survey.[47] The major objections to this act came from two Pacific Coast roads: the Southern Pacific and the Central Pacific as successor to the California and Oregon. In a controversy beginning in 1878 both roads claimed exemption from the act,[48] and the acting commissioner, J. M. Armstrong, supported their claim.[49] But Carl Schurz, secretary of the interior, decided against the companies,[50] and they eventually receded from their position.[51]

Taken together, the suspensions of patenting on the ground of faulty construction or failure to pay the costs of survey were a considerable retarding influence on the issuance of railroad land patents, but in the eighties a new form of suspension, more closely related to anticipated than to existing legislation, produced the greatest barrier to patenting yet encountered. In view of the activities of reformers—and an occasional "railroad statesman"—in Congress who were seeking to settle the questions of indebtedness, forfeiture, and taxation, some secretaries of the interior felt constrained to adjust their patenting policies so as to expedite legislation or at least remove all hindrances to the free action

---

[45] 49 Congress, 1 session, *Senate Executive Document 126* (1886) contains the pertinent documents.

[46] A copy of the resolution is contained in a letter from Henry Villard to H. M. Teller, New York, December 27, 1882, in Record Group 49, Railroad Land Grant Records, box 51. Villard's letter is a thorough defense of the action of the company.

[47] 19 *Statutes at Large* 121 (July 31, 1876). See above, pp. 36–37.

[48] Henry Beard to Carl Schurz, Washington, August 29, 1878, in Record Group 48, Lands and Railroads, Letters Received.

[49] J. M. Armstrong to Schurz, October 29, 1878, in Record Group 49, Division F, Letters Sent.

[50] Schurz to the Commissioner of the General Land Office, February 20, 1879, in Record Group 48, Lands and Railroads, Letters Sent.

[51] See the annual reports of the Commissioner of the General Land Office, 1878–1882, for the report of Division F on the number of acres patented to these roads during each year.

of Congress. Furthermore, once the suspension policies were well established, their application was broadened to include state-contested
dates of final location of granted lands and railroad-contested administrative rulings on methods of selecting indemnity lands and lands in
mineral areas. Thus by the late eighties, despite the removal of the tax-
avoidance device by means of the taxation law of 1886, the annual
volume of patents issued for railroad lands had reached its lowest ebb.[52]

The first important suspension of patenting in anticipation of legislation was made by Secretary of the Interior S. J. Kirkwood. In December of 1880, on the asumption that Congress was about to declare
forfeit all the lands granted to roads that had failed to complete construction within the time limit set in their granting acts, he ordered the
suspension of patenting on all such grants.[53] His expectations did not
materialize. Though a number of forfeiture bills were introduced,
Congress adjourned without taking action. Kirkwood, however, did
not rescind the order.[54] Instead, in March of 1882, he extended it to
the Kansas Pacific. This he did simply by returning to the commissioner
of the General Land Office a list of applications for patents on which
he had taken no action. In the face of a ruling by the attorney general
that he could not withhold patents without an act of Congress, he returned the list "unapproved," he said, not because he disapproved, but
because he was "not disposed at this time to act in the matter."[55]

Henry M. Teller, Kirkwood's successor, at first rescinded the general
suspension order, holding, as had Carl Schurz, that since any forfeiture
must come from Congress, administrative officials could only obey the
law as it existed.[56] This reversal was also temporarily applied to the
Kansas Pacific, when, in connection with one of John A. Anderson's
bills to make the lands of that road taxable, Congressman Benjamin
Butterworth, acting for the House Committee on Pacific Railroads,
requested information on the issuance of patents to the road.[57] Perhaps the commissioner's report on Kirkwood's delaying tactics, together
with the obvious legislative disapproval of slow patenting reported in
Butterworth's letter, produced the change of policy which allowed patents for more than forty-six thousand acres to issue to the company.[58]

[52] Commissioner of the General Land Office, *Annual Report*, 1885, p. 337; 1886,
p. 289; 1887, p. 352; 1882, p. 220; 1889, p. 145; 1890, p. 6.
[53] *Ibid.*, 1883, p. 22.
[54] *Ibid.*, 1882, pp. 10–11.
[55] Samuel J. Kirkwood to the Commissioner of the General Land Office, March 1,
1882, in Record Group 49, Railroad Land Grant Records, box 37.
[56] Commissioner of the General Land Office, *Annual Report*, 1883, p. 22; Schurz
to George F. Edmunds, January 25, 1879, and to Horace White, September 29,
1880, both in Record Group 48, Lands and Railroads, Letters Sent.
[57] Benjamin Butterworth to Teller, Washington, April 10, 1882, in Record Group
48, Lands and Railroads, Letters Received.
[58] N. C. McFarland to Teller, April 18, 1882, in Record Group 49, Division F,
Letters Sent; Commissioner of the General Land Office, *Annual Report*, 1883, p. 72.

Teller, however, soon returned to the suspension policy. He issued no blanket order, but chose instead to apply suspension rulings to individual railroads as occasion arose. Again the Kansas Pacific was interdicted. This time the impetus came from a request of the governor of Kansas, made in October of 1883, that no patents be issued to the Kansas road until a decision had been reached on the question of the erroneous location of a portion of the road filed with the department by S. J. Crawford, attorney for Kansas.[59] The Northern Pacific was again placed on the suspension list and hence, despite its ultimate agreement to pay costs of survey, continued to be denied patents.[60] The Union and Central Pacific roads did continue to receive patents on their main-line grants, and the Southern Pacific on lands on the branch and about twenty-five hundred acres on the main line.[61]

The team of L. Q. C. Lamar and William A. J. Sparks, as secretary of the interior and commissioner of the General Land Office respectively, made suspension in anticipation of legislation established policy. Like their predecessors, they had a choice between issuing patents rapidly in accordance with existing law or withholding them in an effort to promote railroad land reform. Sparks, supported for a time by his superior, chose reform. Indeed, much of his two and a half years in the Land Office was spent in criticism of the land system. His annual reports for 1885, 1886, and 1887 were long indictments of the system, and the railroad grants came in for their share of criticism. During his short career as commissioner Sparks aroused reform elements to the needs of the system and set many precedents in his own office. Not the least of these was his wholesale use of the suspension policy.

Sparks' suspensions of patenting were most widely applied in anticipation of forfeiture. In 1886 and 1887 a total of only 296,858 acres of land was patented to the railroads, and by the end of the fiscal year 1887 patents to selections aggregating over seventeen million acres were suspended in expectation of congressional action forfeiting the grants.[62] The largest area subjected to suspension was the Northern Pacific grant, but in April, 1887, Sparks modified his order to allow the issuance of patents to lands east of the Missouri, opposite that portion of the road which had been constructed on time.[63] This modification resulted in patents for 290,968 acres, the first substantial acreage since

[59] Strother M. Stockslager, Acting Commissioner, to L. Q. C. Lamar, December 17, 1887, in Record Group 49, Division F, Letters Sent.
[60] George Gray, attorney, to Teller, Washington, February 28, 1885, in Record Group 48, Lands and Railroads, Letters Received; W. K. Mendenhall to the Commissioner of the General Land Office, Washington, March 2, 1885, in Record Group 49, Railroad Land Grant Records, box 52.
[61] Commissioner of the General Land Office, *Annual Report*, 1882, pp. 98–101; 1883, pp. 71–73; 1884, pp. 56–58; 1885, pp. 343–345.
[62] *Ibid.*, 1886, p. 288; 1887, pp. 186, 352.
[63] Sparks to Lamar, April 4, 1887, in Record Group 49, Division F, Letters Sent.

1874.[64] Sparks' suspension of patenting in another large area, the grant of the Southern Pacific, was also based on anticipation of forfeiture.[65]

Sparks also applied the suspension policy for reasons other than prospective forfeiture. The question of the adjustment of the debts of the bond-aided railroads was a vexed one, and when these roads fell behind in their payments into the sinking fund established by the Thurman Act, Congress established a Pacific Railway Commission to investigate all aspects of their business.[66] When this commission requested information on certain aspects of the land problems of the companies, Sparks issued orders suspending the patenting of lands to the bond-aided railroads.[67] Another reason for the suspension of part of the lists of the Central Pacific and the Southern Pacific was disapproval of the form of affidavit used in reporting nonmineral lands.[68] All in all, the effect of these suspensions was to put a stop to most patent-issuing activities.

The suspensions ordered by Sparks were continued in force, for a time, by his successors. In March, 1889, patents for more than twenty-one million acres were suspended on the ground of imminent forfeiture, and the lands of the bond-aided roads were under suspension on the indebtedness question.[69] In December, 1889, the new commissioner of the General Land Office, Lewis Groff, recommended that suspension of the Union Pacific patents be terminated, and Secretary of the Interior J. W. Noble, in answer to a Senate inquiry of March 10, 1890, indicated that the question was under consideration in his office.[70] He continued to consider the question until late spring, when he finally decided to return to patenting. In 1891 the Union Pacific received patents for more than 1,200,000 acres, the first since 1886.[71] The suspension of patenting to the Kansas Pacific was also canceled in mid-1890

[64] Commissioner of the General Land Office, *Annual Report*, 1888, p. 248.

[65] Sparks to Henry Beard, March 27, 1887, in Record Group 49, Division F, Letters Sent.

[66] A clear account of these developments is included in Nelson Trottman, *History of the Union Pacific: A Financial and Economic Survey* (Ronald Press, New York, 1923), chapters 6 and 9.

[67] Cadmus M. Wilcox, Chief of Division F, to S. M. Stockslager, March 13, 1889, in Record Group 49, Railroad Land Grant Records, box 86.

[68] Sparks to C. P. Huntington, July 28, 1886, in Record Group 49, Division F, Letters Sent.

[69] Wilcox to Stockslager, March 13, 1889, in Record Group 49, Railroad Land Grant Records, box 86.

[70] Lewis Groff to John W. Noble, December 30, 1889, in Record Group 49, Division F, Letters Sent; Noble to the President of the Senate, March 17, 1890, in Record Group 48, Lands and Railroads, Letters Sent.

[71] George Chandler, Assistant Secretary of the Interior, to Gilbert L. Laws, May 1, 1890, and Noble to C. P. Huntington, June 7, 1890, and to the Commissioner of the General Land Office, June 28, 1890, all in Record Group 48, Lands and Railroads, Letters Sent; Commissioner of the General Land Office, *Annual Report*, 1891, p. 153.

and nearly a million acres, the first since 1884, were patented to it the next year.[72] For the most part suspensions of patent hinging upon prospective forfeiture were continued in force until September, 1890, when the General Forfeiture Act was passed. This measure, which provided for the forfeiture of all lands adjacent to portions of the roads not already built on the date of its passage, settled the question.[73] Though the partial suspension of patenting in mineral areas was continued until 1894 and a temporary suspension on the lands of bond-aided roads was again instituted in 1895, the period of wholesale suspensions was over by the middle of 1891.[74]

During the years when wholesale suspension of patenting was the rule in the Land Office, complaints and arguments regarding the detrimental effects of the policy were received from railroadmen, lawyers, and members of Congress, and occasionally from purchasers of railroad land and officials of local government. The most persistent petitioners were lawyers in the employ of railroads. Especially persistent was Henry Beard of Washington. Among Beard's early complaints was one made in 1879 on behalf of the Kansas Pacific. He requested the patenting of some forty-three thousand acres, contending that the delay in issuing patents to lands selected by the Kansas Pacific was "detrimental to the interests of the company" and held up the collection of payments owed by purchasers of its lands.[75] But it was after 1884, when he was handling the legal affairs of the Southern Pacific, that he became the most unrelenting in his complaints.

Between 1885 and 1890 Beard wrote a series of appeals, first on behalf of the Southern Pacific and later the Southern and the Central Pacific. In importuning Commissioner Sparks in 1885 and 1886 he invoked the strong constitutional argument that "as ours is a government of laws and not of men, the objection of one or of several men to the execution of existing laws, even if these men be Senators and Representatives in Congress, is not good authority for suspending the operation of such laws."[76] Later he told Sparks that no lands adjoining portions of a road completed on time had ever been forfeited, and assured him that these were the lands for which he was seeking

[72] Noble to the Commissioner of the General Land Office, June 28, 1890, in Record Group 49, Railroad Land Grant Records, box 37; Commissioner of the General Land Office, *Annual Report*, 1891, p. 153.

[73] 26 *Statutes at Large* 496 (September 29, 1890); Commissioner of the General Land Office, *Annual Report*, 1891, p. 154.

[74] Secretary of the Interior to the Commissioner of the General Land Office, December 11, 1895, and June 11, 1896, Record Group 49, Railroad Land Grant Records, box 86, and Record Group 48, Letters Sent, respectively.

[75] Beard to Schurz, Washington, January 7, 1879, in Record Group 48, Lands and Railroads, Letters Sent.

[76] Beard to Sparks, Washington, May 18, 1885, in Record Group 49, Railroad Land Grant Records, box 73.

patents.[77] Failing once more to impress the commissioner, he turned to the secretary himself. In this petition he returned to his constitutional argument: "I am demanding a right which is given by law," he said, "and requesting a duty to be performed by the Secretary, which, I believe, the Secretary is required to perform under the law, and the performance of which the Secretary cannot properly delay."[78] Further arguments in the same vein directed to Sparks and to the new secretary in the Harrison administration produced no better results.[79]

The complaint campaign of the Central and Southern Pacific was most intense in mid-1886. At that time high officials of the roads joined Beard in importuning the administrators. In May, Collis P. Huntington forwarded to Secretary Lamar a letter from Alban N. Towne, general manager of the Central Pacific. Towne's central argument, directed against the usual delaying tactics, was based on pure political expediency. "Mr. Sparks," he said, "certainly cannot want a policy which will arrest the development of nearly one half the area of the United States; he must certainly desire that his administration should prove successful, as it seems to me he cannot from a political standpoint, desire to establish the reputation of arresting the growth of the great territories."[80] In support of Towne's proposition Huntington added: "It does seem very hard that the companies cannot get patents for lands which are so clearly theirs in law and which the people want to buy, and the railroad companies want to sell, in part for the money they will receive for the lands, but more particularly that the lands may be settled up and the tonnage thereby produced to support the running of the roads." And he concluded: "I cannot believe that when the Honorable Secretary fully understands this question he will fail to see justice done to the companies and patents granted for the lands."[81]

The campaign was continued by William H. Mills, land agent of the Central Pacific, who told Sparks that the company was anxious to take title to lands aggregating more than two hundred and fifty thousand acres, some of which appeared on lists pending since 1882. "As you are aware," he went on, "legislation looking to forcing title to land by the land-grant companies has already passed the House of Representatives. It is not in excess of exact justice to the companies to state

[77] Beard to Sparks, Washington, October 4, 1886, in Record Group 49, Railroad Land Grant Records, box 73.

[78] Beard to Lamar, Washington, April 14, 1887, in Record Group 49, Railroad Land Grant Records, box 73.

[79] Beard to Sparks, Washington, September 19, 1887, in Record Group 49, Railroad Land Grant Records, box 73; Beard to J. W. Noble, Washington, January 24, 1890, in Record Group 48, Lands and Railroads, Letters Received.

[80] Alban N. Towne to C. P. Huntington, San Francisco, May 11, 1886, in Record Group 49, Railroad Land Grant Records, box 16.

[81] Huntington to Lamar, New York City, May 19, 1886, in Record Group 49, Railroad Land Grant Records, box 16.

that delay in receiving patents as well as obstructions to the survey of land upon which patents are very earnestly desired, has done much to create the abuses, if any such exist, at which this legislation is aimed."[82] The official campaign was climaxed when a New York attorney addressed Sparks to the effect that a client had purchased land in Placer County, California, "sometime ago" and that the company assured him that the land had been listed and only awaited the patent. Where was it?[83] Sparks maintained his policy.

Four years later, in the spring of 1890, Huntington undertook a second, less intensive but perhaps more successful, campaign when he sent Secretary Noble a series of complaining letters from purchasers of railroad land addressed to Jerome Madden, land agent of the Southern Pacific, and Madden's letter explaining them. In his letter accompanying this transmission Huntington said he was quite sure that if Noble realized what inconvenience his policy was causing in California —to the state itself, which wanted to collect taxes on the lands, to the people who wanted to occupy them, and to the railroad company especially—the patents would be issued immediately.[84] Whatever the effect of this latest appeal, the Land Office did in fact return to patenting in 1890 and 1891.

The campaign of the Kansas Pacific and the Union Pacific, jointly conducted after the merger of 1880, was carried on by officials and legal counsel of the company, land lawyers and land agents in the locales affected, and certain Kansas and Nebraska politicians. Again the most intensive efforts were made just before and during the Cleveland administration. In May of 1884 the land agent of the Kansas Division asked Commissioner McFarland when patents could be expected for more than a half million acres selected in 1882 and 1883.[85] In January, 1885, S. J. Gilmore, representing the Platte Land Company, which had acquired land from the Kansas Pacific and had in turn sold much of it to individual purchasers, addressed complaints to McFarland. He asserted that applications for patents had been pending for more than two years and pointed out that purchasers of unpatented land found it difficult to sell it or secure loans on it. The delay in patenting, he said, "is an obstacle to business and retards the development of the country. It seems to me that two years should be more than ample time in which to get out such patents."[86]

[82] Mills to Sparks, San Francisco, June 10, 1886, in Record Group 49, Railroad Land Grant Records, box 16.

[83] B. E. Valentine to the Commissioner of the General Land Office, Brooklyn, June 1, 1886, in Record Group 49, Railroad Land Grant Records, box 16.

[84] Huntington to J. W. Noble, New York City, May 29, 1890, in Record Group 48, Lands and Railroads, Letters Received.

[85] B. M. McAllaster to N. S. McFarland, Denver, May 27, 1884, in Record Group 49, Railroad Land Grant Records, box 37.

[86] S. J. Gilmore to McFarland, Denver, January 6, 1885, in Record Group 49, Railroad Land Grant Records, box 37.

Secretary Lamar had hardly settled in his office when Charles Francis Adams, Jr., the new president of the Union Pacific, brought the patent problem to his attention by forwarding to him a letter he had received from the company's land agent, C. M. Cuming. Cuming stated that patents for more than nine hundred thousand acres were pending in the Land Office. The company's inability to obtain patents for this land, he reminded Adams, "casts a cloud upon its title and retards the settlement of the country tributary to the railroad." Perhaps, he went on, Adams had learned of the tactics of land dealers in Kansas, who were "publishing advertisements inviting people to settle on railroad lands and announcing that the company's title is worthless and the settler's title will be guaranteed."[87] Adams expressed his concern over the problem and suggested that "it would be conducive to the public good" if he could meet and talk with the new secretary.[88]

Even after 1891 and the termination of the policy of wholesale suspensions, Union Pacific officials found occasion to address complaints of Land Office delays to the government administrators. In December of 1894 B. M. McAllaster, the incumbent land agent of the company, asked commissioner of the General Land Office S. W. Lamoreux to take action on a quarter million acres in Utah. The lands had "long since" been sold, McAllaster said, yet he continually received letters from purchasers in which they told him of the great hardships suffered by the owners of land on which the United States patent was not of record.[89]

The Union Pacific, in its own right and as successor to the Kansas Pacific, like the Central Pacific and the Southern Pacific roads, placed most routine business with the Land Office in the hands of railroad attorneys in Washington. After 1882 most of this business was handled by the firm of Samuel Shellabarger and Jeremiah M. Wilson, which regularly filed with the Land Office letters complaining of delays and adverse policies. In October of 1886, for example, Shellabarger and Wilson asked Commissioner Sparks for action on pending selections of nearly eight hundred thousand acres of Kansas Pacific lands. Of these lands more than six hundred thousand acres were in no way involved in the Crawford relocation appeal and were subject to no other adverse claim. Hence the delay, sometimes amounting to years, was completely unjustified; and patents should issue "at the earliest practicable day."[90]

[87] C. M. Cuming to C. F. Adams, Jr., Omaha, September 3, 1886, in Record Group 48, Lands and Railroads, Letters Received.
[88] Adams to Lamar, Boston, September 8, 1886, in Record Group 48, Lands and Railroads, Letters Received.
[89] B. M. McAllaster to S. W. Lamoreux, Omaha, December 12, 1894, in Record Group 49, Railroad Land Grant Records, box 86.
[90] Shellabarger and Wilson to Sparks, Washington, October 22, 1886, in Record Group 49, Railroad Land Grant Records, box 86.

Perhaps the firm's most formidable attempt to earn its fee was made in March of 1889, only a few days after the appointment of Secretary Noble. On March 20 Noble received a multipage brief, in letter form, which reviewed the whole suspension policy as it related to the Union Pacific. The document pointed out that the railroad was not subject to forfeiture and that the only suspension then outstanding against it was the one ordered by Sparks on the occasion when inquires were made by the Pacific Railway Commission of 1887. At that time patents for more than 460,000 acres had been in the last stages of preparation. Other lists pending action included nearly 800,000 acres in Kansas which had originally been suspended on account of the relocation appeal, an additional 459,000 acres in Kansas selected since 1887, and 83,455 acres in Colorado selected in 1885 and suspended because of Commissioner Sparks' disapproval of the traditional form of affidavit for nonmineral lands. "This interminable delay," charged Shellabarger and Wilson, "has been of most serious injury to many persons who have purchased from the Company, and for many reasons are anxious to procure titles. These citizens are constantly appealing to the Company . . . and the Company in turn has during these years been appealing to the Department for action in their behalf."[91]

Politicians also joined the chorus of demands for rapid action on the Union and Kansas Pacific grants. As early as 1883 Governor G. W. Glick of Kansas had asked, on the occasion of the Crawford relocation appeal, that the administrators rush the case through and get the lands patented so that they might be "made to bear their proportionate share of taxation."[92] Another Kansas political figure, Senator Preston B. Plumb, who had been one of the reform leaders in the tax and forfeiture controversy, felt that the suspension question should have been settled long since. In 1888 he reminded Secretary William F. Vilas that numerous complaining letters from his constituents had been forwarded to the department and that he himself had spoken to the secretary about the matter on a number of occasions. As Plumb put it, "If the Government is to issue the patents, they ought to be issued now; if it is not going to issue them, then the parties who have purchased from the road should know it so that they may pursue their remedy against the grantor." Reminding Vilas that the case had been fully argued and only awaited a decision, he said, "I do not urge you to decide it either way, but simply that it be decided some way."[93]

The testimony of settlers regarding the detrimental effects of suspension and delay normally reached the Land Office through political

[91] Shellabarger and Wilson to J. W. Noble, Washington, March 20, 1889, in Record Group 48, Lands and Railroads, Letters Received.

[92] G. W. Glick to H. M. Teller, Topeka, October 1, 1883, in Record Group 49, Railroad Land Grant Records, box 86.

[93] P. B. Plumb to William F. Vilas, Washington, August 20, 1888, in Record Group 48, Lands and Railroads, Letters Received.

channels. Representatives and senators regularly forwarded complaints of this kind to Land Office officials. Senator Plumb, for example, forwarded "perhaps a hundred" such communications.[94] John A. Anderson also passed on a number of them, of which perhaps the most appealing was one he had received from Oak Hill, Kansas, late in 1888. The letter told of a woman who had sold a piece of railroad land she owned and purchased another tract. But she was unable to collect payment for the railroad land because it was unpatented, hence she could not pay for the second tract and was "in danger of losing her home."[95] By 1890, according to testimony of this kind, more than six hundred thousand acres in Nebraska alone were in the pendant state produced by the suspension policies. Requests that something be done had become urgent and numerous.[96] Perhaps this pressure helps explain Secretary Noble's decision, implemented in the summer of 1890, to return to patenting the Union Pacific, Kansas Pacific, and Central Pacific grants.

The Northern Pacific complained that both the alleged liability of the railroad for the costs of survey and the administrative suspension of its patents in anticipation of forfeiture legislation were indefensible in law. The railroad filed elaborate arguments to justify its position and regularly submitted formal demands that patents be issued to the company. It took the ground that the legislation making the road liable for the costs of survey—passed as it had been six years after the grant and as an amendment to an appropriations bill—was not valid law.[97] Attorneys for the road proposed the introduction of a bill to repeal this provision and filed a printed argument in support of their contention that it had been enacted in bad faith, constituted impairment of contract, and was unconstitutional in the light of the Dartmouth case.[98]

[94] *Ibid.*

[95] J. J. Marty to J. A. Anderson, Oak Hill, Kansas, December 26, 1888, in Record Group 49, Railroad Land Grant Records, box 86.

[96] T. S. Clarkson to Lewis A. Groff, Omaha, November 25, 1889 (filed with W. C. Elam, Chief of Division F, to Groff, November 29, 1889, in Record Group 49, Railroad Land Grant Records, box 86); G. L. Laws to Secretary of the Interior, Washington, April 30, 1890, in Record Group 48, Lands and Railroads, Letters Received. See also the Commissioner of the General Land Office to Hugh Alexander, July 30, 1886, in Record Group 49, Letters Sent.

[97] Most of the documents pertinent to this suspension of patenting to the Northern Pacific are printed in 49 Congress, 1 session, *Senate Executive Document 126* (1886), but see also 49 Congress, 1 session, *House Report 1002* (1886). The receipt by the Land Office of lists of selections on which costs of survey had not been paid is chronicled in a series of fifteen letters from local registers and receivers in Minnesota and in Dakota and Washington territories, dated from July 2, 1872, to November 22, 1882, all filed in Record Group 49, Railroad Land Grant Records, box 51.

[98] *Facts and Argument in Support of Senate Bill No. ——*, "*to amend an act in relation to the survey of certain lands granted to the Northern Pacific Railroad Company*" (no imprint), filed in Record Group 49, Railroad Land Grant Records, box 51.

In 1882 the company's general attorney, George Gray, filed what was perhaps the most inclusive of the railroad's arguments. Gray pointed out (1) that the Congress had obviously not originally intended to levy the survey charges on the Northern Pacific, since after due consideration it had rejected the proposal that a provision comparable to section 21 of the act of 1864 be added to the granting bill; (2) that the addition of the requirement was a breach of the private contract between the railroad and its mortgage-holders; and (3) that according to his construction of the granting act the Northern Pacific was also exempted from the costs of survey amendment of 1876.[99]

When, at the end of 1882, by a resolution of its board of directors, the company did agree to pay the costs, it did so under protest and under the provisions of the act of 1876, not that of 1870.[1] Still the dispute dragged on. Between 1882 and 1886 Northern Pacific complaints and demands for action centered upon the problem of arriving at a just rate of assessment for the costs of survey.[2] In 1885 the United States Supreme Court, in the Traill County tax case,[3] established the road's liability for survey costs and early the next year the board of directors resolved, again, to pay them.[4] Now, however, the second problem—that of forfeiture—intervened.

The Northern Pacific, which land reformers viewed as one of the most culpable of the construction laggards, had been since 1880 almost continually on the list of roads whose patents were suspended because of prospective forfeiture. Physical, financial, and strategic difficulties had produced such delays that the road, originally required to complete construction in 1878, had not been completed until 1883. More than half its mileage had been built after the expiration of the time limit. But the suspension of patenting born of the resultant possibility that the grant would be forfeited created no major disagreement between the road and the Land Office until after 1886, simply because the road had outstanding against it a prior suspension of patenting based on failure to pay costs of survey. After 1886, however, when failure to pay

[99] 49 Congress, 1 session, *Senate Executive Document 126* (1886), pp. 13–14.
[1] Enclosed in letter of Henry Villard to H. M. Teller, New York City, December 27, 1882, in Record Group 49, Railroad Land Grant Records, box 51.
[2] W. K. Mendenhall to McFarland, Washington, October 8, 1883, in Record Group 49, Railroad Land Grant Records, box 51; Mendenhall to the Commissioner of the General Land Office, July 8, 1885, in Record Group 49, Railroad Land Grant Records, box 52; Robert Harris, President of the Northern Pacific, to Sparks, New York City, February 12, 1886, in Record Group 49, Railroad Land Grant Records, box 52. See also 49 Congress, 1 session, *Senate Executive Document 126* (1888), pp. 20–21.
[3] 115 *United States Court Reports* 600 (1885).
[4] 49 Congress, 1 session, *Senate Executive Document 126* (1886), pp. 21–22, and two letters to Sparks from the surveyor general of Dakota Territory, dated July 10 and July 17, 1886, transmitting duplicate certificates of deposit for $88,100 of Northern Pacific costs payments, filed in Record Group 49, Railroad Land Grant Records, box 52.

the costs of survey was no longer a ground for suspension, the full impact of the suspension ordered in anticipation of forfeiture was felt and the Northern Pacific directed its complaints and arguments against it.[5] In 1887 Commissioner Sparks did agree to the issuance of patents on lands east of the Missouri River in Dakota—partly in response to attorney Mendenhall's importuning and partly because neither forfeiture bill then in Congress[6] called for recovery of lands adjacent to those parts of the road that had been completed on time. He did not think that patents should issue on "any other portion of the road."[7] This kind of piecemeal retreat from the patent-suspension policy, which continued until the passage of the General Forfeiture Act of September, 1890, was far from satisfactory to officials of the railroad. In June of 1889 company attorney James McNaught summed up the position of the Northern Pacific and of most of its fellow land-grant roads when he wrote that the refusal to issue patents was "in direct disobedience to the mandatory direction of Congress."[8]

The elaborate system of complaints developed and utilized by the land-grant railroads in their opposition to Land Office policies of suspension and delay had its counterpart in an equally involved system of justification presented by government officials. The grounds for Land Office action, or inaction, were three: (1) the enforcement of its own and congressional regulations and requirements; (2) the accommodation of current administrative policy to prospective legislative or executive policy; and (3) the magnitude and complexity of the task imposed upon an inadequately staffed and underfinanced agency.

The responsibility for enforcing regulations, invoked as early as 1868 by Secretary Browning and cited regularly by Cox, Delano, and Chandler, was perhaps the most easily justifiable grounds and the most consistent with past constitutional practices. The setting up of standards for completion and the enforcement of those standards were clearly authorized by legislation.[9] When railroad pressure and congressional

[5] There had been some earlier complaints. See, for example, George Gray to Teller, Washington, February 28, 1885, in Record Group 48, Lands and Railroads, Letters Received. See also George Gray, *Northern Pacific Railroad Company: Summary of Arguments . . . on the Legal Question of Forfeiture, February 6, 1884* (no imprint), and George Gray and J. Lewis Stackpole, *In the Matter of the Northern Pacific Land Grant* (Alfred Mudge and Son, Boston, 1886).

[6] Senate Bill 2172 and House Bill 147.

[7] Sparks to Lamar, April 4, 1887, in Record Group 49, Division F, Letters Sent.

[8] James McNaught to the Commissioner of the General Land Office, St. Paul, June 20, 1889, in Record Group 49, Railroad Land Grant Records, box 53.

[9] *Report of Lieut. Col. James H. Simpson, Corps of Engineers, U.S.A., on the Change of the Route West from Omaha, Nebraska Territory, Proposed by the Union Pacific Railroad Company Made to Honorable James Harlan, Secretary of the Interior, September 18, 1865, with the President's Decision Thereon* (Government Printing Office, Washington, 1865); *Report of Board Convened to Determine on a Standard of Construction of the Pacific Railroad Made to Honorable*

inquiry were brought to bear on the policy and the House passed a bill to force issuance of patents,[10] Secretary Delano justified the position of his department thus: "The subsidy in bonds granted said companies has long since been received in full by them, so that this moiety of lands withheld is the only security of the Government for the completion of the road as required by law."[11] He went on to argue that any mandatory issuance of patents should be made contingent on the satisfaction of all the deficiencies reported by the committee of "eminent citizens."[12] The suspension of patenting for failure to pay the arrears of costs of survey, both the temporary suspension applying to all the roads and the long-term suspension applying to the Northern Pacific, were made on much the same grounds.[13] The early opposition to taxation legislation on the part of such government officials as Commissioner Drummond and Secretary Chandler was expressed in terms of the government's need of a lever for enforcing its requirements, and the suspension of patenting to the Kansas Pacific on account of state agent Crawford's relocation appeal was also undertaken partly in the enforcement tradition.[14]

Less easily justifiable on constitutional grounds was the accommodation policy, the policy of adapting current administrative practice to prospective legislative and executive policies in order to expedite their application. There was plenty of room in the legal tradition, perhaps, for this "loose constructionist" approach—Justice Marshall had seen to that—but the opposition could and did draw upon the equally hoary "strict constructionist" interpretation of the law and bitterly attacked what it viewed as the unprincipled usurpation of legislative authority by the administrators. The position of those government officers who sought

---

James Harlan, Secretary of the Interior, February 24, 1866, with Accompanying Documents (Government Printing Office, Washington, 1866); *Opinion of Hon. Wm. M. Evarts, Atty. General, Upon the Duties of the Executive Relative to the Pacific Railroad, the Acceptance of the Same, and the Issue of United States Subsidies Thereon* (no imprint, September 5, 1868).

[10] William Stewart to Delano, Senate Chamber, June 9, 1874, in Record Group 48, Lands and Railroads, Letters Received. The reference is to House Bill 3281, which passed the House on May 10, 1874.

[11] Delano to Stewart, June 17, 1874, in Record Group 48, Lands and Railroads, Letters Sent.

[12] *Ibid.*

[13] B. R. Cowen to the Commissioner of the General Land Office, September 11, 1873, in Record Group 48, Lands and Railroads, Letters Sent; S. S. Burdett to Delano, December 14, 1874, in Record Group 49, Division F, Letters Sent; Delano to Burdett, December 17, 1874, in Record Group 48, Lands and Railroads, Letters Sent; W. W. Curtiss, Acting Commissioner, to W. K. Mendenhall, May 27, 1874, in Record Group 49, Division F, Letters Sent; 49 Congress, 1 session, *Senate Executive Document 126* (1886), p. 11.

[14] 44 Congress, 1 session, *Senate Executive Document 20* (1876); Chandler to Richard J. Oglesby, Chairman of the Senate Committee on Public Lands, August 8, 1876, in Record Group 48, Lands and Railroads, Letters Sent.

to pursue such an accommodation policy was made doubly difficult by the frequent changes in personnel occasioned by changing political fortunes. Carl Schurz, who had refused to suspend patenting on forfeitable grants, was succeeded by S. J. Kirkwood, who initiated the policy.[15] Kirkwood's justification was simply that it was "not deemed expedient to certify additional lands to the railroad companies . . . pending the determination of Congress in the premises."[16] Teller, at first unable to justify continued suspensions as policy, temporarily dropped them.[17]

Sparks, the great exponent of the accommodation policy, regularly justified his course. In July of 1886 he told Huntington that patenting of a portion of the Southern Pacific grant was being suspended "for the reason that legislation looking to the forfeiture of said grant is pending in Congress."[18] In answer to inquiries from the Pacific Railway Commission of 1887 Sparks countered charges that administrative policies of suspension and delay were causing losses of mineral lands and other benefits to the Central Pacific with the assertion that if such policies often saved the government from relinquishing lands to a company that was not entitled to them, the company had no ground for complaint. The fact that it had complained was itself evidence of its "disposition and desire to wrongfully acquire title to lands to which it has no legal right."[19]

Perhaps the frankest and at the same time most characteristic statement of the position of proponents of the accommodation policy was that made by Sparks in March of 1887, when he told Henry Beard that he did not feel obligated to certify a list of grants referred to him, "thereby defeating the full and free exercise by the 50th Congress . . . of its will on such measure as may come before it, having in view the forfeiture of the grants."[20] In March of 1889 Sparks' successor, S. M. Stockslager, forwarded to the secretary of the interior a statement prepared by the chief of Division F which said in part: "For several years past legislation looking to the forfeiture of the grants to these roads has been pending in Congress and this office, in order to avoid complicating the matter, has suspended their selections and with-

[15] Commissioner of the General Land Office, *Annual Report*, 1883, p. 22; Schurz to G. F. Edmunds, January 25, 1879, and to Horace White, September 29, 1880, both in Record Group 48, Lands and Railroads, Letters Sent; and Stockslager to Lamar, December 17, 1887, in Record Group 49, Division F, Letters Sent.

[16] Commissioner of the General Land Office, *Annual Report*, 1882, pp. 10–11. See also McFarland to Kirkwood, March 30, 1882, in Record Group 49, Division F, Letters Sent.

[17] Commissioner of the General Land Office, *Annual Report*, 1883, p. 22. But see L. Harrison, Assistant Commissioner of the General Land Office, to S. J. Gilmore, February 14, 1885, in Record Group 49, Letters Sent.

[18] Sparks to Huntington, July 28, 1886, in Record Group 49, Letters Sent.

[19] 50 Congress, 1 session, *Senate Executive Document 51* (1888), p. 4396.

[20] Sparks to Beard, March 26, 1887, in Record Group 49, Letters Sent.

held certification or patent, as the case may be."[21] Continuation of Sparks' suspension of patenting because of the Pacific Railway Commission inquiry was justified, he said, in the light of a presidential suggestion that further issuance of patents await settlement of the indebtedness question.[22]

By the beginning of 1890, however, pressure for the relaxation of the suspension policies had become great, and Lewis Groff, Secretary Noble's new commissioner, was anxious to drop them. In an effort to convince the secretary of the wisdom of a change of policy he argued: "The innocent purchasers are the real sufferers, and judging from the numerous letters received, narrating their distressing hardships and urging that their titles be freed from this seeming cloud, both justice and equity warrant an early issue of patents."[23] And Assistant Secretary Chandler, in writing to a congressman, urged that "the present administration ought not to be blamed for the four years delay occasioned by the last."[24] The accommodation policy was dead.

The final argument, the magnitude and complexity of the task devolving upon the Land Office, was also regularly cited as justification for delay. Every commissioner serving between 1872 and 1891 complained of the vast arrears of business that faced him when he took office. These arrears were attributed to two general factors: (1) the lack of office space and office personnel adequate to deal with the ever-increasing land business of the government and (2) the complex character of policy decisions—decisions complicated by the masses of evidence involved and by the conflicting policies of successive Land Office administrators.

The plea for more clerks and more office space was almost unceasing. Commissioner Drummond could not keep abreast of current work. He reported that returns from local land offices often remained unposted for as long as two years and that township field notes had not been indexed for ten years.[25] Commissioner Burdett supported Drummond's request for a thorough reorganization of the Land Office and a large increase in the clerical force. A small increase, granted by Congress in 1874, enabled him to keep up with current work, he said, but he could not bring the arrears up to date. J. A. Williamson, Burdett's

[21] G. M. Wilcox to Stockslager, March 13, 1889, in Record Group 49, Railroad Land Grant Records, box 86. See also T. A. Anderson, Assistant Commissioner of the General Land Office, to W. F. Vilas, September 3, 1888, in Record Group 49, Division F, Letters Sent.

[22] Wilcox to Stockslager, March 13, 1889, in Record Group 49, Railroad Land Grant Records, box 86.

[23] L. Groff to Noble, December 30, 1889, in Record Group 49, Division F, Letters Sent.

[24] Chandler to G. L. Laws, May 1, 1890, in Record Group 48, Lands and Railroads, Letters Sent.

[25] Commissioner of the General Land Office, *Annual Report*, 1871, p. 38; 1872, pp. 5–6; 1873, pp. 5–6.

successor,[26] complained bitterly when, in 1876, Congress reduced his clerical force by twenty-five per cent, and the office fell further in arrears during the remainder of his administration. J. M. Armstrong, reporting as acting commissioner in 1879, complained that Division F in particular was suffering from the clerical drought. In 1880 Commissioner Williamson devoted eleven pages of his report to a summary of his own and his predecessors' complaints and also asked for higher salaries and better office accommodations.[27]

N. C. McFarland, content to cite earlier commissioners in 1881, demanded a hundred new clerks in 1882. A ten per cent increase authorized in that year was quickly absorbed, largely by new business, and in 1883 McFarland, protesting that it would take his present force three years to catch up (even if all new business were suspended), asked for two hundred more clerks. Commissioner Sparks said nothing of clerical shortages in 1885, but in 1886 and 1887 he made his characteristically thorough recommendations. The regular business of the office, he said, was two years behind, and in some divisions, such as those of railroads and private land claims, the much larger arrearages could not even be estimated. He had 377 clerks. He wanted an additional 159 regular and 112 temporary clerks. Sparks' immediate successor, S. M. Stockslager, got 32 new clerks, but he also called for a thorough reorganization of the office. In 1889 Acting Commissioner Stone reorganized much of the business of the Land Office, removing many of the safeguards considered essential by Sparks and thereby managing to increase the output of his office. In 1891 Commissioner Thomas H. Carter requested not clerks but more office space, and a year later jubilantly reported that the Land Office was abreast of current work—for the first time since 1875.[28]

Cited almost as regularly as staff shortages to explain Land Office arrearages were the delays incidental to policy-making. Carl Schurz virtually ceased patenting railroad indemnity lands for three years while he reconsidered the whole policy of selections and identification of them that his predecessors had followed.[29] He decided that designation of each tract lost in the original grant area and of the specific tract selected as indemnity for it was necessary. But in 1883, after three more years of reconsideration, Teller rescinded the order.[30] Then, in

[26] Ibid., 1874, p. 7; 1875, pp. 21–22. See also Delano to J. A. Garfield, December 2, 1874, in Record Group 48, Lands and Railroads, Letters Sent.

[27] Commissioner of the General Land Office, Annual Report, 1876, pp. 14–16; 1877, pp. 1–3; 1878, p. 145; 1879, pp. 85–224; 1880, pp. 2–13.

[28] Ibid., 1881, pp. 14–26; 1882, pp. 15–16; 1883, pp. 31–32; 1887, pp. 182, 188; 1888, pp. 101–102, 200; 1889, pp. 3, 101–102; 1891, pp. 61–66; 1892, p. 3.

[29] Henry Beard, "The Railways and the United States Land Office," in the Agricultural Review, 3:441 (1883).

[30] General Land Office, Circular of November 7, 1879; W. K. Mendenhall to McFarland, Washington, April 2, 1883; Teller to the Commissioner of the General

1885, on the basis of appeals from Washington Territory, the requirement was reimposed by Secretary Lamar.[31]

Policy decisions on land in mineral areas were also complicated and somewhat vacillating. The foothills region of the Sierra Nevada, which was dotted with old worked-out placer mines, had been designated a mineral area by the original surveyors. In 1878 the Central Pacific was allowed to select its lands in the area on the basis of blanket affidavits rather than the individual affidavits normally used for agricultural selections in such mineral areas.[32] In 1886, however, Commissioner Sparks insisted upon a return to the filing of separate affidavits for each forty-acre tract.[33]

The magnitude of the task was constantly cited as cause for delays in making policy decisions. The delay on account of the Crawford relocation appeal was partly attributed to this cause,[34] but more pertinent, perhaps, is Secretary Noble's reconsideration of the suspension of the patenting of Union Pacific lands that had been imposed at the beginning of the investigation by the Pacific Railway Commission of 1887. In answer to an inquiry from Huntington, Noble stated: "The subject, taking all the railroads together, is one of immense magnitude and requires the most deliberate action on my part to avoid injustice to the people on the one hand and the railroads on the other."[35] To the president of the Senate he said: "The question is one of more than ordinary importance, and with the time at the disposal of the Secretary for such business he has not been able to complete the inquiry."[36] And in this instance, as was typical after Sparks left office, it was pleaded that his administration had produced a vast accumulation of unfinished business.[37]

Land Office, May 28, 1883; all in Record Group 49, Railroad Land Grant Records, box 51.

[31] William Walker, Acting Commissioner, to Lamar, August 3, 1885, in Record Group 49, Division F, Letters Sent.

[32] This policy is described in the Central Pacific Railroad Company's *Annual Report* for 1878, pp. 55–56.

[33] Sparks to Beard, October 11, 1886, in Record Group 49, Letters Sent. The conflict over Southern and Central Pacific selections of mineral lands is chronicled in a series of letters and reports filed under Beard to Lamar, May 2, 1886, in Record Group 48, Lands and Railroads, Letters Received. See also J. W. Noble to the Commissioner of the General Land Office, February 29, 1891, in Record Group 48, Letters Sent. See also Henry Beard, *Before the Honorable Secretary of the Interior: The Listing and Patenting of Lands Granted to the Central Pacific Railroad Co.: The "Mineral Lands" Excepted from the Grant* (Judd and Detweiler, Washington, 1890).

[34] 50 Congress, 1 session, *Senate Executive Document 51* (1888), p. 4396.

[35] Noble to Huntington, June 7, 1890, in Record Group 48, Letters Sent.

[36] Noble to the President of the Senate, March 17, 1890, in Record Group 48, Letters Sent.

[37] George Chandler to G. L. Laws, May 1, 1890, in Record Group 48, Letters Sent; Commissioner of the General Land Office, *Annual Report*, 1888, p. 214.

In fact, Commissioners Stockslager, Stone, and Carter all attributed much of their arrears to the suspension policies of Commissioner Sparks on the one hand and to his complicated system of safeguards, including a board of review, on the other. Stone's criticism of Sparks was particularly sharp. He held that many of the safeguards Sparks had instituted were directed "against improbable or impossible irregularities" and proceeded to abandon most of them. Commissioner Carter likewise, in his report for 1891, castigated Sparks for causing complications and delay and expressed the sympathies of the new administrators with the policy of expeditious disposal of public-land business.[38] Land Office policy had taken a new turn. By 1891 the incumbent administrators were viewing the Cleveland-Lamar-Sparks era of suspension and delay as part of the inglorious past.

[38] *Ibid.*; and 1889, p. 3; 1891, pp. 3–5.

Five

The Operators

IN THE beginning the trans-Missouri railroads enjoyed a benevolent atmosphere of public praise, encouragement, and anticipation. Legislators, public officials, private investors, and both resident and prospective settlers in the areas they were to serve lauded them, supported their demands, and supplied their financial wants. But often the promoters undertook to reap a twofold or threefold profit from construction; the roads fought one another for land and trackage rights and for advantageously located terminals and junction points; and the rapid expansion of population engendered by their transportation facilities and land-sale programs created more problems than it solved. For these and many other reasons the operators of the land-grant railroads came to conduct their business—both as transportation agents and as owners and sellers of land—under a cloud of public disapproval and distrust. After 1870 the cloud grew larger and more ominous until, during the storm of the 1890's, the operators were faced with the possibility, remote as in the end it turned out to be, of having their railroads taken from them.

These changes in the attitude of the public toward the railroads were directly reflected in the controversy over the taxation of the railroad lands. Legislative and administrative actions reflected the changes in popular opinion. So did the actions of the railroadmen. As the attitudes of the legislators and administrators evolved from permissive to restrictive to punitive, so also did the attitudes of the railroad operators evolve from presumptive to assertive to plaintive. The operators, at first content to ask for what they considered their due, were by the mid-seventies insisting upon what they considered their right. And from the early eighties on into the nineties they complained with increasing energy of the unjust and prejudicial treatment they were receiving at the hands of public officers. Thus they created, at least for their sympathizers, an image of themselves as the innocent victims of legislative demagogues and administrative incompetents.

At first the operators' requests for administrative services, favors, or changes of policy were made with an air of full expectation that they would be granted—and they usually were. J. P. Usher, as attorney for the Union Pacific, Eastern Division, in 1866, and John P. Devereaux, as land agent for the same road in 1869, expected the accommodation they got when they asked that a program of partial listing of land

87

selections be allowed.[1] When in 1865 Collis P. Huntington, writing to Usher, then secretary of the interior, asked that the government undertake the immediate survey of lands along the Central Pacific route so that the company could protect its holdings from timber depredations,[2] Usher within three days' time instructed the commissioner: "At once give the necessary directions to the Surveyor General to cause the survey of the lands along the route . . . to be prosecuted the coming season as rapidly as possible."[3] Kansas Congressman Sydney Clarke, one of the early practitioners of the art of privately aiding and publicly baiting the railroads, wrote to President Johnson in October of 1865 to urge the early settlement of all questions pertaining to the Union Pacific, Eastern Division, praising the promoters of the road as experienced and able men.[4] In later years "railroad statesmen" had to be more circumspect in seeking aid or favor.[5]

Slowly the attitudes of the administrators changed. Secretary Usher had withdrawn from the public domain broad strips of land for railroad grants: fifty miles wide for forty-mile grants and comparable excesses for others. Usher himself modified this action to permit settlement on the even-numbered sections, but he maintained the excess width. Later, Secretary Browning reduced the width of the tracts withdrawn to the approximate width of the grants, but at first seems not to have contemplated allowing settlement on the even-numbered sections. In 1868, however, he restored these lands to the public domain, leaving for the railroads only the odd-numbered sections within the limits of the grants.[6]

The stiffening attitude of the government—as best expressed in the suspensions of patenting imposed in 1869 and thereafter—was paralleled by a growing impatience and an aggressive assertion of their rights on the part of the railroadmen. This too developed gradually. Many of

[1] See above pp. 61–62.

[2] Huntington to Usher, Washington, February 28, 1865, in the National Archives, Record Group 48 (Records of the Office of the Secretary of the Interior), Letters Received. Hereafter this collection will be cited as Record Group 48.

[3] Usher to the Commissioner of the General Land Office, March 2, 1865, in Record Group 48, Pacific Railroads, Letters Sent.

[4] Sidney Clarke to the President, Washington, October 6, 1865, in Record Group 48, Letters Received. See also Paul W. Gates, *Fifty Million Acres: Conflicts over Kansas Land Policy, 1854–1890* (Cornell University Press, Ithaca, 1954), 179, 179n, 256n, 256–258.

[5] See, for example, Senator John Mitchell's letter to J. A. Williamson, Washington, November 28, 1877, in the National Archives, Record Group 49 (Records of the General Land Office), Railroad Land Grant Records, box 66. Hereafter this collection will be cited as Record Group 49.

[6] J. P. Usher to the Commissioner of the General Land Office, November 4 and November 21, 1864, and O. H. Browning to the Commissioner of the General Land Office, November 10, 1866, all in Record Group 48, Pacific Railroads, Letters Sent; Commissioner of the General Land Office to Browning, November 8, 1867, in Record Group 48, Letters Received; Browning to J. S. Wilson, December 5, 1876, and March 25, 1868, both in Record Group 48, Pacific Railroads, Letters Sent.

the complaints about the suspensions of patenting imposed to force the roads to meet the standards of completion set by the government were conciliatory in tone.[7] And as late as March of 1873 Usher, representing the Kansas Pacific, could request a new procedure for assessing costs of survey, one that would require the roads to pay them only on the lands they were actually to get from any given list. Thus the roads would not just save money on the costs of survey but, more important, would have to pay taxes only on those lands they were assured of receiving immediately.[8] This accommodation, like the relaxation of suspensions of patenting, the Land Office did not provide. The letters of railroadmen became more aggressive and the campaign of public justification of the railroads' position began to take form.

Early expressions of dissatisfaction with the Land Office were comparatively moderate in tone. The Union Pacific published in 1874, as a part of its own annual report, the report of the government directors of the road. Their report blamed much of the taxation controversy in Nebraska on the suspensions of patenting that the General Land Office had imposed on the roads.[9] In the same year the land agent of the Central Pacific excused the small volume of land sales in Utah by telling the stockholders that it was attributable to the failure of the General Land Office to define the boundary between the lands of the Central Pacific and those of the Union Pacific.[10]

By the mid-seventies the criticisms were more outspoken. In 1876 railroad attorney James H. Storrs, pamphleteering against the Crounse tax bill, charged that the Land Office was incapable of conducting the surveys of railroad lands that would be necessary to make the bill operable.[11] When Carl Schurz ruled that the contingent right of preemption was valid law, the Central Pacific told its stockholders that the ruling was illegal; that the company, although it had regularly sold its lands below the market price, had found it "impossible to sell all its lands, and more particularly the very large portion that was withheld . . . as security for the completion of the road according to contract."[12] The Central Pacific continued its attack in 1878 when its land agent reported the failure of all efforts to get the Land Office to rescind its unreasonable ruling designating as mineral land the old placer-mine area in the foothills of the Sierra Nevada.[13]

[7] See above, pp. 66–67.
[8] Usher to the Commissioner of the General Land Office, Lawrence, Kansas, March 1, 1873, in Record Group 49, Railroad Land Grant Records, box 36.
[9] Union Pacific, *Annual Report*, 1874, pp. 41–42.
[10] Central Pacific, *Annual Report*, 1874, p. 38.
[11] *Argument of James H. Storrs, Counsel for Central Pacific Railroad Company, before the Committee on Public Lands, United States Senate . . . in Relation to the Taxation of Lands Granted to Railroad Companies, March 8, 1876* (John L. Ginck, Washington, 1876), 2–3.
[12] Central Pacific, *Annual Report*, 1877, p. 5.
[13] *Ibid.*, 1878, pp. 55–56.

The Northern Pacific began its assault on the Land Office in 1879. In that year its land agent reported that sales in the area east of the Missouri were falling off "for the want of Government surveys," and from 1879 until 1883 every annual report cited the same failure of the Land Office to maintain a satisfactory pace in surveying the grant. By 1881 the road's land department was "much embarrassed" by the lack of surveys. It was particularly anxious that timber districts be sectionalized so that the company's holdings might be segregated and "measures taken to prevent depredations on the timber." In 1883 the land agent reported that the lack of surveys had retarded both sales and settlement. "In many localities of Dakota," he said, "numbers of settlers have gone out and occupied lands in advance of surveys and both the welfare of these settlers and good faith to this Company demand that these lands should be surveyed by the Government at as early a date as is practicable."[14]

The Union Pacific was still the mildest of the critics. In 1882 its land agent referred, in passing, to the lack of surveys, and the next year the report of the government directors, conceding the magnificence of the company's grant but at the same time citing the great benefits the railroad was bringing to the West, was appended to the annual report.[15]

The change of tone that marked the adoption of a more plaintive attitude came in the early eighties. The demarcation line was a classic interchange between Henry Beard, the most widely known of the railroad lawyers, and George W. Julian, one of the early and most inflexible leaders of the congressional land reformers. Julian, in an article appearing in the North American Review for March, 1883,[16] saw the land-grant railroads as an example of "commercial feudalism" and presented a large body of circumstantial evidence to support his contention that they exercised virtual control over the Land Office. As his best evidence he cited the administrative decisions that all lands within the limits of the grant areas lost to other claimants were indemnifiable, not merely those lost sometime between the date of the grant and the date of definite location of the roads. As further evidence he cited the excess acreage "inadvertently" patented to the Santa Fe, the Missouri, Kansas and Texas, and the Kansas Pacific. "The claims of the railroad companies," he wrote, "are always recognized by the Government as paramount while . . . the legal rights of the citizen seem to be regarded as matters of little moment. . . . Every presumption is against him and no mistakes are ever made in his favor."[17]

Julian went on to indict the Land Office for its land-withdrawal policy, citing instances of tracts suspended from the public domain for

[14] Northern Pacific, Annual Report, 1879, p. 11; 1880, pp. 16, 21; 1881, p. 16; 1882, p. 31; 1883, pp. 39–40.
[15] Union Pacific, Annual Report, 1882, p. 10; 1883, Appendix, pp. 16–17.
[16] George W. Julian, "Railway Influence in the Land Office," in the Northern American Review, 136:237–256 (March, 1883).
[17] Ibid., 249.

years to aid roads that had never been constructed. He argued that "these illustrations of the management of the railroads by the Land Department are, in fact, illustrations of the management of the Land Department by the railroads."[18] His cure for the evils he cited was simple: "What is wanted is a thorough reorganization of the machinery and working force of the Department, such additions to the working force as shall be adequate to the work to be performed, and such an increase of compensation as will bring into the service the highest grade of capacity and integrity."[19]

Beard's answer, published in the *Agricultural Review*,[20] ostensibly defended the Land Office. Actually it was a defense of the railroads. He first cited Julian's record in Congress as evidence that at the outset he had favored the grants, failing to point out that more than fifteen years had elapsed since they had been made—thereby using a tactic employed by Julian when he failed to note how the withdrawal policy of the Land Office had changed since the days of John Palmer Usher. He then cited court decisions to show that Julian was misreading the judicial interpretations of the indemnity laws. The core of his criticism, however, was directed not at Julian but at the Land Office. He demonstrated that in thirty years only forty-seven million acres of a prospective hundred and eighty million had been certified, that the pace of certification was slowing up year by year, and that only about six and a half per cent of the land patented in each of the years 1880, 1881, and 1882 had gone to the railroads. Citing Carl Schurz's suspension of the indemnity issues for three years while he investigated them, Beard contended that the railroads "instead of favor only obtained their legal rights after long contention and long delay."[21] This article, in content and in tone, set the fashion for the railroad literature of the eighties. The thesis of such literature was Beard's own—the railroads "have not obtained justice."[22]

The attitudes and policies of the railroads in three broad areas were germane to the waxing controversy: the prosecution and adequacy of the surveys of the public lands; the wisdom of and necessity for the proofs demanded of the roads that specific tracts should be patented and the methods of verification of these proofs used in the Land Office; and the relationship of the acreage selected by the railroads to the acreage patented by the government. The channels commonly utilized for the public presentation of the views of the railroadmen were also three: the annual and special reports to stockholders, pamphlets, and the testimony given before governmental investigative bodies. The views expressed and policies proposed in correspondence with administrative

[18] *Ibid.*, 253.
[19] *Ibid.*, 256.
[20] Henry Beard, "The Railways and the United States Land Office," in the *Agricultural Review*, 3:423–443 (April, 1883).
[21] *Ibid.*, 439.
[22] *Ibid.*, 434.

officials, though often the clearest statements available, were only indirectly designed for or accessible to the public. Congressional committees sometimes did publish such correspondence in conjunction with reports of their investigations or deliberations. And of course there was the great linen-airing of 1887, when the Pacific Railway Commission gathered what was to become five volumes of testimony and appended data on the history, conduct, and general policies of the bond-aided lines. In such hearings railroadmen, usually supported by company counsel, regularly presented the most thorough and most precise of statements of policy and indications of attitude. On these points and through these channels the railroadmen built a strong case.

The most persistent assailant of governmental survey policy was the Northern Pacific. The railroad pressed its attacks on two fronts, arguing its case for the nonpayment of survey fees on the one hand and complaining of the lack of surveys on the other. In its annual report for 1883 the company told its stockholders that the listing and certifying of the road's lands was progressing "without hindrance or delay" so far as they had been surveyed. In the same report the company stated that all the lands in Dakota had been selected so far as the government surveys had been completed. In 1882 the company had finally agreed to pay the costs of survey and in 1883 reported setting aside $601,942 for that purpose. But in 1884 it returned to its argument that it was not liable for such costs. The contention of company attorney George Gray that the amendment to the appropriations bill of 1870 was an "illegal and inequitable oppression" was used to justify the company's early policy of nonpayment and its continued resistence, but after the Traill County decision established the legality of the act, the company, in 1886, once more receded from its position. After that the annual reports concentrated in earnest upon the surveys themselves. The 1887 report, in reviewing the activities of the land department, described "the lack of complete surveys" as "a serious drawback to the settlement of the West Missouri country, more than two thirds of the land within the company's grant in that part of Dakota being yet unsurveyed by the Government." And a year later: "The operations of the Land Department have been retarded and obstructed by the limited area yet covered by Government surveys." Again in 1889: "Selection and sales of lands are retarded, and adequate protection by the company of its timber interests prevented by the failure of the Government to make these needed surveys."[23]

The bond-aided lines, though they said little about the surveys in their annual reports, had much to say about them during the investigation of 1887. The Union Pacific, which as a result of the merger of 1880 spoke also for the Kansas Pacific and the Denver Pacific, was the less outspoken complainant, but its general attorney, Andrew Poppleton, did

[23] Northern Pacific, *Annual Report*, 1883, pp. 40–43; 1884, p. 42; 1886, p. 47; 1887, p. 48; 1888, p. 49; 1889, p. 53.

cite slow surveys as a contributing cause of slow patenting in presenting evidence that the company had pursued the selection of its lands with due diligence. Former land commissioner Leavitt Burnham also defended the company by pointing out that there was "much land that was not surveyed and could not be surveyed at the price paid for the Government survey."[24]

It was the Central Pacific that cited the lack of surveys most effectively. As spokesman for the road its land commissioner, William H. Mills, on a number of occasions condemned the survey policy of the Land Office. He reported that because the rates for government surveys were too low to appeal to responsible surveyors, the road had given them passes as an inducement to accept the contracts. On another occasion, with reference to proofs that given tracts were nonmineral lands, he pointed out that the government on the one hand demanded affidavits for each forty-acre tract and on the other refused to survey units smaller than 640 acres. Finally, in a prepared statement in which he castigated the administrators in detail, Mills stated that during the decade of the seventies surveying proceeded very slowly and that, despite increased activity during the years 1880-1883, about half the lands granted to the Central Pacific were still unsurveyed. Yet, because of the policies of Commissioner Sparks, surveying had been virtually suspended for two full years.[25]

The Railway Commission's general report published, as its own conclusion, Commissioner Sparks' answering testimony that surveys had been adequate, ignoring the arguments of the railroads. According to Sparks the Union Pacific had selected only about two-thirds of its Nebraska lands, though they had all been surveyed for ten years, 640 of its 590,000 surveyed acres in Colorado, 80,317 of its 5,016,000 surveyed acres in Wyoming, and 42,360 of its 480,000 surveyed acres in Utah. The Kansas Pacific had selected less than half its grant in Kansas, though all of it had been surveyed for thirteen years, and only 71,580 of 1,200,000 surveyed acres in Colorado. And the Central Pacific had selected only 819,768 of 1,540,000 surveyed acres in California, 517,322 of 2,000,000 surveyed acres in Nevada, and 517,322 of 850,000 surveyed acres in Utah.[26] There had to be a better argument than lack of adequate surveys.

Unreasonableness of the proofs required and of decisions rendered by government officers, also cited occasionally in the seventies, became a standard topic of published criticism and complaint during the eighties. Here too Henry Beard had set the stage with his censure of Secretary Schurz, but it was during the tenure of Commissioner Sparks that the most violent attacks were made. The Central Pacific, speaking

---

[24] 50 Congress 1 session, *Senate Executive Document 51* (1888), pp. 1024, 1026, 1238.

[25] *Ibid.*, 2424, 2564, 3601.

[26] *Ibid.*, 145, 4397–4398.

also for the Southern Pacific, was at the forefront of the assault, citing the policies of Commissioner Sparks as a major cause of delay and as evidence that the railroads were being unjustly treated by the Land Office. When Sparks proposed a new method of determining the outer limits of the railroad grants, a method designed to solve the old problem of applying a curved line to a rectangular survey pattern, the Central Pacific published a pamphlet by Henry Beard in which he argued that the proposed method was visionary. It would, he said, confuse the adjustment of the grants and thereby further delay issuance of patents. It would also upset the prospective titles of thousands who were purchasing land or who had settled with reference to the old limits.[27]

The mineral-land policies inaugurated by Commissioner Sparks were also attacked. Sparks had ruled that for each forty-acre tract in areas designated mineral land in the original survey and in other areas identified by the Land Office as possibly containing mineral deposits, the railroad must file a separate affidavit, made by a person familiar with the specific tract in question, that there were no indications of mineral deposits. He further ruled that these affidavits must be presented at the time the selections were first filed in the local land office.[28] When the Central Pacific's land agent appeared before the Railway Commission, he argued that the new rules were discouraging, unreasonable, and unjust. They were being applied, he said, to vast areas of land in sparsely settled regions that were suitable only for grazing and were "notoriously free from all mineral indications." It would be almost impossible to find qualified persons who had traversed given forty-acre tracts frequently enough to enable them to make the required affidavits. Moreover, the new rules requiring that such proofs be filed simultaneously with the application for selection were equally onerous: first, because the local registers and receivers could no longer hold hearings preliminary to selection (thus the burden was now on the roads to prove that the lands were not mineral rather than on the government officers to prove that they were) and, second, because lands already selected under the old method were interdicted and the whole process would have to be repeated. "By this ruling," said Mills, "lists of selections long since completed were relegated to a condition of very indefinite delay."[29]

When Sparks' successor did not recede from this policy of requiring affidavits for each forty-acre tract, the railroad published two more pamphlets by Henry Beard. In the first of these, which appeared in January of 1890, he said that the Central Pacific had 18,222 affidavits

[27] Henry Beard, *Protest of the Central Pacific Railroad Company against Interruption in the Administration of Its Land Grant by Executive Action or Decisions Tending to Disturb the Limits of Its Grant as Heretofore Adjusted* (Judd and Detweiler, Washington, 1886).

[28] Sparks' letter of June 25, 1887, to Lamar, in Record Group 49, Letters Received, explains the ruling and defends its propriety.

[29] 50 Congress, 1 session, *Senate Executive Document 51* (1888), pp. 2564–2565.

for 728,869 acres pending in the Land Office, and he castigated Sparks for deliberately blocking the issuance of patents.[30] In the second pamphlet Beard argued that the new policy did not coincide with the survey laws, the grant-conveyance laws, or the mineral laws—in short, that to force the railroads to file nonmineral affidavits on lands returned as agricultural in the original surveys was illegal and oppressive.[31] In 1894, well after the new policy of expeditious patenting had been inaugurated, the administrators receded from Sparks' position. They issued new rules allowing the presentation of a single affidavit covering an entire list of selections instead of requiring the filing of separate affidavits for each tract selected.[32]

Both the Union Pacific and the Northern Pacific were much less outspoken in their criticism of the proofs required and decisions rendered by the Land Office. The Union Pacific's position was presented in a pamphlet written by attorney John S. Blair and addressed to the secretary of the interior. At the outset Blair challenged the legality of withholding patents on the grounds stated, contending that the commissioner of the General Land Office was not empowered to suspend patenting either to meet provisions of prospective legislation or to readjust the land grant. The effect of these policies, he said, was to create "in the minds of the community a needless, but at the same time dreadful, uncertainty." The effect of this uncertainty, in turn, was to retard buyers of railroad land "in their work of improvement." Some even asked "to throw up their contracts." In conclusion he asked that all lands not clearly excepted by the granting act be patented, that the secretary of the interior issue an authoritative statement that the grant could not be readjusted, and that the old method of determining the outer limits of the grant, rather than that proposed by Sparks, be adhered to.[33] Sparks' successor, S. M. Stockslager, agreed with Blair, but the suspension of patenting was continued until 1890 on the ground that the Pacific Railway Commission might make recommendations on the subject.[34]

The Northern Pacific's criticism of the rules and decisions made in the Land Office was made indirectly, probably because a very large number of the patents suspended were its own and because the road was in fact liable to congressional forfeiture. In any event, only twice was

[30] Henry Beard, *Motion Relating to Patenting Lands Granted to the Central Pacific Railroad Company* (Judd and Detweiler, Washington, 1890), 8.

[31] Henry Beard, *Before the Honorable Secretary of the Interior: The Listing and Patenting of Lands Granted to the Central Pacific Railroad Co.: The "Mineral Lands" Excepted from the Grant* (Judd and Detweiler, Washington, 1890).

[32] Commissioner of the General Land Office, *Annual Report*, 1895, p. 262.

[33] John S. Blair, *Before the Secretary of the Interior in the Matter of the Application of the Union Pacific Railway Company for Patents for Lands Along the Line of the Kansas Pacific Railway and the Proposed Readjustment of the Grant* (Gibson Brothers, Washington, 1886), 2, 21–23.

[34] S. M. Stockslager to L. Q. C. Lamar, December 17, 1887, in Record Group 49, Division F, Letters Sent.

reference made to the deterrent effect on patenting which would attend the requirement for separate affidavits that each forty-acre tract of selected land was nonmineral. The company's major criticism of the policies of the Land Office was never stated explicitly. It was only implied in the emphasis placed on the growing list of lands applied for and awaiting action, a list that totaled 21,897,823 acres by 1890, when the General Forfeiture Act was passed.[35]

The case against the Land Office that the railroadmen built in the course of their criticism of its survey policies, its requirements for proof of the railroads' right to specific tracts, and its "unreasonable" decisions on other matters was a weak one. It was weak, first, in that the discrepancy between selections made and the amount of land available for selection could not be attributed to tardiness in surveying it and, second, in that the proofs required and decisions rendered were within the realm of administrative discretion, not of abstract law. The criticisms made in the process of building this case did, however, provide the traditions and much of the material for the far more convincing "selections versus patents" case.

The railroads presented their strongest arguments and their most damning testimony in their analysis of the numerical relationship between the selections they made and the patents they got. In its broadest terms the case they made was simply that the administrators had at no time in the past been able, nor did they show promise or likelihood of being able in the future, to patent the lands selected by the roads as rapidly as the selections were made. In short, it was delay in the Land Office, not in railroad selections, that was producing the lag in patenting. This case was constructed within the framework of three general considerations: the efficiency and productive capacity of the General Land Office; the effects that the "unreasonable" and "illegal" rulings and requirements had on that capacity; and the contradictory policies pursued by the Congress and the administrators. As the key argument the ratio of acres selected to acres patented became the focal point of the controversy, upon which most of the other complaints impinged, until the whole argument over responsibility for the lag in patenting came to revolve around this particular ratio.

The selections versus patents controversy became a major issue in the Pacific Railway Commission hearings of 1887, but it had been presaged by many of the earlier clashes over the prosecution of the surveys, the proofs demanded, and the verification methods used by the General Land Office, and by the emphasis that the Northern Pacific placed on its growing surplus of selections over patents. It was also foreshadowed by the railroad pamphlets on the taxation bill of 1886. Attorney G. H. Tweed argued that the acreage selected by the Central Pacific had always

[35] Northern Pacific, *Annual Report*, 1888, p. 49; 1891, pp. 9–10; 1883, p. 40; 1884, p. 63; 1885, p. 39; 1886, p. 47; 1887, p. 50; 1888, p. 53; 1889, p. 57; 1890, p. 59; 1891, p. 53.

substantially exceeded the acreage patented by the Land Office,[36] and the road's land agent presented a detailed statement of that discrepancy. According to agent Mills the railroad had pending in the Land Office selections for 820,857 acres and was prepared to select 200,000 more. But, he wrote, "it has never been possible at any time, in the history of the administration of the grant, to obtain patents from the General Land Office as rapidly as required." This lag he attributed not to "any dereliction" or to "unnecessary delay, or wanton dilatoriness," but rather to "questions arising out of the construction of the granting act as to whether the lands selected were granted or excepted."[37]

In the Commission hearings, as in the preliminary bout over the tax bill, the Central Pacific was the principal railroad combatant. And in these hearings Mills adopted a more assertive tone. Now he did charge, or at least strongly implied, the "dereliction" and "wanton dilatoriness" he had dismissed the year before. When asked whether the company had failed to patent its land in order to avoid taxation, Mills answered,

No, sir. Under my administration of the land department I have urged upon the Department at Washington continually the subject of survey. I have urged upon their attention selection. I have written frequently, and personally made complaints to the Commissioner of the General Land Office at Washington, of the tardiness of the Government in making response.[38]

He went on to point out that Sparks had promised "to give it his personal attention," implying that he had not done so. Then, using the ammunition supplied him by the government officers themselves, he cited the reports of Commissioners McFarland and Sparks to the effect that the Land Office was then and had been for many years past far in arrears. Pressed on the question of the possible savings the company might derive from delaying patenting until the land was sold, Mills countered by admitting that in the abstract it did seem advantageous to pursue such a policy, but that actually the losses to the railroad far outweighed the gains. Judicial constructions of the minerals-reservation clause of the granting act had established the principle that if land was not known to be mineral land at the time the patent was issued, any minerals later discovered passed with the patent. Thus, Mills alleged, "the one item of loss of lands in consequence of the discovery of minerals would have paid all the taxes that ever could have been assessed against the company if the whole grant had been taxable from the start." The extension of discovery, he concluded, "lost in value more to the company, a great deal more, than the taxes would have amounted to."[39]

[36] G. H. Tweed, *In the Matter of the Payment for Surveys and the Taxation of the Granted Lands of the Central Pacific Railroad* (no imprint).

[37] W. H. Mills, *Payment of Survey Fees upon and the Taxation of Granted Lands: . . . Letter Addressed to the Chairman of the Senate Committee on Public Lands* (San Francisco, March 2, 1886), 13.

[38] 50 Congress, 1 session, *Senate Executive Document 51* (1888), p. 2424.

[39] *Ibid.*, 2424–2425.

Leland Stanford testified to the same effect: "We have never been derelict in taking out patents for such lands. We have not received our patents properly." There were, he claimed, Central Pacific selections of "over one million acres of land pending," and the delay in patenting had caused the company "great loss, not merely in the sales of lands, but more particularly in the business that would have arisen in their occupancy."[40]

Mills' prepared statement, filed in support of the oral testimony, was more inclusive and far more outspoken in its criticism. Tracing the administration of the grant since 1862, Mills cited the several Land Office suspensions of patenting and presented lists of selections made and patents granted. Land had regularly been suspended from each list, with the result that by June of 1887 the road had an aggregate balance of 622,612 acres of listed but unpatented lands. From 1865 to 1883 it had selected 887,728 acres, of which only 780,879 acres had thus far been patented. During the next three and a half years applications had been made for 774,595 acres more. "The policy of increased activity in the application for patents," wrote Mills, "was inaugurated in the hope that a corresponding activity in the examination of the lists would be manifested by the Government." The only effect had been to increase "disproportionately" the acreage listed but unpatented, to retard rather than speed the issuance of patents. The compilation of these lists and their submission to the Land Office had cost a great deal of money, money on which the company received no return while it remained "idle and useless in the Government Treasury." Development of lands adjacent to the road had been retarded. Both the settlers and the company had been subjected to inconvenience and loss, the one because of failure to receive their titles, and the other because of the consequent delay in receiving the purchase price. Finally, the company had suffered great losses by reason of further discoveries of mineral lands within the limits of the grant. To provide the capstone to the indictment of administrative policy and practice, Mills turned to Land Office arrearages. Citing the reports of successive commissioners from 1883 to 1887, he showed that during the five-year period the acreage awaiting action had increased from somewhat less than two million to more than sixteen million. The Land Office had patented in those years an average of only a half million acres annually. At this rate it would require thirty-two years to deal with the selections already at hand. Thus, said Mills, "the uselessness of making further lists of selections, and of devoting further sums of money to that purpose until the lists now before the Interior Department are disposed of, is altogether apparent."[41]

The Union Pacific System also took up the selections versus patents argument. J. S. Blair, in his pamphlet on the Crawford relocation appeal had utilized the principle when he included a county-by-county list

[40] *Ibid.*, 2517–2518.
[41] *Ibid.*, 2562–2568.

of lands selected but unpatented, a list totaling 813,630 acres.[42] It remained, however, for witnesses before the Pacific Railway Commission to state the case fully. Land commissioner Benjamin McAllaster, when questioned on railroad policies of land selection, defended what his interrogators viewed as slow selections on the Kansas Division by saying, "We have applied for patents for nearly a million acres of land and paid the fees—since 1881—that we have got no patents for. Had we got those patents we would have paid on a million more acres."[43]

On another occasion, when drawn out by the company's general attorney, Andrew Poppleton, he repeated the charge of dilatory patenting. Then Poppleton summed it up. The Commission's questioning, he said, "assumes that it is the fault of the company that it has not patented all its lands, when the fact is there are many of them that are not surveyed; and we have had great difficulty in getting the patents when we wanted them." He concluded: "There is an order now prohibiting the issuing of any patents at all until this Commission is all through."[44] As compared with the Central Pacific's statement of its case, that of the Union Pacific was mild indeed—but it was the same case.

When the Pacific Railway Commission's report, ignoring the testimony of the railroads and Land Office arrears, directly charged the roads with delaying patenting to avoid taxation, the Union Pacific offered little defense,[45] but the Central Pacific again took up the cudgels. In 1888, citing the usual figures to show the discrepancy between selections and patents, the land department alleged the same kinds of losses to the company that Stanford and Mills had cited. It told the stockholders that it had virtually run out of patents, that the land was "not as merchantable" without them, that, in short, "it only remains for the Government to respond to the demands of your Company with record evidence of title, to insure record sales in this department for the coming year."[46] In 1889 the road published a pamphlet as a counterweight to the Commission's report. In it Mills' arguments were repeated.[47] Finally, in 1890, two more pamphlets, these by Henry Beard, were added to the accumulated testimony. One of these dealt primarily with the affidavits required of the railroad as proof of the nonmineral character of land,[48] but the other was largely a selections versus patents argument. Beard placed his emphasis on the contradictory policies pursued by Con-

[42] Blair, *Application for Patents Along the Kansas Pacific*, 1.
[43] 50 Congress, 1 session, *Senate Executive Document 51* (1888), pp. 1021–1022.
[44] *Ibid.*, 1023–1026.
[45] *Ibid.*, 145; *The Case of the Union Pacific Railway Company: Statement Made by Charles Francis Adams, before the Committee on Pacific Railroads, March 17, 1890* (Rand Avery Supply Company, Boston, 1890), 90–91.
[46] Southern Pacific, *Annual Report*, 1888, pp. 82, 118–119. The Central Pacific was leased to the Southern Pacific System in 1887.
[47] *Relations between the Central Pacific Railroad Company and the United States Government: Summary of Facts* (H. S. Crocker and Company, San Francisco, 1889), 15–17.
[48] Beard, *Listing and Patenting of Lands*.

gress on the one hand and by the administrators on the other. Asserting that a congressional policy of rapid patenting had been clearly announced by the tax law of 1886 and the adjustment law of 1887, he argued that the administrators had done all in their power to thwart that intent. The company, he said, in accordance with the avowed policy of Congress, had "applied for a larger annual acreage," but the government, "instead of increasing its acreage, as pledged to do, actually stopped issuing patents entirely since July, 1886." Tying in the requirements respecting nonmineral affidavits, he concluded:

An intelligent officer always intends the direct effect of his acts, and hence we are authorized to say that Mr. Sparks intended the delay in issuing patents. He intended to place himself in opposition to the policy of the Government in this thing, and the great wonder is that he has succeeded in producing delay and confusion for so long a time. His action is as clearly a usurpation as was his order suspending several of the Laws of Congress for ninety days.[49]

This was the Beard thesis of 1883 elaborated and refined into the railroad thesis of 1890.[50] Henry Beard had had the first word; now he had the last.

The railroads had made a strong case. It is true that no consideration of the internal operations of the Land Office justifies the allegations of malicious intent and wanton dilatoriness, but it is also true that the administrative contribution to the lag in patenting was great. Just as true as either of these assertions is a third: a consideration of the selection, patent, and sales policies of the railroads, superficial though it must be at this juncture, detracts subtantially from the railroad case. For the operators, like the administrators, ran their business in a context of changing needs, assumptions, and attitudes. Circumstances do, it turns out, alter cases.

Although most of the land policies of the railroads involved in the patent-taxation controversy were strikingly similar to those of the earlier companies receiving federal-through-state aid, the trans-Missouri roads made a number of highly significant innovations. First, they tended to sell their land in larger unit acreages than had their predecessors. Second, they developed the system of partial patenting, of selecting the lands due them from the government in small parcels rather than in larger blocks, the procedure regularly followed before their time. Then they combined the larger unit sale with the smaller selection list to produce the third and most important innovation—selling land before they had title to it. It was out of these innovations that the controversy developed. For, on the one hand, the judges decided that land that was unpatented or unpatentable (because the costs of survey had not been

[49] Beard, *Motion Relating to Patenting*, 5, 8.
[50] See Stuart Daggett, *Chapters on the History of the Southern Pacific* (Ronald Press, New York, 1922), 55–58.

paid) was not taxable and, on the other, land was patented to the railroads more and more slowly. Thus was created the situation, accursed in the eyes of the reform element, that enabled the roads to mortgage, sell, and use their land without paying taxes on it. Here was a classic example of minor changes in policy and interpretation that produced a major political controversy.

That the land policies of the trans-Missouri roads should have been in most respects similar to those of their predecessors was natural enough. Like the government administrators of their grants, they were able to draw upon the experience of the earlier land-grant railroads. As the first of the land-grant roads, the Illinois Central was the greatest source of precedents. Its classification and appraisal system as well as its contract and credit systems were adapted to the use of every major land-grant railroad coming after it. So also were its advertising technique and its colonization methods. Often the adaptation was one or two steps removed. The experience of the Burlington in Iowa, for example, was often drawn on, but the debt to the Central was real and direct. Likewise, there was often a personal connection as men who had had their first experience as underlings in the land departments of the earlier roads moved on to become guiding figures in the trans-Missouri railroad-land programs. Furthermore, land department officials often moved from one trans-Missouri road to another, taking their policies with them.

Thus the land-grant railroads, both east and west of the river, developed land policies that had much in common. (1) They advertised their lands widely in the East and in Europe and often made use of resident agents in those areas. (2) They operated "land looker" programs, which usually included special low transportation rates and often, if the land was purchased, a rebate of the fare in the form of a credit against the price. (3) They utilized model farms, sold seed on credit, transported tools, animals, and even prefabricated houses at reduced rates, and in miscellaneous other ways endeavored to speed buyers into production. (4) They sold land on long-term credit at comparatively low interest and, less frequently because the demand was far less, gave discounts, up to twenty-five per cent, for cash. (5) They usually extended contracts for those who fell behind in their payments, often going to great lengths to avoid cancelling the agreement. (6) They required the purchaser to pay any taxes assessed against the property while the contract was in effect. And (7) they regularly engaged in litigation with counties over the taxation of their landholdings or operating property. Obviously there were many deviations within these norms. The Northern Pacific was probably the most active of the European advertisers. Some others concentrated more heavily on the East. The Santa Fe gave eleven years credit. Six to eight years was more common. The Central itself, after the initial cases establishing its nontaxability, engaged in comparatively little local tax litigation, but others, such as the Santa Fe and the Burlington, maintained and utilized special legal departments for that purpose. Despite the deviations, however, these generalizations do describe the sales and settlement policies of the land-grant railroads.[51] The land policies of the roads involved in the patent-taxation controversy were in most respects typical. Though the energies they expended and the areas in which they concentrated their efforts varied somewhat, they all published and circulated pamphlets, broadsides, immigrant guides, and the like to lure purchasers. This literature, like that of other railroads, was usually overoptimistic about the potentialities of the land it advertised, but at the same time realistic in cautioning prospective settlers of the need for capital at the outset and of the difficulties of farm-making in the new country. All offered long-term credit and low interest rates—from five to ten years and from six to ten per cent.[52]

[51] Paul W. Gates, *The Illinois Central and Its Colonization Work* (Harvard University Press, Cambridge, 1934); Richard C. Overton, *Burlington West: A Colonization History of the Burlington Railroad* (Harvard University Press, Cambridge, 1941); Morris Nelson Spencer, The Union Pacific's Utilization of Its Land Grant with Emphasis on Its Colonization Program (unpublished doctoral dissertation, University of Nebraska, 1950); Nicholas J. Schmidt, Jr., Evolving Geographic Concepts of the Kansas Area with Emphasis on the Land Literature of the Santa Fe Railroad (unpublished master's thesis, University of Kansas, 1949); Glenn D. Bradley, *The Story of the Santa Fe* (Gorham Press, Boston, 1920), 107–138; L. L. Waters, *Steel Trails to Santa Fe* (University of Kansas Press, Lawrence, 1950), chapter 7; William S. Greever, *Arid Domain: The Santa Fe Railway and Its Western Land Grant* (Stanford University Press, Stanford, 1954); Paul W. Gates, *Fifty Million Acres: Conflicts over Kansas Land Policy, 1854–1890* (Cornell University Press, Ithaca, 1954), chapter 8; James B. Hedges, "Promotion of Immigration to the Pacific Northwest by the Railroads," in the *Mississippi Valley Historical Review*, 15:183–203 (September, 1928); Hedges, "The Colonization Work of the Northern Pacific Railroad," *ibid.*, 13:311–342 (December, 1926); and E. L. Lomax, "The Work of the U P in Nebraska," in the *Proceedings of the Nebraska State Historical Society*, 15:181–188 (1907).

[52] Examples of this outpouring include Central Pacific Railroad, *Railroad Lands in California and Nevada* (Record Printing House, Sacramento, 1872); Northern Pacific Railroad, *Guide to the Northern Pacific Railroad Lands in Minnesota* (no imprint [1872?]); R. S. Elliot, Kansas Pacific Industrial Agent, *Report on the Industrial Resources of Western Kansas and Eastern Colorado* (Levison and Blyth, St. Louis, 1871); *Handbook for the Kansas Pacific Railway, Containing a Description of the Country, Cities, Towns, etc., Lying Along the Line of the Road and Its Branches: Extracted from "Tracy's Guide to the Great West"* (Wiebusch and Son, St. Louis, 1870); B. McAllaster, Land Commissioner, *List of Lands of the Union Pacific R'y in Kansas Still for Sale, March 1, 1886* (Ramsey, Millet, and Hudson, Kansas City, 1886); *Union Pacific Railway, Lands in Kansas* (Omaha, 1893); *Weston's Guide to the Kansas Pacific Railway . . .* (Bulletin Steam Printing and Engraving, Kansas City, 1872); J. T. Allan, comp., *Nebraska and Its Settlers: What They Have Done and How They Do It; Its Crops and People* (Union Pacific Land Department, Omaha, 1883); J. T. Allan, comp., *Creameries and Dairying in Nebraska: What Has Been Done and What May Be Done* (Union Pacific Land Department, Omaha, 1883); *Central and Western Nebraska and the Experiences of Its Stock Growers* (Union Pacific Land Department, Omaha, 1883); *Guide to the Union Pacific Railroad Lands: 12,000,000 Acres Best Farming, Grazing, and Mineral Lands in America . . .* (Union Pacific Land Department, Omaha, 1871).

Some offered more than the usual incentives for early production, such as sizable rebates for the cultivation of specified acreages or for other improvements made during the contract period.[53] Most of the roads expressed interest in and encouraged settlement on government lands in areas tributary to the road.[54] In short, like their predecessors, they normally operated as transportation companies first and as land agencies second, seeking above all to create revenue for the road by increasing the production of its hinterland.

The first important deviation from the norm was in the size of the tracts these roads sold. The earlier roads had occasionally sold large tracts; the transcontinentals and some of their feeder lines made a practice of it. All of them, while setting out to sell small tracts to actual settlers—simply because it was good railroad business to do so—eventually sought to dispose of some of their lands in larger blocks.[55]

There were two primary reasons for this policy. Partly it stemmed from the occasional recurrence of a disposition to subordinate the long-term transportation interest to the prospect of early and assured land sales by selling directly to speculators for cash or for the redemption of outstanding capital stock.[56] Closely related to the sales of individual tracts for the sake of profit were the transferrals to wholly-owned land subsidiaries, such as the Kansas Pacific's National Land Company; to director-owned companies, such as the Burlington's South Platte Land and Townsite Company; to investment trusts, such as that of the St. Joseph and Denver City; and the consignments to land agents specializing in speculative sales, such as the Union Pacific's sales to J. W. Reynolds of Omaha.[57] True, the roads sometimes stipulated in their sales contracts that large purchasers must settle a specified number of families in a specified time, thus maintaining the small-tract policy, but

---

[53] See, for examples, the Union Pacific's *Annual Report*, 1881, p. 11; the Northern Pacific's *Annual Report*, 1881, p. 14; and Hedges' "The Colonization Work of the Northern Pacific," in the *Mississippi Valley Historical Review*, 13:327–328.

[54] The pamphlets cited in note 52 regularly described the availability and desirability of adjacent public lands. Northern Pacific annual reports of the 1880's regularly tabulated entries on government lands. See also 50 Congress, 1 session, *Senate Executive Document 51* (1888), p. 2566, and Hedges, "The Colonization Work of the Northern Pacific," in the *Mississippi Valley Historical Review*, 13:321.

[55] Union Pacific, *Annual Report*, 1883, p. 10; Central Pacific, *Annual Report*, 1872, p. 10; Northern Pacific, *Annual Report*, 1881, p. 14; and 50 Congress, 1 session, *Senate Executive Document 51* (1888), pp. 2424, 2518, 2566.

[56] Gates, in his *Fifty Million Acres*, 253–254, 283–287, describes this phenomenon as it manifested itself in Kansas. For further descriptions of such sales see Allan G. Bogue, *Money at Interest: The Farm Mortgage on the Middle Border* (Cornell University Press, Ithaca, 1955), 60; Hedges, "The Colonization Work of the Northern Pacific," in the *Mississippi Valley Historical Review*, 13:327–328; the *Freemont Herald* (Nebraska), July 26, 1883; and the *Hastings Weekly Nebraskan*, November 22, 1883.

[57] Such transfers are described in the *Omaha Daily Herald* (Nebraska), May 17, 1884; the *Hastings Weekly Nebraskan*, April 13, 1884; and the *Kearney County Bee* (Nebraska), March 19, 1880.

such restrictions were not often included,[58] and when they were they were often evaded.

The other reason for most of the large sales was much less illusory. The transcontinentals crossed the West. It was that simple. Westbound, beyond the great bend of the Arkansas, the forks of the Platte, or the southward turn of the Missouri, small-scale agriculture was almost impossible and large-scale agriculture was risky. Eastbound, the Sierra Nevada and the Cascades marked the beginning, and the eastern base of the Rockies the end, of an area chiefly valuable for timber, water power, and minerals or so arid as to require irrigation. The railroads thus adapted their sales policies to the character of the land, selling in blocks to bonanza wheat farmers, grazers, development companies, and lumbermen.[59] Even the tracts sold to individual settlers in these areas were large. For example in western Kansas and Nebraska sales of less than a whole section were rare, of two to five sections not unusual, and of much larger acreages common.[60] And the result of all this, in terms of the patent-taxation controversy, was that the assessment base was a narrow one; a comparatively small number of people paid, or were supposed to pay, the taxes on a comparatively large acreage.

The second and most important deviation from the norm was the system of partial selections developed by the companies—with the full consent of Land Office administrators. In the permissive-presumptive period of government-railroad relationships, before the estrangement of the seventies, there were numerous justifications for this innovation. At the outset few of the lands in these greatest of all grants were surveyed; there were likely to be contests over specific tracts, which might delay patents for large blocks; no one foresaw the administrative log-

[58] Hedges, "The Colonization Work of the Northern Pacific," in the *Mississippi Valley Historical Review*, 13:326, 334–335; 50 Congress, 1 session, *Senate Executive Document 51* (1888), p. 2330; Gates, *Fifty Million Acres*, 283–284. An example of the colonizing efforts of such a buyer is Warren, Keeney and Company's pamphlet, *Trego County, Kansas: Its Soil and Climate* . . . (J. S. Spalding, Chicago, 1878).

[59] Union Pacific, *Annual Report*, 1881, p. 11; 1882, p. 10; Northern Pacific, *Annual Report*, 1876, p. 14; 1886, p. 7; 1890 p. 56; 1891, pp. 47, 49; Gates, *Fifty Million Acres*, pp. 283–285; James C. Malin, *Winter Wheat in the Golden Belt of Kansas* (University of Kansas Press, Lawrence, 1944). Examples of such sales are Union Pacific sales to the Ogallala Land and Cattle Company, to C. W. Payne, and to W. A. Paxton in Keith County, Nebraska, and Kansas Pacific sales to E. S. Beach, Fred Pennington, and others (as well as the better-known Warren, Keeney and Company sales) in Trego County, Kansas. Numerical Lists, Office of the Register of Deeds, Ogallala (Keith County), Nebraska, and Wakeeney (Trego County), Kansas.

[60] Land transfer records cited in note 59 show these tendencies. The disappearance of sales of small acreages beyond the line described is particularly striking when sales are compared with those made in counties to the east. For examples see the Numerical Lists, Office of the Register of Deeds, Hastings (Adams County), Nebraska; Holdredge (Phelps County), Nebraska; and Salina (Saline County), Kansas.

jam of the eighties; and the question of taxability had yet to become paramount.[61] There was also a legal justification, for into section 21 of the act of 1864 had gone the provision that the companies were to receive the patents "as the titles shall be required."[62] This provision was to be a major bulwark of the railroad defense in the patent-taxation controversy,[63] but that had yet to arise. In the beginning the provision simply served to support the requests for partial patenting privileges and to justify the granting of them. In any event, the system of partial selections was established and its establishment made all the rest very nearly inevitable. For without it no long-term prior-sale policy would have been possible and without that policy the taxation controversy would have been mild and short-lived indeed.

The prior-sale program was the third of the innovations and the logical outcome of the first two. This program took two forms: (1) sale of land after it had been selected and the selection approved in the local land office, but before the patent itself had been issued, and (2) sale before selection. In the first instance, according to numerous court rulings, the road had title in fact and the patent itself was only record evidence of it. In the second instance, according to the same rulings, the road did not have title at all, since selection and the payment of costs of survey that accompanied it were the final steps it must take to earn the land. Thus, to sell before patent but after selection was to sell something owned in fact though not in name; whereas to sell before selection was to sell something in fact not salable because it was not in fact owned.

There were three distinct periods during which the prior-sale policy was pursued: (1) until 1875, because it took time to work out the rules of practice and methods of verification in the Land Office, because the first patents were often delayed by reinspections and the formulation of patent policies to be pursued by the government on any given grants, and because the demand for land sometimes preceded the completion of the road and the operators acceded to that demand; (2) between 1875 and 1882, because there were obvious tax and market advantages in such a policy or because long-term disputes between a railroad and the government produced suspensions of patenting; and (3) between 1882 and 1890, because the vexed questions surrounding most of the grants brought the entire patenting process very nearly to a halt.

Some railroads that were not even involved in the patent-taxation controversy utilized one or another form of the prior-sale policy. For example, both the Burlington and the Santa Fe roads—which were exceptional in that they promptly selected the bulk of their lands and received the patents for them almost immediately upon completion of construction—sold lands before they had been selected. Both roads were begun in settled areas and both inspired a vociferous demand for land before

---

[61] See above, pp. 61–62.
[62] 13 *Statutes at Large* 365 (July 2, 1864).
[63] See above, pp. 36, 49–50.

TABLE 4.—SELECTIONS FILED, PATENTS RECEIVED, AND SALES MADE
BY THE UNION PACIFIC, 1868–1890 (IN ACRES)

Year	selections			patents		gross sales	
	lists	in year	to date	in year	to date	in year	to date
1868	10	854,443	854,443				
1869	8	456,942	1,311,385			128,825	128,825
1870	1	1,550	1,312,935			164,058	292,883
1871	2	4,626	1,317,561	639,024	639,024	206,605	499,488
1872			1,317,561		639,024	172,108	671,596
1873			1,317,561	51,694*	690,718	177,083	848,679
1874	7	327,827	1,645,388	58,477	749,195	235,749	1,084,428
1875	6	206,503	1,851,891	901,564	1,650,759	111,965	1,196,393
1876	9	45,777	1,897,668	225,968	1,876,727	128,696	1,325,089
1877	1	1,320	1,898,988	2,065	1,878,792	69,015	1,394,104
1878	1	640	1,899,628	1,173	1,879,965	318,903	1,713,007
1879			1,899,628		1,879,965	243,337	1,956,344
1880	1	640	1,900,268	640	1,880,605	176,201	2,132,545
1881	7	83,176	1,983,444		1,880,605	96,059	2,228,604
1882	1	7,460	1,990,904	67,921	1,948,526	292,159	2,520,763
1883			1,990,904	640	1,949,166	867,871	3,388,634
1884	9	634,495	2,625,399	486,287	2,435,453	4,348,202	7,736,836
1885	1	18,244	2,643,643	159,074	2,594,527	745,744	8,482,580
1886	5	512,982	3,156,625	16,293	2,610,820	146,500	8,629,080
1887	2	114,495	3,271,120	31,190	2,642,010	51,352	8,680,432
1888	1	640	3,271,760		2,642,010	18,505	8,698,937
1889			3,271,760		2,642,010	104,946	8,803,883
1890	5	927,784	4,199,544		2,642,010	163,821	8,967,704

* Jointly with the Sioux City and Pacific.
Data on selections are from the "Selections Docket" in Record Group 48, and from a tabular
statement in Record Group 49, Railroad Land Grant Records, box 47. Data on patents are from
50 Congress, 1 session, *Senate Executive Document 51*, pp. 4250–4254, and from the annual reports
of the commissioners of the General Land Office, 1887–1890. Data on sales are from the annual
reports of the company; interview with Leavitt Burnham in *Grand Island Times*, January 29, 1880;
and 50 Congress, 1 session, *Senate Executive Document 51*, p. 5244. In the 23 year period 865,308
acres, or an average of 37,625 acres annually, were retrieved by cancellation of contract. Though
this distorts the table slightly, it is not misleading because any sale represents a promise of title
and the rate of cancellation was at its highest at the end of the period—when the boom busted.

they were completed. As the board of directors of the Burlington put it,
"Not wishing to wait until the title of the company to the land could
be fully completed, we began to grant preëmptions in April, 1870; and
subsequently, when the patents were made, the regular business of making sales by contracts and by deeds began."[64] Once the selections had
been made and the patents received (in blocks in the traditional
fashion), the occasion for such anticipatory sales was gone. The roads
advertised that holders of preëmption certificates were to redeem them,
then went about the sale of land they had title to.[65]

Every railroad that was involved in the patent-taxation controversy
followed the prior-sale policy. Up to 1879 the Union Pacific selected its
lands before it sold them, but from 1869 to 1874 it regularly sold in advance of patent. This policy was of course occasioned by the suspension
of patenting which the Land Office imposed to insure completion of the
road. Between 1874 and 1879 the company always had patents for more

[64] *Report of the Directors of the Burlington and Missouri Railroad in Nebraska*,
1873, p. 13, in the Burlington Archives, Newberry Library, Chicago.
[65] See, for example, the *Nebraska Statesman* (Lincoln), December 23, 1872.

TABLE 5.—SELECTIONS FILED, PATENTS RECEIVED, AND SALES MADE
BY THE KANSAS PACIFIC, 1868–1890 (IN ACRES)

Year	selections			patents		gross sales	
	lists	in year	to date	in year	to date	in year	to dat e
1868						111,271	111,271
1869						382,885	494,156
1870	6	178,518	178,518			124,168	618,324
1871			178,518			123,935	742,259
1872	1	25,999	204,517			68,851	811,110
1873	4	81,772	285,289	52,914	52,914	25,423	836,533
1874	4	346,896	632,185	378,988	431,902	35,393	871,926
1875	3	65,084	697,269	60,387	492,289	61,366	933,292
1876	2	32,763	730,032	46,505	538,794	74,554	1,007,846
1877	9	241,017	971,049	225,466	764,260	135,994	1,143,840
1878	3	57,194	1,028,243	15,491	779,751	207,938	1,351,778
1879	11	68,165	1,096,408	56,710	836,461	169,328	1,521,106
1880	3	21,245	1,117,653		836,461	100,382*	1,621,488*
1881	5	24,836	1,142,489	81,155	917,616	99,478*	1,720,966*
1882	9	167,006	1,309,495		917,616	105,915*	1,826,881*
1883	9	456,861	1,766,356	46,193	963,809	298,478*	2,125,359*
1884	6	52,580	1,818,936		963,809	475,007*	2,600,366*
1885	8	175,078	1,994,014		963,809	711,960*	3,312,326*
1886	5	46,533	2,040,547		963,809	230,387*	3,542,713*
1887			2,040,547		963,809	522,512*	4,065,225*
1888	7	482,094	2,522,641		963,809	127,393*	4,192,618*
1889	1	236,583	2,759,224		963,809	70,228*	4,262,846*
1890	1	36,902	2,796,126		963,809	28,764*	4,291,610*

* Includes sales from the Denver Pacific grant.
Data on selections are from the "Selections Docket" in Record Group 48, and from a tabular statement in Record Group 49, Railroad Land Grant Records, box 37. Data on patents are from 50 Congress, 1 session, *Senate Executive Document 51*, p. 4253, and from the annual reports of the commissioners of the General Land Office, 1887–1890. Data on sales are from the annual reports of the company to 1880, of the Union Pacific 1880–1890; and 50 Congress, 1 session, *Senate Executive Document 51*, p. 5244. No source or combination of sources presents data on sales in a form that permits effective separation of Kansas and Colorado lands after 1880. This produces misleading excesses after 1880 and especially after 1883. An effort is made to partly correct this distortion in Table 12 below. In the 23 year period 526,209 acres, or an average of 22,878 acres annually were retrieved by cancellation of contract. See the note to Table 4 for a discussion of this.

land than it sold, but thereafter it made sales far in advance of both selections and patents, until, by 1886, it had sold over six million acres more land than it had patents for. From the beginning both the Kansas Pacific and the Denver Pacific always sold far in advance of selection and of patent. By 1886 the two roads had sold a total of almost two and a half million acres more land than had been patented to them. No government suspension explains their early use of the prior-sale policy, though it is true that after 1883 patenting to the Kansas Pacific, at least, was suspended pending a decision on the Crawford relocation appeal. The Northern Pacific, under suspension almost continually after 1874, and after 1879 engaged in a vigorous colonization campaign, quickly exhausted its stock of patents. During its feud with the administrators it also made selections slowly, so that from 1877 to 1882 it sold well ahead of both selections and patents. When, in 1882, it agreed to pay the costs of survey, it began a vast selections program that virtually inundated the Land Office. After 1883 it always had selections pending for millions of acres more than it had sold. The suspension in anticipation of forfeiture, however, precluded much more than token patenting, so that

TABLE 6.—SELECTIONS FILED, PATENTS RECEIVED, AND SALES MADE
BY THE DENVER PACIFIC, 1870–1890 (IN ACRES)

Year	selections			patents		gross sales	
	lists	in year	to date	in year	to date	in year	to date
1870						32,613	32,613
1871						41,543	74,156
1872						19,959	94,115
1873						17,951	112,066
1874	2	49,811	49,811			10,918	122,984
1875			49,811	49,811	49,811	3,676	126,660
1876			49,811		49,811	4,364	131,024
1877			49,811		49,811	26,101	157,125
1878			49,811		49,811	34,523	191,648
1879	2	42,498	92,309		49,811	7,554	199,202
1880	1	640	92,949		49,811		
1881			92,949	36,425	86,236		
1882	4	110,788	203,737		86,236	The data are not	
1883	3	46,187	249,924	78,484	164,720	separable from	
1884	1	10,115	260,039		164,720	those for the	
1885	2	14,252	274,291		164,720	KANSAS PACIFIC	
1886			274,291		164,720	See	
1887			274,291		164,720	Table 5 above	
1888			274,291		164,720	and	
1889			274,291		164,720	Table 12 below	
1890	1	76,274	350,565		164,720		

Data on selections are from the "Selections Docket" in Record Group 48. Data on patents are from a tabular statement in Record Group 49, Railroad Land Grant Records, box 84, and from the annual reports of the commissioners of the General Land Office, 1881–1890. Data on sales are from 50 Congress, 1 session, *Senate Executive Document 51*, p. 5244; data on cancellations are not available. See the note to Table 5 for an explanation of the lack of data on sales after 1879.

by 1886 it too had sold some five million acres more than had been patented to it. The Land Office regularly received reports that the road was selling unpatented land—forfeited land from the point of view of those anxious to enforce the terms of the original granting act.[66]

Both the Southern Pacific and the Central Pacific seem to have planned to wait for patents before they sold land, since they regularly told their stockholders that the lands were not appraised and classified until they had been patented.[67] The southern road maintained the policy until 1884, when suspensions in anticipation of forfeiture resulted in an excess of sales over patents. By 1886 it had sold over a million acres without record title. It never did, however, sell in advance of selection. The Central Pacific sold before patent on two occasions: first, when the patents were under suspension to assure its completion, as had the Union Pacific, and, second, after 1880, when the Land Office backlog began to build up. By 1886 its excess of sales over patents amounted to

[66] See, for example, George W. Sweet to Carl Schurz, St. Paul, November 7, 1887, in Record Group 48, Lands and Railroads, Letters Received; and R. B. Kinne to the Commissioner of the General Land Office, Colfax, Wyoming Territory, November 29, 1879, in Record Group 49, Railroad Land Grant Records, box 51.

[67] Southern Pacific, *Annual Report*, 1876–1877, p. 50; 1881, p. 46; 1882, p. 44; Central Pacific, *Annual Report*, 1876, p. 49; 50 Congress, 1 session, *Senate Executive Document 51* (1888), p. 2934.

TABLE 7.—SELECTIONS FILED, PATENTS RECEIVED, AND SALES MADE
BY THE CENTRAL PACIFIC, 1865–1890 (IN ACRES)

Year	selections			patents		gross sales	
	lists	in year	to date	in year	to date	in year	to date
1865	1	55,259	55,259			*	†
1866	4	94,570	149,829	87,596	87,596	*	†
1867	3	30,355	180,184	56,790	144,386	*	†
1868	2	55,714	235,898		144,386	*	†
1869	3	162,145	398,043		144,386	*	†
1870	4	225,716	623,759	117,138	261,524	*	†
1871	2	35,108	648,867	9,640	271,164	*	†
1872	2	41,257	690,124		271,164	*	250,402
1873	1	13,209	703,333		271,164	58,733	309,135
1874	5	32,677	736,010		271,164	63,846	372,981
1875	9	89,660	825,670	70,330	341,494	29,254	402,235
1876	4	363,184	1,188,854	183,760	525,254	36,503	438,738
1877	4	14,006	1,202,860	165,304	690,558	92,647	531,385
1878	4	2,211	1,205,071	14,703	705,261	78,100	609,485
1879	1	10,439	1,215,510		705,261	43,258	652,743
1880	7	32,800	1,248,310		705,261	114,852	767,595
1881	2	11,019	1,259,329	12,572	717,833	195,254	962,849
1882	4	128,005	1,387,334		717,833	196,472	1,159,321
1883	3	18,399	1,405,733	59,944	777,777	379,787	1,539,108
1884	8	193,916	1,599,649	109,066	886,843	398,021	1,937,129
1885	14	114,535	1,714,184	31,640	918,483	127,045‡	2,064,174
1886	22	373,456	2,087,640	118,123	1,036,606	284,623	2,348,797
1887	4	126,245	2,213,885		1,036,606	*	*
1888	10	95,943	2,309,828		1,036,606	*	*
1889	9	9,942	2,319,770		1,036,606	153,129	*
1890	2	2,631	2,322,401		1,036,606	55,199	*

* No usable data were located.
† No breakdown of sales by year was located. The figure given for 1872 represents the accumulation of sales made up to that time.
‡ Estimated from the financial statement of the land department, at $3.50 an acre.
Data on selections are from the "Selections Docket" in Record Group 48. Data on patents are from 50 Congress, 1 session, *Senate Executive Document 51*, p. 4252, and the annual reports of the commissioners of the General Land Office, 1887–1890. Data on sales are from the annual reports of the company and, after 1885, of the consolidated Southern Pacific company. Data on cancellations are not available.

a million and a quarter acres. It kept its selections ahead of sales until 1883, when they too fell behind. By 1886 the road had sold over a quarter million acres prior to their selection.

By 1886 the prior-sale policy had become so general that the railroads involved in the patent-taxation controversy had sold a total of 16,116,857 acres more land than they had patented and a total of 6,961,487 acres more than they had selected. Tables 4–11 show the annual and cumulative results of these sales systems as they operated in the context of an administrative policy they helped to make. Two roads, the Burlington and the Santa Fe, which were never seriously involved in the controversy and which, after the first two or three years of preëmption sales, regularly had patents for much more land than they sold, are included for purposes of comparison. The statistical key to the character and magnitude of the prior-sales policies lies in the cumulative excesses of sales over selections and patents, given in the sales column. Table 12, which summarizes these excesses, reveals the wide application of the policies,

TABLE 8.—SELECTIONS FILED, PATENTS RECEIVED, AND SALES MADE
BY THE SOUTHERN PACIFIC, 1871–1890 (IN ACRES)

Year	selections			patents §		gross sales	
	lists	in year	to date	in year	to date	in year	to date
1871	3	33,836	33,836				
1872			33,836				
1873			33,836				
1874	3	331,391	365,227	5,966	5,966		
1875	4	77,138	442,365		5,966	*	†
1876	5	338,371	780,736	326,883	332,849	*	†
1877	5	395,138	1,175,874	22,920	355,769	*	†
1878			1,175,874	230,540	586,309	*	†
1879	5	3,682	1,179,556	65,612	651,921	*	†
1880	2	85,644	1,265,200	1,720	653,641	*	314,994
1881	2	17,803	1,283,003	156,662	810,303	186,515	501,509
1882	3	44,429	1,327,432	3,500	813,803	103,537	605,046
1883	28	155,970	1,483,402	2,519	816,322	83,565	688,611
1884	28	128,559	1,611,961	47,599	863,921	354,556	1,043,167
1885	43	371,176	1,983,137		863,921	458,130‡	1,501,297‡
1886	10	218,365	2,201,502		863,921	458,130‡	1,959,427‡
1887	56	713,879	2,915,381		863,921	458,130‡	2,417,557
1888	38	252,476	3,167,857		863,921	174,287	2,591,844
1889	30	180,583	3,348,440	480	864,401	45,281	2,637,125
1890	25	42,326	3,390,766		864,401	98,026	2,735,151

* No usable data were located.
† No breakdown of sales by year was located. The figure given for 1880 represents the accumulation of sales made up to that time.
‡ These are estimates: total sales for the 1885–1887 period are divided equally among the three years.
§ These data are for the fiscal not the calendar year.
Data on selections are from the "Selections Docket" in Record Group 48. Data on patents are from the annual reports of the commissioners of the General Land Office, 1874–1890. Data on sales are from the annual reports of the company. Sales officially began on April 1, 1875. Data on cancellations are not available.

the vast increase in sales over patents that took place in the eighties, and the differences between roads—from the Kansas Pacific, which always sold before either selection or patent, to the Southern Pacific, which never sold before selection and which sold before patent only under pressure of the forfeiture suspensions of the later eighties.

The excesses of sales over selections and patents shown in these tables, though partly explicable in terms of the administrative and railroad policies already discussed at length, can be fully explained only by consideration of two additional characteristics of the trans-Missouri railroads. First, there was the fact that unpatented lands were tax-exempt. Many roads recognized the cash benefits to be derived from this exemption; some felt they could not survive without it; and some used it to protect both themselves and buyers of their lands, settler and speculator alike, from what they viewed as excessive or downright criminal assessments. Second, there was the land boom of the mid-eighties. Sales doubled, trebled, quadrupled. Suddenly slight excesses of sales over patents or selections became vast surpluses. Circumstances outside the direct control of either administrators or operators transformed a minor, if serious, disagreement into a great debate.

TABLE 9.—SELECTIONS FILED, PATENTS RECEIVED, AND SALES MADE
BY THE NORTHERN PACIFIC, 1872–1890 (IN ACRES)

Year	selections		patents		gross sales	
	lists	in year	to date	in year	to date	in year	to date
1872	4	280,175	280,175			*	†
1873	10	710,446	990,621	743,573	743,573	*	†
1874	1	3,773	994,394		743,573	*	†
1875	1	5,234	999,628		743,573	*	695,072
1876	5	122,238	1,121,866		743,573	226,311‡	921,383
1877	4	47,346	1,169,212		743,573	270,996	1,192,379
1878			1,169,212		743,573	875,019	2,967,398
1879			1,169,212		743,573	390,803‡	2,458,201
1880	3	190,777	1,359,989	3,016	746,589	286,330	2,744,531
1881	1	2,288	1,362,277		746,589	839,399	3,583,930
1882	2	3,160	1,365,437		746,589	465,208	4,049,138
1883	81	5,954,224	7,319,661		746,589	761,236	4,810,374
1884	44	1,665,854	8,985,515		746,589	478,116	5,288,490
1885	66	2,126,777	11,112,292		746,589	351,264	5,639,754
1886	61	3,091,662	14,203,954		746,589	383,551	6,023,305
1887	285	6,850,683	21,054,637		746,589	334,814	6,358,119
1888	47	2,884,635	23,939,272	290,968§	1,037,557§	407,969	6,766,088
1889	34	586,506	24,525,778		1,037,557§	641,197	7,407,285
1890	53	406,003	24,931,781	261,773§	1,299,330§	393,110	7,800,395

* No usable data were located.
† No breakdown of sales by year was located. The figure given for 1875 represents the accumulation of sales made up to that time.
‡ A fractional year.
§ These data are for the fiscal not the calendar year.

Data on selections are from the "Selections Docket" in Record Group 48, and 49 Congress, 1 session, *Senate Executive Document 126*, pp. 6–10. Data on patents are from *ibid.*, 10, and the annual reports of the commissioners of the General Land Office, 1887–1890. Data on sales are from the annual reports of the Company. Cancellations for the period 1884–1890 amounted to 269,529 acres, or an annual average of 38,504 acres for the seven year period. See the note to Table 4 for a discussion of this.

The value of the tax-exemption rulings was quickly recognized and, in some cases, capitalized upon. There can be little doubt that the Kansas Pacific sold lands as early as 1870, while the tax cases were still in the lower courts, with the (verbal, not written) assurance that they were not taxable. At least one buyer wrote the secretary of the interior for confirmation.[68] The Union Pacific also promptly recognized the monetary value of the Prescott and McShane decisions. In 1874 its stockholders were told that the rulings were "a great benefit to the Company by relieving it from large expenditures of money."[69] And the company's acting president, John Duff, told the secretary of the interior that "no board of directors would be justified in waiving such exemption."[70] The Central Pacific, faced in the mid-seventies with the legislative effort to end the exemption, asserted that no land-grant road could retain its land if it were taxed—in other words, that taxation would be confisca-

[68] Alfred V. Leaman to C. Delano, New York, November 25, 1870, in Record Group 48, Letters Received; Delano to Leaman, November 28, 1870, in Record Group 48, Pacific Railroads, Letters Sent.
[69] Union Pacific, *Annual Report*, 1874, p. 14.
[70] John Duff to C. Delano, New York, January 23, 1874, in Record Group 48, Lands and Railroads, Letters Received.

TABLE 10.—SELECTIONS FILED, PATENTS RECEIVED, AND SALES MADE
BY THE BURLINGTON—IN NEBRASKA, 1870–1890 (IN ACRES)

Year	selections			patents§		gross sales	
	lists	in year	to date	in year	to date	in year	to date
1870						61,623	61,623
1871						120,757	182,380
1872	12	2,376,278	2,376,278	1,420,178	1,420,178	120,928	303,308
1873			2,376,278	950,474	2,370,652	276,704	580,012
1874			2,376,278		2,370,652	394,261	974,273
1875	1	3,437	2,379,715	3,096	2,373,748	92,251	1,066,524
1876			2,379,715	340	2,374,088	76,816	1,143,340
1877			2,379,715		2,374,088	246,738	1,390,078
1878			2,379,715		2,374,088	512,108	1,902,186
1879			2,379,715		2,374,088	369,431	2,271,617
1880			2,379,715		2,374,088	270,030	2,541,647
1881			2,379,715		2,374,088	129,960	2,671,607
1882			2,379,715		2,374,088	241,175	2,912,782
1883			2,379,715		2,374,088	182,636	3,095,418
1884			2,379,715		2,374,088	56,996	3,152,414
1885			2,379,715		2,374,088	40,851	3,193,265
1886			2,379,715		2,374,088	14,951	3,208,216
1887			2,379,715		2,374,088	7,079	3,215,295
1888			2,379,715		2,374,088	3,713	3,219,008
1889			2,379,715		2,374,088	3,275	3,222,283
1890			2,379,715		2,374,088	1,840	3,224,123

§ These data are for the fiscal not the calendar year.
Data on selections are from the "Selections Docket" in Record Group 48. Data on patents are
from the annual reports of the commissioners of the General Land Office, 1870–1890. Data on sales
are from the annual reports of the company and from "Miscellaneous Sales Records" in the Burlington Archives, Newberry Library, Chicago. The road reported cancellations of 727,161 acres, or an
annual average of 34,626 acres—the highest rate of cancellation of any road studied. It also reported net sales of 117,247 acres in excess of what was patented to it.

tion, would remove the equity of the land-mortgage holders, would
bankrupt the railroads.[71] A decade later it used an almost identical
argument and the legislative defenders of the roads made the same
point.[72] Exemption from taxation was necessary to survival.

Though most roads denied that they made studied use of the exemption feature to their own advantage and that of buyers of their land, at
least two admitted that they did so. Benjamin McAllaster, Kansas Pacific land agent from 1875 to 1887, when called to account in the Pacific
Railway Commission hearings, said in justification of the road's patent-
tax policy: "The Government lands adjoining ours were not taxable.
A man on the Government land had no taxes to pay; therefore the man
buying the railroad land was but getting a fair show if he didn't pay
taxes for two or three years after he bought his land. He was taking up
land by the side of a man who paid nothing for it."[73] Leavitt Burnham, Union Pacific land agent from 1878 to 1886, when asked a similar question, said his company's policy was "to patent as fast as the
lands could be settled or disposed of and the country could be occupied,

[71] Argument of James H. Storrs, Counsel for Central Pacific Railroad.
[72] W. H. Mills, Payment of Survey Fees upon and Taxation of Granted Lands;
G. T. Tweed, In the Matter of the Payment for Surveys. See above, p. 51.
[73] 50 Congress, 1 session, Senate Executive Document 51 (1888), pp. 1020–1021.

TABLE 11.—SELECTIONS FILED, PATENTS RECEIVED, AND SALES MADE
BY THE SANTA FE—IN KANSAS, 1871–1890 (IN ACRES)

Year	selections			patents§		gross sales	
	lists	in year	to date	in year	to date	in year	to date
1871	3	48,922	48,922			71,801	71,801
1872			48,922			45,328	117,129
1873	33	2,670,759	2,719,681	2,456,393	2,456,393	133,507	250,636
1874	4	10,580	2,730,261	15,337	2,471,730	200,459	451,095
1875	4	3,115	2,733,376	2,955	2,474,685	75,415	526,510
1876			2,733,376		2,474,685	122,201	648,711
1877	2	475	2,733,851		2,474,685	85,047	733,758
1878			2,733,851		2,474,685	267,282	1,001,040
1879			2,733,851		2,474,685	104,744	1,105,784
1880	1	280,717	3,014,568		2,474,685	78,241	1,184,025
1881			3,014,568	280,717	2,755,402	50,033	1,234,058
1882	1	189,405	3,203,973	*9,465	2,745,937	189,830	1,423,888
1883			3,203,973	*160	2,745,777	431,755	1,855,643
1884			3,203,973	189,384	2,935,161	353,090	2,208,733
1885			3,203,973		2,935,161	770,494	2,979,227
1886			3,203,973		2,935,161	347,321	3,326,548
1887			3,203,973	*480	2,934,681		3,326,548
1888			3,203,973		2,934,681	5,436	3,331,984
1889			3,203,973		2,934,681	20,830	3,352,814
1890			3,203,973		2,934,681	626	3,353,440

§ These data are for the fiscal not the calendar year.
* A minus quantity.
Data on selections are from the "Selections Docket" in Record Group 48. Data on patents are from the annual reports of the commissioners of the General Land Office, 1870–1890. Data on sales are from the annual reports of the company. Data on cancellations are not available.

or used in such a way that there could be a fair and honest utilization of taxation, after being patented." Burnham justified the policy of selling before patent by asserting that the road had suffered heavy tax stealings in some of the western counties of Nebraska and in Wyoming.[74] Table 12 bears out the testimony of McAllaster and Burnham. The amount of land sold by the Kansas Pacific and its subsidiary Denver Pacific during the period from 1869 to 1883, and by the Union Pacific between 1879 and 1887—when there was no administrative suspension or other external justification for it—was well in excess of both selections and patents. No other road stated its motives so clearly.

All the other roads could cite either administrative policies or external circumstances to explain their excess sales. Even the Northern Pacific, which sold in excess of patents after 1876 and in excess of selections from 1877 to 1882, and which from the standpoint of sheer volume made greatest use of the policy, could and did justify its course on the basis of its feud with the Land Office over the costs of survey requirement. Significantly, it did not take the issue to the courts until 1885, eleven years after it arose. It did, however, have it to fall back on. There were no such retreats for the Union Pacific and Kansas Pacific roads, at least not until the mid-eighties. Manifestly an important part of their motive was to save themselves and the buyers of their lands the cost of local taxation.

[74] *Ibid.*, 1238, 1239–1240.

TABLE 12.—SUMMARY OF SALES BY THE PACIFIC RAILROADS OF LAND

Year	UNION PACIFIC		KANSAS PACIFIC		DENVER PACIFIC	
	Sales over Selections	Sales over Patents	Sales over Selections	Sales over Patents	Sales over Selections	Sales over Patents
1868	†	†	111,279	111,279	†	†
1869		128,825	494,156	494,156	†	†
1870		292,883	439,806	618,324	32,613	32,613
1871			563,741	742,259	74,156	47,156
1872		32,572	606,593	811,110	94,115	94,115
1873		157,961	551,144	783,619	112,066	112,066
1874		335,233	239,741	440,024	73,173	122,984
1875			236,023	441,003	76,849	76,849
1876			277,814	469,052	81,213	81,213
1877			172,791	379,580	107,314	107,314
1878			323,535	572,027	141,837	141,837
1879	56,716	76,379	424,698	684,645	106,893	149,391

Year			Sales over Selections		Sales over Patents	
1880	232,277	251,940	410,886		735,216	
1881	245,160	347,999	485,528		717,114	
1882	529,859	572,237	313,647		823,029	
1883	1,397,703	1,439,468	109,079		996,830	
1884	5,111,437	5,301,383	521,391		1,471,837	
1885	5,838,937	5,880,053	1,044,021		2,183,797	
1886	5,472,455	6,018,260	1,227,875		2,414,184	
1887	5,409,312	6,038,422	1,750,387		2,936,696	
1888	5,427,177	6,056,927	1,395,686		3,064,089	
1889	5,532,123	6,161,873	1,229,331		3,134,317	
1890	4,768,160	6,325,694	1,144,919		3,163,081	

† The road was not selling land in this year.

The effect of the land boom on the ratio of sales to selections and to patents, and consequently on the patent-taxation controversy, was as drastic as it was sudden. Demand for railroad land soared. The Union Pacific had sold 2,132,545 acres up to 1882; between 1882 and 1888 it sold an additional 6,566,392 acres. Comparable figures for the Kansas (and Denver) Pacific were 1,826,881 and 2,365,737 acres; for the Central Pacific 1,159,321 and well over a million and a half acres; for the Southern Pacific 605,046 and 1,986,790 acres; and for the Northern Pacific 4,049,138 and 2,716,950 acres. To put it differently: between the period 1865–1872, when sales began, and 1882 these six roads (counting the Colorado and Kansas roads separately) sold somewhat less than ten million acres of land; between 1882 and 1888 they sold over fifteen million acres—a rate of sale more than three times as rapid as that of the seventies. This boom combined with two other factors to produce an unprecedented proportion of sales before patent or

IN EXCESS OF SELECTIONS AND PATENTS, 1868–1890 (IN ACRES)

CENTRAL PACIFIC		SOUTHERN PACIFIC		NORTHERN PACIFIC	
Sales over Selections	Sales over Patents	Sales over Selections	Sales over Patents	Sales over Selections	Sales over Patents
*	*	†	†	†	†
*	*	†	†	†	†
*	*	†	†	†	†
*	*	†	†	†	†
		†	†	*	*
	37,971	†	†	*	*
	101,817	†	†	*	*
	60,741	*	*		
		*	*		177,810
		*	*	23,167	448,806
		*	*	898,186	1,323,925
		*	*	1,288,989	1,714,628
	62,334			1,384,542	1,997,942
	245,016			2,221,653	2,837,341
	441,488			2,683,701	3,302,549
133,375	761,331				4,063,785
337,480	1,050,286	179,246			4,541,901
349,990	1,145,691	637,376			4,893,165
261,157	1,312,191	1,095,506			5,276,716
*	*	1,553,636			5,611,530
*	*	1,727,923			5,728,531
*	*	1,772,724			6,369,728
*	*	1,870,750			6,501,065

* Data on annual sales are not available.
Compiled and calculated from the data used in the construction of tables 4 through 9 above.

before selection. On the one hand, administrative policy throughout the eighties tended to limit patenting to a rate almost directly inverse to the burgeoning sales rate. On the other hand, some roads had habitually and others at least occasionally sold without title before. As a matter of course they resorted to the practice again, or, if they were already following it, simply increased the volume.

As the boom progressed the lag in patenting increased, and so did the pressure to end it. For now the concerted attack of the railroadmen was added to the familiar appeal of the legislative tax reformers. The roads had sold a promise to convey title. But, as the delay in acquiring title lengthened, sales contracts were completed and they still had no patents. Thus what had been a useful convenience to the operators in the seventies became a positive threat to them in the eighties. They were caught with a vast arrearage of selections and faced with a growing number of buyers demanding their titles, titles the roads could not supply.[75] It was then that they made their concentrated attack, alleging administrative responsibility for the delay, a delay some of them had made good use of in earlier years.

The operators, then, must share responsibility for the delay they lamented. Their contribution to that delay was a very different one from that of the administrators, but it was just as real. To begin with, during the permissive-presumptive period of government-railroad relations, they played a positive role in the creation of a complicated and slow patenting process. Later, partly because the delay gave them a measureable and immediate advantage and partly because they could not foresee the serious difficulties the eighties would bring, they sought no purgative remedies. When the administrative log-jam, the land boom, and the reform movement coincided to demonstrate the error of their ways, they tried to mend them. In the circumstances their only defense was an attack. It was a good one, but it came too late. They had been judged.

[75] For an example of the court decisions establishing the principle that a purchaser who had contracted for a deed need not accept a title that was not supported by a patent see *Ankenny vs. Clark,* 148 *United States Court Reports* 345 (1892).

Six

The National Issue and the
Local Problem

FOR almost twenty years the tax-exemption feature of the corporation grants occupied a small but significant part of the national political and economic scene. Out of it came three things: (1) another article for the political faith of the trans-Mississippi reformers and their spiritual allies; (2) a seemingly substantial saving to many of the Western railroads, one which some at least felt was necessary to their survival; and (3) a number of important influences on state and local government and finance in the areas traversed by the roads. Each of these phenomena was of sufficient importance to attract national attention, and the resulting assessments of their origins and of their effects had a common characteristic: the astonishing rarity of an accurate view.

Tax exemption for railroad land-grant lands provided the reformers another example of the greed and perfidy of the "railroad monopolists" and gave the politicians another rod with which to flay them. Because the origins of the exemption were indirect, deriving from judicial interpretation rather than express legislation, the more extreme of the critics were quick to accuse the roads of engineering it from the start. John A. Anderson, Charles Van Wyck, and William A. J. Sparks made effective use of this charge. So did the anti-monopoly press. Those who were hesitant to charge original intent or who felt it really made no difference, such as Preston B. Plumb and Justice Miller, had no doubt that the roads, by clever manipulation of the court decisions and their own interpretation of administrative procedure, were using the feature to save themselves large sums of money and bilk the states and localities of desperately needed tax revenue. To be sure, an occasional reformer, George W. Julian for example, cast aspersions on the Land Office, but to such men administrative contributions were also engineered by the railroads and were but additional proof of their unscrupulous conduct.

These reform views were superficial, but no more so than those propounded by the railroads and their defenders. The railroads relied almost exclusively on the dual charge of administrative unreasonableness and administrative inefficiency. In the beginning the roads insisted that efforts of the Land Office to insure accuracy and justice in the patenting process were the result of wrongheadedness; later, in Commissioner Sparks' time, they ascribed it to wanton dilatoriness or to that peculiarly

TABLE 13.—ACRES CERTIFIED OR PATENTED TO CER

	UNION PACIFIC	KANSAS PACIFIC	DENVER PACIFIC	CENTRAL PACIFIC	SOUTHERN PACIFIC	NORTHERN PACIFIC
Total area of the grant*	12,000,000	6,000,000	1,100,000	8,000,000	6,750,000	47,000,000
to 1871†	639,024			304,385		
1872				33,379		
1873	15,395	25,999				
1874	50,733	387,001			5,966	374,885
1875	919,771	29,887	49,811	70,247		255,832
1876	219,373	63,665		2,344	326,883	
1877	39,371	32,284		352,662	22,920	
1878	1,842	240,858		14,703	230,540	
1879		43,760			65,612	
1880		12,950			1,720	
1881	640	81,155		12,572	90,050	3,016
1882	67,921		36,425		3,500	
1883	640	46,193	78,484	59,444	2,519	
1884	350,501			32,964	47,599	
1885	294,939			95,997		
1886	16,293			52,440		
1887				77,428		
1888						
1889						290,968
1890					480	
1891	1,290,275	960,485			6,598	261,773
1892		551,853	44,511		804,400	563,868
1893	314	48,794	116	75,382	71,553	361,345
1894				1,486		479,379
1895	274,065	1,439		466,041	689,276	5,743,500
1896				627,849	260,357	12,204,026
Total‡	4,206,911	2,533,858	209,347	2,279,323	2,629,973	20,538,473

* These figures indicate the total prospective acreage covered by the respective grants, as estimated by the commissioner of the General Land Office in 1872.

† This line shows the total number of acres certified or patented prior to June 30, 1871. Each of the others shows the amounts for the twelve-month period from July 1 to June 30 of the years named.

‡ These totals are those reported by the commissioner of the General Land Office in 1896. They are not footings of the columns partly because fractional acreages are not included in this table, and partly because corrections made as the result of periodic "audits" of the annual reports have

administrative brand of perfidy, usurpation. The charge of inefficiency did sometimes take account of a niggardly Congress, but for the most part it was based on what was viewed as wasteful duplication of effort and profitless investigation. The legislative defenders of the roads, above all Senators Conger and Blair, aired these views in Congress and made them part of the public record.

Both sides were wrong. The first common error was to ascribe all responsibility to one side or the other. In both arguments, as a matter of fact, there was an element of truth. The railroads were responsible for holding up the patenting process. So was the Land Office. The second common error was to overlook the responsibility of others than the railroads and the Land Office. Both the courts and the Congress were also responsible. A third usual, but not universal, error was to ignore or underplay the differences between the different railroads and between the different locales. But the primary error was the assumption, made by all parties to the conflict, that it was possible to issue patents quickly. Under the circumstances this was a false assumption.

TAIN RAILROAD CORPORATIONS, 1871–1896

ATLANTIC & PACIFIC	CENTRAL BRANCH U.P.	SIOUX CITY & PACIFIC	BURLINGTON & MO. RIVER	OREGON & CALIFORNIA	ALL GRANTS TO CORPS.
40,000,000	245,166	60,000	2,444,800	3,500,000	150,099,166
496,350				221,896	1,960,722
3,171	183,893		1,420,178	69,061	1,889,382
2,792		29,744	950,474		1,443,339
949	2,560	10,452			736,955
3,744			3,096		1,420,097
642		400	340	14,629	638,910
				86,622	582,553
					498,928
					111,383
	1,154				806,115
23,037					211,992
					122,653
					187,782
					455,580
					1,107,149
	30,528				99,262
	273				77,702
					290,968
40					2,686
					338,986
7,529					2,414,656
373,099					2,337,731
312,386				292,486	1,420,463
				152,409	633,275
				395,108	8,085,187
				1,114,813	15,408,386
790,942	218,248	40,596	2,373,288	2,345,938	42,883,885

not been incorporated here. Corrections made in 1882, for example, reduced the total acreage patented to all corporations by 398,457 acres, and reduced the total for the Central Pacific by 160 acres, for the Atlantic and Pacific by 432,797 acres, for the Burlington by 800 acres, for the Oregon and California by 1,086. The same audit increased the total for the Union Pacific by 25,814 acres and that for the Kansas Pacific by 7,535 acres. A correction in 1883 reduced the total for the Northern Pacific by 119 acres.

Compiled from the annual reports of the commissioners of the General Land Office, 1871–1896

The conveying of lands to the railroads was a process, not an event. Every participant in that process, whether legislator, judge, or railroad land agent, left his impress upon it. By 1890, at which time the process (including federal-through-state as well as corporation grants) had been going on for forty years, it had conveyed to recipients only about a third of the land granted for their use. The task was huge; it was complicated; and circumstances only indirectly related to it affected it mightily. Not that it could not have been done differently. Of course it could. That it was done as it was is attributable not to a single nor even a small number of important policy decisions, but to a large number of cumulatively important smaller semi-routine decisions made over a period of years. Consistently different decisions would have produced a different process. All this may merely document a truism, but it is a truism that was ignored by the assessors of responsibility.

The patenting statistics for the period from 1872 to 1896, which were cited for support by both sides in the argument over responsibility for the delays in the patenting process, are given in Table 13. Only the division of responsibility among all the participants in the process explains them all. Every administrative suspension of patenting was a reaction to railroad laxity, judicial decision, or legislative vacillation and each is clearly revealed: that for inadequate construction, 1869–1874; that for nonpayment of the costs of survey as applied in 1874 to all the roads involved, in 1874–1886 to the Central Branch, and in 1874–1882 to the Northern Pacific; that in anticipation of forfeiture legislation, 1882–1890; and that for failure to make debt payments on time, 1887–1891 and 1895. The various minor suspensions designed to assure compliance with Land Office regulations or to allow time for the reconsideration of Land Office policy are more directly attributable to administrative vacillation and inefficiency. The lack of activity on specific grants in the interim between suspensions is explicable only in terms of partial listing, slow selecting, and clerical insufficiencies attributable to railroad policies, administrative inefficiency, and legislative niggardliness. The virtual cessation of patenting activities in the eighties reflects the accumulation of these influences, and the sudden upswing of the nineties reflects the disappearance of many of them, particularly the administrative policy of retaining every acre possible and the railroad policy capitalizing on the delay.[1]

However responsibility for the lag in patenting is parcelled out among the participants in the process, one fact remains: title to their lands was vested in many of the railroads at a very slow pace. Because the law made unselected and unpatented lands untaxable, numerous political attacks were made on the roads. But more than their political standing was at stake. Tax exemption meant that they paid a smaller land-tax bill. How much they saved was regularly the subject of debate. That they saved something, at least in the short run, was never denied. Railroad pamphleteers James Storrs and William Mills asserted that

[1] Compare James E. Boyle, *Financial History of Kansas* (*University of Wisconsin Bulletin in Economics and Political Science*, vol. 5, no. 1, Madison, 1909), 47–48, 76; Lewis Haney, *A Congressional History of Railways in the United States, 1850–1887* (*University of Wisconsin Bulletin in Economics and Political Science*, vol. 6, no. 1, Madison, 1910), 181–182; Nelson Trottman, *History of the Union Pacific: A Financial and Economic Survey* (Ronald Press, New York, 1923), 113–114; Addison E. Sheldon, *Land Systems and Land Policies in Nebraska* (*Publications of the Nebraska State Historical Society*, vol. 22, Lincoln, 1936), 98–103; Harold H. Dunham, *Government Handout: A Study in the Administration of the Public Lands, 1875–1891* (the author, New York, 1941), 117–118, 281; John D. Hicks, *The Populist Revolt: A History of the Farmers' Alliance and the People's Party* (University of Minnesota Press, Minneapolis, 1931), 86; David M. Ellis, *The Forfeiture of the Railroad Land Grants* (unpublished master's thesis, Cornell University, 1939), 37–38; James C. Olson, *History of Nebraska* (University of Nebraska Press, Lincoln, 1955), 222; Paul W. Gates, *Fifty Million Acres: Conflicts over Kansas Land Policy, 1854–1890* (Cornell University Press, Ithaca, 1954), 264–266, 273–281; Carter Goodrich, *Government Promotion of American Canals and Railroads, 1800–1890* (Columbia University Press, New York, 1960), 339; Stuart Daggett, *Chapters in the History of the Southern Pacific* (Ronald Press, New York, 1922), 55–58.

TABLE 14.—LAND TAXES PAID BY CERTAIN RAILROAD CORPORATIONS FROM
THE BEGINNING OF OPERATIONS THROUGH 1886

Railroad	Total Paid	Annual Average Paid	Annual Tax Per Acre*
Union Pacific	$1,120,526.30	$62,251.46	$.0058
Kansas Pacific	160,927.60	8,469.87	.0014
Central Pacific	458,617.52	21,838.93	.0027
Santa Fe (Kansas)	1,172,832.28	73,302.01	.0244
Burlington (Nebraska)	1,131,072.61	66,533.68	.0272

* Based on the total acreage accruing to the railroad, as estimated by the Land Office in 1872.
Totals paid are from 50 Congress, 1 session, *Senate Executive Document 51* (1888), pages 2446–2451 and 4283, and from the annual reports of the companies. Other data are mathematically derived. No adequate data are available for the other companies concerned.

the roads could not have paid the taxes had they been levied and that therefore they would have lost the lands to tax-sale speculators and land sharks. Had this happened, the mortgage on the land-grant property could not have been met and the companies would have been forced into bankruptcy. Senator Blair, in his defense of the roads, also argued that they would lose the lands if they were taxed—in other words, that taxation was tantamount to confiscation. Late in the controversy, arguments that the savings were much less significant began to appear. Most roads claimed that they did in fact pay large sums in land taxes on those tracts already patented. Finally, Mills asserted that the loss in mineral lands more than offset the tax gain, that in the long run the lag in patenting produced a net loss despite the exemption from taxation. Without considering whether the savings were necessary to survival, those who attacked the roads alleged vast savings. John Anderson asserted that the Kansas Pacific saved $240,000 a year. Others were not so quick to produce figures, but were just as sure that they were huge. Representative Hanback, Senator Van Wyck, Commissioner Sparks, anti-monopoly editor Rosewater, and the Pacific Railway Commission all adhered to this view.

Consideration of railroad land-tax payments, on this the general level and removed from the context of other taxes and tax policies, tends to support the estimate that the savings were large. The data in Table 14 reveal a vast difference between the land taxes paid by roads that were tax-exempt and those that were not. The key figures are those representing the average annual tax per granted acre. The Burlington, a road that got its patents almost immediately and thus paid taxes from the beginning, averaged almost two and three-quarters cents an acre. The Santa Fe, a road that received most of its patents promptly but waited eleven years for the balance, averaged not quite two and a half cents an acre. The Central Pacific, which by 1886 had received patents for only about a million acres of a prospective eight million, paid an average of just over a quarter cent an acre. The Kansas Pacific, a road that by 1886 had received patents for a little less than a million acres of a prospective six million, averaged just under a seventh of a cent. The Union Pacific, which by 1886 had patents for something over two and a half million acres of a prospective twelve million, averaged just under three-fifths of a cent. Had the Union Pacific been taxed on its entire prospective grant from the start, at an average rate comparable to that paid by the Burlington, it would have paid an average of $326,000 a year, instead of $65,250. The Kansas Pacific would have paid $163,200 instead of $8,469. The Central Pacific would have paid $209,600 instead of $21,838. The Santa Fe would have paid $81,600 instead of $73,302. To look at it another way, if the Burlington had paid at the same rate as the Kansas Pacific, it would have saved $63,000 a year. Even at the rate the Union Pacific was paying, it would have saved $52,000 annually. There are no adequate general data for the Northern Pacific, the slowest patenting road of them all, but between 1884, the year after it began its vast program of selections, and 1892 it paid $631,421.84 in land taxes, an annual average of $70,157.98 for the nine years and an average annual tax rate per acre comparable to that of the Kansas Pacific.[2] To have paid the Burlington rate on its whole grant would have cost the Northern Pacific $1,278,400 annually.

In the abstract these savings to the railroads, and the consequent revenue losses to the states and counties, appear tremendous. Actually, a number of factors reduced them. In the first place, railroad *land* paid a great deal more in land taxes than did railroad *companies*. Every land-grant railroad sold much, if not most, of its land on long-term contracts, which stipulated that the buyers pay the taxes. If, as was charged by the reformers, a road could get more for untaxable land or sell it more easily,[3] it would get less for taxable land or find it harder to sell. Tax assessments, then, even when they were paid by buyers (and consequently did not show up in railroad tax payments), cost the roads money and cut sharply into their savings on the tax account.[4] How much this amounted to it is impossible to determine on the general level. Only the study of the sales and tax policies of individual railroads will reveal it.

In the second place, the contrast between the Burlington and the Santa Fe on the one hand and the Western roads on the other is mis-

[2] Northern Pacific, *Annual Report*, 1887, p. 49; 1888, pp. 51, 52; 1889, pp. 55, 56; 1890, pp. 57–58; 1891 pp. 49, 51; 1892, p. 57.

[3] This argument is summarized in Gates, *Fifty Million Acres*, 273, and in Haney, *Congressional History of Railways*, 81–82.

[4] The Burlington tax department, for example, kept two series of tax lists, one for unsold lands on which it paid the taxes and one for lands on which the contracting buyers paid them. The relationship of these lists varied from county to county, but after the first year or two the list of buyers paying taxes covered the bulk of the land. Eventually it included almost all of it. Forty-six volumes of these tax lists are preserved in the Burlington Archives, Newberry Library, Chicago.

leading, for two reasons. (1) Both the roads paying higher taxes received their land quickly and the land they got is the basis for computing the average. Most of the other roads in the end got less than the total prospective grant: the Union Pacific got eleven and a half rather than twelve million acres; the Kansas and Denver Pacific, together, did get nearly all their prospective seven million one hundred thousand acres; the Central Pacific got seven and three-quarters of a prospective eight million acres; and the Northern Pacific received only thirty-eight and a half million of a prospective forty-seven million acres. Thus the per acre averages, particularly those for the Northern Pacific, run somewhat low. (2) Both the Burlington and the Santa Fe had comparatively small grants in the eastern half or two-thirds of their respective states. Counties were organized and local taxes levied from the beginning; county expenses ran high; and the railroads paid taxes in keeping with the costs of local government. Settlement in western Kansas and Nebraska and in Colorado, Wyoming, Utah, Nevada, western Minnesota, the Dakotas, and Montana came later and was never as concentrated. Thus the costs of county government came later and were probably lower. But again the effects of these differences cannot be determined on the general level. Only the study of county government in the locales themselves will reveal them.

In the third place, all these railroads paid county taxes on roadbed and rolling-stock as well as on land. The valuation per mile was normally determined at the state or territorial capital and was uniform. The county, precinct, and school district tax rate per dollar of valuation was locally determined on the basis of the revenue required for local purposes. Thus a local taxing jurisdiction was at least partly compensated for the lack of taxable land by an automatic boost in the tax on railroad operating property, if there was any. How often this happened and what effect it had on the railroad tax bill cannot be determined on the general level. Obviously it sharply curtailed the total tax saving that can be attributed to land-tax exemption.

Despite all these qualifications it appears likely that the tax-exemption feature did produce some savings for most of the slow-selecting, slow-patenting roads. The savings could not have been nearly so vast, however, as the reformers and the early defenders of the railroads thought they were. It is manifest that no useful approximation can be made at this point. Too many local factors must be considered. Only by the study of individual railroads in particular local circumstances can any valid estimate be made.

Though all the participants were vitally concerned with fixing responsibility for the lag in patenting and with estimating the tax savings the roads were realizing as a result of it, their fundamental concern was with the impact of the nontaxability feature on the state and local level. Here was where the effects of legislative enactment, judicial pronouncement, administrative decision, and railroad policy were felt and could be measured. In these areas, because they were in the process of being settled, the exemption of land from taxation could have been catastrophic, for of all forms of property land was potentially the most valuable. Presumably most local revenues would come from land taxes, and the need for revenues would be great in the early years when the building of roads, county buildings, bridges, and schools called for an immediate and substantial investment of public funds. Within the limits of railroad land grants approximately half the land was reserved to the roads. If that land were not taxable, the effective potential tax base of these areas would be halved for as long as it remained off the tax rolls. The implications of such an eventuality were many, and they were readily and regularly cited as justification for criticism of the roads and as motivation for reform proposals.

Among anti-monopoly newspapermen and reforming politicians there was substantial agreement on the local effects of the nontaxability feature. Because railroad land was not taxable, state and county revenues were drastically curtailed. Much-needed roads, bridges, county buildings, and, above all, public schools could be built only in insufficient numbers, if at all. What taxes could be assessed were those against the personal property of the settlers and against adjacent tracts of government land that had come into the ownership of the settlers through preëmption, homestead, or other public-land laws. This meant that the settlers had to pay all the costs of county government and local public improvements. It also meant that the railroad, without paying its just share of the cost of those improvements, benefited from an increase in the value of its own land. It could withhold land from the market until it could get the advanced prices attendant on public improvements and the settlement of public land. This in turn would retard the development of public facilities, curtail settlement, and in general retard the growth of the states and counties. But that was not all. When the road did sell, said the critics, it passed the tax exemption it enjoyed on to the buyers, giving them an unfair advantage over their neighbors on government land. Speculation was encouraged because a buyer could hold the land, escape taxes, and gain for himself the entire increment in value that had been produced by settlement around his holdings, without having to pay anything in the way of taxes for the privilege.

Spokesmen for this viewpoint were numerous and vociferous. On the occasion of the Prescott and McShane decisions Kansas and Nebraska newspapers were often incredulous, usually angry, and sometimes fearful. Paced by the *Omaha Bee,* they protested the injustice done the settler and expressed the fear that many counties, having undertaken ambitious improvements before they discovered that the railroad lands were not taxable, would go bankrupt in efforts to meet bond payments.[5] The *Junction City* (Kansas) *Union,* for example, cited a number of school districts in its own county that had two or three

[5] See above, pp. 26–27.

thousand dollars in outstanding bonds but only one or two legally assessable taxpayers.[6]

Lorenzo Crounse in the seventies and John Anderson in the eighties carried these views to the floors of the national Congress. As Crounse put it, his purpose was

to put the railroad companies on the same footing as the struggling settler, who has to deprive himself of the very necessaries of life to meet the taxation which inexorably comes around with every recurring year. . . . Every day [the railroads'] lands are being enhanced in value by the sweat and toil of the settlers upon the alternate sections. The alternate sections are sold for $2.50 per acre, and the settler strains himself to pay that amount, and by industry labors to meet taxation; and by his building up school-houses, bridges, and courthouses, and in all the various ways that men improve and advance settlements, the lands of the railroad company are also advanced in value. . . . From the moment the settler gets possession of his land he commences to pay taxes; he enhances the value of the railroad lands not only by his improvements, but by paying taxes upon the land which he holds for all purposes, school, local, and general. At the same time these lands held by the railroad companies for speculative purposes are exempted from all taxation.[7]

Anderson repeated the Crounse indictment, giving it his own particular oratorical flavor:

And, too, as adjacent lands are cultivated, as houses are erected and homes beautified, as schools, churches, and towns spring into vigorous life, the value of the company's property is correspondingly and rapidly increased. But these are the indirect benefits of that security and civilization which law begets and law alone maintains. Then, upon what semblance of justice or upon what pretense of soulless legality can it be claimed that so vast a property, receiving such valuable benefits from society, should rightfully evade its quota of the common expenses necessary to the maintenance of society?[8]

Other politicians—among them Kansans Phillips, Hanback, Ryan, Haskell, and Plumb; Nebraskans Laird, Weaver, and Van Wyck; and Payson of Illinois, Cobb of Indiana, and Dunn of Arkansas—repeated and popularized this view until Congress adopted it.

Acceptance of the Crounse-Anderson estimate of the effect of the nontaxability feature on the local level spread beyond the legislators. Commissioners Teller and Sparks both publicized it. Sparks, writing in 1885, asserted: "The non-taxability of railroad lands imposes hardships upon settlers on Government lands by making them bear all municipal expenses, and thus retards local improvements and impedes the development of the country."[9] The Pacific Railway Commission of 1887 was

[6] *Junction City Union* (Kansas), May 3, 1873.
[7] *Congressional Record*, 44 Congress, 1 session, 1521–1522 (March 7, 1876).
[8] *Ibid.*, 47 Congress, 1 session, 664 (January 26, 1882).
[9] Commissioner of the General Land Office, *Annual Report*, 1885, p. 198.

specifically instructed to investigate the effects of the tax-exemption feature. When the Commission asked *Omaha Bee* owner-editor Rosewater about it, he replied that the Union Pacific's successful battle to prevent taxation of its lands had "changed the burdens from the railroad company, who owns the vast tracts of land, and put them upon those of other land and property owners and compelled them to pay all the tax."[10] The Commission itself, accepting this and similar testimony, summed up the political estimate of the effects of nontaxability when it concluded: "The Central Pacific, Union Pacific, and Kansas Pacific have persistently evaded local taxation and have thrust undue burdens on the other taxpayers."[11]

A few contemporaries disagreed. These dissenters cited a series of additional factors and expressed a number of contrary views which, if given credence, detract heavily from the testimony of the reformers and their allies. These contentions fall into four broad categories: (1) the relation of railroad rates to railroad taxes; (2) the relation of taxes on railroad operating property to taxes on other property, especially other railroad property; (3) the relation of those taxes that were paid on railroad land to taxes on other land; and (4) the character of government in sparsely settled areas not yet agriculturally developed.

At the outset *Omaha Weekly Herald* editor "Doctor" Miller argued that the people who ultimately paid railroad land taxes were the shippers: "Every increased dollar added to their valuation for taxable purposes," he said, "seeks and secures remuneration in an increase in the freight and passenger rates."[12] Since, in the early stages of settlement, much more shipping was done by eastern than by western Nebraskans, thought Miller, the true payers of railroad-land taxes levied by the new settlers in the western section of the state were the early settlers in its eastern portion. The effect of exemptions, then, was to help keep transportation rates down. Miller made the mistake of connecting land-tax costs directly with operating costs. All the roads maintained separate land departments with distinct accounts and separate funds. It is unlikely that any road used current operating revenues to pay land taxes, or that any road could have done so, since the land was usually tied up as security for some kind of land mortgage or trust.

A more valid connection between taxes on land and taxes on operating property was made in the argument that excessive taxes were levied on operating property to compensate for the lack of tax revenue from lands that were not taxable. Kansas Pacific land agent McAllaster argued this point before the Pacific Railway Commission.[13] The effect of exemption, according to this view, was simply to shift taxes from one form of railroad property to another. Many dissenters argued that when

[10] 50 Congress, 1 session, *Senate Executive Document 51* (1888), p. 1417.
[11] *Ibid.*, 145.
[12] *Omaha Weekly Herald*, September 5, 1873.
[13] 50 Congress, 1 session, *Senate Executive Document 51* (1888), p. 1022.

railroad land, rolling stock, or both were taxable in a county, local settlers reaped large returns by taking unfair advantage of the road. They
pointed out that because government land was not taxable until the
settler had fulfilled certain requirements and acquired either his title
or his right to it, the interval between settlement and taxability of this
land was seldom less than a year and sometimes as long as seven years
on a homestead entry. The settlers on government land organized school
districts, voted short-term bonds for the construction of expensive
schoolhouses, and paid them off by taxing railroad property heavily
during those few years before their own land was taxable. Other expensive improvements were financed in the same way.[14]

Many examples of these practices were cited. According to one author, writing for the Association of Railroad Land Commissioners, the
Santa Fe, whose lands became taxable very soon after the road was
built, by its land taxes alone financed the construction of five hundred
of some six hundred school buildings erected between 1872 and 1878
in the sixteen Kansas counties in which its lands lay. Thereby "a much
better class of buildings has been erected than would have been the case
had the residents of the districts been compelled to pay for them."[15]
Before any but the railroad property within its boundaries was taxable
the township of Kenesaw in Adams County, Nebraska, voted bonds for
and built a two-story, three-room school, with a bell tower, cloak and
recitation rooms, and other refinements. This was obviously designed,
not for the accommodation of the twenty-seven children between the
ages of five and twenty-one already resident in the district, but for the
children of future settlers there. Four thousand dollars in five-year
bonds were floated to finance it.[16] The Santa Fe, already heavily assessed on its lands, regularly fought excessive county taxation of its
operating property. Between 1872 and 1880 it initiated thirty-nine such
cases. Between 1872 and 1876 alone it obtained $122,000 in tax abate-
ments as a result of this litigation.[17] The Central Pacific fought a long,
and partly successful, legal battle with California over assessments on

[14] The *Junction City Union* of May 3, 1873, and the *Omaha Weekly Herald* of Sep-
tember 5, 1873, recite examples of this. See also James C. Malin, ed., "J. A. Walker's
Early History of Edwards County," in the *Kansas Historical Quarterly*, 9:259–284
(August, 1940).

[15] E. H. Talbott, *Railway Land Grants in the United States: Their History,
Economy and Influence upon the Development and Prosperity of the Country* (The
Railway Age Publishing Company, Chicago, 1880), 44–45. This pamphlet was pre-
pared for the Association of Land Commissioners.

[16] *Adams County Gazette* (Nebraska), March 6, May 1, 1872; William R. Burton
and David J. Lewis, eds., *Past and Present of Adams County, Nebraska* (2 vols.,
S. J. Clarke, Chicago, 1916), 1:372; A. T. Andreas, comp., *History of the State of
Nebraska, Containing a Full Account of Its Growth . . . Description of Its
Counties, Cities, Towns, and Villages . . .* (Western Historical Company, Chicago,
1882), 367–368.

[17] Atchison, Topeka and Santa Fe, *Report of Ross Burns, Attorney* [1876] (George
W. Martin, Topeka, 1877), 3–11; and same for 1880, pp. 3–13.

its operating property that it considered unfair because they exceeded valuations of comparable property in the state and of railroad property in other states.[18]

To those—usually railroadmen or their defenders—who held that some states and localities took unfair advantage of the railroads, tax exemption of any kind reduced the opportunity for doing so by reducing the property on which it could be perpetrated. Even so, the net result of railroad taxation on the frontier, from this viewpoint, was to improve rather than impair the quality of local improvements, to accelerate rather than retard their construction.

Closely associated with this argument was the position taken by the Union Pacific's land agent, Leavitt Burnham, and its general counsel, Andrew Poppleton, before the Pacific Railway Commission. They asserted that settlers in sparsely populated Western areas stole public funds, misappropriated tax money, and carefully gerrymandered taxing jurisdictions so as to get as much from the road as possible. They cited instances of school districts one mile in width and nine, seventy, and ninety miles in length designed to get from the road the highest tax possible. They also maintained that every Wyoming county from Laramie westward extended the whole north-south length of the territory, so that each county could collect taxes from the road. In Sweetwater County, the county seat, where most of the money went, was a hundred and twenty miles from the road.[19] In circumstances such as these, implied the railroadmen, all exemptions were to the good, since they reduced the opportunity for gerrymandering, fraud, and the outright theft of tax funds.

Whichever of these views, or whatever combination of them, was adhered to, one conclusion was inherent in them: the settlers were not suffering unduly from land-tax exemptions. Such exemptions kept their ambitions within reasonable bounds.

It was the hardship interpretation that found widest acceptance. It is true that most of the general testimony was on that side. Still, the volume and character of testimony on the other side was significant, and even if it was not accepted, it must at least be accounted for. There are three possible explanations which individually or in combination serve to explain the differences. First, both political oratory and self-interested testimony are notoriously careless of facts. It may be that, through ignorance, intent, or a combination of both, one or the other (perhaps both) groups distorted their interpretation. This is an obvious possibility, the application of which has been shown throughout the study of the patent-taxation controversy on the general level. It

[18] William W. Fankhauser, *A Financial History of California: Public Revenues, Debts, and Expenditures* (*University of California Publications in Economics*, vol. 3, no. 1, Berkeley, 1913), 260, 265, 271, 301–310; 50 Congress, 1 session, *Senate Executive Document 51* (1888), pp. 145, 2507–2511.

[19] *Ibid.*, 1240–1241.

needs no further elucidation here. Second, land-tax exemption had its primary effect on the local level. Localities differed in physical characteristics, obviously, but in addition the period of intensive settlement varied from place to place and, perhaps most important, the character, origins, and purposes of the inhabitants also varied. Thus the tax policies pursued by school district, precinct, and county governments differed considerably from one locality to another. Differences between the localities from which these examples were derived may, then, explain the varying viewpoints. Third, the local tax policies of at least eight different railroads were involved. As already shown in the survey of the railroads' selection and patent policies, the operators' approach to land-title and land-control problems differed considerably. All roads had their tax problems. How they dealt with them was fundamental to their relations with their tributary locales. Thus differences between the roads themselves may explain the opposing views of the effect of the tax-exemption feature.

Obviously little can be learned of the local effects of the laws governing railroad land taxation by studying the national scene. Effects can be validly studied only on their own level. However, two general distinctions are possible. In the first place, because the most noteworthy practitioners of the art of slow selection and slow patenting were the Northern Pacific, the Kansas Pacific, and the Union Pacific, it can be assumed that the areas in which these roads held land felt the effects of the nontaxability feature most keenly. If so, the states of Minnesota, Oregon, Kansas, Nebraska, and Colorado and the territories of Dakota, Montana, Idaho, Washington, Wyoming, and Utah included within their boundaries the regions most affected. In the second place, because the newspaper complaints and political repercussions of the nontaxability feature came first from Kansas and Nebraska and because the overwhelming weight of political pressure to remove it continued to come from those two states, it seems logical to assume that the local political effects were most pronounced there. Beyond these general observations nothing conclusive can be said at this point. Only the direct study of the areas concerned can produce reliable information.

For a realistic evaluation of the effects of the nontaxability feature on the local level, then, a form of particularism must be resorted to. Generalizations there are, but they can be effectively stated only when undergirded by an analysis of local experience, experience that in many respects differed widely from one locale to another. Coupled with the experience of individual locales must be the experience of individual railroads, which, in turn, differed widely from road to road and locale to locale. The study of the taxation of railroad lands has gone as far as it can effectively go on the general level.

Seven

The Taxability Question

THE study of the local effects of the nontaxability feature of the railroad grants requires two restrictions at the outset. To consider in detail its impact on all the areas in which it was operative is manifestly impossible within the compass of the present study. Hence to render the question manageable the analysis has been narrowed to the area in which two of the three worst offenders among the slow-patenting railroads held land and from which came the most persistent and vociferous of the political repercussions, namely Kansas and Nebraska. The second restriction is dictated less by limitations of time and space than by the nature of the question itself. Final judgments of the total effect of the phenomenon in any given area can be made only after the legal context, revenue machinery, railroad policies and practices, local policies and ambitions, and the personal careers of the inhabitants have been fully elucidated. All these considerations, however, hinge upon and thus are secondary to a more general initial question—the question of taxability. Because these states were being carved out of the public domain, determination of who was liable for taxes was, in the final analysis, a matter of chronology. All personal property values were either imported or created, over time, and all landed property values were rendered taxable only when title or the right to title had passed from public to private hands. Thus the initial and all important question around which all the others revolve is the problem of whose property became taxable when.

Since land was potentially, if not immediately, the basis of most wealth in the area, one overriding fact governed all others in matters of taxability in Kansas and Nebraska. All land titles derived either directly or indirectly from the United States. As public domain or as Indian land allotted in severalty or sold to private parties on behalf of the Indians, the land was the property of the United States and passed into private hands only when proof of title, in the form of a final receiver's receipt or the patent itself, was issued or at least was issuable. And, of course, the property of the United States was not taxable by any state or local jurisdiction. This fact tied the revenue systems of the two states directly to the land system of the United States.

There were numerous methods by which land in Kansas and Nebraska passed into the hands of parties other than the United States. Though the methods were different most of them had a common char-

130

acteristic, a time-lag between the "occupation" of the land by the party who was to receive it and the actual transfer of a taxable title.[1] On the face of the law a preëmption entry took a year to complete, and homestead entries, unless commuted at the end of six months, took five years. An entry under the Timber Culture Act took eight years and under the later Kinkaid enlarged-homestead law five years. In actual fact delays were common and continued failure to prove up, or the relinquishment or abandonment of an entry and selection by a new entryman, could extend the time considerably. With unselected and unpatented land in railroad grants the lag in many instances ran to more than twenty years, and such lands, though they were finally made taxable even if they were unselected, did not reach the tax rolls until 1887. There were more Indian lands allotted in severalty or sold directly by the Indian Office in Kansas than in Nebraska. The bulk of the Kansas Indian lands reached private hands in the fifties and sixties, most of those in Nebraska not until the seventies and eighties. Thus, whereas former Indian lands were among the first to reach the tax rolls in Kansas, they were well behind much preëmpted, homesteaded, and granted land in Nebraska. Only with agricultural college scrip, military bounty land warrants, and certain miscellaneous and minor other types of certificate and direct-sale entries was the lag between entry and alienation of title insignificant. Usually there was a delay, never less than six months and sometimes as long as twenty years, between original entry and the vesting of taxable title.[2]

[1] Public officials and local newspapermen were often acutely conscious of this lag and proposed methods of expediting the process in order to broaden the tax base. See, for examples, the "Message of Charles Robinson, 1861," in *Messages of the Governors of Kansas* (variously printed), vol. 1, n. p., in the Kansas Historical Society, Topeka; the report of Mary H. Higby, Superintendent of Labette County, in the *Annual Report of the Superintendent of Public Instruction* [Kansas], 1876, p. 40; *Russell Record* (Kansas), November 19, 1881; *Omaha Weekly Herald* (Nebraska), August 27, 1873; *Juniata Herald* (Nebraska), April 6, 1882; and Othman A. Abbott, *Recollections of a Pioneer Lawyer* (Nebraska State Historical Society, Lincoln, 1929), 126.

[2] Benjamin H. Hibbard's *A History of the Public Land Policies* (Macmillan, New York, 1924), and Roy M. Robbins' *Our Landed Heritage* (Princeton University Press, Princeton, 1942), the general works on the land system, have been supplemented and corrected for Kansas by Paul W. Gates' *Fifty Million Acres: Conflicts over Kansas Land Policy, 1854–1890* (Cornell University Press, Ithaca, 1954), and for Nebraska by Addison E. Sheldon's *Land Systems and Land Policies in Nebraska* (*Publications of the Nebraska State Historical Society*, vol. 22, Lincoln, 1936).

Less general but useful and more technical studies include the following: Arthur F. Bentley, *The Condition of the Western Farmer as Illustrated by the Economic History of a Nebraska Township* (*Johns Hopkins Studies in Historical and Political Science*, eleventh series, nos. 7 and 8, Baltimore, 1893); John Arnett Caylor, The Disposition of the Public Domain in Pierce County, Nebraska (unpublished master's thesis, University of Nebraska, 1951); and Evan E. Evans, An Analytical Study of Land Transfer to Private Ownership in Johnson County, Nebraska (unpublished master's thesis, University of Nebraska, 1950).

TABLE 15.—PUBLIC LANDS TRANSFERRED TO PRIVATE HANDS
IN KANSAS, 1868–1890 (IN ACRES)

Total area of state: 52,631,040 acres

Fiscal Year	Homestead		Timber Culture		Railroad†	Cash, Scrip, and Warrant‡	Total Final Entries§
	Original	Final	Original	Final			
1867*	623,551					2,908	6,139,886	6,142,794
1868	166,214	68,602					157,590	226,192
1869	225,518	48,571					56,820	105,391
1870	646,609	37,143					258,386	295,529
1871	1,261,622	39,346				92,019	215,032	346,397
1872	1,224,830	65,086				781,966	133,112	980,164
1873	806,881	156,269	9,642		2,821,150	146,715	3,124,134
1874	838,511	216,673	282,479		574,914	139,255	930,842
1875	362,283	344,880	168,269		125,329	27,748	497,957
1876	423,844	437,593	185,596		82,677	33,167	553,437
1877	435,857	568,153	238,020		227,269	294,811	1,090,233
1878	1,103,203	670,337	593,295		18,235	360,109	1,048,681
1879	1,584,377	514,816	1,167,582		48,546	94,995	658,357
1880	1,059,047	496,713	408,261		8,146	677,177	1,182,036
1881	447,247	477,247	268,575		360,352	781,128	1,618,727
1882	537,349	499,300	273,053	7,435	160	306,446	813,341
1883	508,780	506,081	237,860	24,965	215,872	395,487	1,142,405
1884	514,720	698,271	397,525	23,093	40	748,469	1,469,873
1885	1,530,372	601,478	1,169,303	27,133	160	1,123,294	1,752,065
1886	3,224,214	394,387	1,920,802	42,657	30,802	1,642,391	2,110,237
1887	1,974,549	306,336	732,545	56,502		2,261,971	2,624,809
1888	876,484	323,903	689,256	26,202		2,395,461	2,745,566
1889	344,890	302,831	457,047	16,853		1,135,818	1,455,502
1890	222,649	392,004	292,735	78,767	779,853	329,162	1,579,786
Total	20,943,601	8,166,020	9,491,845	303,607	6,170,398	19,854,430	34,494,455

* This line includes all entries made up to and including fiscal 1867.
† These data are for calendar year, not fiscal year.
‡ This classification includes all forms of "cash" disposal—preëmption, commutation, auction and private sale, Indian lands, abandoned military reservations, and scrip locations. It does not include lands granted to Kansas by the United States.
§ Original homestead and timber culture entries are not included.
Compiled from the annual reports of the commissioners of the General Land Office, 1868–1890, and from 58 Congress, 3 session, *Senate Document 189* (1905). See also Gates, *Fifty Million Acres*, 209, 228. After 1880, purchasers of Osage Indian lands in Kansas, buying on a three year contract, were required to pay taxes after the first payment, even though title did not pass for three years. See *ibid.*, 267–268 and 21 *Statutes at Large* 144 (May 28, 1880).

The general chronological pattern as well as the relative importance of the various methods followed in the alienation of federal land is presented in Tables 15 and 16. Original homestead and timber-culture entries are also included. Though these figures for original entry are not a wholly reliable measure of actual occupancy of a given tract—because the same parcel could be entered more than once, when an unsuccessful entryman was superseded by a new one or when overlapping entries were inadvertently allowed by busy land office officials—they do give some indication of the vast gap between acreages in the process of alienation and acreages to which taxable title had passed. Unfortunately no effective distinction can be made between preëmption entries and other forms of cash disposal.

These data on federal alienation shed much light on the taxability question. Up to July of 1867, thirteen years after the opening of the territory, 11.67 per cent of Kansas land but only 3.84 per cent of Ne-

TABLE 16.—PUBLIC LANDS TRANSFERRED TO PRIVATE HANDS IN
NEBRASKA, 1868–1890 (IN ACRES)

Total area of state: 49,619,840 acres

Fiscal Year	Homestead		Timber Culture		Railroad†	Cash, Scrip, and Warrant‡	Total Final Entries§
	Original	Final	Original	Final			
1867*	710,136					1,905,045	1,905,045
1868	325,459	20,536				515,229	535,765
1869	376,860	41,687				232,934	274,621
1870	509,062	42,134				613,855	655,989
1871	713,306	61,465			639,024	209,672	910,161
1872	696,620	91,446			2,412,651	160,780	2,664,877
1873	742,884	220,420	21,858		195,557	124,034	540,011
1874	615,424	321,743	312,712		121,125	41,409	484,177
1875	265,548	344,345	130,894		863,089	11,833	1,219,267
1876	237,786	418,962	106,499		327,771	13,218	759,951
1877	163,312	422,147	90,812		4,508	7,544	434,199
1878	407,949	456,075	195,306		5,236	40,072	501,383
1879	703,750	349,373	465,968		160	82,416	431,949
1880	827,112	315,501	475,275		1,809	83,992	401,302
1881	365,922	202,241	240,306		320	91,546	294,107
1882	471,939	258,393	298,520	9,775	67,921	322,581	658,670
1883	716,509	241,511	481,704	42,522		256,548	540,581
1884	1,362,186	375,128	1,068,189	30,040	475,056	375,020	1,255,244
1885	1,748,841	393,239	1,468,114	24,767	159,074	455,278	1,032,358
1886	1,590,410	328,968	969,706	28,278	16,293	730,931	1,104,470
1887	1,098,636	292,874	794,047	52,541	469,884	1,098,838	1,914,137
1888	839,675	331,409	660,915	48,264		1,076,442	1,456,115
1889	622,626	467,373	501,078	7,433		798,815	1,273,621
1890	475,188	651,732	399,514	120,087		572,203	1,344,022
Total	16,587,140	6,648,702	8,681,617	363,707	5,759,478	9,820,235	22,592,122

* This line includes all entries made up to and including fiscal 1867.
⸰ These data are for calendar year, not fiscal year.
‡ This classification includes all forms of "cash" disposal—preëmption, commutation, auction and private sale, Indian lands, abandoned military reservations, and scrip locations. It does not include lands granted to Nebraska by the United States.
§ Original homestead and timber culture entries are not included.
Compiled from the annual reports of the commissioners of the General Land Office, 1868–1890, and from 58 Congress, 3 session, *Senate Document 189* (1905).

braska land had passed into private hands through the agency of the general government—that is, had become taxable. The difference is probably partly explained by the initial surge of population into much-publicized Kansas and the early sales of large areas of Indian lands there. Whatever the reason, the lead early established by Kansas was maintained in varying degrees for more than two decades. By 1890 land reaching private hands through federal channels represented more than 65 per cent of the state's area; in Nebraska it amounted to only 45.53 per cent. In 1871, when litigation over the taxation of railroad lands began to plague the district courts of Nebraska, only 8.63 per cent of the land in the state had been alienated through federal channels, and a year later, when Kansas and Nebraska congressmen began the first campaign to achieve immediate taxation of the 15,239,276 acres[3] of unpatented railroad land in the two states, only 8,096,467 acres, or 15.38 per cent, of Kansas lands and 6,946,458 acres (of which

[3] Based on the acreage actually received up to June 30, 1904. 58 Congress, 3 session, *Senate Document 189* (1905), pp. 148–149, 152–153.

3,051,675 acres belonged to the railroads), or 13 per cent, of Nebraska lands had reached private hands through federal channels. Had the congressmen been successful, the land-tax base in the two states would have been doubled, and more than half of it would have been railroad land. In 1880, when John A. Anderson began his tax fight, 17,182,144 acres, or 32.65 per cent, of Kansas land had passed and of that land 4,783,159 acres, or 27.84 per cent, belonged to railroads. This taxable railroad acreage represented over 44 per cent of all railroad land in the state. Finally, in 1887, when all railroad lands, unpatented as well as patented, were made taxable, still only 54.56 per cent of Kansas and 37.32 per cent of Nebraska lands had reached private hands through the agency of the federal land system.

It would be a mistake to take these figures at face value as evidence that the discrepancy between granted and taxable railroad lands as compared with other lands in given areas was less than was commonly alleged. Railroad grants did not cover either state uniformly. Nor was settlement evenly distributed. Neither are these figures correlated either to the total population or to the population distribution within the two states. Nothing conclusive can be said about local tax structures from these data. However, subject to an additional reservation, these figures do give some indication that for purposes of *state* revenue the railroad lands, constituting 18.11 per cent of the area of the two states (20.63 per cent of Kansas and 15.44 per cent of Nebraska), though they made up only .0004 per cent of federally alienated land in 1867, accounted for 26.12 per cent in 1872, 32.38 per cent in 1880, and 25.02 per cent in 1886. Had all railroad lands been made taxable in 1872, though they made up only 18.11 per cent of the area of the two states, they would have constituted approximately 54 per cent of taxable land, and when they were made taxable, fifteen years later, they still accounted for about 34 per cent of the land-tax base.

The additional reservation is that federally alienated land did not constitute quite all the land reaching private hands. Each state in its turn also had a small, but important, land system. In Kansas and Nebraska, as in other public-land states, the central government used its landed wealth to subsidize the new state government. Each state received the equivalent of two sections, with some exceptions, for each township as a subsidy for the common school system. In addition, each state received lands for the endowment of public buildings, a state university and an agricultural college, and a quantity of saline lands as well. Finally, each state received a half million acres of internal improvement lands. Thus each state, with a land endowment of approximately three and a half million acres, was also in the land business and, because state like federal land was not ordinarily taxable, its land policies had a direct bearing on the operation of its revenue system.

The speed with which state lands reached private hands varied a great deal. Both Kansas and Nebraska disposed of their internal improvement and miscellaneous noneducational lands comparatively quickly. Nebraska received, between March of 1870 and February of 1874, 500,812 acres designated for internal improvements. Under legislative acts passed in 1867 and 1869 the state had by 1871 disposed of 257,312 acres to various feeder railroads. By 1878 railroads had received an additional 273,791 acres, and 2,000 acres had been used to aid bridge-building projects in two counties.[4] Kansas had intended to use its internal improvement lands for school purposes, but in 1866 the legislature provided for their immediate sale and the establishment of a fund to aid local railroads. By August 7, 1873, the state had sold 495,000 acres. At that time an injunction, based on a disclaimer of interest filed by the roads, directed cessation of sales. The state land agent did sell 800 acres in 1874, but the injunction was modified to legalize this transaction. The remaining 4,200 acres and the funds still in the account were transferred to the general fund after 1877.[5]

The career of the miscellaneous other noneducational lands was checkered. Nebraska received 32,391 acres of saline lands in addition to the 12,722 acres it set aside for the state normal school. All but 13,605 acres of these "additional saline lands" had been deeded by 1878 and little more was sold before 1892. In that year the state retained 11,124 acres, all leased and all in Lancaster County. Nebraska also received 12,751 acres as an endowment for public buildings and 32,044 acres for the support of the penitentiary. By 1878 all save 4,479 acres of these two classes of land had been deeded.[6] Kansas used all its saline lands for educational purposes and it received neither "additional saline" nor penitentiary lands. It did receive ten sections as an endowment for public buildings. All but 160 acres of these so-called "State Capitol Lands" were deeded by August of 1870.[7]

Though the fragmentary data on these noneducational state lands permits no precise conclusions, it seems probable that both states disposed

[4] *Biennial Report of the Commissioner of Public Lands and Buildings of the State of Nebraska*, 1878, pp. 28–29, 30–32; *Biennial Message of His Excellency, David Butler, to the Legislature of Nebraska, 1871* (Mills and Company, Des Moines, Iowa, 1871), 7; *Laws of Nebraska*, 1869, pp. 153–157. The excess of 32,291 acres disposed of over those actually received was apparently made up by book transfers of saline lands and by voluntary relinquishments.

[5] "Special Message of George T. Anthony, 1877," in *Messages of the Governors of Kansas*, vol. 1; James E. Boyle, *Financial History of Kansas* (*University of Wisconsin Bulletin in Economics and Political Science*, vol. 5, no. 1, Madison, 1909), 40–41; *Compiled Laws of Kansas, 1862*, pp. 33, 48, 84; *Laws of Kansas*, 1862, chapter 84; 1863, chapter 84; 1886 special session, chapter 156. See also Thomas LeDuc, "State Administration of the Land Grant to Kansas for Internal Improvements," in the *Kansas Historical Quarterly*, 20:545–552 (November, 1953).

[6] *Nebraska Public Lands and Buildings Report*, 1878, pp. 35–36; 1892, p. 41.

[7] 58 Congress, 3 session, *Senate Document 189* (1905), p. 157. Data on the disposal of the "State Capitol Lands" are from a manuscript tabular statement provided the author by the State Auditor's Office, Topeka. See also Robert Taft, "Kansas and the Nation's Salt," in the *Transactions of the Kansas Academy of Science*, 49:258 (December, 1946).

TABLE 17.—DISPOSAL OF COMMON SCHOOL LANDS IN KANSAS AND
NEBRASKA, 1865–1890

	Kansas	Nebraska
Total acreage received from U. S............	2,910,151	2,729,849
Acreage deeded in:		
1865................................	523	
1866................................	2,499	
1867................................	4,234	
1868................................	6,624	*
1869................................	10,183	*
1870................................	9,680	*
1871................................	15,037	*
1872................................	21,816	*
1873................................	19,911	*
1874................................	22,044	*
1875................................	21,119	*
1876................................	24,789	*
Total to date.......................	158,459	110,362
1877–1878...........................	56,757	6,770
1879–1880...........................	117,557	7,991
1881–1882...........................	117,989	15,143
1883–1884...........................	103,017	24,804
1885–1886...........................	177,569	35,603
1887–1888...........................	286,403†	42,833
1889–1890...........................	116,867‡	65,405
Total to date.......................	1,134,618	308,911
Undeeded in 1890....................	1,775,533	2,420,938

* No yearly breakdown is available.
† Includes only a part of sales for 1888.
‡ Includes the remainder of sales for 1888.
Data for Kansas are compiled from the Kansas *Auditor's Report*, 1890, pages 512–513 and 58 Congress, 1 session, *Senate Executive Document 189* (1905), page 157. Data for Nebraska are compiled from the reports of Nebraska's commissioner of public lands and buildings, 1878–1892. See also the *Message of James W. Dawes, Governor, to the Legislature of Nebraska, Twentieth Session, 1887* (Journal Company, Lincoln, 1887), pages 45–46.

of them quickly. Certainly by 1878 nearly all the 1,084,398 acres (577,998 in Nebraska and 506,400 in Kansas) save the few thousand acres that would be retained more or less indefinitely had been deeded to private parties.

By far the greater portion of state lands were designated for educational purposes. Of the Nebraska total of 3,455,438 acres, 2,877,440 were educational lands, and of the Kansas total of 3,585,688 acres, 3,079,288 were thus earmarked. The distribution of these tracts had an important bearing on the taxability question. Special and miscellaneous lands were often concentrated in, or at least were selected early from, lands in the eastern third of each state, but the greater part of the educational lands were distributed more or less evenly, two sections to

TABLE 18.—DISPOSAL OF LANDS FOR HIGHER EDUCATION IN KANSAS,
1868–1890

	University	Agricultural College	Normal School
Total received from U. S.	44,073	78,366	46,698
Year	Acres Deeded	Acres Deeded	Acres Deeded
1868		83	
1869		160	
1870		480	
1871		472	
1872		320	
1873			
1874		638	
1875		2,703	
1876		20,696	160
1877			
1878*	40	10,152	320
1878–1880†	1,120	4,160	1,520
1880–1882	5,064	8,600	2,966
1882–1883	4,886		1,366
1883–1884	3,480	5,395‡	3,431
1884–1885	3,426	4,966	
1885–1886	5,240	7,116	560§
1886–1887	3,000	4,799	1,440
1887–1888	1,915	3,018	4,280
1888–1889	1,115	1,288	2,160
1889–1890	480	1,157	2,394
Total to 1890	29,766	76,203	20,597
Undeeded in 1890	14,307	2,163	26,101

* To June 30.
† July 1, 1878 to June 30, 1880.
‡ July 1, 1882 to June 30, 1884.
§ July 1, 1884 to June 30, 1886.
Compiled from the *Kansas Auditor's Report*, 1890, pages 512–513, and 58 Congress, 1 session, *Senate Document 189* (1905), page 157.

a township, throughout each state. Forming as they did one-eighteenth of the land in most townships, their rate of disposal had both a more general and a more measurable effect on the whole taxability question. The disposal of these educational lands, most of which were of the evenly distributed "common school" variety, is shown in Tables 17–19.

Analysis of the disposal of educational lands yields one major conclusion: Kansas deeded its lands at a much more rapid rate than did Nebraska. Sales of common school lands started first in Kansas because it acquired statehood earlier, and in the first twelve years the state sold its common school lands at a rate comparable to that adopted by Nebraska when it began selling in the sixties. After 1876, however, Kansas sold these lands at a faster rate than Nebraska ever did. This difference

TABLE 19.—DISPOSAL OF LANDS FOR HIGHER EDUCATION IN NEBRASKA, 1879–1890

	University	Agricultural College	Normal School
Total received from U.S.	45,439	89,452	12,722
Year	Acres Deeded	Acres Deeded	Acres Deeded
1879–1880	80		
1881–1882			
1883–1884	120	80	160
1885–1886	480	480	241
1887–1888	1,291	416	533
1889–1890	613	1,272	1,281
Total to 1890	2,584	2,248	2,115*
Undeeded in 1890	42,855	87,204	10,607

* This total was listed as 2,335 but the extra 220 acres is nowhere reported.
Compiled from the reports of Nebraska's commissioner of public lands and buildings, 1878–1892

in policy was more pronounced in the sales of lands for higher education. Kansas began selling its agricultural college lands very early and sold them rapidly. By mid-1880 it had deeded more than half of them. Nebraska did not even begin deeding until 1883 and by 1890 had passed title to only about 2.5 per cent. Kansas began selling its university and normal school lands in the mid-seventies and by 1890 had deeded more than 55 per cent of them. Nebraska, which began deeding in 1880, had by 1890 alienated only about 8 per cent.

To illustrate the combined effects of the federal and state systems of disposal on the rates at which lands reached private hands, the data in Tables 15–19 have been combined in Table 20. Though the integrated data are not wholly accurate because of the varying forms in which they were reported, they do come close enough to a chronicle of the process to permit two general conclusions. First, the creation of the state land systems, operating simultaneously with the federal land system, had no profound effects on the comparative rates at which public lands reached private hands. Kansas outstripped Nebraska with both systems, the total area disposed of always running from at least one to more than twenty-one percentage points ahead of that in Nebraska. This difference, beginning at over seven per cent in 1867, was reduced to the low point in 1872 by the Nebraska rush of the early seventies and then gradually increased until the proportionately greater Kansas boom of the eighties carried it to the high point reached in 1890. Kansas, then, always had the larger proportion of privately held land.

Second, in both states title usually passed to railroad lands at a faster rate, often a far faster rate, than it passed to lands as a whole. By 1872 about 8 per cent of Kansas and almost 40 per cent of Nebraska

TABLE 20.—FEDERAL AND STATE LANDS ALIENATED IN KANSAS AND
NEBRASKA, 1868–1890

	KANSAS			NEBRASKA		
Year	Acreage in Year Cited	Acreage to Date	Percent-age to Date	Acreage in Year Cited	Acreage to Date	Percent-age to Date
to June 30, 1867		6,150,290	11.69		1,905,045	3.84
1868	315,399	6,468,477	12.29	548,033	2,453,078	4.94
1869	198,234	6,666,711	12.67	286,889	2,739,967	5.52
1870	388,189	7,058,248	13.41	803,477	3,543,444	7.14
1871	444,406	7,502,654	14.26	1,057,649	4,601,093	9.27
1872	1,084,800	8,587,454	16.32	2,723,108	7,324,201	14.76
1873	3,226,545	11,813,999	22.45	598,242	7,922,443	15.97
1874	954,324	12,768,323	24.26	542,508	8,464,951	17.06
1875	521,779	13,290,102	25.25	1,277,498	9,742,449	19.63
1876	599,082	13,889,184	26.39	818,186	10,560,635	21.28
1877	1,118,611	15,007,795	28.52	483,553	11,044,188	22.26
1878	1,090,972	16,098,767	30.59	550,737	11,594,925	23.37
1879	720,535	16,819,302	31.96	435,984	12,030,909	24.25
1880	1,244,972	18,064,274	34.32	405,338	12,436,247	25.06
1881	1,681,879	19,746,153	37.52	301,678	12,737,925	25.67
1882	880,651	20,626,804	39.19	666,242	13,404,167	27.01
1883	1,202,862	21,829,666	41.48	553,163	13,957,330	28.13
1884	1,530,991	23,360,657	44.39	1,267,826	15,225,156	30.68
1885	1,849,521	25,210,178	47.90	1,050,759	16,275,915	32.80
1886	2,211,658	27,421,836	52.10	1,122,873	17,398,788	35.06
1887	2,777,249	30,199,085	57.38	1,936,672	19,335,460	38.97
1888	2,897,981	33,097,066	62.89	1,478,653	20,814,113	41.95
1889	1,518,498	34,615,564	65.77	1,307,905	22,122,018	44.58
1890	1,642,251	36,257,815	68.89	1,378,309	23,500,327	47.36

Compiled and calculated from the data in Tables 15 through 19. The accuracy of this table is impaired by three factors. (1) The data cover overlapping periods of time. Federal data are consistently for fiscal year, railroad data for calendar year, and state data in part for calendar year and in part for biennium. Moreover, some data are reported as summaries of several years' operations. Adjustments have been made with respect to data covering these longer periods on the principle of equal division by year. (2) Since the disposition of internal improvement lands and miscellaneous other state lands is not chronicled by year, the equal-distribution technique has been applied to such lands in Kansas for the years 1868–1874, and in Nebraska for the years 1870–1878. (3) 4,360 acres of Kansas state lands, the disposal of which is nowhere reported, are excluded from the tabulation, as are 2,481 acres of "additional saline lands" in Nebraska which were disposed of sometime between 1878 and 1892.

railroad land had passed. A year later, with the issue of major patents to the Santa Fe and the Kansas Pacific, the Kansas proportion rose to over 34 per cent. By 1880 Kansas was up to about 44 per cent and Nebraska to 59.63 per cent. In 1886, when all such lands were made taxable, nearly 50 per cent of the railroad lands in Kansas and over 69 per cent of those in Nebraska had been patented. After 1886, of course, all the railroad lands in both states were subject to taxation, even though there was little additional patenting of railroad lands until 1890. Over the whole period, it seems clear, Nebraska railroad lands were patented at a faster rate than comparable lands in Kansas—the reverse of the situation with regard to other lands.

The general statistics of land alienation in the two states, considered apart from less easily measurable legal and administrative factors, chronicle a process by which lands became taxable over a long period of time and in which railroad lands regularly made up a larger proportion of the land-tax base in relation to their total acreage than did other lands. In other words, on this comparative basis railroads and the buyers of railroad lands were liable for a larger, not a lesser, proportion of land taxes than were buyers of and settlers on other lands.

Questions of taxability were infinitely more complicated than the simple determination of the date on a deed or patent. In a growing territory, where half a dozen methods of acquiring title to formerly nontaxable property and an indeterminate number of factors adding to its value were operating, many fine distinctions were necessary. It was a well established and regularly cited principle that all equities not specifically exempt were subject to taxation.[8] Thus, since both federal and state land systems either required extended residence and some improvements or allowed from seven to ten years for payment, taxable equities were built up before final title passed. In these circumstances taxability and nontaxability could be decided only through constant litigation and repeated tinkering with the tax laws. Two opposing trends developed. On the one hand, the tax liability of many varieties of property, especially minimum quantities of individual personalty, was regularly restricted. On the other hand, the liability of land in process of alienation, from either federal or state ownership, was gradually extended.

Added to the problems created by the system of acquiring equities were those created by the system of identifying and assessing them. Both Kansas and Nebraska labored under a decentralized, overlapping, and amateur-operated tax system. Almost all the responsibility for uniformity in valuations, thoroughness in listing property, impartial and nonpolitical assessments, scrupulous honesty when dealing with neighbors, resistance to corporate (and local) pressures for compromise, and careful allocation of available revenues to most-needed investments was placed on locally elected officials subject to no checks except taxpayers willing to go to court, an occasional local newspaperman, and distant state supervisory boards and officials. The question of

[8] Judicial decisions on all levels regularly so ruled. Examples include *Carroll vs. Safford*, 3 *Howard* 441 (1845); *Witherspoon vs. Duncan*, 4 *Wallace* 210 (1866); *Wisconsin Central Railroad Company vs. Price County*, 133 *United States Court Reports* 496 (1889); *Hussman vs. Durham*, 165 *United States Court Reports* 144 (1896); *Astrom vs. Hammond*, 2 *Federal Cases* 71 (Michigan, 1842); *Carrol vs. Perry*, 5 *Federal Cases* 167 (Michigan, 1845); *Bronson vs. Kukuk*, 4 *Federal Cases* 221 (Iowa, 1874); *Saline County vs. Young*, 18 *Kansas* 440 (1877); *Kohn vs. Barr*, 52 *Kansas* 269 (1893).

taxability thus became a problem not only of who was liable but also of who was assessed.

The tax systems of both states had two outstanding characteristics: minimum differentiation between forms of property and the pyramiding of taxing jurisdictions. There were, in general, three forms of taxable property. Real estate was by far the most widely held and the most valuable, and once title had passed to private hands it bore the greater portion of the burden of taxation. Personalty in general was of course also widely held, but its valuation, and consequently the proportion of the tax load it bore, was normally low. The third form of taxable property, special forms of personalty, of which corporate property—largely that of railroads—was the most significant, varied widely in location and in value and, all other things being equal, was liable for a smaller portion of the whole tax than was real property.

These three forms of property were taxable in five different taxing jurisdictions. All property not exempted by legislative act or judicial construction was liable for state taxes. Once a county had been organized, all such property within its boundaries was also subject to county taxes. Within the county there were three further taxing jurisdictions. Property located in rural areas and in villages was subject to taxation by the township or precinct, and property located in municipalities, though not subject to the township or precinct tax, was liable for taxation by the city. The fifth taxing jurisdiction was the school district, which levied taxes on all nonexempt property within its boundaries, boundaries which regularly crossed township or precinct lines and occasionally crossed county lines as well. Thus any piece of private property in either state was subject to taxation by at least one and commonly four different taxing jurisdictions.[9]

Assessment was amateurish and notoriously unequal. Though the revenue laws of both states required that all property not specifically exempt be listed at fair cash value,[10] it was rarely indeed that assess-

[9] The tax system of Kansas has been much studied. See Boyle, *Financial History of Kansas;* E. J. Benton, *Taxation in Kansas (Johns Hopkins University Studies in Historical and Political Science,* vol. 18, Baltimore, 1900), 113–176; Jack F. McKay, Property Tax Assessment in Kansas: An Administrative History (unpublished master's thesis, University of Kansas, 1950).

The Nebraska system has been studied only from the present-day point of view. See E. B. Schmidt, *An Appraisal of the Nebraska Tax System* (University of Nebraska Press, Lincoln, 1941) and his "Tax Systems in Nebraska," in *Nebraska Studies in Business* (Number 46, Lincoln, February, 1940); G. G. Virtue, ed., *The University of Nebraska Tax Primer* (Nebraska Agricultural Experiment Station, Lincoln, 1933); Howard W. Ottoson *et al., Valuation of Farm Land for Tax Assessment* (University of Nebraska, College of Agriculture, *Experiment Station Bulletin 427,* Lincoln, December, 1954).

[10] *Compiled Laws of Kansas, 1862,* chapter 197, section 11; *Laws of Kansas, 1876,* chapter 34, section 15; *Laws of Nebraska,* 1854–1857, 2d session (1855–1856), chapter 26, section 7; 1869, section 4 of the Revenue Law of February 15; 1879, p. 276; Article 9 of the Nebraska Constitution of 1875, in the Preface to *Laws of Nebraska,* 1879.

ments even approached this level. Much more common, under either the precinct assessor or the county assessor system—both used by each state at one time or another[11]—was the practice of agreeing beforehand to assess at from one-sixth to one-third of actual value. Complaints of injustice under both systems of assessment were myriad.[12] The evils cited fell into three general categories: imbalance between real and personal property values and listing; wide divergence in valuations as between one precinct and another; and great discrepancies in the levels of valuation as between one county and another.

Imbalance between real and personal property assessments was natural. Real estate was hard to hide; personalty, especially mortgages, notes, stocks, bonds, money, and the like, was susceptible of easy concealment from and undervaluation by untrained assessors more familiar with land as a form of wealth. Titles to or rights in land were somewhat harder to identify and value than land itself, but efforts were made to remedy this by requiring that the auditor of state obtain from the local land offices lists of land entered each year. But Kansas, in 1870, turned this duty over to the county clerks. Under this system titles and rights often went unlisted for many years.[13]

Divergencies in valuations between precincts reflected, as one commentator put it, "'a spirited competition' between assessors to see which can return the lowest assessment."[14] Another charged, "Almost every individual assessor has personal friends he would like to favor

[11] McKay's Property Tax Assessment in Kansas, 18–19, 35ff., chronicles the changes in assessment methods. For the major provisions of and changes in the Nebraska system see Laws of Nebraska, 1854–1857, 2nd Session (1855–1856), chapter 26; 1879, pp. 276ff.

[12] See the Manhattan Nationalist (Kansas), March 8, 1872; January 23, 1885; Russell Record, March 4, August 5, 1882; Omaha Weekly Herald, May 17, 1872; Beatrice Express (Nebraska), May 1, 1873; Omaha Weekly Bee, April 27, 1881; Nebraska City News, June 21, 1884; Lincoln County Tribune (Nebraska), March 19, 1887; March 31, 1888; Kansas Auditor's Report, 1873, p. 16; 1876, pp. 116–117; 1888, p. i; 1890, pp. i–iv; Biennial Report of the Treasurer of the State of Kansas, 1886, pp. 89–95; 1888, p. 4; Nebraska Auditor's Report, 1886, p. 4; 1892, p. 3; the "Message of G. W. Glick, 1883," in Messages of the Governors of Kansas, vol. 2; the messages of John A. Martin, 1885, pp. 8–10, and 1889, pp. 17–19, ibid.; Message of Robert W. Furnas, Governor of Nebraska to the Legislative Assembly, Tenth Regular Session, 1875 (Journal Company, Lincoln, 1875), 7; Message of Albinus Nance, Governor, to the Legislature of Nebraska, Eighteenth Session, 1883 (Journal Company, Lincoln, 1883), 23; Message of [Nebraska] Governor Dawes (1887), 10; and Message of John W. Thayer, Governor, to the Legislature of Nebraska, Twenty-First Session, 1889 (Gibson, Miller, and Richardson, Omaha, 1889), 9, 38–39. See also Addison E. Sheldon, Nebraska, the Land and the People (3 vols., Lewis Publishing Company, Chicago, 1931), 1:668; Boyle, Financial History of Kansas, 34–35; and Benton, Taxation in Kansas, 155, 159–160.

[13] Laws of Nebraska, 1857, p. 247; 1869, section 78 of the Revenue Law of February 15; Laws of Kansas, 1870, p. 246. Hundreds of examples of late listings—often ten or more years late—are entered in the ledger of Lands Entered in Russell County, in the Office of the County Commissioners, Russell, Kansas.

[14] Kansas Auditor's Report, 1876, p. 116.

if he could, and enemies he would like to punish. . . . Each . . . is a special agent for his constituents."[15] According to still another, precinct assessors were "an unmitigated and unendurable humbug."[16] Variations within counties and from year to year also reflected the short tenure and rapid turnover of assessors. The effect of it all was the situation described by Nebraska's Governor Robert Furnas:

On the same land, divided only by a precinct line, one tract is valued as low as $5.00 per acre and the adjoining at $25.00. The average value of lands in one county in this state as returned shows a gradual increase in five years, from $5.00 an acre to $16.90, and for the next four, a variable gradation . . . to $9.00 per acre. Another county, from an average valuation of $12.95 per acre in 1872, runs down to $3.46 in 1874. Still another county shows a variation in three years from $2.50 per acre to 48 cents per acre, and from 48 cents per acre, the next succeeding year, up to $7.40 and down again in 1874 to $3.50.[17]

The remedy proposed by Governor Furnas was to adopt the "true principle" and "exempt nothing. Let the property of each individual who enjoys the protection of the government, be taxed to sustain it, at actual cash value."[18] Another proposal frequently made was to return to the county assessor system, but such movements failed in these years. The only remedy lay in the county boards of equalization provided for in the original tax systems of the two states. But the county boards, made up of county commissioners or supervisors, were subject to many of the same political pressures as the precinct assessors, and neither traditional practice nor the reactions of their constituents when assessments were changed prompted them to attempt very drastic alterations. Furthermore, when they did raise low assessments they automatically increased the share of state taxes collected from the county. In these circumstances attempts at reform were rare.[19]

The divergencies of valuation between counties, though partly a direct reflection of assessment practices followed in the precincts and the timidity of local equalization boards, were also (perhaps mostly) attributable to the desire of county commissioners to keep the amount of state taxes paid by the county as low as possible and to the weaknesses in the state machinery designed to prevent them from succeeding. The state itself, except for corporate personalty, assessed no local property. Its valuations were based directly on those returned by local officers, and its taxes, levied at a mill rate established by the legislature, were collected by the county treasurers and remitted to the capitol.[20] Both states, in an effort to forestall underassessment in the counties,

---

[15] *Manhattan Nationalist,* January 23, 1885.

[16] *Omaha Weekly Herald,* May 17, 1872.

[17] *Message of* [Nebraska] *Governor Furnas* (1875), 7.

[18] *Ibid.,* 8.

[19] See especially the "Message of [Kansas] Governor Martin, 1885," page 9, for a description of the results of such moves for reform. All sources cited in note 12 report the same pressures.

[20] Sources cited in note 11 provide descriptions of the system.

made a state equalization board part of the revenue system. It worked well in neither state. In both Kansas and Nebraska membership on the board was ex officio. In Kansas the members were the secretary of state, the auditor of public accounts, and the state treasurer. In Nebraska at the outset they were the auditor and the treasurer. The governor was added in 1864 and the secretary of state in 1869.[21] Snatching time from their regular duties and unfamiliar with the areas they sought to equalize, they tended to let low assessments—especially in eastern long-settled counties (hence the counties most heavily represented in state government)—go unchallenged. When they did raise valuations they explained the action carefully, even apologetically.[22]

And well they might, for the local press could be venomous. In 1882, for example, when the Kansas board raised the Russell County general rate by ten per cent (the assessment had been made at thirty-three and a third per cent) while leaving the railroad rate untouched (it had been fifty per cent),[23] the "official" county newspaper published a letter from the county clerk, in which he said,

... we are happy. The poor railroad company must be protected, and the homesteaders living in their magnificent dugouts—living on the healthy and vigorous diet of bread and water, or perchance the county may have the much sought after privilege of boarding them. They, to pay for all these glorious privileges must have 10 per cent added to their taxable property. . . . Why should they not be happy. In the name of the homesteaders I would say that if the State Board has any more favors to deal out—to shove them right along—they are here and cannot get out unless the walking is extremely good.[24]

Even when the state board was anxious to do its duty there was, in fact, little it could do to bring about equality. In neither state did the board have the power to make differential changes within any given category of property. General adjustments—as percentages of the total in Kansas and as changes in the state levy in Nebraska—could not remedy inequalities built into the valuations made on the precinct and county level. And proposals to give the boards such power came to nought.[25] The net result was that the state equalization machinery, like that of the counties, could do virtually nothing to render taxable the property that had been exempted on the local level as a result of political pressure, personal interest, and traditional practice.

Railroad operating property, like the property of individuals, was regularly underassessed, but because assessment machinery was created

[21] Laws of Kansas, 1855, chapter 137; Compiled Laws of Kansas, 1862, chapter 90; Laws of Nebraska, 1857, p. 232; 1864, chapter 38, section 29; 1869, section 29 of the Revenue Law of February 15.

[22] Kansas Auditor's Report, 1871, p. 5; 1872, p. 5; 1874, pp. 76–77; Kansas Treasurer's Report, 1886, pp. 94–95; Message of Governor Albinus Nance . . . of Nebraska, 1883, p. 23; and Nebraska Auditor's Report, 1892, p. 3.

[23] Russell Record, March 4, 1882.

[24] Ibid., August 5, 1882.

[25] Nebraska Auditor's Report, 1886, p. 4; "Message of [Kansas] Governor Martin, 1889," pp. 17–19; Kansas Auditor's Report, 1890, pp. iii–iv.

that took the process out of local hands, the underassessment tended to be uniform. Kansas experimented with several forms of railroad taxation. It took the first step toward special valuations for railroad property in 1869, when it created a system of assessment by a board consisting of the county clerks of the counties along each railroad line. In 1871 a special board of assessors, made up of two elected members from each judicial district in the state, was organized. But charges of excessively low valuations led to its abolition in 1874 and a return to individual county assessments. Two years later, partly as a result of the wide variations in values returned (the Santa Fe was assessed at $3,067 per mile in one county and $6,254 in another, for example) the state board was revived, but this time its members were ex officio: the lieutenant governor, secretary of state, treasurer, and attorney general.[26] Nebraska's first step toward special valuations was a provision that the state auditor receive and apportion reported valuations among the several counties through which each road passed. In 1872 Nebraska, too, adopted the board system, making the governor, auditor, and treasurer its members and subjecting its assessments to review by the state equalization board (on which, incidentally, they all served). Nebraska also experimented with the law, removing railroad property outside the right of way from local jurisdiction in 1880 and putting it back again in 1881.[27]

Dissatisfaction with the levels of railroad valuation was rife throughout the period. Most critics, however, failed to connect low railroad assessments with low general assessments and usually their suggestions for reform ignored the possibility of making all property valuation conform more closely to true monetary values. Instead they contemplated boosting railroad values and leaving general values strictly alone. For example, in 1873, when Kansas Congressman Sidney Clarke was making political capital of popular dissatisfaction with the new railroad assessment board, he held out the enticement of a reduction of everyone else's taxes by more than thirty per cent simply by raising railroad values. By this method he proposed to "transfer from the people to the railroad corporations the annual payment in taxes of the immense sum of $1,814,368.82."[28] What Clarke and others wanted was to use the

[26] Benton, *Taxation in Kansas*, 134–135; Boyle, *Financial History of Kansas*, 57–59; McKay, Property Tax Assessment in Kansas, 32ff.; *Kansas Auditor's Report*, 1873, pp. 21–22; 1876, pp. 110–111; *Laws of Kansas*, 1871, chapter 150; 1874, chapter 96.

[27] *Beatrice Express*, April 24, May 8, 1873; *Omaha Weekly Bee*, September 22, 1880, June 8, 1881; *Message of Governor Albinus Nance . . . of Nebraska, 1883*, pp. 22–23; *Laws of Nebraska*, 1869, p. 75; 1881, chapter 70.

[28] Sidney Clarke, *The Taxation of Railroads in Kansas: Speech of Hon. Sidney Clarke, Delivered before the Anti-Monopoly Clubs of Lawrence, December 12th, 1873. A Startling Array of Facts and Figures* (published by the Anti-Monopoly Clubs and Tax Reform Association of Lawrence, Kansas. Standard Book and Lot Office, Lawrence, 1873), 10 and *passim*. See also the *Beatrice Express*, April 24, May 8, 1873, March 4, 1875; the *Omaha Weekly Bee*, June 8, 1881; and the *Kansas Auditor's Report*, 1873, pp. 21–22.

capital accounts of the railroads as the assessment base. What the railroads wanted was a taxable valuation based on depreciated physical property.[29] When, later, it came to valuations for purposes of ratemaking the positions were of course exactly reversed, the railroads demanding valuations based on capital account and the reformers valuations based on physical property.

Another complaint grew out of the method of financing local railroads and its relation to tax levels. Having failed in attempts to get further railroad subsidies from the central government and having exhausted their own land resources, both Kansas and Nebraska had created a system by which local governments could vote bond aid to local railroads. Both states, however, required that the aiding agency apply the tax monies collected from the railroad toward paying the interest on and retiring the bonds voted to aid it.[30] Difficulty arose when, in some instances at least, because of low valuations of railroad property returned by state boards, the local jurisdictions could not collect enough in taxes to pay the interest on their railroad bonds, let alone the principal. Thus were they forced into taxing other property to help meet these obligations, a contingency they had seemingly expected to avoid by collecting the necessary funds from the road itself.[31] Higher railroad assessment levels, especially if they could be arranged without corresponding increases for other property, would help correct the difficulty.

Though the net effect of the system of assessing railroads was to keep railroad valuations down—well below cash value even of depreciated physical assets—they were not as low as other valuations. Assessments of railroad property were proportionately higher partly because local assessors either failed to raise or actually lowered other property valuations as time passed and partly because the boards of railway assessors usually raised or at least maintained the valuations of the preceding years. It was not until the late eighties and the early nineties, when other property valuations were plummeting, that the railroad

---

[29] See, for examples, Edgar W. Dennis, *Tabulated Statement Relating to Taxation of Railroads, 1873* (Kansas State Record Office, Topeka, 1873); *Message of Governor Albinus Nance . . . of Nebraska, 1883,* pp. 22–23; *Nebraska Auditor's Report,* 1872, p. 8.

[30] Benton, *Taxation in Kansas,* 121, 137–138; Boyle, *Financial History of Kansas,* 45–91 *passim; Laws of Kansas,* 1862, chapter 52; 1876, chapters 106 and 107; *Laws of Nebraska,* 1869, pp. 67–157; 1871, pp. 72–74, 233–235, 237–238; 1873, pp. 101–102; 1875, pp. 110–111, 166–169; 1879, pp. 116–118, 151–165.

[31] Boyle, *Financial History of Kansas,* 57, 63–64, 91; *Kansas Auditor's Report,* 1873, p. 28; "Message of Governor Silas Garber, 1875," in the *Messages and Proclamations of the Governors of Nebraska* (4 vols., Works Projects Administration Project 165-1-81-317, Lincoln, 1941), 1:491–492; *Omaha Weekly Bee,* September 22, 1880; C. E. Tingley, "Bond Subsidies in Nebraska," in the *Quarterly Journal of Economics,* 6:347–348 (April, 1892). For examples of predictions of the cost of specific bond issues see the *Beatrice Express,* September 2, 1871; the *Nebraska State Journal* (Lincoln), July 24, 1874; the *Grand Island Times* (Nebraska), May 15, 1879; and the *Kearney County Bee* (Nebraska), May 7, 1880.

boards made slight reductions, explaining that they did so only because local returns had dropped by 15 to 83 per cent since the early eighties, despite the general increase in the amount and value of taxable property. These reductions did not accomplish much by way of making assessments uniform, but they did do a little toward reducing the discrepancies in valuation as between railroad and other property.[32]

The various exemptions born of assessment methods and practices were supplemented by another series of exemptions. These, however, were an outgrowth of legislative policy. In both Kansas and Nebraska certain amounts and certain kinds of personal property as well as some classes of individuals were accorded tax exemption. Public property— federal, state, county, city, town, village, and school district—was exempted, in keeping with traditional American policy. The personal property and the real estate actually occupied and used by literary, benevolent, and charitable organizations was also, and traditionally, nontaxable.[33]

Each state also exempted a portion of the personal property of individuals. Kansas, in the Wyandotte Constitution, provided a two-hundred-dollar "family exemption" for each household and also exempted, by legislation, livestock to the value of a hundred dollars, agricultural tools and implements, and mechanics' tools. Later it added the wearing apparel of each person and books up to fifty dollars in value.[34] Nebraska's personal exemptions, established by territorial legislation in 1857 and re-enacted as state law in 1869, included animals other than horses, neat cattle, mules, asses, sheep, and swine; libraries not exceeding a hundred volumes and family pictures; and such family necessaries as kitchen furniture, beds and bedding, food for consumption, and wearing apparel.[35] Both states gave special exemptions to some classes of persons. Kansas allowed a thousand-dollar exemption for orphans and widows, but later reduced it to five hundred dollars and excluded the orphans. Nebraska from the outset exempted the polls and estates of those "judged aged and infirm and unable to contribute" and in 1869 added a two-thousand-dollar exemption for widows and minor heirs of soldiers.[36]

[32] Kansas Auditor's Report, 1892, pp. v–viii; below, Table 43. See also the Railroads of Nebraska, Railroad Taxation in Nebraska (no imprint, [1902]).

[33] Laws of Kansas, 1855, chapter 137, sections 1–8; 1860, chapter 114, section 5; 1862, p. 48 (the Wyandotte Constitution); 1863, chapter 60, section 19; Laws of Nebraska, 1854–1857, pp. 33, 147–148; 1869, Revenue Law of February 15, section 1; Constitution of 1875, Article 9.

[34] Laws of Kansas, 1862, p. 48; 1863, chapter 60, section 19; 1876, chapter 34, section 3; 1899, chapter 249; Compiled Laws of Kansas, 1862, chapter 198, section 2.

[35] Laws of Nebraska, 1854–1857, pp. 147–148; 1869, Revenue Law of February 15, section 1.

[36] Laws of Kansas, 1855, chapter 114, section 9; 1860, chapter 114, section 5; Laws of Nebraska, 1854–1857, pp. 147–148; 1869, Revenue Law of February 15, sections 1 and 20.

Both states also used the tax-exemption mechanism to correct what the legislature viewed as inequities and to encourage property improvements. Both, on grounds that it was unfair to tax real estate and not mortgages upon it, debated taxation of mortgages with a proportionate exemption for the mortgaged property, and Nebraska enacted such a law in 1873. Legal problems, difficulties of enforcement, and the unpopularity of what in practice was a double tax that was compensated for by increased mortgage-commission rates prompted early repeal.[37] Improvements in general and the cultivation of trees in particular were encouraged. Kansas, in the first legislative session after statehood, exempted improvements on real estate to a total value of five hundred dollars. In 1872 it also gave a two-dollar per acre twenty-five-year bounty to encourage tree planting, but repealed the act within two years.[38] The Nebraska constitution of 1875 empowered the legislature to exempt improvements, but Nebraska's encouragement of tree cultivation had begun much earlier, when in 1860 it had provided a fifty-dollar exemption for each acre upon which there had been planted a hundred fruit or ornamental trees or four hundred forest trees. In 1879 the subsidy system was adopted when the state agreed to pay $3.33 per acre for timber cultivation.[39] Nebraska's eagerness for economic improvement and diversification also led it, in 1875, to exempt mining machinery from taxation and to offer an award of four thousand dollars for each discovery of coal and two thousand dollars for each discovery of iron ore within the state.[40]

All the complexities and innovations introduced into the tax systems of Kansas and Nebraska thus far discussed were derogatory of the interests of the taxing jurisdictions in that they limited the amount of assessable propery. But almost from the beginning of organized government another tendency developed: the bases for taxation of land were gradually modified by both legislation and litigation to increase the speed with which real property reached the tax rolls. Two major categories of land were affected: (1) homesteads and preëmption claims, which were forced on to the assessment rolls before final patent had issued, and (2) state lands in the process of contractual sale, which were also made taxable before final title had passed.

At the outset both Kansas and Nebraska, as was standard practice with new states in the public domain, had abrogated their right to tax

[37] *Laws of Nebraska*, 1873, chapter 140; 1874, chapter 130; address of Governor Robinson of Nebraska to the Farmers' Convention, April 27, 1873, quoted in A. T. Andreas, comp., *History of the State of Nebraska, Containing a Full Account of Its Growth . . . Description of Its Counties, Cities, Towns, and Villages . . .* (Western Historical Company, Chicago, 1882), 264; "Message of Thomas Osborn, 1875," in *Messages of the Governors of Kansas*, vol. 1; *Manhattan Nationalist*, March 17, 1876.

[38] *Compiled Laws of Kansas, 1862*, chapter 198, section 1; *Laws of Kansas*, 1872, chapter 204; 1874, chapter 76.

[39] Nebraska Constitution of 1875, Article 9; *Laws of Nebraska*, 1860, p. 45; 1879, pp. 187–188.

[40] *Laws of Nebraska*, 1875, pp. 156–157.

federal land in process of alienation even though it was recognized that this would seriously handicap local government in the first years of settlement. The traditional compensations were viewed as worth the sacrifice: payment of territorial debts, grants of land for public institutions, buildings, and railroads, and a small percentage of the income from the disposal of public lands.[41] But hardly had the deal been made when a disposition to regret it became manifest.

Complaints of the effects of the nontaxability of government lands were voiced even before the decisions in the railroad tax cases were handed down. Afterward they multiplied as the counties, constrained to exempt unpatented and unselected railroad lands, discovered that there was little else to assess. When they turned to improvements on government land, as Kansas had done in the territorial period, they were blocked by decisions that they too were untaxable until the land title had passed.[42] Only personalty, railroad operating property, and settler implements and goods in excess of the exempted minimums were taxable. School districts were especially hard pressed. According to one Kansas school official the decisions making unpatented railroad lands untaxable worked "greater hardships than did grasshoppers and drouth." Bonds had been issued and school houses built before the decisions were rendered. He concluded: "Now the burden falls on those who unfortunately have paid for their lands in cash or years of pioneering. . . . If there is no relief next year many school terms will be shortened, and perhaps school houses sold."[43]

Such difficulties prompted suggestions for changes in the Homestead Law. One proposal, which made no reference to railroad lands, was for a residence period of only two years instead of the standard five, on the ground that this would enable the localities "to pay as they go" instead of having to carry a heavy burden of debt for ten to twenty years. County organization and government were necessary as soon as there were a few hundred settlers, said its proponent, but the exemption of homesteaded lands from taxation for five to seven years so curtailed the public revenues that virtually every western county was forced to carry a burden of indebtedness ranging from twenty to thirty thousand dollars during the first decade of its history.[44] But even before this proposal was made, local jurisdictions had succeeded in placing some unpatented government lands on the tax rolls.

For the homesteaders and preëmption claimants, just as for the railroads, there was often considerable delay between the filing of final

---

[41] *Laws of Nebraska*, 1854–1857, p. 33; *Laws of Kansas*, 1862, p. 48; "Message of Charles Robinson, 1861," in *Messages of the Governors of Kansas*, vol. 1; "Message of George T. Anthony, 1873," *ibid.*; Boyle, *Financial History of Kansas*, 16.

[42] *Laws of Kansas*, 1855, chapter 137, section 3; *Commissioners of Chase County vs. J. S. Shipman*, 14 *Kansas* 532 (1875).

[43] Report of D. H. Emery, Superintendent of Dickinson County, in the *Annual Report of the Superintendent of Public Instruction* [Kansas], 1873, pp. 100–101. See also *ibid.*, p. 112; 1874, p. 57; 1876, p. 40; Othman A. Abbott, *Recollections of a Pioneer Lawyer* (Nebraska State Historical Society, Lincoln, 1929), 126.

[44] *Russell Record*, November 19, 1881.

proof and the receipt of patent from the Land Office. Other homesteaders simply postponed making final proof as long as possible in
order to avoid taxation.[45] These delays became the subject of litigation
in both Kansas and Nebraska. The rulings—rendered in 1875 in Kansas
and in 1877 in Nebraska—made the land taxable after the statutory
period of residence had elapsed or final proof had been made, even if
no patent had yet been issued.[46]

Popular reaction was varied. The *Hamilton County* (Nebraska)
News, for example, in an editorial entitled "State Courts vs. The People" lamented: "Our poor homesteaders—the men to whose enterprise
and brawn, and privations, the county owes more than to ought else,
without whom it were still a wild desert—these men must pay the
taxes!"[47] The *News* called for the election of a new judge, then for protest meetings. An organization was created to fight the tax, but the second meeting was adjourned for lack of attendance, and the few present, rather than do battle alone, decided "to pay the tax, though it be
unjust."[48] In the years that followed, occasional homesteaders continued
to object to paying taxes before the patent was received, as is attested
by the receipt of complaints by the General Land Office,[49] but most of
them seemingly accepted the practice or were apathetic about fighting
it and a few were even pleased with it.[50]

State lands in process of alienation were also the subject of taxability
litigation, and in most cases their status too was altered in favor of the
taxing agencies. In Nebraska the assumption that state lands were untaxable until patent issued was overturned in 1873, when the state
supreme court ruled that such lands sold on credit were liable for taxation as soon as the sale was contracted. If the lands were sold for taxes,
the state, said the court, would not lose its lien for the purchase price:
the liability would simply be transferred to the purchaser of tax title.[51]
However, the inclusion of leased, as opposed to sold lands in the tax-
free category was not overthrown, and in Nebraska this was of prime
significance. Most of the state's land sales were slow as compared with

[45] See, for example, John Ise's *Sod and Stubble* (Wilson and Erickson, New York, 1936), 81.

[46] 14 *Kansas* 412 (1875) ; 5 *Nebraska* 399 (1877) ; 6 *Nebraska* 124 (1877) ; 38 *Nebraska* 723 (1894). For the Supreme Court's refusal to render a decision on the question see 159 *United States Court Reports* 491 (1894).

[47] *Hamilton County News,* July 20, 1877.

[48] *Ibid.,* April 19, 1878. Calls for and reports of meetings were published on March 1, March 22, and April 19, 1878.

[49] Carl Schurz to James B. Weaver, February 7, 1880, in the National Archives, Record Group 48 (Records of the Office of the Secretary of the Interior), Lands and Railroads, Letters Sent; Letters to the Secretary of the Interior from John P. Cook, October 4, 1881, Lucy Jane Davis, October 8, 1881, and J. A. Buckney, July 12, 1886, all in the National Archives, Record Group 49 (Records of the General Land Office), Letters Received.

[50] See, for examples, the *Russell Record* of July 14, 1877; *Annual Report of the Superintendent of Public Instruction* [Kansas], 1876, p. 40; 1878, vol. 2, p. 75.

[51] *Hagenbuck vs. Reed,* 3 *Nebraska* 17 (1873).

those in Kansas. Common school lands in particular were sold but slowly, perhaps partly because the minimum price was high.[52] Furthermore, by the mid-eighties strong sentiment had developed for a permanent leasing policy, a policy formally adopted in 1897. Thus the common school lands in many jurisdictions were exempt from taxation. This was especially true in the western and northwestern parts of the state, where there was little settlement until the leasing period. The exemption eventually created such difficulty that a system was adopted whereby income from the general school fund was allocated on the basis of the amount of leased school land in each county.[53]

In Kansas the trend was also toward taxation of state lands that were under sales contract. In the territorial period the legislature had stipulated that educational lands were not to be taxed until "sold or leased."[54] Among the first acts of statehood was the classification of internal improvement and university lands as educational and the establishment of a system of sales by long-term contract.[55] Apparently most state lands under sales contract were not returned as taxable by local assessors, on grounds that the lands were state-owned until actually deeded. By 1873, however, the assumption of the legislature seems to have been that these lands were taxable, since it made provision for tax-sale purchases in that year. It was not until 1876 that the question was clarified. It was then that the state supreme court decided that such lands were subject to taxation even though they had "neither been patented nor paid for."[56] By the late seventies the legislature was specifically making land under sales contract taxable in every revision and re-enactment of law concerning sales of state land.[57] Because sales contracts ran either seven or ten years, much of this land became taxable long before title passed. Local tax revenues were undoubtedly increased appreciably by this means, because Kansas sold its lands rapidly and not until the twentieth century was there much interest in a permanent leasing policy for Kansas state lands.[58] One restriction, adopted in 1886, that no school land be sold for three years after the organization of a county government, did withhold such lands in some late-settling far-southwestern counties from taxation during the early years.[59]

Kansas agricultural college lands were for a time in a special category. Selected in 1863, most of them were well situated and in great

[52] *Laws of Nebraska*, 1869, p. 23.

[53] Sheldon, in his *Land Systems and Land Policies in Nebraska*, 215–284, gives a detailed account of the development of these policies.

[54] *Laws of Kansas*, 1855, chapter 7, section 4, and chapter 131.

[55] *Compiled Laws of Kansas, 1862*, chapter 104. See also *Laws of Kansas*, 1870, chapter 110; 1872, chapter 189; *Kansas Auditor's Report*, 1871, p. 6; 1872, p. 6.

[56] *Laws of Kansas*, 1873, chapter 129; 17 *Kansas* 320 (1876); 25 *Kansas* 25 (1881); 26 *Kansas* 341 (1881).

[57] *Laws of Kansas*, 1876, chapter 122, article 14; 1879, chapters 161 and 169.

[58] See the "Message of John P. St. John, 1879," in *Messages of the Governors of Kansas*, vol 1, for an expression of the "quick sale" philosophy of the public officials of Kansas.

[59] *Laws of Kansas*, 1886, chapter 150.

demand, but they were withdrawn from the market pending the price increase that would accompany settlement of lands around them and were not again opened to sale until the early seventies. At that time they were advertised and sold, on seven years' credit, as nontaxable until the patent was due.[60] But when county officials, following precedents being set for other lands, assessed them anyway, the state supreme court decided that they were taxable.[61] Though the attorney general questioned the ruling and the governor advised the exemption of all state lands in process of sale,[62] the legislature, in 1876 and 1877, accepted the decision by requiring the college board of regents to use the endowment funds to clear the lands, almost thirty-one thousand acres, of the nearly eleven thousand dollars in back taxes outstanding against them.[63]

The rules of taxability thus worked out in Kansas and Nebraska by the 1880's can be summarized as five broad principles. (1) Levels of liability, as opposed to simple liability, varied widely in both states, largely because they were determined by local assessors subject to little effective equalization control. (2) Only railroad operating property and a few other special forms of personalty were assessed by state officers. (3) Minimum amounts of the personal property of individuals, ranging from specified items or a blanket two-hundred-dollar valuation to an occasional two-thousand-dollar valuation, were exempt. (4) State lands under contract for sale were taxable from the date of contract, but state leased lands were exempt from taxation, provisions which did little to keep lands off the tax rolls in Kansas but which made great quantities untaxable in Nebraska. (5) Federal land in process of alienation was taxable when the right to a patent had been earned—that is, when the homesteader or preëmptor had finished the statutory period of residence or paid his final fees or, if it was railroad land, when the selection had been made, the fees paid, and the land certified to the railroad by the local land office. In none of these instances of federal alienation was it necessary that patents should have been issued, though, obviously, some record of the completion of requirements had to be filed in the county deed registry or other register so that assessors could identify the tracts. For all federal lands this record had to be, in practice, the final receiver's receipt, showing payment of the last of the government's claims against the land.

The implications of these taxability rules and of the history of their construction for the attempt to analyze the relationship of railroad

---

[60] *Annual Report of the Kansas State Board of Agriculture*, 1874, p. 333. See also pages 34–35 in the "Message of Governor Anthony, 1877," in *Messages of the Governors of Kansas*, vol. 1.

[61] 15 *Kansas* 154 (1875).

[62] Taxation of College Lands: Attorney General Randolph's Opinion, a broadside dated January 24, 1876, in the Kansas State Historical Society. See also page 12 of the "Message of Governor Anthony, 1877," in *Messages of the Governors of Kansas*, vol. 1.

[63] *Laws of Kansas*, 1876, chapter 128; 1877, chapter 177.

property, particularly granted lands, to other property, particularly other lands, on the county tax rolls are numerous and significant. Because of the complexity and frequent modification of the rules, the tax rolls themselves—showing the assessment and noting the receipt of payment or the sale of tax title—should provide the most reliable single source of information on both liability for taxation and levels of assessment. However, two characteristics make them unusable except as corroborative evidence. First, in many sections of both states, but especially in Kansas, hundreds of thousands of acres were at one time or another erroneously assessed, sold for taxes, and later redeemed by the county. For example, eleven Kansas counties assessed and sold for the taxes of 1869-1872 the railroad lands in their jurisdictions and were later forced to refund the money. In Dickinson County this amounted to a $24,000 and in Saline to a $40,000 reduction of the original tax roll.[64] Records of such transactions appear in later legislation and in county proceedings, not on the tax rolls. Second, the assessment rolls themselves are not all available nor all complete.[65] This fact, since comparative study must be based on comparable quantitative data, makes them unusable. Another possible source, the local land office records, must also be ruled out, simply because what federal alienation records show has no application to the county if the county's records do not show it. County officials could operate only on the basis of what they knew.

Thus the only records that can be regarded as all but universally applicable are the county title records. Since these documents show all matters of record—including the final receiver's receipt (usually), the patent, and all subsequent contracts, deeds, mortgages, and other encumbrances—and since they are county documents, a careful analysis of them—the first item of record for each tract being taken as indicative of knowledge on the part of county officials of its liability for taxes—comes closest to a reliable and at the same time universally applicable measure of taxability. Whenever documents went unfiled the land probably escaped. This is particularly likely with final receiver's receipts for privately entered tracts; the settlers may simply have neglected to file them. When final receipts for costs of survey were not filed there was less likelihood of escape, simply because most railroad entries ran to substantial acreages, but some of them too may have been missed. But in a comparison of railroad with settler land these difficulties tend to cancel one another out and therefore any conclusions

[64] *Ibid.*, 1874, chapters 77 and 17. The counties involved were Dickinson, Clay, Saline, Lincoln, Ellsworth, Russell, Wabaunsee, Morris, Ottawa, Ellis, and Jefferson.

[65] See the manuscript records of the Work Projects Administration's Historical Records Survey, held by the Manuscript and Archives divisions of the Nebraska State Historical Society at Lincoln and the Kansas State Historical Society at Topeka. Although indicative of the range of records available they are not completely reliable. A number of counties do not hold some of the reported documents, or hold only fragments, or used a form of record that is not comparable to forms used by other counties.

drawn from such comparisons should not be invalidated by these possible errors. In any event, because no other valid source is available, the data derived from the title records come closest to indicating which lands became taxable and when.

That the complexities of taxability principles in the two states and the nature of the sources available to the student both dictate analysis on the county level is clear. It is equally clear that within the limits of this volume it is impossible to present a thorough study of all counties directly involved—nearly half of the 105 counties in Kansas and an equal proportion of the 93 counties in Nebraska, or nearly a hundred separate units. It becomes necessary to work out selection techniques which reduce the analysis to manageable proportions and at the same time guarantee, so far as possible, a selection that will not distort any more than is intrinsically unavoidable the general applicability of the results obtained. That a selection of areas for specific study cannot utilize the statistician's random sample is obvious; the statistical universe is too small to insure that such a sample would encompass all the variables. For the variables—physical, chronological, and economic and social—are myriad. Topography, soil types, rainfall, drainage, and underground water supply all helped to determine the attractiveness and the productivity of the land. In addition, pre-agricultural history, available access routes and facilities, and the periods of intensive settlement determined who came and why he came. And finally, all these forces influenced and were influenced by the social structure and both general and local economic conditions, as well as the governmental structure of the communities and the political organization and habits of the settlers.

The methods of selection utilized here identify and measure the most significant of these variables, first by comparative physical and chronological description and second by a series of tabulations showing growth and structure of population, changes in and levels of the valuations of specific types of property, and county expenses and ambitions as reflected in the pattern of debt and in the total tax levy. This is done for each state as a unit and for a group of individual counties—thirteen in Kansas and eleven in Nebraska—at five-year intervals, or at other intervals when the available data forces adaptation. From these twenty-four counties are then selected three counties in each state which, though they cannot be called representative, can at least be viewed as not unrepresentative of the experience of the railroad land-grant counties. These six counties are then subjected to the detailed title survey dictated by the nature of the source materials and the complexity of the principles of taxability found in the two states. Only thus are reliable answers found to the fundamental question asked at the outset: whose property became taxable when?

Eight

The Kansas Tax Base

LYING south and west of the last great bend of the Missouri, stretching westward over four hundred miles, covering a swath more than two hundred miles wide, and enclosing more than fifty-two million acres within its boundaries, Kansas contains a multiplicity of geological formations, topographical features, and land-use classifications hardly matched elsewhere in the United States. And the history of Kansas settlement is as diverse and as complicated as the state's geography. The range of national origins, religious convictions, political persuasions, and economic ambitions is as wide and the period of settlement as various as any in American history. It is from these diversities that the selections for this analysis are made.

Even the most superficial survey of the physical characteristics of Kansas reveals tremendous variety.[1] By use of a highly simplified classification the state can be divided into nine physiographic regions. (1) The Glaciated Region, lying in the northeast corner of the state, is a large area covered principally with pleistocene glacial deposits; the ridges and the bluffs along the Missouri are of loessial origin. The area as a whole is a highly productive corn region. (2) In the southeast corner lies a tiny area of Mississippian limestone and a larger area of flat marine and non-marine shale, limestone, and sandstone soils under-

---

[1] The physiographic descriptions that follow are summarized from data largely derived from John C. Frye and A. Byron Leonard, *Pleistocene Geology of Kansas* (State Geological Survey, Bulletin 99, Lawrence, 1952) ; Walter H. Schoewe, "The Geography of Kansas, Part II, Physical Geography," in the *Transactions of the Kansas Academy of Science*, 52:261–333 (September, 1949) ; and O. W. Bidwell, *Major Soils of Kansas* (Agricultural Experiment Station, Circular 336, Manhattan, July, 1956). Note that land-use classifications referred to here are for modern crops and modern practices and are therefore only indicative of potentials for nineteenth-century agriculture.

See also the outline maps prepared and distributed by the Kansas State Geological Survey, Lawrence; William Frank Zornow, *Kansas: A History of the Jayhawk State* (University of Oklahoma Press, Norman, 1957), 3–8, which adopts the complicated Schoewe classifications; and James C. Malin, *Winter Wheat in the Golden Belt of Kansas: A Study in Adaption to Subhumid Geographical Environment* (University of Kansas Press, Lawrence, 1944).

Professor Malin's *The Grassland of North America: Prolegomena to its History* (the author, Lawrence, 1948) and his *Grassland Historical Studies: Natural Resources Utilization in a Background of Science and Technology:* Volume One, *Geology and Geography* (the author, Lawrence, 1950) are both drawn upon. His "The Turnover of Farm Population in Kansas," in the *Kansas Historical Quarterly*, 4:339–372 (November, 1935), has been used throughout this section.

lain with heavy claypan that together make up the Cherokee Plain, which is subject to poor drainage in spring and to drought in summer. (3) South of the Glaciated Region and west of the Cherokee Plain is the Osage Cuestas region, an area which is more than twice the size of its northern neighbor and which is characterized by Pennsylvanian deposits of residual soils, some of them sandy, that are best suited to mixed farming. (4) West of these three regions is a strip of thin-soiled Permian limestone hills, called the Flint Hills, which runs the full breadth of the state, varying in width from a few miles at the north to nearly fifty miles at the center. These are the famous bluestem pastures, a broad strip of which runs out at the northern and western edge to finely textured claypan soils well-adapted to wheat cultivation. (5) West of the Flint Hills region, in the northern half of the state, its western boundary trending sharply southwest, is the Smoky Hills region (including the Blue as well as the Smoky hills). This is an area of conglomerate rocks of cretaceous origin. The eastern parts of it have sandy, rolling soils suited to pasturage; its western sections contain heavier soils suited to corn in parts of the far north along the Nebraska line and to wheat and sorghum farther south. (6) The Great Bend Prairie, lying south of the Smoky Hills region, is largely an area of Pleistocene soils of both sandy and claypan texture. There is also some dune-sand topography. Wheat is grown here and so is sorghum in the areas where sufficient water is available. South of the Great Bend Prairie lie two small regions associated with the Oklahoma border: (7) the Wellington Area and (8) the Red Hills region. The Wellington Area (the easternmost) and part of the Red Hills region are composed largely of sandy outwash over clay and pack sand. In the level areas wheat is grown. In much of the Red Hills the relief is too sharp for anything but native grasses. (9) The westernmost and by far the largest region, covering nearly a third of the state, is the High Plains region. These high, gently rolling plains stretch eastward for two hundred miles from the western border in the north and equally far in the south. In the central section they extend eastward less than a hundred miles. In the north, except for a combination of shallow cretaceous soils and some recent alluvium along the Smoky Hill and lesser streams, the soils, which are deep and comparatively level, are for the most part comprised of old alluvial deposits overlaid by wind-deposited sand and silt. In the south this structure has been modified by the more recent alluvial deposits, bluffs, breaks, and dune sands of the valleys of the Arkansas (the so-called Finney Lowland) and Cimmaron rivers and by more varied wind deposits. Most of the soils of the southern High Plains are fine-textured and hence subject to wind erosion. Many are good producers of wheat when sufficient moisture is available. These nine regions, though susceptible of subdivision into at least as many more classifications, differentiate the most important large areas of potential land use in the state —always subject to the availability of adequate water supplies.

The availability of water in Kansas, as elsewhere, is governed by precipitation, evapotranspiration, runoff, and supplies of ground water.[2] The average annual precipitation for the state as a whole is just over twenty-seven inches, but the range is from forty-one inches in the southeast to sixteen inches in the southwest. The traditional twenty-inch line, west of which standard humid agricultural practices fail, runs roughly north and south in a course wavering between seventy and ninety miles of the western border and more or less close to the hundredth meridian. The traditional thirty-inch line, east of which humid agricultural practices are considered safe in "normal" circumstances, begins on the Nebraska line about sixty miles west of the Missouri and trends south-southwest to a point on the Oklahoma border about a hundred and fifty miles west of the eastern boundary of Kansas. Thus the area of uncertain rainfall—the transitional zone, where only a slight variation can produce either crop failures or bumper yields—constitutes about half the state's area, beginning in the Flint Hills and ending in the High Plains. In the southwestern quarter of the state, evapotranspiration serves to move the western boundary of this transitional area sharply eastward. West of the Flint Hills ninety per cent or more of all precipitation is consumed by the process, but in the far southwest ninety-nine per cent succumbs to this combination of evaporation and transpiration through vegetation.

Runoff is carried by two chief and two minor river systems. The north half of the state is drained by the Kaw, or Kansas, River and its principal tributaries—the Blue, Republican, Solomon, Saline, and Smoky Hill. The Arkansas River system drains most of the southern half of the state, though the Marais des Cygnes drains a small section of east-central and the Cimmaron a small section of southwestern Kansas. Supplies of ground water are available in almost directly inverse proportion to rainfall. Deep wells that will yield five hundred gallons or more a minute can be sunk in many parts of the western and south-central area, whereas eastern Kansas wells, except on the flood plains of the Missouri, Kaw, Blue, and Republican, will normally yield less than fifty gallons. Thus although surface water is usually scarce in the western sections, ground water is often abundant. The precise reverse is true of the eastern sections. During much of the period of settlement, when streams and shallow wells were the chief sources of water, these characteristics had the effect of confining settlers in the west to the vicinity of stream beds, since it was expensive to drill or dig deep wells, and efficient drilling and pumping equipment had yet to be developed.

[2] The data on availability of water summarized here are drawn almost exclusively from a study made by the Kansas Water Resources Fact-Finding Research Committee, *Water in Kansas, 1955: A Report to the Kansas State Legislature* (Topeka, 1955), 13–38. Also useful is the summary map of the findings of more than forty individual studies of county and area ground-water supplies published and distributed by the State Geological Survey. See also the publications by Professor Malin cited in note 1 and Zornow, *Kansas*, 9–13.

On this land and water base the settlement of Kansas proceeded. Four general characteristics of that settlement must be considered in connection with the land and water base to insure that the counties selected for detailed study reflect conditions that are not excessively dissimilar to others in the state.[3] First, Kansas was settled in what might be loosely called "decade belts." From the opening of the territory in the mid-fifties until the late sixties the eastern third of the state was the principal objective in the quest for land. During the next decade the central third was gradually settled, especially heavily in its eastern half. From the late seventies until the late eighties the western third was the chief area of settlement, for the most part in a boom atmosphere. And, finally, in the decade after 1888 much of Kansas, but especially the western half, lost population.

Second, for the most part settlement at first proceeded most rapidly along the streams and rivers; later it was most rapid along the railroad routes. Settlement along the streams was a result of natural conditions, but settlement along railroads stemmed in part from conditions of railroad development. As transportation for the settlers and their products the roads were obviously a factor in attracting population. An equally important factor was their lands, which most roads advertised and colonized.[4] Seven roads had federal grants. All but two, however, were small and were confined to the eastern third of the state. The St. Joseph and Denver City traversed the northeast corner, the Glaciated Region, and received just over eighty thousand acres. The Union Pacific, Central Branch, which crossed the same area, received almost a quarter million acres. The remaining three of these short eastern roads were north-south lines. The easternmost, the Missouri River, Fort Scott and Gulf, which paralleled the eastern border, received only about twenty thousand acres. The Leavenworth, Lawrence and Galveston, starting at Leavenworth, trended southwest, and the Missouri, Kansas and Texas, starting at Junction City in the Flint Hills region trended southeast. The two roads crossed in southeastern Kansas. Their combined grants amounted to about three-quarters of a million acres, most of it going to the Katy. The two great land-grant roads, the Santa Fe and the Kansas

[3] The characteristics cited are revealed in most works on the history of the settlement of Kansas and in the census reports, both state and federal. See Zornow, *Kansas*, 161–171, for a summary description of the process. See also John A. Martin, "The Development of Kansas," in the *Garden City Sentinel* (Kansas), January 1, 1888; Raymond Miller, "The Background of Populism in Kansas," in the *Mississippi Valley Historical Review*, 11:469–489 (March, 1925); Hilda Smith, The Advance and Recession of the Agricultural Frontier in Kansas, 1865–1900 (unpublished master's thesis, University of Minnesota, 1931).

[4] See Paul W. Gates, *Fifty Million Acres: Conflicts over Kansas Land Policy, 1854–1890* (Cornell University Press, Ithaca, 1954), 250ff., for summaries of railroad grants, and *passim* for a detailed description of land policies operative in the eastern third of the state. The figures given in *Fifty Million Acres* for the St. Joe and Denver are for its entire grant. Only about a quarter of it was actually located in Kansas.

Pacific, received between them almost seven million acres. Though both started from the eastern border, they held most of their land in the western two-thirds of the state. It was their advertising, colonization, and sales policies that constituted the railroad-land factor in Kansas settlement in the west, after 1870. The settlement of the southern half of central and western Kansas was closely associated with the history of the Sante Fe, that of the northern half of the state with the history of the Kansas Pacific.

Third, federal land policy in Kansas can be divided into two distinct periods. From the opening of the territory in 1854 into the mid-sixties land was disposed of chiefly by means of the Preëmption Act, cash sales, grants to railroads, and sales of Indian reserves. From the mid-sixties onward lands not already granted or engrossed were disposed of chiefly through the homestead and preëmption systems. Thus—after initial delays in extinguishing Indian title and subject to new modes of disposal of Indian lands—much of the eastern third of Kansas was settled under the old cash, warrant, scrip, and grant system with but short periods of delay between entry and patent, whereas the western two-thirds was settled under a combination of the delayed-title homestead, preëmption, and timber-claim systems and the railroad land-grant system of disposal.

Fourth, and finally, many areas of central and western Kansas, occupied after the Civil War during the period of heavy immigration from abroad, were settled by concentrations of immigrants partly in response to railroad colonization schemes. Where they did settle in large numbers—especially those who settled in compact national groups, as did the migrants to southern Saline County, or in religious groups, as did the Mennonites and Catholics in various counties—they created special patterns of land settlement and land cultivation and a tenacity uncommon among the native-born settlers and in less well-knit communities.[5]

Thirteen counties have been selected as a basis for the survey of growth in Kansas, a survey designed to establish the general characteristics of population, property values, and public policies as reflected in county finance. The location of these counties is shown on the accompanying map. The fact that they are concentrated in the northern half of the state is dictated by the subject under discussion, the effects of nonpatenting on the relation of railroad lands to other lands and to

[5] See Malin's "Turnover of Farm Population in Kansas," in the *Kansas Historical Quarterly*, 4:340–341, and Zornow's *Kansas*, 175–185, for general discussions of the effects and character of immigrant colonies. A serious problem of identification is inherent in the colonizing experience. Many such "colonies" were no more than concentrations of foreign-born settlers. Some were only promotion gimmicks. Others were nebulous projects that never really materialized or that were abandoned so quickly as to exert no important effect on anything but local historical mythology. However, where persistent reference is made to such an enterprise it is common practice to apply the nomenclature. That practice is followed here.

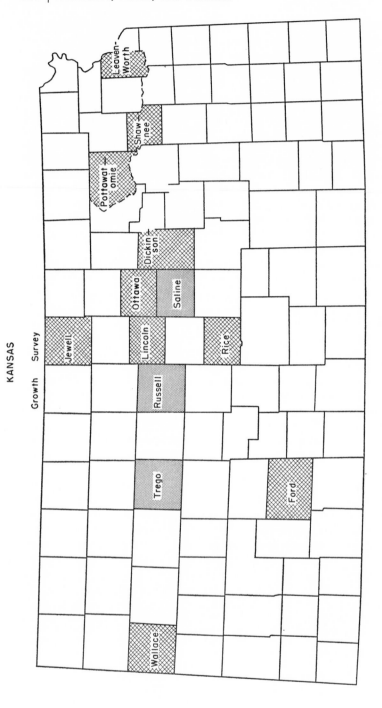

the tax toll. Aside from this reservation the selection is designed to cover the most significant variables.[6]

Three eastern counties are included. The easternmost, Leavenworth County, lying on the southeastern edge of the Glaciated Region and touching on the Missouri in the northeast and the Kaw in the south, was among the areas of the state to be settled earliest and one that figured prominently in pre-territorial and territorial history. Its fort, the early development of the city of Leavenworth and numerous small towns, and its agricultural potential combined to make it a wealthy, well-populated, and important entrepôt for Kansas throughout most of the period. The county was eventually served by two land-grant railroads, the Leavenworth, Lawrence and Galveston and the Leavenworth, Pawnee and Western (predecessor of the Kansas Pacific).

Shawnee County, in which the capital is situated, also had two land-grant railroads, the Kansas Pacific and the Santa Fe. Lying as it does across the Kaw River and therefore including the soils and topography of both the Glaciated and the Osage region, as well as the bluffs and alluvial soils along the river, it too had good agricultural potential as an area of mixed farming. Topeka, the capital, also served as a stimulus to settlement and, at times, to land values.[7]

Pottawatomie County, west of Shawnee County and wholly north of the Kaw, lies about a quarter in the Glaciated Region and about three-quarters in the Flint Hills Region. Its western boundary is the Blue River. Its agricultural potential was thus divided between pasture lands in the west and corn-farming and mixed-farming areas in the east and along the streams. The Kansas Pacific was built along its southern border, but the center of the county, including the county seat, Westmoreland, was never served by a railroad. After 1872 small feeder roads were built in the north and east. Settlement was partly by immigrant colonies: Swedes, first in Mariadahl beginning in 1855, and later in the southwest; Irish in the north, beginning in 1878. There was also a small French colony. All three of these eastern counties were organized before 1861 and had received the major portion of their populations by 1872, though Pottawatomie County was far enough west and so ill-served by railroads that it was not until the next decade that its agricultural population increased rapidly.[8]

[6] The general descriptions that follow are principally based on A. T. Andreas, comp., *History of the State of Kansas* (2 vols., A. T. Andreas, Chicago, 1883), *passim*; Frank W. Blackmar, ed., *Kansas: A Cyclopedia of State History* . . . (2 vols., Standard Publishing Company, Chicago, 1912), *passim*; Zornow, *Kansas*, 55–189; *Weston's Guide to the Kansas Pacific Railway* . . . (Bulletin Steam Printing and Engraving Service, Kansas City, 1872); and descriptive materials cited in notes 1 and 2. Additional sources applicable to specific counties are cited in connection with the material they document.

[7] James L. King, ed. and comp., *History of Shawnee County, Kansas, and Representative Citizens* (Richmond and Arnold, Chicago, 1905).

[8] See the *Handbook of Pottawatomie and Riley Counties* (published by the Modern Argo, n. p. [1883]), a boomer publication.

Dickinson, Ottawa, and Saline counties are in the transition zone between the Flint and Smoky Hills regions. Dickinson County, on the Smoky Hill River and the western edge of the Flint Hills, is part of the finely textured claypan-soil area of the region. It became a major wheat-producing county. Some of these soils are also present in east-central Saline County, but most of the remainder and all the soils of Ottawa County, save only the bottom lands along the streams, are the naturally infertile Lancaster, Hedville, and Longford soils, which produce well only with heavy liming and fertilization. Saline County is watered by three rivers: the Saline joins the Smoky Hill just northeast of the center of the county, and the Solomon, after flowing southeast through Ottawa County, also joins the Smoky Hill, in the northeast corner of the county. After 1861 both Dickinson and Saline counties were on the Butterfield Overland Mail route and still later both were traversed by the Kansas Pacific. Besides Kansas Pacific lands Dickinson County also had some Katy lands. Both counties were in the spearhead of central Kansas settlement and both were organized before 1861; each had a major cattle-shipping point in the early seventies, Salina and Abilene respectively. Dickinson County was also the site of T. C. Henry's large-scale wheat-farming experiments. Both counties received heavy complements of immigrant and religious colonies. Dickinson County received many Swedes and Irish and some Germans, and, in 1879, a colony of some three hundred "River Brethren." Saline County's immigrant settlements consisted mostly of Swedes, who were concentrated largely in the southern half of the county, but included also settlements of Irish, Dunkards, River Brethren, and German Baptists.[9] Ottawa County, off the trails and the route of the Kansas Pacific, was not organized until 1866. Its railroad, the Solomon Valley branch of the Union Pacific, was not built until 1878. No major immigrant colonies settled there.

Jewell, Lincoln, and Rice counties lie across that first guide meridian west, near the center of the state. The first two had no land-grant railroads. Rice County was traversed by the Santa Fe. Jewell County is divided between the High Plains region, in the northwest, and the Smoky

[9] Malin, in his *Winter Wheat*, presents a detailed history of the experiments of T. C. Henry, of the development of the wheat regions, and of the derivation of the varieties of hard winter wheat. See also the *Directory of Dickinson County, Kansas* (Kansas Directory Company, Salina, 1887), *passim*, but especially pp. 37–39; Stuart Henry, *Conquering Our Great American Plains: A Historical Development* (E. P. Dutton, New York, 1930), for cowboy Abilene; George L. Cushman, "Abilene, First of the Kansas Cow Towns," in the *Kansas Historical Quarterly*, 9:240–258 (August, 1940); "Along the Line of the Kansas Pacific Railway in Western Kansas in 1870," *ibid.*, 19:207–211 (May, 1951); Federal Writers' Project, *A Guide to Salina, Kansas* (*Advertiser-Sun*, Salina, n.d.), 20–36; *Directory of Saline County, Kansas* (J. M. Davis and Warren Knaus, Salina, 1885); N. H. Loomis, comp., *Directory of Saline County, Kansas* (J. S. Boughton, Lawrence, 1882); J. C. Ruppenthal, "The German Element in Central Kansas," in the *Collections of the Kansas State Historical Society*, 13:513–534 (1913–1914).

Hills region, in the southeast. Most of the soils yield excellent crops of corn and wheat. Hence, though the county had no railroad until the late seventies, it grew rapidly after the Indian scares of the early years of the decade had subsided. Like Ottawa County, it attracted only a few foreign-born settlers.[10]

Lincoln County was long regarded as a grazing area, though its western half contained potentially good Crete, Hastings, and Nuckolls soils like those of Jewell County and though it was bisected by the Saline River. The slow development of agriculture is attributable to the fact that much of it is in the heart of the Smoky Hills region, and that it had no railroad until the late eighties. The first "settlers" were the members of the 1st Colorado Cavalry who filed on most of the river lands while passing through Salina in 1865. Six of them eventually did return to their claims after they were mustered out. A small group of Danes settled in the county in 1869. In the same year a settlement was established by Swedes (who were promptly massacred by Indians) on Spillman Creek, and other Swedes settled in the county during the eighties. A few Dunkards also settled there. The county was organized in 1870.[11]

Rice County, located for the most part in the Great Bend Prairie and crossed on the southwest corner by the Arkansas River, is possessed of good, relatively level wheat soils in a broad belt running through its center and in the Arkansas bottoms. There are some sandy soils in the southeast corner and some of the infertile Lancaster, Hedville, and Longford soils in the northeast. The original Santa Fe crossed the county in a northwesterly direction on its way to the Great Bend of the Arkansas. The Santa Fe's McPherson cutoff later crossed the center through Lyons, the county seat after 1876. The first land claim was filed in 1870 and the county was organized in 1871. Few immigrants settled as groups in the county, but one non-immigrant religious group, a Quaker colony, was established at Sterling in the early seventies.[12]

The western sections of the state are represented here by Russell, Trego, Ford, and Wallace counties. Russell County, at the western edge of the Smoky Hills region, is crossed by two major streams, the Smoky Hill through the middle of the southern half and the Saline through the center of the county. South of the Smoky Hill and in the northwest corner of the county the soils are the excellent Hastings, Holdrege, and Colby classifications, well suited in this section to wheat cultivation if adequate moisture is available. The rest of the county is river bottom, low bluff, or Crete, Hastings, and Nuckolls soils. The center of the county was traversed by the Butterfield route and the Kansas Pacific.

[10] Henry E. Ross, *What Price White Rock? A Chronicle of Northwestern Jewell County* (*Burr Oak Herald*, Burr Oak, 1937).

[11] Elizabeth N. Barr, *A Souvenir History of Lincoln County, Kansas* ([*Kansas Farmer* Job Office, Topeka], 1908).

[12] Horace Jones, *The Story of Early Rice County* ([*Wichita Eagle* Press, Wichita], 1928).

Cattlemen used the area even before 1870, and its northern parts in particular remained important for grazing. The first permanent settlement was made in 1871 by a group of sixty Congregationalist families from Ripon, Wisconsin. The county was organized the next year. In 1874 a group of Pennsylvania Dutch settled in the southeastern section of the county. There were also Bohemian settlements in the extreme southeast and a large and important settlement of Germans (by way of Russia) in the southwestern corner of the county. An English colony settled Gorham, on the Western border, in the mid-seventies.[13]

Trego County is in the High Plains region and its soils are the Hastings, Holdrege, Keith, and Colby wheat-producers. Because of the uncertainty of rainfall, however, the county is largely devoted to grazing. The Plains topography is broken by the Smoky Hill and Saline rivers and by Big Creek, all of which cross the county from west to east. The area of Trego County, like that of Russell County, was crossed by the Butterfield route and the Kansas Pacific. Though the first settlements were made in the early seventies, the major inrush of population came only with the promotion, after 1878, of Kansas Pacific lands purchased by Warren, Keeney and Company. The boom was short-lived and after 1880 the population dwindled until the second boom, this time statewide, got under way in the mid-eighties. A Swedish colony, established in the late eighties, and a small group of Austrians made up the bulk of foreign group immigration. The county was organized in 1879.[14]

Ford County, in the southwest, is another Santa Fe county. It is bisected by the Arkansas River. The bulk of the county's soils are of the Richfield and Colby classifications, soils on which wheat yields well when moisture is available. There is also a large area of dune-sand topography south of the river in the western half of the county. The remainder is made up of the Arkansas bottoms and the bluffs along the river. The area was traversed by the Santa Fe trail and the Santa Fe Railroad. Fort Dodge was located near what became the site of Dodge City. The county was organized in 1873. As in Dickinson and Saline counties, its principal town and county seat (Dodge City) was an important cattle-shipping point. No immigrant colonies as such

[13] Elmer L. Craik, *A History of the Church of the Brethren in Kansas* (the author, McPherson, Kansas, 1922), 132–133, 233–234; Ralph Geist, "Early Days in Russell County," in *The Aesend, A Kansas Quarterly* (Kansas State College, Hays), 10:51–53 (Winter, 1939); *The Leading Industries of the West* (H. S. Reed and Company, Lincoln, 1886), 8:567–568, 590–591, 599–605 (October, 1886); Resources of Russell County, Kansas! Cheap Farms! Healthy Climate! Mild Winters! Best Soil in the World!, a broadside published by the Russell County Immigation Association about 1889, in the Kansas Historical Society; *Russell Record*, February 23, 1888.

[14] Warren, Keeney and Company, *Trego County, Kansas: Its Soil and Climate* . . . (J. J. Spalding and Company, Chicago, 1878); Mrs. Norah Yette Tawney and Mrs. Hattie Ridgeway Clark, *In Remembrance: Early Pioneer Settlers of Ogallah and Community, 1877–81* (no imprint); *Topeka Commonwealth*, February 5, 1880; *Hays News*, November 11, 1929, November 30, 1932.

were established in the county, but a considerable number of individual Germans settled at the county seat.[15]

The area of Wallace County was traversed by both the Butterfield route and the Kansas Pacific. Fort Wallace was located in it. More than half its soils are the canyon soils associated with the Smoky Hill River and the numerous creeks flowing into it from the north. Even native grasses do poorly on these slopes. The southern half of the county is comprised of high, undulating Keith, Colby, and Richfield soils which but for lack of rainfall would be good wheat producers. Some of these soils irrigate well. The county was first created in 1868, on the basis of a reported population of more than six hundred, mostly connected with the fort or the railroad. Faced with grasshopper plagues, drought, and the reduction of the garrison at the fort, the population dwindled. In the election of 1875 only twenty-four votes were reported. The state census of that year treated the county as unorganized and in 1879 the legislature officially disestablished it. The boom of the eighties reached the area, however, and after 1885 the county was recreated. A small Swedish colony, begun after 1887, was the only settlement established by an immigrant group.[16]

Each of these thirteen counties is of course different from the others and from every other county in the state. Each has its own history. Yet for present purposes they serve as not unrepresentative examples of physiographic regions, decade belts of settlement, and populations. A summary view of the growth and structure of their populations, property valuations, and indebtedness bears this out.

The growth of population and the percentage of foreign-born inhabitants in each of the counties and in the state as a whole is shown, for selected years, in Tables 21 and 22. These tables reveal a number of patterns. The east to west movement in decade belts is graphically illustrated, as is the boom of the eighties and the decline that had set in by 1890. The gradual development of large and relatively stable populations (in terms of numbers, not necessarily of persons) in the better agricultural counties is also revealed. And of course the further individual characteristics of each county are also reflected in the data. Leavenworth County, as an entrepôt, felt the influence of both the booms and a pronounced reaction to both the busts—in the early seventies in the first instance and the early and mid-eighties in the second. The data for Shawnee County reflect its role as the location of the capital; it was the only county in which there were significant gains in population between 1887 and 1890. In Pottawatomie, Dickinson,

[15] *Handbook of Ford County, Kansas* (C. S. Burch Publishing Company, Chicago, 1887); Leola Howard Blanchard, *The Conquest of Southwest Kansas* (*Wichita Eagle* Press, Wichita, 1931).

[16] Mrs. Frank C. Montgomery, "Fort Wallace and Its Relation to the Frontier," in the *Collections of the Kansas State Historical Society*, 17:1–95 (1926–1927); *Kansas City Star* (Missouri), May 21, 1911; *Topeka Commonwealth*, December 1, 1886.

TABLE 21.—POPULATION OF SELECTED KANSAS COUNTIES, 1870–1890

County	1870	1875	1880	1885	1887	1890
Leavenworth	32,444	27,698	32,360	42,799	46,500	38,503
Shawnee	13,121	15,417	29,094	40,579	46,360	49,018
Pottawatomie	7,848	10,344	16,347	18,139	18,310	17,681
Dickinson	3,043	6,841	14,973	20,366	23,087	22,267
Ottawa	2,127	4,429	10,308	12,740	15,806	12,509
Saline	4,246	6,360	13,810	15,381	20,100	17,326
Jewell	207	7,651	17,477	18,998	19,483	19,326
Lincoln	516	2,493	8,582	8,269	11,232	9,699
Rice	5	2,453	9,292	11,939	15,484	14,417
Russell	156	1,052	7,351	6,665	9,073	7,337
Trego	165	*	2,535	1,886	3,258	2,526
Ford	427	813	3,122	7,778	9,218	5,305
Wallace	538	*	686	197	2,000	2,463
All Kansas	364,399	527,070	995,966	1,268,530	1,514,574	1,423,485

* Unorganized.

Compiled from *Annual Report of the Kansas State Board of Agriculture*, 1872–1876; *Biennial Report of the Kansas State Board of Agriculture*, 1878–1890; *Annual Report of the Secretary of State of Kansas*, 1870, pages 35–52; *Kansas Auditor's Report*, 1880, page 314; and the *Compendium of the Eleventh Census of the United States* (1890), Part I, pages 486–487. There are slight discrepancies between the federal and state returns for 1880. The state returns are used here.

TABLE 22.—PERCENTAGE OF FOREIGN-BORN IN SELECTED KANSAS
COUNTIES, 1870–1890

County	1870	1875	1880	1885	1890
Leavenworth	21.31	17.01	16.51	14.64	17.88
Shawnee	11.16	11.75	10.21	10.29	10.61
Pottawatomie	19.67	18.38	16.75	15.92	15.57
Dickinson	28.49	23.86	17.63	15.80	14.53
Ottawa	21.86	14.88	10.50	10.25	9.88
Saline	34.74	31.01	24.70	22.85	20.07
Jewell	9.18	8.35	6.09	5.81	5.83
Lincoln	23.84	13.44	10.43	12.08	12.49
Rice	20.00	9.29	8.01	7.71	7.40
Russell	39.74	10.74	16.09	16.80	15.98
Trego	48.80	*	14.83	17.13	13.33
Ford	27.87	25.22	17.77	9.00	10.10
Wallace	40.33	*	19.24	12.18	15.72
All Kansas	13.28	12.23	11.05	10.46	10.36

* Unorganized.

Calculated from *Annual Report of the Kansas State Board of Agriculture*, 1872–1876; *Biennial Report of the Kansas State Board of Agriculture*, 1878–1890; *Annual Report of the Secretary of State of Kansas*, 1870, pages 35–52; *Kansas Auditor's Report*, 1880, page 314; and the *Compendium of the Eleventh Census of the United States* (1890), Part I, pages 486–487. There are slight discrepancies between the federal and state returns for 1880. The state returns are used here.

and Jewell counties, and to a lesser extent in Rice County, the beginnings of major settlement took place in precise relationship to their distance from the eastern border and their railroad connections, but, as the better agricultural counties, they were all quickly settled thereafter. All reflected only slightly the boom of the eighties, and suffered little loss of population when the bubble burst. Saline County benefited from its spearhead character and its strategic location, participating in the boom of the eighties and holding its population relatively well thereafter. The booms and busts were greatest in those counties that were off the trunkline railroads (Ottawa and Lincoln), on the border of the boom belt of the eighties (Russell), or in the far west and southwest (Trego and Ford). Wallace County did not follow the bust pattern, but did follow the boom pattern.

The addition of data on the foreign-born not only reflects the history of settlement but also reveals some general characteristics. The three eastern counties established their ratios of foreign-born to native population early and continued to hold them, the ratio in Shawnee County running well below that in both of its neighbors. Beyond the first decade belt foreign-born populations were, with one exception, high at the outset, after which the counties developed three divergent trends. In all the Kansas Pacific counties the percentage of foreign-born residents declined somewhat in the early seventies, the greatest decline taking place in those farthest west. Then the percentages in all these counties rose once more and maintained significant levels. In the Santa Fe counties the percentages of foreign-born dropped, sharply in Rice and more slowly in Ford County, until by 1890 they were very low. In the third group, counties off the railroads, the percentage of foreign-born tended to drop quickly and to remain low or, as in Jewell County, never to reach high levels. The Kansas Pacific land-grant area seems to have drawn a relatively large proportion of the foreign-born, its hinterland a lesser but still significant proportion, and the distant counties and the Santa Fe counties a still smaller percentage. Perhaps this is attributable to the promotion and colonization schemes; perhaps there are other explanations. Whatever the reason, the Kansas Pacific land-grant counties selected for detailed study would be unrepresentative if they did not contain a significant percentage of foreign-born.

Data on assessed valuations serve to buttress the conclusions drawn from the population data. Tables 23 and 24 show valuations in the same counties for roughly equivalent years (though, because of the nature of the data, not always identical years). Distance from the eastern border and railroad connections seem to have been the determining factors in the periods of earliest settlement, agricultural potential adding its weight later. The periods of boom and bust are also clearly revealed. In 1871 both land and personal property valuations were lowest in the western counties. Ottawa County, though just north of Saline County, also had low valuations because it still had no railroad to feed settlers

TABLE 23.—ASSESSED VALUATION, EXCLUSIVE OF RAILROAD OPERATING PROPERTY, IN SELECTED KANSAS COUNTIES, 1871–1890

County	1871		1875		1880	
	Land & Lots	Personal	Land & Lots	Personal	Land & Lots	Personal
Leavenworth	$ 7,693,210	$ 2,347,557	$ 6,133,019	$ 927,760	$ 4,841,173	$ 887,284
Shawnee	4,611,926	1,879,989	4,042,143	1,165,388	4,836,431	1,082,521
Pottawatomie	1,584,095	926,679	1,948,451	439,340	2,228,347	848,681
Dickinson	1,217,912	230,821	1,150,490	250,476	2,279,271	571,275
Ottawa	563,413	163,031	430,949	136,565	900,282	271,848
Saline	963,478	703,988	1,368,604	294,107	1,952,961	471,818
Jewell	81,758	52,230	230,401	170,600	1,017,380	630,440
Lincoln	84,080	72,329	131,255	80,286	475,596	238,936
Rice	*	*	528,511	56,354	685,420	246,535
Russell	*	*	127,024	98,609	466,553	272,226
Trego	*	*	*	*	341,438	115,425
Ford	*	*	122,185	60,732	276,740	73,164
Wallace	*	*	*	*	*	*
All Kansas	73,671,344	31,839,933	89,755,784	19,422,637	108,432,050	20,922,012

County	1885		1887		1890	
	Land & Lots	Personal	Land & Lots	Personal	Land & Lots	Personal
Leavenworth	$ 6,431,555	$ 1,193,284	$ 6,794,841	$ 1,214,920	$ 6,906,190	$ 1,119,138
Shawnee	8,044,897	2,181,508	9,020,568	2,671,061	12,990,360	2,814,680
Pottawatomie	2,737,477	1,312,844	2,987,436	1,192,246	2,863,502	937,866
Dickinson	2,647,910	1,097,288	3,078,862	964,081	3,205,115	811,640
Ottawa	1,629,786	610,104	1,746,342	552,601	1,949,452	496,684
Saline	2,426,170	809,327	2,727,177	813,046	2,995,251	547,828
Jewell	1,609,429	1,038,659	1,955,913	1,108,449	2,267,317	892,428
Lincoln	900,240	461,770	1,578,613	648,108	1,672,039	290,066
Rice	1,151,469	629,606	1,540,179	623,398	1,924,066	382,279
Russell	539,275	288,430	1,327,929	319,617	1,102,882	244,946
Trego	206,387	316,218	710,870	208,813	985,064	62,726
Ford	531,089	348,407	2,094,096	404,818	1,829,440	135,266
Wallace	*	*	491,950	92,238	342,577	49,746
All Kansas	161,291,641	56,502,133	208,847,539	60,796,746	241,100,072	48,750,913

* No report.
Compiled from the *Kansas Auditor's Report*, 1871–1890.

TABLE 24.—ASSESSED VALUATION OF RAILROAD OPERATING PROPERTY
IN SELECTED KANSAS COUNTIES, 1871–1890

Country	1871	1875	1880	1885	1887	1890
Leavenworth	126,414	636,298	647,298	790,170	784,215	1,223,352
Shawnee	*	396,163	579,045	849,665	1,171,349	1,212,684
Pottawatomie	*	270,208	347,113	466,593	479,646	477,715
Dickinson	175,622	168,683	207,415	225,518	360,967	1,023,172
Ottawa	*	*	168,127	183,034	258,339	448,427
Saline	200,003	149,412	400,150	437,017	704,080	986,474
Jewell	*	*	90,731	152,205	153,167	441,474
Lincoln	*	*	*	*	80,839	211,853
Rice	*	82,772	185,474	418,430	710,800	922,663
Russell	*	143,072	276,633	296,937	305,898	459,513
Trego	*	*	262,069	299,262	616,626	309,172
Ford	*	159,429	329,113	533,643	413,867	742,158
Wallace	*	*	*	*	281,141	325,121
All Kansas	3,242,298	12,277,931	20,547,803	30,367,817	41,222,605	57,866,232

* No report.
Compiled from the *Kansas Auditor's Report*, 1871–1890.

to it. Saline County's high percentage of personalty probably represented cattle and other property connected with the shipping business. By 1875 more western counties had been organized, the personal property ratio in Saline County had dropped (the cattle business was moving on), and Ottawa County and two of the three eastern counties had failed to recover fully from the depression of the early seventies produced by panic, drought, and grasshoppers. By 1885 property valuations were reflecting agricultural potentiality, strategic location, and the beginnings of the new boom. Leavenworth County valuations had found their level. So had those of Pottawatomie County. Of the eastern counties only Shawnee reflected the boom in the making. The counties without railroad facilities still lagged, though each either had or was about to get its feeder. Jewell County—which had obtained its road in the late seventies and was a good corn and wheat producer—had pulled ahead. The western counties in general but the Kansas Pacific counties in particular reflected the major growth of the 1885–1887 period and the drastic curtailment after 1887.

Valuations of railroad operating property reveal two things in addition to these patterns. First, the through-line counties held property yielding more revenue than did the feeder counties. Second, when considered in connection with increases in population and with general valuations, the addition of or a major increase in railroad property on the tax roll was common during the boom years in general and during the boom periods of the individual counties in particular. The data for Saline County, Rice County, and Lincoln County reveal this characteristic especially clearly. Third, sometimes during and almost always after the first years and again in 1890 railroad property constituted a large proportion of personal property, especially in the western counties. In these areas the Kansas Pacific counties and the Santa Fe counties con-

TABLE 25.—TOTAL INDEBTEDNESS OF SELECTED KANSAS COUNTIES, 1874–1890

County	1874	1878	1880	1882	1884	1886	1888	1890
Leavenworth	$1,037,193	$1,812,432	$1,272,846	$1,370,311	$1,621,401	$1,664,521	$2,069,334	$2,041,174
Shawnee	298,000	714,848	600,200	590,540	596,137	668,595	899,070	969,825
Pottawatomie		149,687	162,106	154,840	152,746	172,805	178,860	181,610
Dickinson	64,200	135,235	123,218	98,450	54,845	115,645	541,163	505,821
Ottawa	3,871	113,917	155,649	148,658	158,278	146,335	278,680	227,325
Saline	126,113	155,006	134,329	136,733	125,083	215,600	524,794	527,450
Jewell	9,538	48,263	95,067	112,015	120,745	117,133	195,900	190,200
Lincoln	28,121	36,750	55,300	49,900	47,739	48,821	228,304	295,604
Rice	13,822	63,415	115,050	132,925	128,562	161,278	433,604	461,869
Russell	*	42,496	29,580	37,189	36,437	34,340	71,964	74,184
Trego		*	6,570	8,277	12,400	12,588	44,500	52,400
Ford	13,991	38,587	62,078	63,241	66,194	116,416	336,454	383,809
Wallace	*	*	*	*	*	*	8,929	55,339
All Kansas	6,650,915	13,473,198	13,998,604	14,472,020	15,951,930	17,779,299	31,107,647	37,119,977

* No report.
Compiled from the *Kansas Auditor's Report*, 1874–1890.

TABLE 26.—BONDED INDEBTEDNESS OF SELECTED KANSAS COUNTIES, 1874–1890

County	1874	1878	1880	1882	1884	1886	1888	1890
Leavenworth	$ 881,350	$ 1,491,561	$ 1,272,846	$ 1,148,074	$ 1,157,539	$ 1,664,396	$ 1,994,044	$ 2,041,174
Shawnee	298,000	714,087	600,200	590,540	596,137	668,595	899,070	969,825
Pottawatomie		149,687	161,277	154,840	152,200	171,805	178,860	181,610
Dickinson	61,200	135,235	123,218	98,450	54,845	115,645	540,615	505,821
Ottawa		108,329	153,975	148,658	158,278	146,335	278,680	227,325
Saline	117,500	150,985	129,945	136,195	123,670	215,600	521,900	527,450
Jewell		41,392	91,325	104,125	117,745	108,400	195,900	190,200
Lincoln	24,000	35,600	53,362	37,272	34,012	48,821	228,304	295,604
Rice	8,000	62,434	114,874	131,732	128,562	161,278	433,604	461,269
Russell	*	38,130	23,300	35,370	36,437	34,340	71,964	74,184
Trego	*	*	*	*	12,400	12,300	44,500	52,400
Ford	10,000	30,000	37,932	52,277	51,734	103,251	257,890	335,610
Wallace	*	*	*	*	*	*		41,350
All Kansas	6,125,053	12,730,032	13,497,710	13,791,993	15,091,900	17,376,367	30,126,813	36,316,338

* No report.
Compiled from the *Kansas Auditor's Report*, 1874–1890.

sistently held the advantage over their neighbors. They always had a high railroad valuation to tax.

The amount and character of local indebtedness is the third major consideration in identifying the patterns of settlement and the financial characteristics and ambitions of the counties during the period of growth. Tables 25 and 26 show both the total and the bonded debt of each county. Although the data on debt structure do not follow as clear a pattern as do the data on population and valuation, some useful conclusions can be drawn from them. Most counties in their early years tended to operate on a floating debt, in the form of county warrants. This debt reflected the operating expenses of the newly organized county government before tax revenues were collected and can be taken only as an indication of the magnitude of initial expenses. No useful pattern appears except the usual east to west and railroad and non-railroad distinctions.

Bonded debt is a much better indicator of long-term expenditures and ambitions and, perhaps, of difficulty in the collection of taxes. Here some conclusions are possible. First, and of fundamental importance, all the counties without land-grant railroads except one refrained from bonding themselves heavily in the early years (Lincoln County is the exception and it had Kansas Pacific lands in its southern half). Railroad land-grant counties all bonded early. Whether this reflected an inability to collect needed taxes from railroad lands, an attempt to tax them heavily before private lands reached the tax rolls, or some other characteristic that such counties had in common remains to be seen. Second, counties that eventually got feeders (often by bonding themselves to aid construction) were still far less deeply in debt than were the railroad land-grant counties. Third, in the early years the Kansas Pacific counties bonded sooner and at higher levels than did the Santa Fe counties, but by 1890 the Santa Fe counties were among the most heavily bonded in the group studied. And, fourth, most counties bonded heavily in the boom periods—the eastern and central counties in both such periods and the western counties only in the second.

Finally, no summary of settlement and financial history can provide a basis for selection without reference to levels of taxation. These data are given in Table 27. The levels of tax levies coincide almost exactly with the decade, railroad, and land-quality patterns that have been established. They also reflect the booms, the levels of the eighties far surpassing those of the seventies in all counties. There is one significant variation in the pattern. The Santa Fe counties levied higher taxes and levied them sooner than did either the non-railroad counties or the Kansas Pacific counties in their decade belt. The non-railroad counties did not levy as high taxes nor increase them as much in the eighties as did most of the railroad counties. The Kansas Pacific counties eventually raised taxes to a high level but were relatively restrained in the early years. This is of considerable significance in view of the early date

TABLE 27.—TAXES LEVIED IN SELECTED KANSAS COUNTIES, 1874–1891

County	1874	1876	1880	1885	1887	1891
Leavenworth	$ 295,321	$ 284,566	$ 199,832	$ 375,691	$ 415,850	$ 365,270
Shawnee	217,353	208,013	230,599	392,133	626,386	529,213
Pottawatomie	67,121	76,610	82,889	*	135,260†	133,080
Dickinson	62,005	77,402	100,422	131,536	184,808	215,137
Ottawa	25,425	34,625	63,983	118,014	111,129	112,136
Saline	81,477	92,559	99,745	121,653	169,256	160,511
Jewell	16,920	22,924	41,634	106,504	122,111	144,841
Lincoln	8,283	14,576	26,760	42,682	66,208	70,038
Rice	24,986	39,803	49,650	95,202	142,726	137,375
Russell	*	21,871	34,617	42,964	71,610	43,394
Trego	*	*	18,626	25,596	55,188†	31,176
Ford	14,230	17,327	42,282	56,899	89,759‡	96,879
Wallace	*	*	*	*	24,547	22,358
All Kansas	4,179,469	4,325,184	5,699,408	8,890,024	11,496,708	12,683,649

*No report.
† 1886. No report for 1887 or 1888.
‡ 1888. No report for 1886 or 1887.
Compiled from the *Kansas Auditor's Report*, 1874–1891.

at which the Santa Fe received patents for most of its lands. Clearly the counties derived considerable revenue from them.

From the foregoing general survey of topography, availability of water, and history of settlement, and the tabular summaries of population and financial growth, a group of general characteristics common to specific types of counties becomes clear. For this study of the effects of unpatented railroad land on the tax base, the counties selected must be counties having not only unpatented land but certain other attributes in common with other counties in their class. Significant variations would make any county an even more special case than, by its very nature, it already is. The characteristics they have in common are these: (1) They are Kansas Pacific counties, the Santa Fe counties being disqualified because that road received most of its land patents early. (2) They are not counties with high agricultural potentials; only one of the Kansas Pacific counties west of the Flint Hills included in the selection (Dickinson County) was such a county. (3) They fall into the decade belt classifications applicable to the period after 1868 and to the western two-thirds of the state, the problem of nontaxability having been confined to the period between 1868 and 1886. (4) They had a higher proportion of foreign-born inhabitants and more numerous immigrant colonies than did their neighbors. (5) Their taxable valuations were a direct reflection of their position in the decade belts and tended to be higher than those of non-railroad counties but lower than those of Santa Fe counties. (6) They tended to bond themselves earlier than either non-railroad or Santa Fe counties. And (7) their tax levies reflected the booms and were also, usually, higher than non-railroad counties but lower than Santa Fe counties in the same decade belt.

The positions of the three counties chosen for the detailed study of railroad land taxability—Saline, Russell, and Trego—are shown on the map on page 160. Each has its own peculiarities but each also has a modicum of the seven characteristics listed above. From the analysis of these three counties precise information concerning the relationship of railroad land to other lands on the tax roll can be obtained and, if the selections are valid, some tentative generalizations can be made.

Saline County lies in the decade belt settled most heavily between 1868 and 1878, the central third of the state. A number of factors, however, encouraged earlier attempts to establish settlements there: its strategic location, the establishment of the Butterfield Overland Mail route, the confluence of three rivers within a twelve-mile area, and the salt springs located in the bowl-like depression in the northeastern sections of the area. The first such attempt was made in 1856 by a group led by Preston B. Plumb, but came to nothing. Shortly thereafter, in 1857, the Buchanan Town Company tried to establish a settlement at the mouth of the Solomon River, in the northeastern corner of the area. This also failed. The third attempt was a success. Under the leadership of William A. Phillips, Salina was established in 1858 and the next year the county was organized.[17] The government townships included within its boundaries are shown on the map of the county included in the Appendix (page 253).

Because the county attracted a number of settlers in these early years and because of the saline lands within its boundaries, numerous individuals and the State of Kansas had established claims to land there before lands were withdrawn for the railroad and long before the railroad reached Salina, in 1867. These claims fell into two categories: (1) lands taken up by settlers, usually along one of the three rivers, near Salina, or on one of the many creeks; and (2) Kansas state saline lands. The railroad lands lost to prior claimants were located along the Smoky Hill in Township 16, Range 3, in Townships 16, 15, and 14 of Range 2, and in Township 13, Range 1; along the Saline in Township 13, Ranges 3 and 4; along the Solomon in Township 13, Range 1; around Salina in Township 14, Range 3; and along the creeks in the eastern half of the county. Altogether the railroad lost 35,680 acres and ultimately received only a little more than 42 per cent of what would have been, had all the grant accrued, almost half of the county's area. Of the portion of the grant lost in place—nearly 16 per cent—a large part was river bottom lands and the finely textured claypan wheat soils of the east-central portion of the county. The best land was gone before the railroad arrived.

Saline County's inrush of population came after the railroad. Salina soon became a cowtown, but by 1874 the business had moved west. The county grew most rapidly in the seventies, though it did suffer a setback, as did most of Kansas, in the panic and drought years of the early part of the decade. By 1883 all land was reportedly engrossed and prices had risen to twenty dollars an acre and higher. By this time also

[17] Andreas, *History of Kansas*, 1:696–709.

Salina had embarked on its campaign to obtain additional railroad connections and was fast becoming a grain-shipping center. A branch line up the Solomon was built in 1878. Another branch south to McPherson and still another through the southern part of the county and eastward to Topeka was built in the eighties. Eventually the county was served by all four of the major Kansas lines.[18]

The alienation of title into taxable form of all the land in Saline County is shown on the twenty township-diagrams of this county included in the Appendix (pages 254–273). The data, which are mapped cumulatively at five-year intervals, show the gradual filling in of taxable title over the twenty-five-year period between 1872 and 1897. All railroad lands, whether title had passed to the company or not, became taxable in 1887.

The history of taxability in Saline County pictured in these diagrams demonstrates conclusively that: (1) The railroad held no patents for its lands in the county in 1872, at the time of the Prescott decision, nor when, shortly thereafter, William A. Phillips, Salina's founder and representative of the First Congressional District of Kansas, joined Lorenzo Crounse of Nebraska in the first major legislative effort to make the lands taxable though unpatented. (2) By 1877 the road held patents to the bulk of its lands in the county, and to all except 32,160 acres by 1882, when John A. Anderson, Phillips' successor, was waging his taxation campaign. (3) It was not until 1887, when legislation made unpatented lands taxable, that all railroad lands in the county reached the tax roll. Some of these lands had remained off the tax roll for twenty years.

However, the alienation history demonstrates just as conclusively that: (1) In 1872, when the first effort was made to render all 194,720 acres of railroad land taxable, only 66,960 acres of private land had reached the rolls. (2) Even in 1877, when the road held patents to the bulk of its lands, only about half of the non-railroad lands had been alienated. (3) By 1882 the gap was closing. Untaxable private land was becoming more rare. The ratio of taxable railroad lands to the total land-tax base was approaching the ratio of total railroad lands to the total area of the county. (4) When the act of 1886 made all the road's lands taxable, the position of 1882 was nearly restored. Again the ratio of taxable railroad lands to total taxable lands was greater than the ratio of total railroad lands to the total area of the county. This graphic picture, which also, incidentally, shows the movement of titles from northeast to southwest and the gradualness with which private lands in the southern (the Swedish) parts of the county reached private hands, is summarized more precisely in Table 28.

---

[18] *Ibid.*; "Along the Line of the Kansas Pacific Railway in Western Kansas in 1870," in the *Kansas Historical Quarterly*, 19:207–211 (May, 1951); Federal Writers' Project, *Guide to Salina*, 20–36; *Directory of Saline County*, 1882; *Directory of Saline County*, 1885, p. 5; *Saline County Journal*, October 24, 1878, May 17, 1883, March 6, 1884.

TABLE 28.—TAXABLE LANDS IN SALINE COUNTY, KANSAS, 1872–1897

Total area of county, 460,800 acres
Total lands lost in place, 35,680 acres
Percentage of total area accruing to railroad, 42.26

Year	Kansas Pacific Railroad Land			Privately Entered Land		
	Acres in County	Per Cent of the Taxable Land		Acres in County	Railroad Land Lost in Place	Acres of All Taxable Land
		in County	in Grant Area*			
1872				66,960	24,290	66,960
1877	144,760	51.26	64.24	137,620	30,520	282,380
1882	162,560	44.81	54.40	200,240	32,000	362,800
1887	194,720	45.36	53.56	234,580	32,880	429,300
1892	194,720	43.53	51.24	251,560	33,120	446,280
1897	194,720	43.16	50.79	256,400	33,880	451,120

* In this county a great deal of railroad land was lost to prior claimants. In order to avoid distortion, therefore, the half-area character of the grant is maintained for each year for which the percentages are calculated by doubling the acreage of all lands lost in place and actually entered and subtracting that figure from the total of the privately entered land for that year.

Computed from plattings of the Saline County numerical indices, Office of the Saline County Register of Deeds, Salina, Kansas.

If what the tax-exemption feature accomplished, as every critic from Lorenzo Crounse to Edward Rosewater insisted, was to shift the bulk of the tax burden to settlers on non-railroad lands—that is, onto privately entered land—while the majority of railroad acres escaped, the ratios shown in this table are especially illuminating. According to the critics' formula, the liability of non-railroad lands should have exceeded that of the granted lands. Actually, at all save the first of the five-year intervals shown, the proportion of the potential railroad land that was taxable was greater than the proportion of the potential privately entered land that was taxable. In other words, a greater proportion of railroad land than of privately entered land was on the tax roll.

What the years between demonstrate can be stated only generally, but they also tend to reflect the same degree of tax liability for railroad lands. The first Saline County railroad patents, issued in June of 1874, were among the first to be issued to the company from lists it had submitted in 1870 and 1872. Major patents were also issued in 1875 and 1877, building up the railroad's liability to the 144,760 acres appearing in the table for 1877. In 1881 most of the additional patents showing up in the table for 1882 were issued. The equivalent of two more sections was patented in 1883. From 1883 until 1890 the road was under patent suspension. In 1890 all the remaining lands were patented. These may have been among the "nearly a million acres" selected but not patented that land agent McAllaster had complained of to the Pacific Railway Commission in 1887.[19] Furthermore, of the 234,580 acres

[19] See above, p. 99.

privately held in 1887, over ten thousand acres had been patented in the preceding two years, reflecting the pressures created by the boom of the eighties. Even so, it would appear that by 1886 the roads' lands were liable for not much more than forty-two per cent of the taxable acreage in the county, or perhaps even a little less. By 1886, in other words, the railroad lands had become liable for a proportion of taxes just about equal to, or possibly a little less than, the proportion of the county's acreage held by the railroad. The act of 1886 temporarily reversed the situation by putting railroad lands in a position where they were again liable for a large proportion of total taxes, a position they had held during most of the period under review.

For Saline County, then, the nontaxability feature of the unpatented railroad lands was a valid issue in 1872 and 1873, when there were few taxable acres of any kind in the county and no taxable railroad acres at all. From 1874 until 1882 the railroad lands were liable for more than their proportion of taxes. After 1882, with the land boom on the one hand and the suspension of patenting by the General Land Office on the other, the gap was gradually closed—until the tax law of 1886 opened it once more. Perhaps this explains why Congressman Phillips was an ardent backer of the tax legislation proposed in 1873 and 1875 but perfunctory in his support after 1876. Perhaps it also explains why Anderson's opponents in the district argued that his tax campaign of 1880 and 1882 was a ruse, designed to win votes without harming anyone.[20]

Russell County lies in the western half of the 1868–1878 decade belt, in the central third of the state. This position gave its settlement a transitional quality, gave the county a role in the expansion of the seventies and at the same time gave it a role in the boom and bust of the eighties. Its settlement history spans a longer period than does that of either of the two other Kansas counties studied in detail.

The early history of the county is closely associated with grazing. Cattle were being ranged in the area before 1870, and the first permanent resident, H. E. Mathews, who filed at the mouth of Coal Creek in the southwest corner of the area in 1869, was a cattle trader. In the spring of 1870 a number of similar claims were filed in the northeast corner, along Wolf Creek. In 1871 the first town settlements were made. In April of that year the Northwestern Colony, a group of about sixty families from Ripon, Wisconsin, purchased the east half of section 27 in Township 13, Range 14, from the Kansas Pacific and established the town of Russell, on the railroad at the site of a company well and water tower. At about the same time the partnership of Harbaugh and Cobbet purchased section 31 in Township 13, Range 12, and founded Bunker Hill, also a railroad water stop. A locating committee sent from Berea, Ohio, inspected the townsite in 1871, but although the committee remained, the colony never came. Both Russell and Bunker Hill served

[20] See above, pp. 29–30, 33, 35, 37, 41.

during their first years as suppliers of grazers, and agricultural settlements built up only gradually. Neither town became a major shipping point. Instead the cattle were driven a little over thirty miles east to Ellsworth for shipment. On the basis of this early, largely nonagricultural, settlement the county was organized in 1872.[21] The government townships included in its boundaries and the route of the railroad are shown on the map of the county included in the Appendix (page 274).

The county was settled almost entirely with reference to flowing water, alluvial soils, and towns on the railroad. The road lost only one quarter section in place, the southwest quarter of section 9 in Township 11, Range 11, one of the early claims on Wolf Creek. Public lands were first taken up (1) on the Saline River, which crosses the county through the townships numbered 12; (2) on the Smoky Hill, which in Range 15 is in Township 15, and in Ranges 14 through 11 is in the high-numbered sections of the townships numbered 14; and (3) on the feeder creeks. They were also engrossed early around Russell and Bunker Hill. The northern tier of townships, watered largely by Wolf Creek and its tributaries, remained important for grazing, were the slowest to be settled, and boomed only after the establishment of Lucas (in Township 11, Range 11) and the building of the railroad branch line from Lincoln to Colby, begun by the Union Pacific in 1887. The influence of the towns was pronounced. Russell early became a mild "boomer's town," and after the drought of 1872–1875 and the Panic of '73 had subsided, undertook to attract settlement by advertising. The chief medium, the *Russell Record,* began continuous publication in November of 1875 and boomed the county regularly thereafter. Besides land, it advertised small lignite deposits along the Smoky Hill and "an abundance" of sandstone suitable for building.

The population of the county grew steadily, though not spectacularly, until 1880, by which time all but the very poorest of government land had been filed upon. Then a period of drought forced retrenchment, and growth ceased until 1883, when Russell County, like the rest of western Kansas, experienced a boom in settlement and land values. Despite the booming of Russell County as a wheat area, however, the danger of drought, the difficulties of getting water for domestic use, and the considerable quantity of rough land along the streams combined to make it an important grazing and woolgrowing county rather than a grain producer throughout this period.[22]

[21] *Report of the Kansas State Board of Agriculture,* 1875, pp. 397–398; Andreas, *History of Kansas,* 2:1283–1289; *Russell Record,* March 27, July 13, 1876, December 18, 1897, January 29, 1914; *Junction City Union,* May 13, 1871; *Manhattan Nationalist,* September 17, 1875; *Lucas Independent,* September 30, 1937; Kansas Pacific, *Annual Report,* 1871, p. 12.

[22] These articles appeared regularly in the *Russell Record.* Some of the best examples are those in the issues for April 23, 1875, May 25 and June 1, 1876 ("Facts for Immigrants" section), November 22, 1877, May 2, 1878, August 10, 1880, February 28 and July 17, 1884, March 10 and May 19, 1887. See also

The taxability history of Russell County is pictured in the twenty-four township-diagrams of this county included in the Appendix (pages 179–299). One important reservation must be made about these data, the most unreliable of any on the six counties studied in detail. Analysis of the other counties is based on the county title records. In Russell County these records are not organized in usable form. Thus it is necessary to rely upon the county lists of lands entered. Two things make these sources less reliable than the title records. First, certificates of location and other forms of nontaxable instrument are often recorded without effective identification. Second, it is the date on the instrument rather than the date on which it was filed that is recorded. These two characteristics make it necessary (1) to treat all instruments not clearly identified by other entries as alienations of taxable title and (2) to consider the date on the instrument the date of its application, even though—as revealed by its late position on the entry lists—it was not filed until ten years or longer thereafter. Both these rules of evidence tend to skew the results in the same direction: they show more public lands taxable and at an earlier date than would otherwise be the case. All errors in these records are, by definition, in favor of government land. There is no way to make an accurate estimate of the degree of this skew. It could be as high as twenty or as low as five per cent in any given year. Because it cannot be determined precisely it is ignored in the plats and in the tabulations. It could have no greater effect on the conclusions than to change the chronology somewhat.

The history of taxability in Russell County shows, first of all, that much of the government land was homesteaded, since the heavy settlement of the seventies did not show up in the alienation records until the early eighties and thereafter. It also shows clearly that railroad patenting followed the settlement pattern; the road selected first the lands along the river bottoms and creeks and the areas around the towns and later the other lands. It further demonstrates that: (1) No railroad land in Russell County had been patented by 1872, which fits the pattern set in Saline County and which could be assumed in any event simply because no patents for railroad land (even land selected as early as 1870) were issued by the General Land Office until 1873 and 1874. (2) Unlike the railroad lands in Saline County, those in Russell County were not patented in bulk by 1877. Only about fifteen per cent had been patented by that time. (3) Even as late as 1882 large areas of railroad land—apparently as much as seventy-five per cent—remained unpatented. (4) The bulk of Kansas Pacific land in the county re-

Andreas, *History of Kansas*, 2:1284–1289; *Report of the Kansas State Board of Agriculture*, 1886, pp. 370, 496–498; *Russell Independent*, August 6, 1880; *Dorrance Nugget*, September 29, 1887; *Line Etchings: A Trip from the Missouri River to the Rocky Mountains via the Kansas Pacific Railway* (Woodward, Tierman and Hale, St. Louis, 1875), 16–17; Stephen F. Smart, *Colorado Tourist and Illustrated Guide via the Golden Belt Route . . . to the Rocky Mountain Resorts* (Ramsey, Millett and Hudson, Kansas City, 1879), 46, 59.

TABLE 29.—TAXABLE LANDS IN RUSSELL COUNTY, KANSAS, 1872–1897

Total area of county, 576,000 acres
Total lands lost in place, 160 acres
Percentage of total area accruing to railroad, 49.97

Year	Kansas Pacific Railroad Lands		Acres of Privately Entered Land	Acres of All Taxable Land
	Acres in County	Per Cent of the Taxable Land		
1872			640	640
1877	42,000	73.27	15,320	57,320
1882	62,920	47.79	68,740	131,660
1887	287,840	62.97	169,290	457,130
1892	287,840	57.20	215,340	503,180
1897	287,840	55.08	234,720	522,560

Computed from plattings of "Lands Entered in Russell County" (a ledger of entries reported to the county officers from the local land office), in the Country Commissioners' Office, and spot-checked against the assessment rolls, in the County Treasurer's Office, Russell, Kansas. Russell County's numerical indices are not usable for these purposes.

mained off the tax rolls until 1887. The alienation of government land was slow at first but was accelerated later, especially after 1877. Only the equivalent of one section had been alienated by 1872, and even five years later only about five per cent had been alienated. By 1882, however, more than twenty-five per cent of these lands had reached private hands, and in 1887 nearly sixty per cent appears on the plats. The alienation of Russell County lands is summarized in Table 29.

For all practical purposes the railroad eventually got half the area of Russell County. Thus, if railroad lands were to bear a share of liability proportionate to the total acreage of such lands in the county, they should have constituted half the taxable lands. In two of the six years tabulated they were liable for a smaller proportion than that: in 1872, when they constituted less than the one section required to balance private land, and in 1882, when they constituted 4,820 acres less or something over forty-seven per cent. In the other four years tabulated they were liable for more—in one year almost fifty per cent more—than their proportionate share.

Data for the intervening years yields comparable results. The first of the railroad land patents in this county, like those in Saline County, were issued in 1874. The first patent was for 24,480 acres, almost twice the total area of alienated private land three years later. In 1875 another ten thousand acres of railroad land was patented. Subsequent patenting of smaller lots brought the total to 42,000 acres in 1877 and to 48,800 acres in 1878. Further patenting in 1881 brought it to the 1882 level. The only other patent issued before 1891 was issued just before the General Land Office applied the suspension of 1883. This brought the total to 68,040 acres. Taxation of most of the remaining railroad lands had to await the tax law of 1886, since patenting was not resumed in the county until 1891, after the ban was lifted.

The pattern that developed here was similar to that in Saline County, but much more pronounced. No patents had issued when the tax fight was begun, but in Russell County this was of little moment, since almost no land was yet taxable. The issue, in terms of proportions of taxability, disappeared in 1874—further documentation for the suggested explanation of Congressman Phillips' growing coolness on the tax law. By 1877 the railroad lands were liable for more than seventy-two per cent of the taxable acres in the county. During the next few years that percentage dwindled rapidly. By 1880 it had dropped almost to fifty per cent, at which point Congressman Anderson began his campaign. Then gradually—here the trend was much more marked than in Saline County—an imbalance developed. The small patent of 1883, made when the Land Office suspension of 1882 was temporarily lifted, was not adequate to restore the balance. After 1883, with the county booming and the Land Office withholding railroad patents, the imbalance became so pronounced that by 1886, when the tax law was passed, the proportion of railroad lands was reduced to about thirty-four per cent of all taxable acres.

The only qualification of the above analysis that the unreliability of the data for this county requires is that, on the basis of comparative taxable acreage, railroad lands were probably liable for a somewhat greater proportion of total taxes throughout the period after 1874, and that the period when they were liable for less than fifty per cent was probably somewhat shorter than five years.[23] It is unlikely that the data could be skewed enough to invalidate the general conclusion that at the end of the first fourteen years and just before the passage of the 1886 tax law, railroad lands in this county were liable for less than what the reformers called "their share" of land taxes.

Trego County lies on the eastern edge of the 1878–1888 decade belt. It played no real part during the first two periods of Kansas settlement, and its first permanent settler did not arrive until sometime in 1876 or 1877. In 1878 and 1879 the county experienced a quick boom, connected with the colonizing schemes of Warren, Keeney and Company of

[23] The data on percentages of taxable land have been checked against some of Russell County's extant tax rolls. In 1876, according to tax rolls for the entire county, 10,080 acres of government land were taxable and accounted for only 17.5 per cent of the roll. In 1882, only 66,800 government acres (68,740 in the table) were on the rolls and accounted for only 46.7 per cent (52.21 in the table). In 1886, according to these same all-county rolls, railroad lands were liable for 45.97 per cent of the area taxed, not the 34 per cent shown by the ledger of land entries.

In all cases checked, government land shows a *reduction* of two to five thousand acres, representing six to nearly fifteen percentage points. In the same cases railroad land shows an *increase* of up to eighty thousand acres, representing six to fifteen percentage points. Thus all skewing inherent in the data is undoubtedly prejudicial to the estimate of the railroad position and tends to reduce sharply the railroad proportion pictured as compared to the railroad proportion actually collected upon by the county treasurer.

Chicago. Then it steadily lost population until the mid-eighties, when it felt the effects of the all-Kansas boom, only to slump again after 1888.

The early history of settlement in the county is inseparable from the story of the Warren, Keeney and Company promotion, one of the most ambitious colonization schemes undertaken in Kansas Pacific territory. Apparently the two promoters, John M. Keeney and Henry A. Warren, proposed to settle the county with Chicago workingmen.[24] The first arrangement, made with the road late in 1877, included the purchase of the railroad lands in two entire townships. Of the thirty-six sections . involved only twelve seem to have been paid for at the outset. The other twenty-four were mortgaged to the Kansas Pacific and Andrew Crawford. There also seems to have been some agreement that Warren and Keeney would sell some of the other railroad lands in the county on some kind of commission. During the course of the promotion the Chicago firm handled all or parts of a hundred and twenty sections in eleven of the twenty-five townships in the county. A total of about fifty thousand acres was sold by the company at prices ranging from $2.50 to $5.00 an acre. Keeney came to the county, homesteaded a quarter section next to the townsite, and seemingly acted as the company agent on the scene. It is not clear whether Warren came or not. In 1881 and 1882 Keeney deeded all the unsold lands to Warren, who made his last sales in 1885. The Union Pacific, as successor to the Kansas Pacific, recovered and sold the rest.[25]

The population attracted by the promotion was sufficient to permit organization of the county in June of 1879. The county seat was the promoters' town, WaKeeney. The townships included, the route of the railroad, and the location of the lands outside the grant area are shown on the map of the county included in the Appendix (page 300). The townships involved in the promotion were the elevens in Ranges 23, 24, and 25; the twelves in Ranges 22, 23, 24, and 25; the thirteens in Ranges 22, 23, and 24; and fourteen in Range 22.

Spectacular as was the Warren and Keeney promotion, it was short-lived. The promoters claimed too much and charged too little. In their literature they talked more of crops than of livestock, professed to have control of most of the county, and required only five hundred dollars capital of a prospective settler. There was a heavy influx of settlers in 1878 and an even heavier one the next year. Homesteaders took up government land and by late summer of 1879 a population in excess of thirty-five hundred was claimed. Then the bottom dropped out. In two successive seasons the crop failed. By 1881 fewer than fifteen hundred people remained, and they had turned to raising livestock for a liveli-

[24] *Joliet Republican* (Illinois), reprinted in the *Russell Record*, November 22, 1877.

[25] Summarized from the deed records in the Office of the Trego County Register of Deeds, Washington, Kansas.

hood. The new boom brought another influx of settlers, however; by 1885 the population was approaching two thousand, and two years later it exceeded three thousand. Then the boom busted. The census of 1890 tabulated only 2,536 inhabitants.[26] The taxability history of Trego County is shown in the twenty-four township-diagrams for this county included in the Appendix (pages 301–325). Though a taxable title had passed to a section of railroad land and to a quarter-section of government land by 1877, neither was taxed. There was no county organization to levy the tax. The first tax in the county was levied in 1880.

The history of taxability in Trego County reveals most strikingly the influence of the railroad, the promoters, and the water courses—in the order named—on passage of title. The area along the road produced the earliest titles, first for the railroad lands, then for the government lands. The earliest and most concentrated of these railroad-oriented titles were those issued in the area of Warren and Keeney's promotional activities. The effects of the rivers and creeks—the Saline in the northern sections of the townships numbered 11; Big Creek in Township 13 of Ranges 21 and 22 and in Township 12 of Ranges 23, 24, and 25; and the Smoky Hill on the line between Townships 14 and 15 across the county—is perhaps most evident in the rapid alienation of the lands along the Smoky Hill, despite their distance from the railroad. Second only to the factors determining the location of earliest settlement was the impact of the tax law of 1886. The county was blanketed with taxable railroad land at a time when very little government land had passed into private hands.

The picture presented by these plats also demonstrates that: (1) There was no tax problem in Trego County during the first period of congressional agitation over the nontaxability feature of the railroad grants. There was not even a taxing jurisdiction until 1879. (2) From 1877 onward, railroad land in most areas of the county, but especially in the WaKeeney area, made up the bulk of the taxable land, even as late as 1897. And (3) although the railroad lands comprised only about forty-seven per cent of the area of the county, they were liable for far more than forty-seven per cent of the taxes throughout the period.

These relationships are shown with more precision in Table 30. The ratio of taxable railroad lands to all taxable lands in the county ranged from as high as over eighty-two per cent in 1887 to a low of about sixty per cent in 1897. Within the limits of the grant the range was from about eighty-four per cent in 1887 to about sixty-three in 1897.

[26] Andreas, *History of Kansas*, 2:1295–1297; Warren, Keeney and Company, *Trego County, Kansas: Its Soil and Climate, passim; Rush County Progress* (Kansas), January 11, 1878; *Topeka Commonwealth*, May 5, 1879, February 5, 1880; *Wa-Keeney World*, December 22, 1879; *Western Kansas World*, June 2, 1888.

TABLE 30.—TAXABLE LANDS IN TREGO COUNTY, KANSAS, 1872–1897

Total area of county, 576,000 acres
Total area outside grant limits, 32,080 acres
Percentage of total area accruing to railroad, 47.43

Year	Kansas Pacific Railroad Land			Privately Entered Land		
	Acres in County	Per Cent of the Taxable Land		in County	Acres Outside Grant	Acres of All Taxable Land
		in County	in Grant Area			
1872						
1877	640	80.00	80.00	160		800
1882	41,520	77.75	77.99	11,880	160	53,400
1887	273,200	82.41	84.24	58,320	7,200	331,520
1892	273,200	67.03	70.35	134,360	19,240	407,560
1897	273,200	59.77	63.22	183,860	24,920	457,060

Computed from plattings of the Trego County numerical indices, Office of the Trego County Register of Deeds, Wakeeney, Kansas.

Consideration of the years between serves only to confirm the conclusion that the railroad lands constituted the great majority of the taxable lands in the county. Aside from the single section in Township 12, Range 21, selected by the road in 1874, no land in the county was selected by or patented to it until 1878. The first general selection was made in May of 1878 and patented a year later. It became taxable as soon as the county was organized. No land in the county was patented to the railroad in the years 1882–1887, but 7,360 acres were selected and final receipts issued in 1883 and 1884. No more selections were made until 1890, when the Land Office suspension was lifted. These selected lands, under rulings made in the seventies by both state and federal courts, were taxable, however, from the date the final receipt was issued by the local land office. Thus by 1884 a total of 48,880 acres of railroad land was taxable. Yet in 1885 only 37,240 acres of government land were in private hands. By 1886 the total had risen to approximately 48,000 acres. If the tax law had not been passed in 1886, private lands in the county as a whole would have been subject the next year to a larger proportion of taxes than railroad lands. The tax law placed the railroad lands far in the lead again and kept them there. Most railroad lands in the county were not finally patented until the middle and late nineties and some not until after the turn of the century.

The story of Trego County, although it includes none of the problems of the early seventies encountered by the other two, does have two characteristics similar to those of Russell and Saline counties. First, in all the counties studied the percentage of taxable acres for which the railroad was liable was higher, during the greater part of the period studied, than the percentage of the total area held by it. In Trego County rail-road land never quite lost this edge over government land. Second, in the years from 1882 to 1886, during the boom period and the period of Land Office suspensions, that ratio dropped steadily. By 1886 it was approaching, in Trego County as in Saline County, a level commensurate with railroad land holdings. It was then that congressional action re-turned the lands to the position they had held in the first years. For Trego County this was a costly position, for it was not until after the turn of the century that enough government land had been alienated to restore the ratio to the levels of the mid-eighties. In the meantime the railroad and the buyers of its lands had to meet a disproportionate part of the costs of debt payment and retrenchment that came in the wake of the busted boom.

The survey of growth in thirteen Kansas counties and of taxability in three of those counties shows clearly that the range of experience was broad, that taxability reflected characteristics of growth, and that each county was distinctive and had its own problems. The validity of any general conclusions about the relationship of railroad lands to the tax rolls rests upon the validity of the selections made for study, selections that, for the analysis of taxability, are two steps removed from the experience of the state as a whole. Only to the extent that the three counties finally selected are not unrepresentative of the experience of the whole area in which the taxability question had application—the Kansas Pacific land grant—is their taxability history likewise not un-representative. The general conclusions drawn here are subject to that reservation.

The history of taxability fits the decade belts; that is, a county clearly within one or the other belt had few problems deriving from the tax exemption of railroad land. In only one of the counties studied, the transitional county, Russell, was the taxability of railroad land seriously curtailed in relation to other lands. Once the initial pre-patent period had passed, the county in the 1868–1878 belt, Saline County, possessed a percentage of taxable railroad land either in excess of or roughly equivalent to the ratio of total railroad acres to the total area of the county. The county in the 1878–1888 decade belt, Trego County, was not occupied in the pre-patent period of the early seventies. Once settlement did begin railroad lands were always liable for a proportion of taxes at least equivalent to the ratio of the road's total prospective holdings to the total area of the county, and they were often liable for a far greater proportion. It was in Russell County, the county in which most government lands were alienated between 1881 and 1886, that a prob-lem developed. The county's pre-patent experience was exactly like that of Saline County except that, because settlement was only beginning, the problem was not great. By 1877 the ratios were comparable to those that existed in Trego County five years later. The appearance of either a Saline or a Trego County pattern was forestalled when, with the cessation of patenting in the years 1883 to 1891, there developed in Russell County the only serious railroad patent lag found.

The implications of these patterns for the western two-thirds of the Kansas Pacific land-grant area can be derived from the summary presented in Table 31. Of the total 1,612,800 acres included in the survey,

TABLE 31.—SUMMARY OF TAXABLE LANDS IN SELECTED KANSAS
COUNTIES, 1872–1897

Total area surveyed, 1,612,800 acres
Total area outside grant limits, 32,080 acres
Total lands lost in place, 35,840 acres
Percentage of total area accruing to railroad, 46.86

| Year | Railroad Land | | | Privately Entered Land | | | |
| | Acres | Per Cent of the Taxable Land | | Acres | Outside Grant Area | Lost in Place | Acres of All Taxable Land |
		in Entire Area	in Grant Area*				
1872				67,600		24,290	67,600
1877	187,400	55.04	67.13	153,100		30,680	340,500
1882	267,000	48.74	55.24	280,860	160	32,160	547,860
1887	755,760	62.05	66.02	462,190	7,200	33,040	1,217,950
1892	755,760	55.69	59.41	601,260	19,240	33,280	1,357,020
1897	755,760	52.82	56.50	674,980	24,920	34,040	1,430,740

* These data include those for Saline County, where a great deal of railroad land was lost to prior claimants. For that county the half-area character of the grant is maintained for each year for which the percentages are calculated by doubling the acreage of all lands lost in place and actually entered and subtracting that figure from the total of privately entered land for that year.

only 67,600 acres, all privately held, had been alienated by 1872. In 1877, of a total of 340,500 acres alienated, 187,400, or about fifty-five per cent, were railroad lands. By 1882 the ratio had dropped to just under forty-nine per cent. The tax legislation of 1886 brought the ratio up to sixty-two per cent, the highest up to that time. Between 1887 and 1897, with the continued alienation of government lands, the ratio gradually dropped until it was just under fifty-three per cent in the last year cited. If analysis is limited to the area of the railroad land grant, the preponderance of taxable railroad lands is even more pronounced, ranging from sixty-seven per cent in 1877 down to fifty-five per cent in 1882, rising again to sixty-six per cent in 1887, and thereafter declining once more, to fifty-six and a half per cent ten years later. Over the whole period, then, exclusive of the 1872 pre-patent period, railroad land in the three counties as a whole was consistently liable for more than a proportionate share of land taxes.

Most of the causes of the two instances of lapse or tendency toward lapse in this general pattern of preponderant railroad liability have already been brought out. Railroad selections made between 1870 and 1873 were not finally acted upon by the General Land Office until 1873 and 1874. This is part of the explanation for the pre-patent tax lag of the early seventies. The movement in the direction of lapse (and, in the case of Russell County, the actual lapse) in preponderant liability in the eighties is partly explained by two factors: (1) Beginning in 1882 the Land Office suspended patenting to the Kansas Pacific and, except for a small acreage patented when the suspension was temporarily lifted in 1883, did not return to patenting until 1890. (2) The land boom of the eighties, creating a great demand for government land and a high rate of alienation, forced it on the tax rolls at such a rate as to close the gap quickly. In neither instance was the railroad itself entirely responsible.

The railroad must not be absolved of responsibility, however. There can be no doubt that throughout the period the company consistently postponed selections as a matter of policy, a policy designed to keep railroad acres untaxable, just as government acres were, until the purchaser had made his payments, until the deed was due. Land Agent McAllaster told the Pacific Railway Commission that this was his policy;[27] in at least two instances a local railroad land agent advertised the nontaxability feature as part of the sales conditions;[28] and the title records utilized in this study demonstrate the workings of the program.

Though no exact tabulation of the relationship of date on patent to date on deed has been made, in most cases in which land was deeded before 1883 the deed was dated only a few months or a year after the patent. This means that five- or seven-year sales contracts had run the greater part of their term before the buyer had to pay taxes on the land, though he was in possession of it. In these circumstances the buyer of railroad land was in precisely the same position as his neighbor on government land—no better and no worse. In practice, clearly, the policy of the railroad, because it had overestimated the market for land or because of other miscalculations, did not work perfectly. The taxability plats show that railroad land was regularly patented in advance of the alienation of government land. Still, whatever its shortcomings, there is little question that the aim of the railroad was both to equalize the tax burden of the buyers of its land and to save itself tax expenses on uncontracted lands.

After 1883, when patents were no longer issuing, the contract for a deed or the deed itself was often dated before the patent. This was a result of Land Office suspensions which had placed the road in the position of a short seller in a bull market, of having promised to deliver at a later date something which changing conditions made undeliverable.

[27] See above, p. 112.
[28] *Russell Record*, May 26, 1876, November 22, 1877.

Thus, the Kansas Pacific was eventually caught in its own selection-sales program. Had it not sold in this way, however, railroad lands unpatented before 1883 would necessarily have remained unoccupied until 1891 or even later—unless, of course, the road had applied for and received its patents in the western third of the state before there were either markets for them or county organizations to tax them. It would have had to anticipate both the patent lag and the land boom. Apparently the Santa Fe had done something closely approximating this and as a consequence had experienced both the economic penalties and the political rewards of its policies. Clearly the Kansas Pacific had not done it and as a consequence experienced the economic rewards and the political penalties of its actions.

Nine

The Nebraska Tax Base

NEBRASKA, like Kansas, is large in area and varied in topography. Its settlement, though never as extensive, as rapid, or as spectacular as that of Kansas, was complicated by many of the same factors. At its greatest extent Nebraska stretches more than four hundred and twenty-five miles westward from the Missouri, which forms its eastern and part of its northern boundary. At its widest point on the north-south axis it measures just over two hundred miles. Almost fifty million acres lie within its borders. The two most striking geographical features, the Platte River Valley and the Sandhills, are supplemented by a large number of topographical variants and soils associations.

These characteristics make the selection of areas for study as serious a problem in the analysis of the tax base of Nebraska as it is in the analysis of the tax base of Kansas, but two others, one growing out of special topographical attributes and the other out of a political characteristic, make it doubly so. First, largely because of topography the movement and density of population in Nebraska does not fall into the relatively neat decade belts discernible in Kansas. Second, whereas Kansas counties are reasonably equivalent in area, Nebraska counties vary greatly in size—ranging from Cherry County with almost four million acres to the many eastern counties with less than a quarter million. This makes trustworthy comparisons difficult.

The topographical character of Nebraska is dominated by one feature above all others, the Platte River. Sweeping in gentle curves across the entire east-west length of the state, its valley provides some of the most fertile and most valuable soils in the area and its waters effectively divide the state. Thus there are two Nebraskas, one north of the river and one south of it.

Beyond this general division of the state an additional breakdown into at least nineteen topographic regions is possible, but for present purposes a simpler classification into seven general categories is used.[1]

---

[1] The data on physiographic regions and water resources summarized below are drawn from the following: Nebraska State Planning Board, *Water Resources of Nebraska* (Lincoln, December, 1936) ; United States Department of Agriculture, Soil Conservation Service, "Soil Conservation Problem Area Map—Nebraska" (February, 1949; revised December, 1952) ; John Franklin Gaines, Geographic Study of the Nebraska Loess Plain (unpublished doctoral thesis, University of Nebraska, 1951) ; and H. E. Bradford and G. A. Spidel, *Nebraska: Its Geography and Agriculture* (Macmillan Company, New York, 1931). For a convenient summary see James C. Olson, *History of Nebraska* (University of Nebraska Press, Lincoln, 1955), 7–14. Land-use classifications referred to here, as

(1) North of the Platte and stretching westward from the Missouri for more than half the length of the state, but narrowing toward the river in the west, is the large Loess Hills region. Its eastern third is underlain with glacial drift, which crops out in the stream beds. The region's principal soils are the Moody associations in the east and the Holdrege-Hall associations in the west, both good corn producers whenever adequate moisture is available. (2) West and north of the Loess Hills region is the Sandhills region, beginning near the point at which the Missouri meets the state boundary and extending to within fifty miles of the western border. There are also small outliers of this region south of the Platte, principally in the corner formed by the Kansas and Colorado boundaries. This area, the largest single topographic region and soils association in Nebraska, is composed of dune sands laid down in Pleistocene time by prevailing westerlies blowing over the Arikaree sandstone formation. Most of the hills are grass-covered and stable, but some are still on the move. When properly managed these soils can be used for grazing and for small grains, though insufficient rainfall is often a problem in the western sections. (3) The third general topographic region really consists of a number of small intrusions in the Sandhills north of the Platte and in the low plains south of the river. These are the Nebraska outcroppings of the Dakota, Wyoming, and Colorado tablelands. Part of this region is north of the Sandhills in a series of tables and plains associated with the Niobrara River; part is west of the Sandhills in the Pine Ridge and Box Butte tables north of the Platte; part is in the Wildcat and Cheyenne tables between the north and south branches of the Platte; and part is in the Perkins Table south of the River. The soils are of two general types: Boyd-Holt (a mixture of crop and range soils) in the Niobrara-associated tables and Rosebud-Bridgeport (mixed-farming soils but for the lack of rainfall) in the western tablelands. (4) In the southeastern section of the state lies the Drift Hills region. The deep prairie soils of this area, like those of the Glaciated Region of northeastern Kansas, which they much resemble, are excellent corn producers. (5) West of the Drift Hills, stretching all the way to the Perkins Table near the Colorado line and lying between the Platte River on the north and the Republican River on the south, is the second and largest region south of the Platte, the Loess Plain. These are the excellent Crete, Hastings, Holdrege, and Hall soils that are also present in Kansas, top producers of corn and wheat when adequate moisture is available.

These five regions—the Loess Hills, the Sandhills, the Tablelands, the Drift Hills, and the Loess Plain—are separated, sometimes subdivided and broken by two other types of topography which, because of their wide distribution and large acreages, are considered regions. (6) The more important of the two is the Alluvial Lowland region, of which there are three chief and several lesser components. The Platte Valley

in Kansas, are for modern crops and modern practices and are therefore only indicative of potentials for nineteenth-century agriculture.

Lowland, dividing the state into roughly three-quarters north of it and one-quarter south of it, is the largest, richest, most varied, and most significant. Second only to the Platte Valley is the valley of the Republican, running eastward through the southern tier of counties to within a hundred miles of the eastern boundary, then turning south into Kansas. Closely associated with the alluvial bottom lands of this valley are the Republican Breaks, hilly and broken topography useful in many sections chiefly for pasturage. The third major component of this region is the Missouri River Bottomland, on the eastern border of the state. The lesser components include the relatively narrow valleys of the Niobrara, Elkhorn, and Loup rivers north of the Platte and such minor streams as the Big and Little Blue and the Big and Little Nemaha south of it. Much of this Alluvial Lowland region is productive and well-watered, although, like most alluvial soils, these vary widely in texture and fertility. (7) The designation for the second minor region—the Badlands—is a catchall for the various isolated sections of badlands in the western portions of the state. These include the White River and Hat Creek basins in the northwestern corner; Pine Ridge, lying just south of the basins; and the Wildcat Range, on the western border between the forks of the Platte. These areas are used for pasturage.

The factors governing the availability of water in Nebraska are as varied as the topographic regions they affect. Average annual precipitation lines, unlike those in Kansas, are serpentine. The traditional twenty-inch line enters the state from the south just west of the center and the hundredth meridian. Then it swings abruptly westward, touches the Colorado line only about twenty miles north of the Kansas boundary, leaves the Colorado line again, and trends sharply eastward almost to the hundredth meridian at its crossing of the Platte. North of the Platte, in the Sandhills, it trends northwestward to within fifty miles of the northern border, then swings eastward once more to leave the state just thirty miles west of the hundredth meridian. The area east of the thirty-inch line comprises two small regions close to the eastern boundary of the state. Thus the western sections of the state, save only the westward loop associated with the Colorado border and the Loess Plain, are beyond the boundary line of safe standard agricultural practices, and the remainder of the state, except for two small regions on the eastern border, is in the transition zone—where slight variations can produce crop failures or bumper yields. The mean annual precipitation for the state as a whole is approximately twenty-three inches. Data on evapotranspiration are not available. Most of the runoff is carried by the Platte and its chief tributaries, the Loup and the Elkhorn. These streams and their feeders carry well over eighty per cent of the water. The Niobrara on the northern border (tributary to the Missouri) and the Republican, Little Blue, and Big Blue in the south (all tributary to the Kaw) carry most of the rest. Supplies of ground water, especially in the western sections, are immense. The Sandhills region is a vast underground storage reservoir, the most significant in the entire plains area. Deep wells usually yield high returns in the western two-thirds of the state.

The effect of these topographical characteristics and water resources was to produce three general areas that seemed suited to the traditional agricultural practices the settlers of Nebraska brought with them. The eastern quarter of the state seemed but a continuation of the corn belt and was sought as such. The remainder of the Platte Valley and the Loess Hills regions, west of the hundredth meridian and south of the Sandhills, was viewed as chancy corn but likely wheat country. The area south of the Platte, almost all of it, seemed possible corn and sure wheat country and only trial and error—and rainfall—was to determine how far westward this prospective extension of the corn belt would reach. Most of the rest of the state—sandhills, tablelands, and badlands—was left to the grazers until, in the optimistic aura of the eighties and again under the liberalized land laws of the early twentieth century, farmers at last pushed into it.

Thus the settlement of Nebraska occurred not in decade belts, as in Kansas, but in an expanding right triangle, with its base moving westward on the southern boundary and its perpendicular leg remaining nearly stationary close to the Missouri. If the decades used for Kansas are applied here this characteristic is clearly revealed. Until 1868 settlement was confined almost exclusively to the eastern quarter of the state, with a heavier concentration south of the Platte and a westward-extending spearhead along it. Between 1868 and 1878 the supremacy of the country south of the Platte became even more pronounced as the southern point of the triangle crept toward the Colorado line. In the next decade the country south of the Platte was gradually filled, as was the eastern and central Platte Valley. Also, after 1883, settlement began breaking the triangle as it pushed at the edges of the Sandhills and further westward along the Platte. Throughout the period many points, especially in eastern Nebraska, began to develop urban concentrations, usually small but always significant, and in the eighties Nebraska was the scene of some of the most spectacular of the urban booms. Omaha, Fremont, Nebraska City, Lincoln, Beatrice, Grand Island, Hastings, Kearney, and North Platte were among the most important of these "gems of the prairie." In the late nineties and the twentieth century there was significant settlement in the northwestern extremities of the state and the Sandhills, though there were major concentrations of rural population only in the western Platte Valley.[2]

For the most part the effect of railroad development in Nebraska was to intensify the expanding triangle pattern. The early influence of the

[2] The characteristic pattern of settlement is described by most and recognized by some writers of Nebraska history, but see especially Lloyd Bernard Sellin, The Settlement of Nebraska to 1880 (unpublished master's thesis, University of California at Los Angeles, 1940); Olson, History of Nebraska, chapters 8, 13, 14, 16, and 20; and above all, the maps on pages 38, 89, 110, 146, 147, 168, and 274 of Addison E. Sheldon's Land Systems and Land Policies in Nebraska (Publications of the Nebraska State Historical Society, vol. 22, Lincoln, 1936).

Missouri and the Platte was supplemented, not altered. Five railroads, only four of them actually located in the state, received federal land grants. Three of these grants were small and four were confined to the eastern sections. The Sioux City and Pacific, which built westward from the Missouri north of the Platte, received only about thirty-eight thousand acres. The St. Joseph and Denver City entered Nebraska from Kansas about ninety miles west of the Missouri, trended northwestward to Hastings on the Burlington, then northward to Grand Island on the Union Pacific. It eventually received about three hundred and eighty thousand acres. The Union Pacific, Central Branch, though a Kansas road, also received about twenty-five hundred acres in the extreme southeastern corner of Nebraska.

The two chief recipients of federal grants were the Burlington and the Union Pacific. The Burlington, whose original line entered the state at Plattsmouth on the Missouri, traversed the eastern half of the area south of the Platte, and joined the Union Pacific about a hundred and sixty miles west of the boundary. But because of its close proximity to the Union Pacific, whose claim was a prior one, the Burlington received only a portion of its land in the region south of the Platte. Instead, a ruling was obtained which allowed the company to select "outside" lands north of the Platte in the eastern third of the state. Nearly half of the Burlington's grant of more than two and a quarter million acres was thus separated from the company's line. The Union Pacific, which followed the Platte Valley all the way across the state, was granted the alternate sections in a forty-mile strip along its entire length. It eventually received over four and a quarter million acres in Nebraska. Seven more railroads, built as feeders to the main-line routes, and two of the federal-grant roads also received small acreages in eastern Nebraska from the state's grant for internal improvements. Of the total of more than eight million acres of railroad land in the state over half was located in the eastern third and the rest was in or near the valley of the Platte. Railroad land-promotion and colonization schemes, conducted principally by the Burlington and the Union Pacific, thus served to strengthen the trends in settlement already determined by geography. Furthermore, when the Burlington built on west through the Republican Valley its transportation facilities, townsite promotions, and general advertising served the same end.[3]

[3] Land-grant acreages are summarized in the following: Federal Coordinator of Transportation, *Public Aids to Transportation* (4 vols., Government Printing Office, Washington, 1938–1940), 2:107–114; Sheldon, *Land Systems and Land Policies in Nebraska*, 87n; and Olson, *History of Nebraska*, 170.

The colonization practices of Nebraska railroads have been described by Richard C. Overton, in his *Burlington West: A Colonization History of the Burlington Railroad* (Harvard University Press, Cambridge, 1941), and by Morris Nelson Spencer, in his The Union Pacific's Utilization of Its Land Grant, with Emphasis on its Colonization Program (unpublished doctoral thesis, University of Nebraska, 1950). See also Ray H. Mattison, "The Burlington Tax Controversy in Nebraska over the Federal Land Grants," in *Nebraska History*, 28:110–131 (April, 1947), and Thomas M. Davis, "Building the Burlington through Nebraska—A Summary View," *ibid.*, 30:317–347 (December, 1949).

For purposes of this study the land system operating in Nebraska, like that in Kansas, can be divided into two periods. From the organization of the territory until 1863 land was alienated under the old preëmption and cash sales system, which was supplemented in 1862 and 1864 by the railroad land-grant and agricultural-college scrip systems. After the war the homestead system and the state land system became important and the cash sales system was all but abandoned. In Nebraska, as in Kansas, then, the eastern parts of the state were alienated by quick-title methods entailing only short delay, and the central and western sections by the more time-consuming process-title methods adopted in 1862 and thereafter. In Nebraska, however, because the territory was comparatively slow to develop (the population of Kansas was three times that of Nebraska in 1870) and because early settlement was concentrated in the extreme east, the process-title system was by far the more widely applied. In addition, because settlement continued to lag in Nebraska, a third method, the enlarged homestead, became very important in the twentieth century. This last method had no application in the period under review, however.[4]

Nebraska attracted even larger numbers of immigrants, both as individuals and as colonies, than did Kansas. As early as 1870, even before the first major influx of population into Nebraska and before the intensive colonization campaigns were begun by the railroads of the two states, a full quarter of Nebraska's population was foreign-born, as against only about thirteen per cent of the population of Kansas. Ten years later Nebraska was still far ahead of Kansas in number of foreign-born, the respective percentages at that time being twenty-one and a half and eleven, and in 1890 the percentage of foreign-born in Nebraska was still almost double that in Kansas.[5] Immigrant colonies were established throughout much of the eastern half of Nebraska, chiefly German, Swedish, and Irish groups, but also substantial settlements of Bohemians, English, Danes, Russians, and many others. Religious groups, most of them also made up of immigrants, established many settlements. Most of the Scandinavian groups were Lutheran, but Catholic groups, Protestant sects, and Mennonites also established colonies.[6]

To these demographic and economic factors Nebraska added another, one that has important implications for this analysis. When a few settlers arrived in an area it organized its counties on a piecemeal, temporary basis and thereafter changed boundaries often and without dis-

---

[4] Sheldon, *Land Systems and Land Policies in Nebraska, passim,* especially chapters 2, 3, 5, and 6.

[5] See Tables 22 and 33.

[6] Summarized in Olson's *History of Nebraska,* 179–180. See also Gustav Adolph Bade, A History of the Dutch Settlement in Lancaster County, Nebraska (unpublished master's thesis, University of Nebraska, 1938) ; Joseph Alexis, "Swedes in Nebraska," in the *Publications of the Nebraska State Historical Society,* 19:78–85 (Lincoln, 1919) ; and Sarka B. Hrbkora, "Bohemians in Nebraska," *ibid.,* 19:141–147.

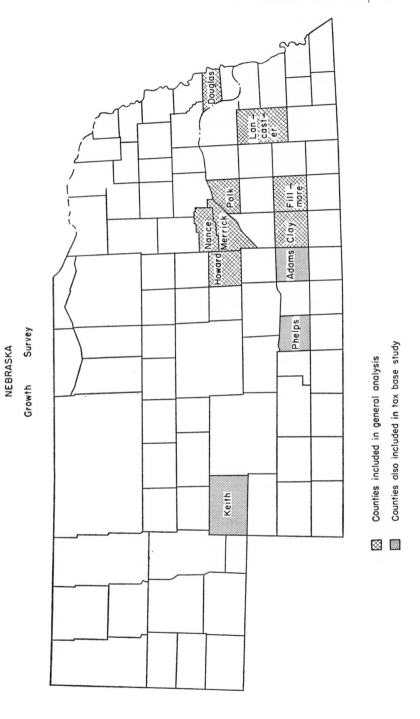

NEBRASKA
Growth Survey

Counties included in general analysis

Counties also included in tax base study

cernible pattern. The areas of some counties were reduced and new ones were added where population became concentrated, but vast areas in the less heavily populated sections were left within the borders of a single county. Whereas Kansas had developed a pattern of counties roughly equivalent in area, Nebraska's counties varied greatly.[7] This makes it nearly impossible to select counties comparable in size which meet at least a modicum of the other requirements dictated by the patterns of topography, transportation, and population.

The eleven counties selected for analysis of the growth of Nebraska represent, so far as possible, the same variables as the Kansas counties selected for this purpose. The location of the selections is shown on the accompanying map. The concentration of these counties in the southern and eastern half of the state is dictated both by the demographic characteristics of the state and by the question at issue—the effects of non-patenting on the relation of railroad lands to other lands and to the tax roll. In the western sections settlement came too late and the political subdivisions vary too much to affect the results greatly or to permit valid comparison with eastern counties.

In general the growth characteristics of the counties selected coincide with those of the state as a whole, already summarized.[8] In addition, of course, each county had its own distinctive attributes. The two eastern-most counties were both influenced by urban development. Douglas County was the entrepôt of Nebraska throughout the period. Omaha, after a combination of territorial politics and natural advantages gave it victory in its contest with Bellevue, became the territorial capital, the first state capital, and the eastern terminus of the transcontinental. It developed into Nebraska's metropolis, and Douglas County grew in importance. Located in the well-watered east, across the peninsula formed by the Platte just before it joins the Missouri, and endowed with the rich Tama-Marshall associations of corn-producing soils, Douglas became a prime agricultural county. By 1880 land was selling for more

[7] This variety and its evolution are pictured effectively in the organization maps on pages 162 and 163 of Olson's *History of Nebraska*. See also the map of Nebraska in the present volume.

[8] The general descriptions that follow are based principally on the pertinent sections of A. T. Andreas, comp., *History of the State of Nebraska, Containing a Full Account of Its Growth . . . Description of Its Counties, Cities, Towns, and Villages . . .* (Western Historical Company, Chicago, 1882); Harrison Johnson, *Johnson's History of Nebraska* (Henry Gibson, Omaha, 1880); J. Sterling Morton, *Illustrated History of Nebraska* (3 vols., Jacob North and Company, Lincoln, 1905–1913); J. Sterling Morton and Albert Watkins, *History of Nebraska from the Earliest Explorations of the Transmississippi Region* (rev. ed., Western Publishing and Engraving Company, Lincoln, 1918); Grant Lee Shumway, *History of Western Nebraska and Its People* (Western Publishing and Engraving Company, Lincoln, 1921); Addison E. Sheldon, *Nebraska: The Land and the People* (3 vols., Lewis Publishing Company, Chicago, 1931); and Olson, *History of Nebraska*. Additional sources particularly applicable to specific counties are cited in connection with the material they document.

than ten dollars an acre. Though Omaha lost the capital before 1870, it gained industry, notably meatpacking, and it was the eastern terminus of a number of the feeder railroads built in the period. Partly because of its entrepôt character it was greatly influenced by the boom of the eighties. Its population doubled between 1880 and 1885 and doubled again in the next two years. Douglas County had a large foreign-born population, but few organized colonies. The largest element was the Bohemian, which was attracted to Omaha and South Omaha by the packing industry, especially after 1885.[9]

Lancaster County is located in the Drift Hills and is possessed of about one-third Tama-Marshall and two-thirds Carrington-Clyde soils. In 1867 Lincoln was made the state capital, but the county never lost its position as one of the most important agricultural areas in the state. Only Saunders County, immediately to the north, outranked it as a corn producer. The county is watered chiefly by the minor tributaries of the Platte, but its southeastern corner is in the drainage basin of the Nemaha. The original Burlington line crossed the county from northeast to southwest. Other railroads, the Atchison and Nebraska and the Nebraska Railway, were built in the seventies and eventually Lincoln itself was served by every major railroad in Nebraska. Lincoln, like Omaha, was influenced by the urban boom of the eighties, though growth was never as spectacular. Lancaster County was settled in part by immigrant colonies, most important of which were a number of large Mennonite settlements south and west of Lincoln.[10]

The eastern Loess Plain region is represented here by two adjacent counties, Fillmore and Clay. Both are covered almost completely by the Crete-Hastings soils, which are good corn and wheat producers but which (because the imperviousness of the underlying claypan subjects them to drought at times) occasionally suffer corn crop failures. Both counties are in the 26–28 inch rainfall belts and both are drained by the branches of the Blue. Both were also crossed in the northern tiers of townships by the original Burlington line. Fillmore County, the easternmost, was the first to attain a large population, but was not organized until 1873. It enjoys the distinction, rare in southeastern Nebraska, of having avoided a county-seat fight. Geneva has been from the first the county capital. In the seventies and eighties the Burlington, in the process of what contemporaries called "system-perfecting," added sev-

[9] Hrbkora, "Bohemians in Nebraska," in the *Publications of the Nebraska State Historical Society*, 19:143. See also the *Omaha Weekly Bee*, July 22, 1885, and January 18, 1888.

[10] Edwin August Schaad, An Agricultural History of Lancaster County, 1856 to 1900 (unpublished master's thesis, University of Nebraska, 1939); Bade, A History of the Dutch Settlement in Lancaster County, Nebraska. See also Abram W. Epp, An Economic History of Agriculture in Gage County, Nebraska (unpublished master's thesis, University of Nebraska, 1937), and the *Omaha Weekly Bee*, January 18, 1888.

eral branch lines. In Fillmore County this process added one east-west and three north-south feeders to the railroad property in the county. Significant numbers of Germans settled there. Clay County was organized in 1871, and almost immediately there began a series of county-seat fights that is classic in southeastern Nebraska. At the end of the decade, after moving from town to town, the county capital finally came to rest at a new town in the exact center of the county, the only solution that could end the travels of the county offices. Clay County, too, was criss-crossed by Burlington feeders, three in all, but it also had another road, the St. Joseph and Grand Island (originally the St. Joseph and Denver City), which crossed the southwestern half of the county. Clay County's foreign-born element was large, the most significant group being a large Mennonite colony that settled in the vicinity of Sutton in the mid-seventies. Both these counties were considered good agricultural areas by the early comers and both grew rapidly. In neither of them did a prairie metropolis develop.[11]

Adams County, just west of Clay, is a third Loess Plain county. It differs markedly from its eastern neighbors, however. Though the eastern third of it is covered by the Crete-Hastings soils associations, it also includes a large concentration of Holdrege-Hall soils in its central sections and a substantial group of Sandhills outliers in the northwest and west. This variety of soils makes it a mixed-farming area. It lies almost wholly in the 24–26 inch rainfall belt and is drained by the Little Blue in the south, the Big Blue in the northeast, and the Platte in the northwest. The county was first organized in 1871 with its county seat at Juniata, but it too experienced a protracted fight over the county seat, which ended only with the victory of Hastings in 1878. On the original Burlington line and soon to be crossed by the St. Joseph and Denver City, but also close enough to the Union Pacific to fall partly within its land-grant limits, the county included some of the granted lands of all three roads. It was also the locus of further railroad construction. The Burlington left the original line at Hastings to build south to the Republican Valley, and the later Holdrege cutoff to Denver also started in the county. Two other minor feeders were built in the eighties. In the early years the population of Adams County included a large percentage of foreign-born, largely because the original settlement at Hastings was established by Englishmen, but the county never

---

[11] G. R. McKeith, comp., *Pioneer Stories of the Pioneers of Fillmore and Adjoining Counties* (*Fillmore County News*, Exeter, 1915) ; *The Centennial Sketch of Clay County, Nebraska* (E. H. White, Publisher, Sutton, 1876; reprinted by the *Clay County Sun*, Clay Center, 1933) ; *Biographical and Historical Memoirs of Adams, Clay, Hall, and Hamilton Counties, Nebraska* (Goodspeed Publishing Company, Chicago, 1890), 341–411; George L. Burr and O. O. Buck, eds., *History of Hamilton and Clay Counties* (S. J. Clarke, Chicago, 1921) ; *Pioneer Story of Harvard* (reprinted from a pamphlet published at Harvard in 1894 by the *Clay County Sun*, Clay Center, 1933) ; *Nebraska Herald* (Omaha), September 15, 1870; *Omaha Weekly Bee*, February 27, 1878.

attracted the large immigrant population that counties both east and west of it did. The county seat did become a prairie metropolis. It was one of the more noteworthy of the boom towns of the eighties.[12]

Three counties—Polk, Merrick, and Phelps—represent the sections of the state lying in the Platte Valley and east of the hundredth meridian. All three of these counties figured in the cattle trade prior to 1870, and unmarketable beef continued to be wintered in them until agricultural settlement drove the grazers further west. Polk County, the easternmost of the group, is divided about equally between the Loess Plain and the Alluvial Lowland. Its drainage is divided in the same fashion. The southern half of the county is tributary to the Big Blue and the northern half to the Platte. The county was delimited in 1865 but was not organized until 1870. Because it lies on the south side of the Platte, and the Union Pacific was built on the north bank, the county had no railroad until Union Pacific system-perfecting reached it in the late seventies with the David City-Central City feeder. The Burlington also built a short feeder between Fairmont in Fillmore County and Stromsburg, on the Union Pacific branch, in Polk County. The county attracted large numbers of immigrants, notably Swedes, who settled around Stromsburg in the late seventies.

Merrick County, contiguous to Polk County at its eastern point but almost twice as large, lies north of the Platte and is traversed by the main line of the Union Pacific. Its soils are a combination of alluvium and loess-capped terraces and a long arm of Sandhills outliers that crosses the county in the northwest. The Platte drains all but its northwest corner. The county was organized in 1858. The only railroad constructed in it besides the Union Pacific was the Burlington's Loup River branch, built in the eighties to tap the Sandhills cattle country. There were no important immigrant settlements in the county.

Phelps County, the farthest west of this group, lies just halfway between the ninety-ninth and hundredth meridian on the south side of the Platte. The soils are, for the most part, the Holdrege-Hall associations of the Loess Plain, but there is some Platte River alluvium along the northern edge of the county, and the breaks of the Republican touch a section of the southwest corner. There is also an area of Sandhills outliers in the northeast, close to the Platte. The northern half of the county is in the Platte River drainage basin and the southern half in the Republican. The twenty-four inch rainfall line crosses the county from southeast to northwest. Wheat is the principal crop. Like Polk County, Phelps County had no railroad in the early years, but did include a large area of Union Pacific land. The first railroad came to the county

---

[12] William R. Burton and David J. Lewis, eds., *Past and Present of Adams County, Nebraska* (2 vols., S. J. Clarke, Chicago, 1916) ; *A Descriptive Review of Adams County, Nebraska* . . . (Pagett and Stinchcomb, Omaha, 1879) ; *The Leading Cities of Southeastern Nebraska* . . . (H. B. Reed and Company, Chicago, 1883), 29–58.

in the early eighties, when the Burlington built the Holdrege cutoff to Denver. The Burlington's branch line to Grant was built through the county in the mid-eighties. Though the county was organized in 1873, there was no major settlement in it until 1879, when the Union Pacific colonized a large group of Swedes there. The greatest upsurge in population came even later, with the completion of the Holdrege cutoff. Phelps County, like Polk County, became an area of concentrated Swedish settlement.[13]

The central agricultural area lying north of the Platte is represented by Howard and Nance counties, both principally in the Loess Hills region and the drainage basin of the Loup River. The southeast corner of each county lies in the Platte drainage basin. The soils are mostly the Holdrege-Hall associations, but Sandhills outliers occur in south-central Nance and southeastern Howard County. Loup River bottom lands are also present in both counties. The Loup crosses Nance County from southwest to northeast. The North Loup enters Howard County near the northwest corner and in the east-central portion of the county meets the Middle Loup, which flows in from the southwest.

Nance County has a special history of land alienation. Until 1876 it was the Pawnee Indian Reservation. Under the provisions of the cession made in that year the lands were sold, on three years credit, in a public sale held in 1878 and a series of private sales lasting until 1884. Many large purchases were made by speculators, who thus created a "speculators' desert" which apparently retarded the growth of the county.[14] There was no major influx of foreign-born in Nance County.

Howard County, like Adams County, was blanketed by two railroad grants—ninety thousand acres of Union Pacific lands in the south and sixty thousand acres of Burlington "outside" lands in the north. Unlike its southern counterpart, however, Howard County was not on a trunk line, and it was not until the early eighties that a Union Pacific branch from Grand Island crossed it. Another Union Pacific branch was built up the Middle Loup, and the Burlington's Greeley extension was put through the northeast corner. Howard County received large numbers of German settlers and smaller numbers of other groups. In 1880 one of every three of the county's residents was foreign-born.[15]

Keith County is a part of the Platte Valley cattle country tributary to the Union Pacific. It lies west of the hundred and first meridian in the 18–20 inch rainfall belt and is crossed by both branches of the Platte. The northern third of the county is in the Sandhills. The central section, between the branches of the river, is part of the Rosebud-Bridge-

[13] Alexis, "Swedes in Nebraska," in the *Publications of the Nebraska State Historical Society*, 19:81–85; Norbert R. Mahnken, "Early Nebraska Markets for Texas Cattle," in *Nebraska History*, 26:3–25, 91–103 (March, June, 1945).

[14] See Sheldon, *Land Systems and Land Policies in Nebraska*, 21, 204–206.

[15] *Official State Atlas of Nebraska* (Evarts and Kirk, Philadelphia, 1885), 37, and Table 33 below, p. 202.

port soils association and is a lowland. The area south of the rivers is part of the Perkins Table. Cattle were probably ranged in the area even before the Union Pacific was built, and the period before 1873 saw the gradual establishment of ranches to the west, in the Nebraska panhandle, under the protection of Fort Laramie and to the east around the forks of the Platte and near Fort McPherson. These years also saw the removal of the Indian threat from the Republican Valley and the movement westward of agricultural settlement in the country south of the Platte. This process of trail-clearing in the west and trail-closing in the east conspired, after 1874, to make Ogallala, the county seat, the logical successor of Schuyler and Kearney as Nebraska's principal cattle-shipping point. Ogallala held its position until the end of the long drive in the mid-eighties. The cattlemen eventually purchased some railroad land and fenced both railroad and government property, so that Ogallala continued to serve as a market long after the flow of Texas cattle had ceased.[16] Large acreages of the government land in the county were not alienated until the Kinkaid enlarged homestead system was applied to Nebraska in the twentieth century.

Though these descriptions of the land and water resources, transportation facilities, and population components of the eleven counties demonstrate clearly that each county is a unique entity, they also help to substantiate some of the general trends characteristic of the state as a whole. First, and perhaps most important, the development of the group of counties selected was lopsided. The eastern counties (with the exception of Nance) were settled, organized, and farmed first and continued to maintain their relative lead. After statehood was achieved the promising agricultural counties south of the Platte were quickly organized and settlement moved rapidly westward. The settlement of those in the valley of the Platte was hardly keeping pace, and those in the area north of the river were lagging behind. In the eighties the counties south of the Platte were populated, and intensive settlement moved on west along the Platte and north to the Sandhills, but the predominance of grazing in Keith County, the westernmost of the group, continued throughout the nineteenth and in the twentieth century. As late as 1883 the land department of the Union Pacific considered its lands west of Phelps County best suited for grazing.[17] Sec-

[16] Mahnken, "Early Nebraska Markets for Texas Cattle," in *Nebraska History*, 26:3–25, 91–103, and his "Ogallala—Nebraska's Cowboy Capital," *ibid.*, 28:85–109 (June, 1947). See also William D. Aeschbacher's "Development of the Sandhill Lake Country," *ibid.*, 27:205–221 (September, 1946), and his "Development of Cattle Raising in the Sandhills," *ibid.*, 28:41–64 (March, 1947).

[17] *Central and Western Nebraska and the Experiences of Its Stock Growers* (Union Pacific Land Department, Omaha, 1883); J. T. Allan, comp., *Nebraska and Its Settlers: What They Have Done and How They Do It* (Union Pacific Land Department, Omaha, 1883), largely confined to Hall and Howard counties; J. T. Allan, comp., *Creameries and Dairying in Nebraska: What Has Been Done and What May Be Done* (Union Pacific Land Department, Omaha, 1883).

TABLE 32.—POPULATION OF SELECTED NEBRASKA COUNTIES, 1870–1890

County	1870	1875	1880	1882	1885	1890
Douglas	19,982	24,698	37,645	*	72,658	158,008
Lancaster	7,074	15,224	28,090	*	39,719	76,395
Polk	136	3,031	6,846	6,942	9,805	10,817
Fillmore	238	4,731	10,204	9,750	13,452	16,022
Clay	54	4,183	11,294	10,259	14,201	16,310
Adams	19	3,093	10,235	8,580	18,004	24,203
Phelps	*	110	2,447	2,922	6,073	9,869
Nance	*	*	1,212	1,419	3,829	5,773
Merrick	557	3,101	5,341	5,041	7,223	8,758
Howard	*	1,708	4,391	*	7,129	9,430
Keith	*	124	194	115	1,140	2,556
All Nebraska	122,993	247,280	452,402	*	740,645	1,058,910

* No report.
Compiled from the *Biennial Report of the Secretary of State of the State of Nebraska*, 1886, pages 190–192, and from the *Compendium of the Eleventh Census of the United States* (1890), Part I, pages 496–497.

ond, railroad development in the area, especially of feeder lines, proceeded at a rapid pace south of the Platte until every county described had at least two and many had four or five. Feeders north of the Platte, many of which were designed to tap the cattle country, came later and were fewer. Third, and finally, as in Nebraska as a whole, the role of the prairie metropolis in county development, especially south of the Platte after 1883, was of considerable importance. Two of the six selected counties south of the river had such a town.

TABLE 33.—PERCENTAGE OF FOREIGN-BORN IN SELECTED NEBRASKA COUNTIES, 1870–1890

County	1870	1880	1890
Douglas	37.72	32.24	25.79
Lancaster	24.73	21.54	14.53
Polk	10.29	29.16	25.64
Fillmore	14.29	17.71	17.21
Clay	11.11	25.31	21.94
Adams	36.84	15.89	16.70
Phelps	*	38.05	30.18
Nance	6.82	15.43	12.97
Merrick	30.70	16.29	14.89
Howard	*	38.49	33.83
Keith	*	26.29	16.78
All Nebraska	25.00	21.53	19.13

* No report.
Calculated from the *Biennial Report of the Secretary of State of the State of Nebraska*, 1886, pages 190–192, and from the *Compendium of the Eleventh Census of the United States* (1890), Part I, pages 496–497.

Quantitative data on these counties substantiate still further the generalizations derived from description. The growth of population and of taxable valuation is chronicled in Tables 32–35. These data provide an excellent picture of the basic pattern in Nebraska's growth: the early and massive advantage of the entrepôt county, the concentrated settlement of the country south of the Platte, and the character and influence of railroad system-perfecting. They also demonstrate the effects of the boom in general and the urban boom in particular in the eighties. Most important of all, they show the great importance of individual variations in all locales and in all periods. Each county was unique.

In the east, Douglas County's large initial population only serves to emphasize the contrast between the growth rate of the seventies and that of the eighties. Part of the explanation probably lies in Nebraska's drought and grasshopper plagues, especially since property valuations in this county (and in most others) dropped sharply between 1870 and 1875 and remained low until 1880. In Lancaster County the pattern of property values was the same, but its population pattern was considerably different, doubling by 1875, almost doubling again by 1880, and doubling once more in the eighties. Perhaps the early variant is partly explicable in terms of Lancaster's greater agricultural potential and its attraction as the location of the capital city, both factors that had greater drawing power in the first than in the second decade.

Fillmore and Clay counties, agriculturally the best of the counties south of the Platte and west of Lincoln, had almost identical growth rates, comparable slumps, and almost equal population by 1890. Property valuations also paralleled each other after the initial higher level in Fillmore County in 1872, which derived from the taxability of Burlington lands in the county for that year but not until 1873 in Clay County.[18]

Adams County fits the growth pattern of the area south of the Platte except in two respects: its property valuation dropped sharply between 1872 and 1875 (because although it had assessed all railroad lands in 1872, only part of them were taxable as late as 1875);[19] and both its population and its valuations exceeded those of the neighboring counties after 1882, the Hastings boom being the explanation here.

Of the river valley counties Merrick was the earliest to be settled and the fastest growing in the seventies, but in the eighties both Phelps and Polk County outstripped it in population and Phelps County in valuation levels as well. Here the explanation undoubtedly lies in the early start that Merrick County, not an inherently wealthy area, had in consequence of its location in the Platte Valley and on the transcontinental railroad. An additional individual peculiarity in this group was the high land valuation returned by Phelps County in 1875 and its drop

[18] See above p. 21.
[19] See below pp. 211–213.

TABLE 34.—ASSESSED VALUATION, EXCLUSIVE OF RAILROAD OPERATING PROPERTY, IN SELECTED NEBRASKA COUNTIES, 1872–1890

County	1872		1875		1880	
	Land & Lots	Personal	Land & Lots	Personal	Land & Lots	Personal
Douglas	$ 6,788,514	$ 1,896,099	$ 5,963,588	$ 2,187,890	$ 5,049,272	$ 2,401,481
Lancaster	3,188,014	749,100	3,055,403	771,981	3,161,568	1,173,402
Polk	557,651	46,142	625,661	166,237	868,986	304,591
Fillmore	1,009,704	127,958	883,126	251,790	1,067,145	502,732
Clay	616,902	86,298	748,843	238,254	1,133,562	608,756
Adams	937,150	2,003	671,780	216,683	1,133,497	492,288
Phelps	*	*	405,398	7,849	10,676	115,605
Nance	*	*	*	*		158,850
Merrick	850,371	123,139	988,252	226,507	715,090	314,266
Howard	197,254	30,142	449,994	100,306	375,523	239,429
Keith	*	*	30	78,410	3,065	171,802
All Nebraska	48,456,117	20,246,193	50,363,052	17,760,353	53,850,147	26,706,278

County	1885		1887		1890	
	Land & Lots	Personal	Land & Lots	Personal	Land & Lots	Personal
Douglas	$ 8,891,958	$ 3,354,540	$15,098,857	$ 4,032,300	$ 20,162,967	$ 4,100,195
Lancaster	4,169,030	1,349,556	6,564,760	1,684,268	7,343,322	1,560,244
Polk	993,766	493,562	1,033,074	455,079	1,006,323	427,208
Fillmore	1,283,822	587,528	1,505,890	792,690	1,486,532	646,841
Clay	1,480,413	918,561	1,634,488	781,882	1,617,922	722,718
Adams	1,634,213	792,509	2,161,759	928,338	2,293,260	795,361
Phelps	518,293	264,950	733,640	335,842	727,624	343,624
Nance	679,912	182,481	635,229	175,814	597,880	306,247
Merrick	965,178	413,975	973,972	437,980	1,112,468	382,387
Howard	671,684	398,345	759,749	418,452	849,096	332,705
Keith	16,271	248,925	1,049,247	256,131	671,153	157,108
All Nebraska	77,139,596	27,744,315	96,358,889	40,546,015	115,360,973	39,445,124

* No report.
Compiled from the *Nebraska Auditor's Report*, 1872–1890.

TABLE 35.—ASSESSED VALUATION OF RAILROAD OPERATING PROPERTY
IN SELECTED NEBRASKA COUNTIES, 1872–1890

County	1872	1875	1880	1885	1887	1890
Douglas	$ 426,634	$ 474,073	$ 416,079	$ 520,649	$ 637,288	$ 779,467
Lancaster	565,004	590,725	594,413	932,999	1,093,107	1,204,384
Polk	*	*	62,944	77,345	79,310	105,210
Fillmore	299,301	186,989	193,121	303,318	518,630	776,693
Clay	296,114	323,977	276,146	422,635	613,950	771,617
Adams	*	228,863	317,275	492,578	552,861	805,559
Phelps	*	*	*	95,057	220,908	214,184
Nance	*	*	*	152,675	166,985	169,700
Merrick	672,391	528,510	454,697	531,216	523,759	617,466
Howard	*	*	*	150,115	252,691	418,790
Keith	*	485,850	417,995	467,043	465,721	480,907
All Nebraska	9,507,095	9,768,523	9,943,193	18,534,789	23,601,362	29,964,208

* No report.
Compiled from the *Nebraska Auditor's Report*, 1872–1890.

by 1880. This reflects, as in Adams County, an unsuccessful attempt to tax unpatented railroad lands.[20] The counties in the Loess Hills are not comparable with the other counties. Neither Nance nor Howard County had a railroad. Nance County, which had a special history of land alienation, shows the lag produced by a late start and, perhaps, by speculator engrossment of lands. Howard County, with a similar late start, had by 1890 caught up with agriculturally comparable counties, such as Phelps and Polk.

Keith County, likewise, is not really comparable with the others. Its tiny population, low land valuation before 1887, and lack of major growth until the mid-eighties reflect its nonagricultural character. Its large size, comparable to that of many other western and northwestern counties, also makes indiscriminate comparison with eastern counties misleading.

The data on the foreign-born contribute nothing of value except to reinforce the conclusion that individual peculiarities were of prime significance in Nebraska, that happenstance was often a potent force. Only Nance County, in which the land was sold for cash by the federal government, shows a variation that might have some significance. Perhaps few of the foreign-born were prepared to buy land on the short-term and solid-block basis that was offered. When they bought from the railroads they at least got long-term credit and the opportunity to homestead, preëmpt, and timber-claim adjacent government land.

Uniqueness does not make all generalization impossible, however. When valuations of railroad operating property are considered, either independently of, or in comparison with, other personal property valuations, four general characteristics become apparent. As in Kansas, the counties with the trunk-line roads possessed a valuable property, and where feeders were added that initial value was increased. All the trunk-line counties demonstrate this. Again as in Kansas, railroad property in

[20] See below pp. 214–215.

TABLE 36.—INDEBTEDNESS OF SELECTED NEBRASKA COUNTIES, 1875–1890

County	Total Debt 1875	Bonds Registered with State†						
		1876–1878	1878–1880	1880–1882	1882–1884	1884–1886	1886–1888	1888–1890
Douglas	$ 650,000	*	*	$125,000	*	*	$ 187,000	$ 108,000
Lancaster	493,812	$ 183,500	$ 14,825	*	*	$145,000	450,000	*
Polk	17,500	*	60,000	3,000	*	*	12,000	*
Fillmore	20,980	*	*	*	*	4,500	85,000	37,600
Clay	51,190	*	251	*	*	*	119,000	*
Adams	82,700	*	316‡	*	*	*	208,000	115,000
Phelps	*	*	445	*	$ 35,000	*	*	8,000
Nance		*	*	*	*	7,000	8,000	12,000
Merrick	58,000	*	*	61,500	*	4,000	20,000	17,500
Howard	19,000	*	300‡	65,000	*	34,500	20,000	5,400
Keith	*	*	*	*	12,000	24,000	30,000	50,000
All Nebraska	4,442,273	1,550,000	510,481	665,750	862,800	887,700	2,949,060	2,894,805

* No report.
† November 30 to November 30. Does not include school district bonds after 1880.
‡ With adjoining county.
Data for 1875 are from the *Message of Robert W. Furnas, Governor of Nebraska, to the Legislative Assembly, Tenth Regular Session, 1875* (Lincoln, 1875), pages 41–42. Other data are from the *Nebraska Auditor's Report*, 1872–1890, and from the *Biennial Report of the Secretary of State of Nebraska*, 1878–1890.

TABLE 37.—STATE TAXES LEVIED IN SELECTED NEBRASKA COUNTIES, 1873–1890

County	1873	1875	1877	1880	1882	1885	1887	1890
Douglas	$ 56,624	$ 63,427	$ 46,412	$ 31,467	$ 56,139	$ 95,434	$ 160,619	$ 153,831
Lancaster	26,687	32,383	23,334	19,718	36,376	47,097	78,240	70,936
Polk	3,601	5,384	5,319	4,637	8,540	12,478	13,427	10,799
Fillmore	6,290	9,722	8,323	7,052	11,495	17,343	21,613	19,695
Clay	6,304	9,636	7,768	7,569	10,755	22,502	24,624	21,452
Adams	6,702	8,212	5,888	7,772	11,352	23,281	30,510	27,329
Phelps	*	2,521	1,364	605	2,129	6,785	10,162	7,896
Nance	*	*	*	635	1,931	8,095	8,191	7,536
Merrick	9,219	11,983	8,644	5,936	10,458	14,758	15,728	13,503
Howard	3,470	4,042	2,272	2,306	5,030	9,426	11,626	10,632
Keith	3,229	4,188	3,638	2,371	4,290	5,473	13,947	6,733
All Nebraska	477,726	547,325	440,425	356,491	597,090	1,027,018	1,305,660	1,171,524

* No report.
Compiled from the *Nebraska Auditor's Report*, 1872–1890, and from the *Biennial Report of the Secretary of State of the State of Nebraska*, 1878–1890.

the areas where only feeders were built was much less valuable, and no county without a trunk line to start with ever built up a level of taxable railroad property comparable to that in the original railroad counties. Only the taxable valuation of Keith County, which never added a feeder, was approached, and then by only one county, Howard. Also as in Kansas, though valuations of personal property dropped, often drastically, in every county except Phelps between 1887 and 1890, railroad valuations rose to some extent in all counties and sharply in many. Finally, the railroad supremacy of the country south of the Platte is clearly demonstrated. These counties had by far the most extensive and by far the most valuable railroad mileage.

Debt and tax data for the Nebraska group, shown in Tables 36 and 37, though in neither instance adequate for detailed analysis, tend to help clarify those patterns already identified. Data on bond registrations reveal the early involvement of the area south of the Platte in debt-contracting, and also the upsurge of bonding, throughout the state, in the years 1886–1888. By 1875 all the counties then organized south of the Platte were bonded—two for railroads, one for lesser services, and one for a combination of both. Along the Platte and north of it only Merrick, the Union Pacific county, had a major debt, which had been contracted to aid the Upper Loup railroad branch. Howard and Polk counties had only small debts. System-perfecting in the late seventies and early eighties accounted for most of the scattered bonding in the period. Only the Phelps County and Keith County debts represented funding and courthouse bonds. The bonding of the period 1884–1890 was significant for its wide distribution; even the entrepôt and capital counties and the eastern counties south of the Platte, which had been so heavily bonded in the seventies to aid railroads, began to issue bonds again. Western counties tended to restrict themselves to constructing county buildings and funding floating debts. Another factor showing up clearly is the high level of bonding adopted and maintained by the prairie metropolis counties—Douglas and Lancaster counties markedly in both periods and Adams County slightly in the first and heavily in the second. County borrowing clearly followed the triangular pattern of population expansion and reflected the booms.

State tax data serve little purpose here other than to summarize effectively the valuation trends in various parts of the state. No effective summary of local taxation data is available for Nebraska. These data show only the state levy on property returned to the state equalization board by the county commissioners. As a summary of valuation they do show (1) the early and massive advantage of the extreme eastern section and that south of the Platte; (2) the tremendous initial and substantial continuing advantage of the counties crossed by the land-grant railroads; and (3) the two periods of major decline: 1875–1880, in the wake of grasshoppers, drought, and financial panic; and 1887–1890, after the bursting of the land- and town-promotion bubble. They also, incidentally, show, for Keith County, the impact of the tax law of 1886. The county's valuation more than doubled in two years, a far greater increase than in any other county.

On the basis of the analysis of topographic, water, and settlement characteristics and the tabulated data on population, valuation, and financial status, the selection of counties for intensive study is made. It is clear, however, that no selection of Nebraska counties can come as close to having general validity for the whole land-grant area in the state as does such a selection of Kansas counties. Only a limited pattern appears. (1) As in Kansas, only one railroad, this time the Union Pacific, was involved on a wide scale. The only other large grantee, the Burlington, received all its patents in 1872. (2) The Union Pacific lands were located, for the most part, in an area of less intensive and later settlement than were those of the other roads. (3) The bulk of the Union Pacific lands were west of the major agricultural settlement of the period, had only a minimum of precipitation, and were in sandhill and other undesirable terrain. (4) All the Union Pacific lands were associated with the valley of the Platte. (5) In the counties through which the road passed—that is, those on the north side of the river—taxable valuations of railroad property were higher than in other counties, except those south of the river through which the Burlington's original line had been built. But (6) with the exception of counties in the extreme east, those on the south side of the river and west to the hundredth meridian were settled sooner than those on the north side. And finally (7) since the history of the nontaxability feature in Nebraska began after 1871, by which time the wave of intensive settlement had passed beyond most of the state's eastern quarter, the counties affected lay in the western three-quarters. Other patterns found in Kansas did not develop in Nebraska. The foreign-born did not become preponderant in any specific type or types of counties. The concentration of bonded debt was usually in Burlington counties, but many of them had Union Pacific lands. Agricultural potential was uneven. Furthermore, disparate county sizes, the influence of town booms, and unusual land policies (in one county) add a large number of features characteristic only of specific counties. Thus the three Nebraska counties selected for close analysis—Adams, Phelps, and Keith (see the map on page 195)—are less likely than those in Kansas to be representative of others or to provide valid indications of the experience of others.

Adams County lies south of the Platte, on the western edge of the rich agricultural region served by the original Burlington. It also lies close enough to the river to place about forty-three per cent of its area within the limits of the Union Pacific land grant. Furthermore, because still another land-grant road, the St. Joseph and Denver City, entered the county from the southeast and received the odd sections in twenty-two per cent of the area, the county includes three different sets of railroad land-grant lands. The county area attracted settlers in sub-stantial numbers only after the Burlington built across it in 1872. Though Burlington lands constituted only about eighteen per cent of its area, the county was a "Burlington county" throughout most of the period. This is reflected in the first major settlements and in the or-ganization of the county government. In Adams County, as in every other Burlington county west of Lancaster, the railroad's town-promot-ing subsidiary, the South Platte Land Company, arranged with pre-ëmptors to purchase government land for townsites. The towns planned for the county were, from east to west, Inland, Juniata, and Kenesaw— named in accordance with the policy that produced, again from east to west, Crete, Dorchester, Exeter, Fairmont, Grafton, and Harvard. Jun-iata was intended as the county seat. The railroad sank an eighty-eight foot well in the center of the section selected (12 of Township 7, Range 11) and in February of 1871 the brothers Titus and Russell Babcock and Isaac Stark and his son John filed preëmptions, which they as-signed to the Burlington trustees in the following April and which the trustees in turn assigned to the South Platte Land Company in March of 1875. Kenesaw has a similar history, as does Ayr, the first town south on the Republican Valley extension, built in the late seventies. In 1878 Inland was moved three miles east, into Clay County. The preëmptors homesteaded their own land while preëmpting for the com-pany, and the Babcocks, at least, stayed on to become leading citizens of the county.[21]

The first substantial settlement in the county was established around Juniata by a colony from Michigan, which was located in the spring and summer of 1871 by D. N. Smith, the Burlington land agent. Other settlers moved into the county in the summer and fall, and many of these, too, settled either in or near Juniata. One group, a small colony from Liverpool, England, established the settlement of Hastings six miles to the east on the line of the railroad (section 12 of Township 7, Range 10). The county organization elections took place in December of 1871 at Juniata. As had been planned, Juniata became the county seat. The votes of the Hastings group were disallowed on technical grounds, and members of the Michigan colony, voting as a bloc, elected members of the Juniata group to all the county offices. Titus Babcock and Isaac Stark were also elected to office, as probate judge and sheriff respectively.[22] The government townships included in the new county,

---

[21] Burton and Lewis, *Adams County*, 1:351, 365; *Juniata Herald*, May 14, 1879, January 11, 18, 25, 1883; Andreas, *History of Nebraska*, 335, 364, 367; A. V. Cole, "Early Experiences in Adams County," in Nebraska Daughters of the American Revolution, *Collection of Nebraska Pioneer Reminiscences* (Torch Press, Cedar Rapids, Iowa, 1916), 18; Adams County title records, in the Office of the Adams County Register of Deeds, Hastings, Nebraska.

[22] Burton and Lewis, *Adams County*, 1:41–42; Cole, "Early Experiences in Russell County," in *Pioneer Reminiscences*, 19; G. F. Work, "First Things in Adams County," in *Pioneer Reminiscences*, 11–14; *Juniata Herald*, January 18, 1883; *Beatrice Express*, May 2, October 28, 1871.

the site of Hastings, and the original railroads are shown on the map of the county included in the Appendix (page 326).

The development of the county in the seventies revolved around these themes: the Hastings-Juniata rivalry; the Burlington's gradual loss of control, first of politics, then of town promotion; and the development of agricultural settlement, first of the north, then of the south half of the area. Further railroad construction was among the chief reasons for each development. In 1873 the St. Joseph and Denver City reached Hastings. From this time Hastings began to outgrow Juniata. In 1875 an election was held to decide the location of the county capital. By obtaining judicial reversal of the canvassing board's rejection of one precinct's votes on grounds of irregularity, Juniata retained the county seat. In 1877 the Burlington began negotiations with both towns for the junction point of the Republican Valley branch. This contest Hastings won, but the battle occasioned a new county-seat election. Hastings won handily, but new charges of irregularity produced a court case— complete with a courthouse fire that destroyed the records of the election—which awarded the county seat, finally, to Hastings.[23]

The loss of complete control by the Burlington is well illustrated by the outcome of the fight over the county seat, but perhaps its weak hold on the settlers is better demonstrated by the efforts to tax both Union Pacific and Burlington property at high rates during the first five years. At least three school districts—Kenesaw, Juniata, and Hastings—built expensive schoolhouses financed by short-term bonds. County Superintendent Adna Bowen stated the position of the settlers: "Now what constitutes the taxable property of this district? First, 15 sections of land claimed by the UP Railroad which at a low estimate is worth $75,000; besides this we have the village of Juniata, all taxable; this constitutes all of the taxable property in the district except a little personal property—and all that will become taxable for the next five years."[24] Furthermore, in 1872 Adams County officers were among the more adamant proponents of the taxation of Burlington lands.[25]

The county developed rapidly. The settlement of the early and middle seventies concentrated in the north half of the county, in Burlington transportation territory but within the limits of the Union Pacific land grant. The Panic of '73 and the grasshopper visitations of 1874–1877 retarded settlement somewhat, perhaps, but thereafter the pace of expansion increased markedly. The southern sections of the county, along the Little Blue and in the St. Joseph and Denver City land-grant area,

[23] Work, "First Things in Adams County," in *Pioneer Reminiscences*, 16; Burton and Lewis, *Adams County*, 1:43–53; Andreas, *History of Nebraska*, 1:359, 360, 367–368; *Adams County Gazette*, May 1, 1872; *Juniata Herald*, October 2, 1878, January 25, 1883, March 1, 1883. The controversy over the county seat is chronicled in the Proceedings of the Board of County Commissioners of Adams County, 1:78–79, 81, 141–142, 143, 150, 157, 160–162, 207–209, 332–333, 343–345, 362–363, 448.

[24] *Adams County Gazette*, March 6, 1872.

[25] See above, pp. 21, 28–29.

were settled slowly until, in 1878, the Republican Valley branch of the Burlington provided a basis for rapid development. In the eighties railroad construction went on apace and Hastings made its bid for gem-of-the-prairie status. Hastings was connected with Grand Island, on the Union Pacific, by the construction of the Hastings and Grand Island, and in 1882 Kenesaw became the junction point of the Burlington's Holdrege cutoff to Denver. In 1884 the Burlington's branch to Minden was built through the southern half of the county. Hastings was a boom town in the mid-eighties. It voted bonds for county buildings and public improvements of all sorts and advertised its advantages through its own immigration and publicity agency. The boom came to its peak in the late eighties, but Hastings retained its boom psychology into the second decade of the twentieth century.[26]

The taxability history of Adams County is shown in the sixteen township-diagrams for this county included in the Appendix (pages 327–342). As elsewhere, the data are mapped for five-year intervals between 1872 and 1897. Railroad lands, whether patented or not, became taxable in 1887, but this development had no effect in Adams County. The pattern of settlement is revealed in the diagrams. In the southern and southwestern portions of the county settlement had a distinct tendency to lag behind the northern and northeastern sections. In the areas of poorest land, the Sandhills outliers, it lagged even more. Perhaps most clearly shown is the concentration of early settlement in the townships surrounding Hastings, around Juniata, and close to the St. Joseph and Denver City.

Each of the three varieties of railroad land had a somewhat different career. Some Union Pacific lands in the county became taxable first, others not until a few years later, and a very few not until 1884. The first Union Pacific patents in Adams County were issued in 1871. These covered—in conformity with the partial Land Office suspension of 1869–1874 designed to insure satisfactory completion of the road—most alternate odd-numbered sections within the grant limits in the northern tier of townships. Most of the remaining Union Pacific lands were patented in March of 1875 and June of 1876, after the Land Office ban had been lifted. Two more sections, on the line between the Burlington and the Union Pacific grant limits, were not patented until 1884. All but three sections of Burlington lands were patented late in 1872—late enough to escape taxation for that year, it later developed. Of the remaining three sections, all on the lines between the Burlington's and

[26] *Juniata Herald*, February 5, May 14, 1879; *Beatrice Express*, December 3, 1874; *Nebraska Auditor's Report*, 1880, p. 117; *Official State Atlas of Nebraska* (1885), 16; Johnson, *History of Nebraska*, 147; Andreas, *History of Nebraska*, 359; *Omaha Weekly Bee*, July 22, 1885, January 18, 1888; *Descriptive Review of Adams County, Nebraska* (1879); *Leading Cities of Southeastern Nebraska* (1883), 29–58; Henry G. Smith, comp., *The Book of Hastings* (The Tribune, Hastings, 1906); *Hastings, Nebraska* (Hastings Chamber of Commerce, Democratic Press, Hastings, 1921).

other land-grant limits, two and a half sections were patented in 1873 and the final half section in 1882. St. Joseph and Denver City lands were patented in three steps: one section late in 1872, most of the remainder in 1873 and 1874, and the final 3,520 acres in 1878. Most of these lands were sold by the Burlington trustees, who purchased them and retailed them to individuals as part of the development of the Republican Valley extension. The railroad's deed was the instrument in sales made in the eighties. A few of these lands were supposed to have been involved in the Knevals case—a case in which parts of the St. Joseph and Denver City grant, considered lapsed by some settlers, were validated in the courts, with the result that settlers on them had to buy

TABLE 38.—TAXABLE LANDS IN ADAMS COUNTY, NEBRASKA, 1872–1897

Total area of county, 360,960 acres

Percentage of total area accruing to railroads, 49.60

Year	Railroad Land				Per Cent of the Taxable Land	Acres of Privately Entered Land	Acres of of All Taxable Land
	Acres						
	Union Pacific	Burling-ton	St. Joe and Denver	Total			
1872	12,800	62,720	640	76,160	98.27	1,440	77,600
1877	76,000	64,000	33,920	173,920	80.95	40,920	214,840
1882	76,000	64,320	37,440	177,760	58.87	124,200	301,960
1887	77,280	64,320	37,440	179,040	54.29	150,724	329,764
1892	77,280	64,320	37,440	179,040	52.22	163,800	342,840
1897	77,280	64,320	37,440	179,040	51.07	167,160	346,200

Computed from plattings of the Adams County numerical indices, office of the Adams County Register of Deeds, Hastings, Nebraska.

their lands from the speculators who had purchased the railroad's rights.[27] No instance of such transactions is found in the Adams County title records. Furthermore, when Commissioner Sparks later reversed the decisions of the court and decided that the St. Joseph and Denver City, because it had failed to build within the specified time limit, was not entitled to the lands and declared them open to settlement, purchasers of the railroad titles expressed dismay when the squatters descended on their farms and delight when the decision was overthrown.[28]

The precise taxability relationships of railroad lands to other lands during the five-year periods mapped on the diagrams are shown for Adams County in Table 38. Clearly there was never any problem of an excess of privately entered land over railroad land on the tax rolls of Adams County. Initial railroad patents greatly exceeded private pat-

[27] See Sheldon, *Land Systems and Land Policies in Nebraska*, 92–93, and the *Juniata Herald* of April 15, 1886.

[28] *Hastings Gazette Journal*, April 28, 1886; April 24, 1888.

ents. Even in the spring of 1872, when the first assessment was made and before the Burlington lands were patented, the only privately entered land taxable was the townsite of Juniata. At that time the Union Pacific already had patents for 12,800 acres—ninety-five per cent of all taxable land. Nearly all railroad lands were taxable by 1877. Thus at no time during the entire period did the taxable acreage of the roads drop below taxable privately entered acreage. The approach to a proportion commensurate with the area of the railroad land grants in the county, achieved after 1882, was the result not of legislative reform making railroad lands taxable but of patents to settlers that made privately entered lands taxable.

The vociferous objection to the nontaxability of Burlington lands which Adams County officialdom voiced late in 1872 obviously stemmed not from fear that they would have to pay an excessive and unfair share of the taxes, but rather from concern that they would be unable to finance their ambitious program of school and county improvements with revenues from railroad land taxes and hence would be faced with financing the improvements themselves. The whole problem was settled for them in the next assessment year, and thereafter they did have the opportunity they sought, namely to collect heavy revenues from the railroads and the buyers of their land. The Union Pacific escaped the tax on some of its lands for another year, thanks to the Land Office suspension of patenting in effect against the road. By 1877, when nearly all railroad lands had finally been patented, the roads and the buyers of their land held over eighty per cent of the taxable titles in Adams County. Even in 1882, when the agricultural settlement of the county was essentially complete and the Hastings boom was beginning, they still held more than fifty-eight per cent.

Phelps County lies just west of Fort Kearney but just south of the Platte. These two facts explain its early development. The Union Pacific was separated from it by the river, and between 1869 and 1874 the town of Kearney was an important cattle-shipping point on the railroad. The cattle trails crossed the county and its eastern neighbor (Kearney County), and grazers pastured their cattle on the south side of the river. Though these conditions alone were potent enough to retard agricultural settlement, another deterrent was added by Union Pacific policy. In 1870 the company announced the opening to sale of the land grant along the first two hundred miles of the road. The two-hundred-mile line, beyond which no sizable areas were sold until 1879, fell near the eastern edge of Phelps County. A few settlers did venture into the county after 1870, enough to produce a county organization in 1873. But the organization was premature. Drought and grasshoppers pushed settlement back, and unpatented railroad land was declared untaxable. In 1875 the resident population of the entire county was only 110 persons, 49 horses, 5 mules, and 133 cattle. Two years later, in 1877, it had increased to 326 persons, 99 horses, 24 mules, and 305 cattle. In

1877 there were only ten quarter sections or 1,600 acres of taxable land in the entire county, though the assessors regularly returned all Union Pacific lands—about thirty-four per cent of the total area—at a valuation of approximately two dollars an acre.[29]

Then two developments brought the languishing county to life. First, the cattle market had moved west after 1875 and the Union Pacific, either because it was no longer interested in protecting its shipping point or for some other reason, lifted the sales ban and, in 1879, settled a large colony of Swedes in Phelps and Kearney counties. Other settlers came in too and the census of 1880 enumerated 2,447 persons, 1,065 horses, 191 mules, and 1,233 cattle in the county. It grew steadily thereafter. Second, in 1882 the Burlington completed the county's first railroad, the Holdrege cutoff, and the county seat was eventually moved to the railroad town. Phelps County, at last, was a going concern.[30] The government townships, the site of Holdrege, and the route of the railroad are shown on the map included in the Appendix (page 343).

The vitalized county grew rapidly, followed conservative financial policies, developed into an important mixed-farming area, and acquired another railroad. By 1882 the population numbered almost three thousand persons; in 1885 it exceeded six thousand; by 1890 it approached ten thousand. The average increase was about a thousand a year. No railroad bonds were voted and the only major debt, a $35,000 bond issue of 1883, was designed in large part to fund the debts of the old county organization. In 1881, 39,000 acres of wheat and 17,000 acres of corn were planted; in 1885, 24,872 and 25,808 respectively; in 1888, 19,952 and over 41,000. In 1890, however, chastened by drought, the crop farmers of the county returned to the old ratio of two acres of wheat to one of corn, planting 20,000 and 10,000 acres respectively. The increase in numbers of cattle was persistent, continuing to grow even in the dry years. From 2,028 in 1881 the cattle population rose to 6,194 in 1885, 14,464 in 1888, and 19,947 in 1892. The second railroad, the Colby extension of the Burlington (the Nebraska and Colorado) entered the county in 1884, made its junction with the cutoff at Holdrege, and built on through in 1887.[31]

The taxability history of Phelps County is shown in the sixteen township-diagrams for this county included in the Appendix (pages 344–

[29] Johnson, *History of Nebraska*, 520; *Report of the Nebraska Secretary of State*, 1886, p. 181; *Nebraska Auditor's Report*, 1875, p. 55; 1877, p. 61; 1880, p. 63.

[30] Mahnken, "Early Nebraska Markets for Texas Cattle," in *Nebraska History*, 26:96–102; *Guide to the Union Pacific Railroad Lands* (Union Pacific Land Department, Omaha, 1871); Andreas, *History of Nebraska*, 326; Alexis, "Swedes in Nebraska," in the *Publications of the Nebraska State Historical Society*, 19: 84–85; Davis, "Building the Burlington Through Nebraska," and his "Lines West—The Story of George W. Holdrege," in *Nebraska History*, 31:25–47, 107–125, 204–225 (1950).

[31] *Report of the Nebraska Secretary of State*, 1886, p. 191; *Compendium of the Eleventh Census of the United States* (1890), Part 1, p. 497; *Nebraska Auditor's Report*, 1882–1892, *passim*.

359). Two distinct title periods are pictured. Before the railroads came to the county settlement was determined by the water courses. The banks of the Platte were alienated first, then the banks of minor tributaries of the Republican, in the southwest corner of the county. With the coming of the first railroad both Union Pacific and government land patents were issued for lands along the route and in the eastern sections of the county. The Nebraska and Colorado, in the southern sections, had a similar effect on government lands. By that time, however, all railroad lands were patented.

A comparison of the taxability of railroad and of privately entered land shows that (1) two and a half sections of privately entered land were taxable by 1877, four years after the organization of the county, but no railroad land was patented; (2) by 1882 railroad land patented in the eastern sections of the county constituted a little less than two-thirds of the taxable area, and scattered privately entered sections and

TABLE 39.—TAXABLE LANDS IN PHELPS COUNTY, NEBRASKA, 1872–1897

Total area of county, 325,800 acres
Total area outside grant limits, 82,600 acres
Percentage of total area accruing to railroad, 33.96

| Year | Union Pacific Railroad Land | | | Privately Entered Land | | Acres of All Taxable Lands |
| | Acres in County | Per Cent of the Taxable Land | | Acres | | |
		in County	in Grant Area	in County	outside Grant	
1872						
1877				1,600	40	1,600
1882	34,000	60.34	84.90	22,340	16,240	56,340
1887	110,640	46.95	63.86	125,020	60,280	235,660
1892	110,640	38.46	52.88	177,060	78,480	287,700
1897	110,640	37.45	51.96	184,760	82,480	295,400

Computed from plattings of the Phelps County Numerical Indices, Office of the Phelps County Register of Deeds, Holdrege, Nebraska.

parts of sections somewhat more than one-third; and (3) by 1887 the railroad lands and the privately entered lands in the county were roughly balanced. However, if comparisons are restricted to the land-grant area, taxable railroad acres continued to exceed privately entered lands after 1882. More than a quarter of the total area of the county was outside the limits of the railroad land grant.

These relationships are shown more precisely in Table 39. The proportion of taxable acres comprised of railroad land demonstrates that in Phelps County, as elsewhere, there was little taxable acreage until the railroad began getting patents and that thereafter railroad land was liable for a proportion of taxes well in excess of the ratio of the road's total prospective holdings to the total area of the county.

Data for the years between tend to reveal that after 1880 the comparative liability of railroad land was even greater. Railroad selections were begun soon after the Swedish colony was established. The first patent, for 34,000 acres, was issued in June of 1882 and a second, but minor, patent in 1883. All the remaining railroad acreage in the county was patented in June and November of 1884. Taxable privately entered lands, which had increased to 22,340 acres by 1882, were concentrated in the southern and eastern sections of the county, near Holdrege. Only 6,100 acres were within the limits of the grant. After 1882 privately entered lands became taxable at the rate of about 15,000 acres a year, two-thirds of them in the land-grant area. By 1885 the total for the county was 90,740, as compared with 110,640 railroad acres. Just over half of these were also outside the grant limits, near Holdrege and along the tributary creeks of the Republican.

In Phelps County, then, there was a short period, from the fall of 1879 to mid-1882, when population was growing and privately entered land was gradually being patented, but the railroad had patented no land, though it had begun selecting a few months after the area was opened to purchasers. Thereafter railroad land, in the county as a whole until 1887 and in the land-grant area until 1892, made up the bulk of the lands liable for taxes. In Phelps, as in Adams County, once intensive settlement had begun—with but temporary delay before the lands were selected—the railroad lands, not the government lands, bore the burden of tax liability. Also, again as in Adams County, the tax law of 1886 had no effect whatever.

Keith County, lying across both branches of the Platte and touching the eastern edge of the Nebraska panhandle, is in the heart of what was, in this period, the Nebraska cattle country. Its area, though approximately equal to that of Adams and Phelps counties combined, is small for western Nebraska counties. In one sense it is ideal for present purposes in that its size in relation to that of the land grant acquired by the railroad in the western half of the state is roughly proportionate to the size of Adams or Phelps County in relation to the size of the land grant acquired by the railroad in the eastern portions of the state. If there is any validity in citing the experience of Adams and Phelps County as representative of the eastern parts of the grant, the western county used for comparison would indeed need to be twice their individual sizes. In many ways Keith County is, as a matter of fact, the most representative of its area of all the counties studied in Nebraska.

Keith County's history is peculiar to the cattle country. The Union Pacific built through, along the north bank of the South Platte, in 1867, and cattle drovers, bound for markets at Forts Kearney, McPherson, and Laramie, moved an occasional herd through the area. By 1869 considerable numbers of cattle were being ranged in the Platte

Valley, both east and west of the section. After 1870 Ogallala, a water stop on the Union Pacific, attracted Louis Aufdengarten, who opened a drover's store. A few others also settled there. In 1873 Aufdengarten and several others organized a county government, dragged a small house to Ogallala from another water stop eight miles west for their courthouse, and awaited developments. In 1874 the Union Pacific built stock pens west of the town. Ogallala's future was assured, for a time at least, and so, only incidentally, was that of Keith County.[32] The government townships in the county, the route of the railroad, and the site of Ogallala are shown on the map included in the Appendix (page 360).

For the first ten years Keith County's existence was almost entirely dependent on Ogallala, which in turn was dependent on the trail herds. The permanent population of the county fluctuated between the low of 95 reported in 1874 and the high of 274 reported in 1879. In 1882 the nearly average 115 was reported. Union Pacific lands in the county were opened to sale in 1884, but no report of cultivated acreages of cash crops was issued until 1886. In that year 195 acres of wheat, 1,476 acres of corn, and 578 acres of oats were returned in the auditor's census. By this time, however, some permanent settlement outside Ogallala, along the South Platte both east and west of town, had begun. In 1885 the state census reported 1,140 inhabitants in the county. Five years later the federal census reported 2,556. The end of the cattle drives was thus marked by the development of some agriculture; it was also marked by the establishment of cattle ranges along the rivers and back into the Sandhills.[33]

The taxability history of Keith County, shown in the thirty-four township-diagrams for this county included in the Appendix (pages 361–395), reflects its range character and its development as permanent-pasture ranch country. As late as 1882, nine years after the county was organized, the townsite of Ogallala and a single eighty-acre tract on the eastern border constituted the sum total of taxable land in the county. No further alienation took place until 1886. All the government land shown on the plats as taxable in 1887 was patented in either 1886 or 1887, except, of course, the 520 acres already taxable in 1882. The railroad patented 320 acres in 1886 and most of its sections west of Range 36 and south of Township 16 in 1887, just before Commissioner Sparks suspended patenting to it. The remainder of the railroad land in the county, except one section not received until 1911, was patented in 1890 and 1891, after the Land Office ban was lifted. But of course all railroad land, whether patented or not, became taxable in 1887 anyway.

[32] The development of the cattle industry in Nebraska is summarized in Olson's *History of Nebraska*, 191–201. See also Johnson, *History of Nebraska*, 413–415; Mahnken, "Early Nebraska Markets for Texas Cattle," in *Nebraska History*, 26:98–103; and his "Ogallala—Nebraska's Cowboy Capital," *ibid.*, 28:85ff.

[33] Mahnken, "Ogallala—Nebraska's Cowboy Capital," in *Nebraska History*, 28:87–109; *Keith County News*, May 13, 1887; *Nebraska Auditor's Report*, 1873–1890, *passim*; and *Compendium of the Eleventh Census of the United States* (1890), Part 1, p. 497.

Government lands reached the tax rolls more slowly. This was partly because a large patent of even-numbered sections was made to the state in 1899 as indemnity school lands, and they were placed in the permanent leasing program. Two other factors also help explain the delay. First, the land was not susceptible of agricultural settlement under the homestead and preëmption laws. It was not until the Kinkaid enlarged-homestead program was adopted that a great deal of the land, especially that north of the river, was entered. Most of this land was not patented until the 1909–1911 period. Second, after 1891 the Union Pacific sold much of its land, notably a large tract west of Ogallala on the North Platte, to the Ogallala Land and Cattle Company and other ranchers. These grazers enclosed their ranges, effectively excluding prospective settlers from the government land behind their fences. Some of these fences came down during the Theodore Roosevelt administration, but much of the land settled thereafter (under the Kinkaid system) quickly found its way back to the ranchers who had enclosed it or to new ranchers building up fenced ranges.[34]

TABLE 40.—TAXABLE LANDS IN KEITH COUNTY, NEBRASKA, 1872–1897

Total area of county, 784,890 acres
Total area outside grant limits, 5,760 acres
Percentage of total area accruing to railroad, 49.56

| Year | Union Pacific Railroad Land | | Acres of Privately Entered Land | Acres of All Taxable Land |
	Acres in County	Per Cent of the Taxable Land		
1872				
1877			240	240
1882			520	520
1887	389,000	97.57	9,700	398,700
1892	389,000	85.00	68,620	457,620
1897	389,000	76.27	121,000	510,000

Computed from plattings of the Keith County Numerical Indices, Office of the Keith County Register of Deeds, Ogallala, Nebraska.

Table 40 summarizes the taxability relationships between Union Pacific and privately entered lands during the years 1872–1897. It shows that there was no problem of privately entered land liability in excess of railroad-land liability in Keith County. In one year, 1886, there was an excess of almost three thousand acres of privately entered land, but railroad patents received the next year made about half the Union Pacific lands in the county taxable, regardless of the tax law. Under the tax law the railroad lands represented more than ninety-seven

[34] Data on titles and sales are summarized from the Numerical Indices of Keith County, in the Office of the Keith County Register of Deeds, Ogallala. A summary of the fence cases is in Sheldon's *Land Systems and Land Policies in Nebraska*, 177–187.

per cent of all the taxable land in the county. Even as late as 1897 railroad lands accounted for over seventy-six per cent of taxable acreage. In Keith County, as in Adams and Phelps counties, the railroad lands were liable for the larger part of land taxes during the era of concentrated settlement (never very concentrated in this county). The difference here was that, because of the slow pace at which government lands reached the rolls after 1887, the railroad lands maintained their preponderance into the twentieth century, providing a tax base that would have been restricted indeed without them.

The data on growth and taxability in Nebraska are less susceptible of generalization than those for Kansas. As the eleven-county growth survey has shown, Nebraska experience varied widely, often without any identifiable pattern or assignable cause. The general patterns discovered were fewer and often less pertinent to the analysis of taxability. The preponderance of railway mileage and gem-of-the-prairie development in the southeastern sections, the comparatively slow growth of the western half and the northwestern two-thirds of the state, and the inapplicability of this particular tax problem to the Burlington Railroad are the only positive generalizations that are usable. There are also negative factors. Foreign-born elements showed no preference for one area or another; debt characteristics were largely a reflection of position in the lopsided development pattern, having no measurable relationship to land-grant railroads; and neither available debt data nor available tax data are adequate enough to be useful. Finally, the variations in the size of counties make both selection and comparison difficult.

The selections made represent a compromise with the diversity of the area and the insufficiency of the data. A southeastern county involved in both the surge of settlement during the seventies and the urban boom of the eighties; a central Platte Valley county settled in the eighties which was neither a multi-grant nor a gem-of-the-prairie county and which lacked a railroad until 1882; and a central-western county in the heart of the slow-developing cattle country that was more than twice the size of the others—these can hardly be other than somewhat unrepresentative of the general experience of the area. Furthermore, each had its own distinctive characteristics: Adams County its multiple grants and its boom town; Phelps County its premature county organization and large Swedish population; and Keith County its own premature organization, forty-one miles of trunk-line railroad, and cattle-shipping point. For these reasons generalizations made here must be viewed as less reliable than those made for Kansas. On the basis of the limited selection studied, findings can only be described as possibly indicative of the experience of similar counties, not, as they were in Kansas, as probably indicative of the experience of the western two-thirds of the grant area.

In the three counties studied one common characteristic is discernable. At no time in one of the counties and in two of them only during the first year or two of intensive settlement was there any lag in the comparative tax liability of railroad land. In all three counties, once serious settlement had begun, railroad lands soon exceeded privately entered lands on the tax rolls. Then, for a period varying in inverse proportion to the speed at which settlement proceeded, railroad land continued to bear the burden of tax liability. In these Nebraska counties, then, it was government land that lagged behind, usually far behind. It was not railroad land. These characteristics as manifested in the three-county area as a whole are summarized in Table 41.

TABLE 41.—SUMMARY OF TAXABLE LANDS IN SELECTED NEBRASKA
COUNTIES, 1872–1897

Total area surveyed, 1,471,740 acres
Total area outside grant limits, 88,360 acres
Percentage of total area accruing to railroads, 46.11

Year	Railroad Land			Privately Entered Land		Acres of All Taxable Land
	Acres	Per Cent of the Taxable Land		Acres		
		in Entire Area	in Grant Area	in Grant Area	outside Grant Area	
1872	76,160	98.27	98.27	1,440		77,600
1877	173,920	69.15	69.16	78,000	40	251,520
1882	211,760	59.01	61.82	147,060	16,240	358,820
1887	678,680	70.39	75.09	285,444	60,280	964,121
1892	678,680	62.36	67.22	409,480	78,480	1,088,160
1897	768,680	58.93	63.48	472,920	82,480	1,151,600

Of the total of 1,471,740 acres included in the survey of the three counties, only 77,600 acres were or became taxable in 1872. Of that taxable area more than ninety-eight per cent were railroad lands. By 1877 the total taxable area had increased to 251,520 acres, and the percentage of railroad land had dropped to about sixty-nine. By 1882, with a further increase of the total, to 358,820 acres, the railroad percentage had dropped again, to fifty-nine. All these changes in the direction of proportionate liability were similar to the trend apparent in Kansas, especially in the eighties, the period during which the reformers won their battle for taxation of all railroad lands. In 1887, partly because of the new tax law—but only partly and in only one of the counties— the level of railroad liability rose to an approximation of what it had been ten years earlier. After 1887, as the government acreage climbed— sharply until 1892, less so thereafter until 1897—the railroad percentage dropped again until, by 1897, it had fallen slightly below that of 1882. If analysis is limited to the limits of the railroad grants, the preponderance of railroad liability is accentuated, by very little before

1882 and by two to almost five percentage points thereafter. Throughout the period, then, the Union Pacific (and the Burlington and the St. Joseph and Denver City in Adams County) and the buyers of railroad land were liable for many more of the assessable acres in these counties, taken as a group, than were the settlers on government land. Without this tax liability of railroad land grant lands these counties would have had serious difficulty in finding significant acreages to tax.

This preponderance of taxable railroad land cannot, however, be attributed to railroad company planning, in the Union Pacific case at least. True, the suspension of patenting by the Land Office in 1869–1874 provides part of the explanation for the patent pattern that developed in the Union Pacific land grant in Adams County. It may also be true that the Union Pacific would have patented most of the lands it threw open to sale in 1870 much earlier had the Land Office not denied the patents. But there is no doubt that the railroad did develop a program of partial patenting for the specific purpose of protecting itself and the buyers of its lands from taxation during the first years of settlement in a new area. Union Pacific land commissioner Leavitt Burnham and general attorney Andrew Poppleton both testified that this was the policy,[35] and in part the land-title records bear them out. Often sales were contracted before patents were issued and often, as in Phelps County, before selections were made. But the Union Pacific agents, unlike those of the Kansas Pacific, tended to select contiguous, if small, blocks rather than individual small tracts, an outgrowth, perhaps, of a recurring effort to predict the market. Apparently, however, the Nebraska line developed this policy later than did the Kansas line and manifestly the Union Pacific was much the less successful in keeping its lands off the tax rolls. But of course the Union Pacific did not have the advantage of a total Land Office suspension until 1887. The Kansas Pacific interdictment, begun in 1883, vastly increased the effectiveness of its original delaying tactics, ever more so as the land boom progressed. The Nebraska boom never developed the proportions of the Kansas boom; hence overly optimistic market predictions (and consequent over-selections) were more costly, because the effects lasted longer, than they were in Kansas.

Finally, in these Nebraska counties, in virtually all periods, the critics of the tax exemption feature of the land grants were wrong when they charged that settlers on government land were burdened by heavy land taxation because their lands were taxable whereas the bulk of neighboring railroad lands escaped. There would have been some justification for the charge in Phelps County in 1881 (though no reformer from Nebraska made it then) and there was an equally slight justification for the charge in Keith County in 1886. That was all.

[35] See above, pp. 112–113.

Ten

The Taxpayers of Kansas and Nebraska

A TENTATIVE evaluation of the effects of the nontaxability feature of the railroad land grants on local tax bases in Kansas and Nebraska can perhaps be induced from the foregoing study of three counties in each state. That any such general evaluation is most tentative, that any conclusions drawn from the study pursued thus far are to be viewed as merely indicative of possible general conditions must be emphasized once more. The selections made for the analysis are too few, too scattered, too unrepresentative, especially those for Nebraska. The information utilized as the criteria of selection is too restricted, too diverse, too inconclusive. Most important, the area from which the selections are made is too large, too disparate, and at the same time too narrowly restricted to land-grant limits. Only when the entire area of the railroad land grants, at the very least, or at the very best, the full extent of both states has been analyzed for patterns of alienation and of taxability will it be possible to draw final conclusions.

Still, on the basis of the limited study reported here a limited answer to the basic question—whose lands became taxable when—does seem possible. It also seems possible, with the addition of some further information, to arrive at a partial and tentative estimate of who actually paid to the county what share of the taxes collected, to what degree taxability was translated into tax payment.

When the data on land taxability in all six counties are combined with a view to deriving a general picture of the relationships of railroad lands to other lands, the resultant summaries demonstrate conclusively that a preponderance of railroad-land liability was the rule, not the exception. Of the 3,084,540 acres studied, only 145,200 were or became taxable in 1872, at which time railroad lands already amounted to 76,160 acres (or 52.45 per cent). By 1877 a total of 592,420 acres were on the tax rolls, of which 361,320 acres (or 68.08 per cent) were railroad lands. In 1882 a total of 906,680 acres were taxable; 478,760 acres (or 52.80 per cent) were railroad lands. A rapid trend toward a balance between railroad land-grant and privately entered taxable acres was developing.

The effect of the continued decline in the preponderance of railroad lands cannot be shown quantitatively on the basis of the material presented here, but it is clear that from 1882 to 1887 the reduction con-

223

tinued until the proportion of taxable railroad land in the area as a whole had dropped to well below half of all taxable land. In the six-county area studied the effect of the tax law of 1886 was to reverse the relationship—that is, to return the railroad proportion to a high level. In 1887, of the 2,182,074 acres taxable, 1,434,440 acres (or 65.74 per cent) were railroad lands. Even as late as 1897, of the 2,582,340 acres of taxable area 1,434,440 acres (now reduced to 55.55 per cent) had originally been or still were railroad lands. When percentages of railroad land are adjusted to the grant limits and account is taken of lands lost in place, an even greater preponderance is revealed. Within the limits of their own land grants these roads or the buyers of their lands were liable for almost seventy-nine per cent of the taxable area in 1872, a proportion which dropped to about fifty-eight per cent by 1882 and undoubtedly to approximately half in 1886, rose to seventy per cent in 1887, and dropped again, but this time more slowly, to about sixty per cent in 1897. These figures are presented in summary Table 42.

TABLE 42.—SUMMARY OF TAXABLE LANDS IN SELECTED KANSAS AND NEBRASKA COUNTIES, 1872–1897

Total area surveyed, 3,084,540 acres
Total area outside grant limits, 120,440 acres
Total lands lost in place, 35,840 acres
Percentage of total area accruing to railroads, 46.50

Year	Railroad Land			Privately Entered Land			Acres of All Taxable Land
	Acres	Per Cent of the Taxable Land		Acres	outside Grant Area	lost in Place	
		in Entire Area	in Grant Area*				
1872	76,160	52.45	78.82	69,040		24,290	145,200
1877	361,320	60.99	68.08	231,100	40	30,680	592,420
1882	478,760	52.80	57.96	472,920	16,400	32,160	906,680
1887	1,434,440	65.74	70.02	747,634	67,480	33,040	2,182,074
1892	1,434,440	58.64	62.86	1,011,740	97,720	33,280	2,446,180
1897	1,434,440	55.55	59.60	1,147,900	107,400	34,040	2,582,340

* These data include those for Saline County, Kansas, where a great deal of railroad land was lost to prior claimants. For that county the half-area character of the grant is maintained for each of the years for which their percentages are calculated by doubling the acreage of all lands lost in place and actually entered and subtracting that figure from the total of privately entered land as of that year.

These data on land taxability indicate that (1) railroad lands constituted more than half the taxable acres in the six-county area as a whole at all six dates for which calculations have been made; that (2) within the limits of their own grants railroad lands accounted for more of the taxable area than did government acres at the six selected dates, the range being from about fifty-six per cent more (in 1872) to about sixteen per cent more (in 1882); and that (3) although railroad lands constituted less than fifty per cent of the total six-county area in the period 1882–1887, the approach to half in the grant area occurred only in the period just before 1887, and undoubtedly, in the six counties as a whole, never did fall below fifty per cent.

Land, however, was only one of the major components of the tax base and any proper evaluation of the relation of railroad property to the tax roll must include consideration of all forms of taxable value. Personalty was always a significant part of the tax roll, despite the important exemptions granted by both states for family or individual possessions. The portion of the tax burden borne by this variety of property was affected by two factors: (1) the amount of taxable real estate and (2) the amount of railroad property, a special form of personalty, located in the county. Thus there were three elements in every county's valuation structure. One category consisted of lands, either government lands alienated to private parties or patented railroad lands that were either still held by the road (for which the road itself was liable) or contracted or deeded to buyers (for which the buyers were liable). A second category consisted of personalty in general, which usually meant the unexempted belongings of residents in the county, but which could also mean the property of nonresidents, especially (as in Saline or Ford or Keith County) livestock either grazed in the county or being held for shipment at the time the assessment was made. The third category consisted of railroad roadbed and rolling stock and other operating installations, including the property of the original high-value trunk-line roads or that of the later low-value branch and feeder lines or, in some instances, both. Table 43 shows, for selected years, the amount of railroad property as compared with general personal property on the one hand and with all taxable property on the other in the twenty-four counties included in the analysis of growth.

These tabulations supply a number of valuable insights into the relation of railroad operating property to the tax bases of Kansas and Nebraska. Most striking is the relation of railroad operating property to other personalty. Such railroad property was always a significant part of non-real property, but it was particularly important in the early years of county organization and settlement and again in 1890. Only in the easternmost, early-settled counties and in some counties without trunk-line railroads did railroad operating property constitute a small proportion of total valuation at the outset. In all others—nineteen of the twenty-four counties—it was more than twenty per cent to begin with and in all but one county continued to be more than that. In most counties, as a matter of fact, it was over fifty per cent, sometimes over eighty per cent at the start, and remained at comparably high levels. Particularly significant in this respect are the western counties with the original land-grant lines, Keith and Merrick in Nebraska and Russell, Ford, Trego, and Wallace in Kansas. The only exceptions to the high percentage of personalty in land-grant railroad counties are the Burlington counties in Nebraska and the easternmost of the Santa Fe counties in Kansas. These counties were settled early and rapidly and their

TABLE 43.—COMPARISON OF RAILROAD OPERATING PROPERTY VALUATIONS AND OTHER PROPERTY VALUATIONS IN SELECTED KANSAS AND NEBRASKA COUNTIES, 1871–1890 (IN PERCENTAGES)

A. KANSAS

County	1871		1875		1880		1885		1887		1890	
	of Personality	of Total	of Personality	of Total	of Personality	of Total	of Personality	of Total	of Personality	of Total	of Personality	of Total
Leavenworth	5.11	1.24	40.68	8.27	42.18	10.15	39.84	9.39	39.23	8.92	52.22	13.23
Shawnee	†	†	25.37	7.07	34.85	8.91	28.03	7.67	30.48	9.27	30.11	7.13
Pottawatomie	†	†	38.08	10.17	29.03	10.14	26.22	10.33	28.69	10.29	33.75	11.16
Dickinson	42.22	10.81	40.24	10.75	28.62	6.90	17.05	5.68	27.24	8.20	55.76	20.31
Ottawa	†	†	†	†	38.21	12.54	23.08	7.55	31.86	10.11	47.45	15.49
Saline	22.12	10.71	33.69	8.25	45.89	14.16	35.06	11.90	46.41	16.59	64.29	21.78
Jewell	†	†	†	†	12.58	5.22	12.78	5.44	12.14	4.76	33.10	12.26
Lincoln	†	†	†	†	†	†	†	†	11.09	3.50	42.21	9.75
Rice	*	*	59.49	12.40	42.93	16.60	39.92	19.02	53.28	24.73	70.71	28.57
Russell	*	*	59.20	38.84	50.01	27.24	50.73	26.40	48.90	15.66	65.23	25.42
Trego	*	*	*	*	69.42	36.45	48.62	36.41	74.70	40.14	90.43	22.78
Ford	*	*	72.41	46.57	81.81	48.47	60.50	37.76	50.55	14.21	84.58	27.42
Wallace	*	*	*	*	*	*	*	*	75.30	32.49	86.73	45.32
All Kansas	9.24	2.98	38.73	10.11	49.55	13.71	34.96	12.24	40.41	13.26	54.27	16.64

B. NEBRASKA

County	1872		1875		1880		1885		1887		1890	
	of Personality	of Total	of Personality	of Total	of Personality	of Total	of Personality	of Total	of Personality	of Total	of Personality	of Total
Douglas	18.37	4.68	17.81	5.50	14.77	5.29	13.44	4.08	13.64	3.22	15.97	3.11
Lancaster	43.00	12.55	43.35	13.37	33.62	12.06	40.88	14.46	39.36	11.71	43.56	11.92
Polk	†	†	†	†	17.13	5.09	13.55	4.94	14.84	5.06	19.76	6.84
Fillmore	70.05	20.83	42.62	14.15	27.75	10.95	34.05	13.95	39.55	18.41	54.56	26.69
Clay	77.43	29.63	57.62	24.71	31.21	13.68	31.51	14.98	43.98	20.26	51.64	24.79
Adams	†	†	51.37	20.48	39.19	16.33	38.33	16.87	37.33	15.18	50.32	20.69
Phelps	*	*	†	†	†	†	26.40	10.82	39.68	17.12	38.40	16.66
Nance	*	*	*	*	†	†	45.55	15.04	48.71	17.07	35.65	15.80
Merrick	84.52	40.85	70.00	30.32	59.13	30.64	56.20	27.81	54.46	27.06	61.76	29.23
Howard	†	†	†	†	†	†	27.37	12.30	37.65	17.65	55.73	26.16
Keith	*	*	86.10	86.10	70.87	70.50	65.23	63.78	64.52	26.29	75.38	36.73
All Nebraska	31.95	12.16	35.48	12.54	27.13	10.99	32.93	13.89	36.79	14.71	43.17	16.22

* No report.
† No railroad operating property reported.
Computed from the *Kansas Auditor's Report, 1871–1890*, and from the *Nebraska Auditor's Report, 1872–1890*.

large populations produced high enough valuations of private personalty to reduce the proportion of railroad property from about sixty per cent to less than forty per cent of the total. It was in the western counties that the relatively slow settlement and continued lack of large populations kept the proportion of railroad personalty high. Also notable is the sharp rise in that proportion which took place between 1885 and 1890, a rise explained partly by the burst of branch-line construction in the period and partly by the gradual, then sharp, decline in the valuations of private personal property.

The relation of railroad personalty to total taxable property was similarly significant but more complex. In the early-settled eastern counties railroad personalty rarely constituted as much as ten per cent of the total tax base. In the originally non-railroad counties, once branch lines had been built, it tended to range between ten and fifteen per cent, though in Polk County it never reached seven per cent and in Phelps County it exceeded seventeen per cent. These low ratios are probably explained by the substantial pre-railroad settlement in these counties. In the western railroad land-grant counties two patterns appeared. First, in the Burlington and Santa Fe counties railroad personalty fluctuated between ten and forty-six per cent of the tax base, the average approximating twenty-five per cent. This is probably explained by the patenting of railroad lands, which broadened the tax base at an early date. Second, in the Kansas Pacific and Union Pacific land-grant counties, where there was delay in patenting railroad lands, the share of taxes paid by railroad personalty ranged markedly between a high in Keith county of eighty-six per cent and a low in Russell County of fifteen per cent, the average being thirty-five per cent. This was simply because the low level of the land-tax base was automatically compensated for by an increase in the share of railroad personalty subject to taxation and, of course, of whatever other personalty was found in the counties. As has been shown for some of these counties at least, a substantial portion of the taxable land also belonged to the railroads, or to those who had purchased land from them.

Railroad property, then, both real and personal, always constituted a major part of the tax base in both states. In Nebraska as a whole, railroad personalty accounted for about thirty-two per cent of all personalty in 1872, dropped to just over twenty-seven per cent by 1880, but rose again, to just over forty-three per cent, by 1890. The ratios for all taxable property in Nebraska were less spectacular but also significant, ranging from about twelve per cent of the tax base in 1872 down to about eleven per cent in 1880 and up again to over sixteen per cent by 1890. In Kansas railroad personalty constituted a small percentage of the tax base in 1871, but after that it was, as in Nebraska, significant. Of personalty, railroad property constituted nearly thirty-nine per cent in 1875 and over forty-nine per cent in 1880. Five years later the ratio dropped to about thirty-five per cent, but rose again, to over fifty-four per cent, by 1890. The share of the total Kansas tax base made up of railroad personalty was about ten per cent in 1875, approached fourteen per cent in 1880, dropped to just over twelve per cent in 1885, and soared to nearly seventeen per cent in 1890.

The significant place that railroads and railroad lands had in the total tax bases of the two states was enhanced in the early years of settlement in all counties populated principally after 1871 and especially in those located in the western two-thirds of the two states. Probably during most of the period and certainly after 1886, when all railroad land joined railroad personalty on the rolls, these counties found the greater portion of their assessable property in railroad-owned personalty and in railroad lands held either by the roads or by their land customers. Without this contribution deriving from the railroads, most of these counties, especially in their early years, would have been virtually destitute of taxable property.

Liability for taxes did not guarantee payment of them. Tax levels were high and the levies were often made by county or school district officials who failed to comply with state laws prescribing forms or limits of assessment. Sometimes the levels were simply excessive. Occasionally they were set by crooks—"bond rangers" Nebraskans called them—who were trying to line their own pockets. These conditions plus the wide fluctuations in land values and crop prices and the effects of natural and financial catastrophes—drought, grasshoppers, and the Panics of '73 and '93—produced considerable deliquency. They also produced at least part of the motivation and much of the opportunity for some individuals and most railroads to fight the collection of almost any tax that appeared either questionable or beatable. Each of these factors—the levels and purposes of taxation and the means employed and success achieved in the various efforts to avoid payment on the county level—is a significant enough aspect of the relationship of railroad property to other property on the tax rolls to require a volume for its proper elucidation and analysis. Here only a generalized picture can be drawn and a tentative evaluation made.

In Nebraska tax levels varied a great deal. Unimproved land in the sparsely settled area north of the Platte averaged about ten cents an acre, but in 1873, for example, taxes on Burlington "outside lands" ranged from a low of about three cents an acre in Greeley County to a high of about fifteen cents in Dixon County. By 1876, after some settlement had taken place, the average for the area as a whole was still about ten cents, but the range was now from about five cents in Dixon to about forty-three cents in Buffalo County.[1] Taxation of Burlington lands south of the Platte followed a common pattern. Here the general levels were usually high in the first few years, dropped gradually until 1880,

[1] Tabular statement, Taxes Levied in Outside Counties, in the Burlington Archives, Newberry Library, Chicago.

and rose during the eighties to new high levels in 1892. In Fillmore County, for example, the rate was twenty-four cents an acre in 1872, seventeen cents in 1876, nine cents in 1880, about eleven cents in 1884, and nearly thirty-one cents in 1892. In Adams County the 1873 rate of twenty cents declined in 1887 to seventeen cents, and in 1884 to ten cents, but by 1888 it had climbed again, to almost fourteen cents an acre. Individual tracts, of course, were subject to both much higher and much lower rates.[2]

The existence of a school district or the levy of a tax judgment against any jurisdiction (usually the school district), sometimes drove taxes to fantastic levels. In Adams County, in 1872, some of the lands in the Juniata school district paid taxes totaling as much as seventy-six cents an acre. In 1876 lands in this district, still almost entirely railroad sections, were down to about twenty-five cents an acre, but the newly organized neighboring districts were collecting from thirty-four to fifty-seven cents an acre. In 1882 lands in these districts were taxed from eighteen to thirty-seven cents an acre, in 1886 from fifteen to thirty cents, and in 1888 from twenty-six to almost forty cents. The southern and western sections of the county, slower to develop, and less valuable land anyway, were chiefly responsible for keeping Adams County averages down.[3]

In the Union Pacific counties of Nebraska similar general patterns tended to develop, except that the upturn usually came later, after 1890. In Merrick County, for example, 1875 taxes were about twenty-four cents an acre, in 1882 about nineteen cents, in 1884 sixteen cents, and in 1889 eight cents. In Hall County in 1878 the rate was about fifteen cents an acre, in 1879 and 1880 about twenty-five cents, in 1886 about thirteen cents, and in 1889 ten cents. In Phelps County the rate dropped from about eleven cents an acre in 1884 to about eight cents in 1888 and about five cents in 1890. Dawson County, a cattle area, levied a tax of about three cents in 1884, eight cents in 1885, about five cents in 1888, and about nine cents in 1890. In Keith County the tax was just under twelve cents in 1887, the first year that large acreages in the county were taxable, and about nine cents in 1890.[4] In these areas, as in Burlington territory, the pattern of high rates at the first stage of major county development and a decline thereafter was common. All these averages of course obscure the great differences within counties and

[2] Tax Receipts—Records by County and Description, 1872 (vol. 1), 1873 (vol. 2), 1876 (vol. 6), 1880 (vol. 11), 1884 (vol. 16), 1888 (vol. 20), and 1892 (vol. 24), in the Burlington Archives.

[3] Summarized from the assessment rolls of Adams County for parts of Cottonwood, Little Blue, Ayr, Juniata, and Verona precincts for the years 1872, 1876, 1878, 1882, and 1888, in the County Treasurer's Office, Hastings, Nebraska.

[4] Union Pacific Tax Vouchers, vol. 2, pp. 13, 27; vol. 3, pp. 69, 94, 147, 150; vol. 4, p. 191; vol. 6, pp. 16–17, 96–97; vol. 8, pp. 458–459; vol. 10, p. 238; and vol. 13, pp. 697–707, 889–893, in the Records of the Union Pacific Properties Division, Omaha, Nebraska.

fail to show the impact of school district financing or of court tax judgments against specific jurisdictions.

In Russell County, Kansas, patterns of taxation were similar. In Russell Township in 1873, at the very beginning of settlement, the total tax was $21,658, apportioned as follows: non-railroad land and private personalty, $2,416; railroad personalty, $4,095; and railroad land, $15,147. Only $1,876 was school district tax, $15,923 county tax. Most unimproved land in the township was taxed at three cents an acre although one tract was taxed at sixty cents and several other tracts at rates between these two extremes. As it turned out, only the personal property taxes were collectable, since neither railroad land nor privately entered tracts had been patented. In Center Township, which included the village of Bunker Hill, the taxes on seven quarters of selected but still unpatented railroad land were paid before delinquency, by contractors purchasing the land from the road. Later, in 1874, the taxes for 1873 were paid on sixteen and a half additional quarters of railroad land. No taxes were paid on privately entered land for the year 1873. Together these railroad-derived titles paid $1,219, of which $426 went for the school, the average tax per acre being about seventeen cents. Railroad personalty paid $4,494, of which $1,053 was school tax.

As population increased, tax levels declined. By 1876 the rate in Russell and Center townships was only about eleven cents an acre. Russell Township collected $1,289 on its land and Center Township $2,190. Private personalty in the two townships paid $1,168 and $627 respectively. In both areas school levies accounted for nearly half the tax. In 1882 the land tax brought $3,434 in Russell Township and $3,768 in Center Township. Of these amounts $1,219 and $1,861, respectively, represented school tax. Private personalty brought $2,824 in Russell and $1,417 in Center Township. Railroad personalty is not listed in the available sources for either 1876 or 1882, but in 1878 it brought $4,213 in Russell and $3,170 in Center Township. The 1882 per acre tax averaged about twelve cents in both townships. In 1886 Russell Township collected $9,327 and Center Township $6,212 in land taxes. On private personalty they received $1,820 and $1,654 respectively. School taxes accounted for $4,617 in Russell and for $3,427 in Center Township. The per-acre rate varied widely—between nineteen and eight cents, the average being about thirteen cents. By 1888 Russell Township's southern portions had become Lincoln Township; together they collected only $8,961 on real property and $883 on private personal property. Of the total, $4,377 was school tax. Center Township's real property paid $7,757, of which $3,427 was for schools, and its private personalty paid $446, of which $208 was school district tax. The average land tax in the three-township area had taken a downturn, to about ten cents an acre.[5]

[5] Summarized from the assessment rolls of Russell County, for the whole county, for the years 1873, 1876, 1878, 1882, 1886, and 1888, in the County Treasurer's Office, Russell, Kansas.

The tax levels in Russell County, then, had the same tendency to start low, climb rapidly, and gradually drop again that was characteristic of Nebraska, but because of its slower rate of settlement and late boom, the movement was much less rapid. The new upswing of rates that took place in the nineties also developed more slowly in Russell County. Furthermore, average per-acre rates in this county, despite occasional excessive taxes on individual tracts, were usually considerably lower than in eastern Nebraska, perhaps partly because the county was settled in a later period and never as completely as eastern Nebraska.

Data on Kansas per-acre tax levels drawn from railroad records, less valuable because less complete, yield similar figures. Kansas Pacific lands in Dickinson County paid sixteen cents in 1889, between nine and twenty cents in 1890, and, to judge from the single entry in the records, eleven cents in 1891. In Rice County they paid from ten to fourteen cents in 1889 and from seven to seventeen cents in 1890. In Russell County the railroad tax vouchers show a per-acre tax of thirteen cents for 1888 (as compared with the general assessment roll average of about ten cents). In 1890 the railroad paid sixteen cents. In Osborne County, just north of Russell County, the railroad paid twelve cents in 1890. In Ellis County the rate for the years 1887–1890 seems to have averaged eight cents. In Trego County the rate in the years 1888–1891 ranged between eight and fifteen cents. In Graham County, north of Trego, the 1888–1890 rate was twelve cents. In Gove County it was nine cents in the years 1886–1892. And in Wallace County in 1889 and 1890 it ranged between seven and fifteen cents.[6] The general pattern here also seems to have been progressively lower from east to west, the average rate in the west being about eleven cents an acre at the end of the period, after the boom had collapsed—a high rate on land that was actually worth only about two dollars an acre and that even the most optimistic, in any but boom times, viewed as worth no more than five dollars an acre.

Relatively high, occasionally fantastic, tax rates partly account for the widespread practice of nonpayment in both states, though they do not serve to explain it completely. State officials were wont to blame much nonpayment on "the evident neglect of official duty"[7] by county officials. The "neglect" they lamented was the disposition of county treasurers to forgo the collection of taxes from the destitute in bad years and to refuse to bring the property to tax sale. That William B. Thorne, county treasurer of Adams County, Nebraska, for example,

[6] Union Pacific Tax Vouchers, vols. 9–13, *passim*. No Kansas Pacific records have been located. The Union Pacific Tax Department paid Kansas taxes occasionally throughout the period after the merger of 1880 and regularly after 1888.
[7] *Message of Governor Albinus Nance to the Legislature of Nebraska, Sixteenth Session, 1881* (Journal Company, Lincoln, 1881), 8; "Message of George T. Anthony, 1877," in *Messages of the Governors of Kansas* (variously printed), vol. 1, n.p., in the Kansas Historical Society, Topeka; and *Biennial Report of the Auditor of State and Register of the State Land Office* [Kansas], 1872, p. 4; 1876, p. 107.

followed this practice is evidenced by his efforts to collect back taxes in good years. In February of 1879 he advertised that all delinquent taxes for the years 1873–1877 which had not been paid by May 1 would be collected "as the law directs."[8] Similarly, R. P. Stein, treasurer of Kearney County, Nebraska, advertised in 1881: "Owing to good crops and good prices this year I deem it to be the case that [the delinquents] are able to pay, and they are notified that longer delay in the payment thereof must not be expected."[9] Tax delinquency reached significant proportions in both states. In Nebraska unpaid state taxes aggregated $861,213 in 1881. In Kansas they totaled $400,000 in 1872 and $387,302 in 1876. Delinquencies in Kansas increased steadily in the eighties, from $492,741 in 1882 to $559,592 in 1886, and to a maximum of $754,053 in 1890.[10]

The collection of unpaid taxes by means of the tax sale, when it was resorted to, was far from successful in bringing revenues into the treasuries. When tax delinquency was subject to a high enough penalty and interest rate, most delinquent lands could apparently be sold. In the early years in both states, a buyer at tax sale could collect up to a fifty per cent penalty plus interest from the owner when the land was redeemed. If the land was not redeemed the buyer could eventually obtain a tax title. But there were also deterrents to such sales. Local buyers at tax sale were, understandably, unpopular. In Minden, Nebraska, the local paper described such a buyer as "a little sneak thief loafer, who seeks whom he may devour. . . . A man who will thus take advantage of a neighbor's mistake and cause him trouble and costs is but, to say the best of him, a small pattern of a man. A man of no more principle than that, will steal if he can get a chance to do it on the sly."[11] Such unpopularity may have served to discourage prospective buyers, local ones at least.

Doubtless a more potent curb on tax sales was the revision downward of penalty and interest rates. In 1874 the Kansas penalty was lowered to twenty-five per cent, with the result, according to the state treasurer, that tax sales were sharply reduced. Only a small portion of the real estate offered was sold.[12] By 1875 the Nebraska penalty was down to twenty-four per cent, but counties were authorized to buy the lands at sheriff's sale if they found no other market.[13] In 1883 the Nebraska penalty for late payment of taxes was set at five per cent and the inter-

---

[8] *Juniata Herald* (Nebraska), February 5, 1879.

[9] *Kearney County Bee* (Nebraska), October 14, 1881.

[10] *Message of Governor Albinus Nance . . . of Nebraska, 1881*, p. 8; *Kansas Auditor's Report*, 1872, p. 4; 1876, p. 107; 1882, pp. 256–257; 1886, pp. 299–300; 1890, pp. 318–320.

[11] *Kearney County Bee*, November 12, 1880.

[12] *Biennial Report of the Treasurer of Kansas*, 1875, pp. 4–5. See also the *Junction City Union* (Kansas), August 30, 1873, and the "Message of Thomas Osborne, 1874," in *Messages of the Governors of Kansas*, vol. 1.

[13] *Laws of Nebraska*, 1875, pp. 93–97, 105–106.

est rate at ten per cent. The penalty was repealed in 1885, however.[14] The imposition of interest without penalty, seemingly, was the system under which most late tax payments were collected. Tax sales are few and tax deeds rare in the title records of the counties surveyed in this study, at least for the seventies and eighties.

Taxes on railroad-derived titles were of course collectable in the same fashion as others. If the land had been contracted for sale, the buyer was required by the railroad company to keep up the taxes. The company kept close account of each contract, published warnings to its contractors to pay their taxes, and usually had county officials send it duplicate lists of taxes collected on these lands or otherwise assured itself that the taxes were being paid. When a contractor failed to pay, the Burlington usually paid the tax and charged it, with interest, to the contractor. When such lands were sold for taxes the road instituted redemption proceedings. The Union Pacific often followed a similar policy with respect to delinquent taxes, except that it usually insisted that the contractor pay the tax himself and redeem the land. Usually the company redeemed land only after a contract had been cancelled. Much of the time of railroad tax and legal departments was devoted to this tax-supervising function.[15]

The significance of these railroad policies for the relationship of tax liability to tax payment is obvious. Since the road was careful to see that until title had actually passed all tax obligations against the land were discharged, large delinquency lists of lands in which the railroad had an interest appeared only when the company was arguing that the lands were not liable or, more often, that the levies were illegal. Once title had passed to the buyer, the railroad no longer had an interest and the settler on railroad acres was free to pay or not, as he was able or as he chose.

The railroads persistently scrutinized the tax levies, assessment procedures, and appropriations of the counties, precincts, municipalities, and school districts taxing their properties. Whenever they saw an opportunity to defeat a tax or part of a tax and obtain an abatement or compromise, they were usually quick to take advantage of it. The large numbers of such cases and the significant measure of success the railroads had is explained in large part by three factors growing out of

[14] *Ibid.*, 1885, chapter 68; *Juniata Herald*, June 28, 1883; *Kearney County Gazette*, December 18, 1884.

[15] The best-organized and clearest records of this supervisory, payment, and redemption system are the forty-six volumes of Tax Receipts—Records by County and Description, in the Burlington Archives. Examples of advertisements urging contractors to pay their taxes are in the *Beatrice Express* (Nebraska), August 13, 1874; the *Juniata Herald*, October 16, 1878; and the *Kearney County Bee*, October 22, 1880. The Union Pacific methods are shown in Union Pacific, Letters and Delinquent Tax Vouchers, Books A and B, *passim*, but especially in Book A, pp. 73, 86, 96–114, 213, 313–314, 327–330, 345, 375–376, and in Book B, pp. 180–181, 244, 246, 325, 397, 406, 782–785, 801–802.

the decentralized and amateur-operated characteristics of the tax systems of the two states. First, in a large majority of cases the irregularities in the levy (the usual reason a tax was fought) were the result of innocent mistakes made by county or school district officers—who were notoriously careless of the letter of the law until a railroad challenge made them cautious. Second, some of the irregularities represented an attempt to collect a tax ostensibly for one public purpose but to apply it to another, and thus circumvent the maximum mill rates set by state law. The levy for the sinking fund was particularly susceptible of such use. In Butler County, Nebraska, for example, according to one account, "the sinking fund tax became quite a joke as the years went by, there being no bonds or any kind of indebtedness to be provided for." The Union Pacific finally protested and the tax was dropped.[16] Third, occasionally taxes were levied or bonds voted for fraudulent purposes. Bogus county organizations were established in both Kansas and Nebraska. In Harper County, Kansas, a ring of adventurers floated $40,000 in bonds and pocketed the proceeds. In Barbour County the take was $31,300. In Holt County, Nebraska, "Baby Smith" and his "bond rangers" pocketed the proceeds from the sale of $75,000 worth of county bonds. In Cherokee County, Kansas, the nonexistent cities of Budlong, Cloud, and Gregory issued bonds that were sold to a New York firm for $68,000. Numerous bogus school district bonds were also issued in Kansas.[17] This combination of weaknesses in the tax system provided the occasions and some of the motivation for railroads to fight taxes where they could. The chief motive was the obvious one: if the policy resulted in net savings to the railroad it seemed good business to pursue it.[18]

Of the four major land-grant railroads in the two states the Burlington was, without doubt, the most persistent and the most successful in its efforts to defeat or compromise taxes on its property. It is true that the Burlington's Kansas counterpart also fought county taxes, especially operating property taxes, with much success; for example, it instituted

---

[16] Anna M. Bunting, *Our People and Ourselves* (n. p., Lincoln, 1909), 97.

[17] James E. Boyle, *The Financial History of Kansas* (*University of Wisconsin Bulletin in Economics and Political Science*, vol. 5, no. 1, Madison, 1909), 89; Alan G. Bogue, *Money at Interest: The Farm Mortgage on the Middle Border* (Cornell University Press, Ithaca, 1955), 149; Addison E. Sheldon, *Nebraska: The Land and the People* (3 vols., Lewis Publishing Company, Chicago, 1931), 1:512; *Kansas Auditor's Report*, 1873, pp. 9–11; "Message of [Kansas] Governor Osborne, 1875," pp. 29–32; *ibid.*, 1876, pp. 13–14; *Message of Robert W. Furnas, Governor of Nebraska to the Legislative Assembly, Tenth Regular Session, 1875* (Journal Company, Lincoln, 1875), p. 27. See also the *Newark Herald* (Nebraska), August 11, 1881, and the *Kearney County Bee*, January 7, 1881.

[18] For a statement of the motives of the railroadmen and their estimates of prospects see T. M. Marquett, attorney for the Burlington, to J. M. Woolworth, Omaha, February 20, 1873, in B. & M. Misc. Legal Papers, 1873–1884, in the Burlington Archives.

thirty-nine cases in the years 1873–1882 and by 1876 had won $122,000 in tax abatements.[19] But the Nebraska road far outstripped the Santa Fe. In the year 1875 alone the Burlington brought fifty-seven suits to restrain taxes,[20] and this was only the most active of many active years. During the 1872 fight over the taxability of unpatented lands a battery of lawyers had been recruited,[21] and the tax department thus formed continued to operate throughout the period. Usually the road succeeded in restraining at least a part of the taxes—on any ground from exceeding the maximum mill rate to improper posting of notices of school district meetings—but often it not only lost the case but was required to pay costs and penalties. Almost every original Burlington county was the scene of at least one such case. Of forty-eight minor, single-county cases of this sort recorded in the ledgers of the railroad's tax department for the period 1874–1883, the company paid in full, with costs and penalties, in ten cases, settled at slight reductions by stipulation in seven cases, obtained significant reductions by court decree in nineteen cases, secured permanent injunctions in five cases, and still had five cases in litigation at the close of 1883.[22]

The most important tax litigation in the "inside" counties was that initiated in 1872 on the question of tax-before-patent, a case involving $190,000. The road lost, but at that it was able to settle by compromise for about $154,000.[23]

Precisely what the actual savings of the road were in all these cases cannot be determined on the basis of the records available, but it is manifest that they ranged from fifteen to twenty per cent. In the years before 1875 this percentage represented a major saving, since 1873 taxes levied amounted to $195,000 and 1874 taxes to $160,000. With the rapid sale of Burlington lands in the region south of the Platte such savings were greatly diminished, and by 1878 both the totals levied and the actions at law pending had been sharply reduced.[24]

Though the Burlington's savings south of the Platte were significant, the company had greatest success north of the river on its "outside" lands. This section of the Burlington grant totaled 1,204,085 acres. These lands were not taxable in 1872 because they had not been pat-

[19] Atchison, Topeka and Santa Fe, *Report of Ross Burns, Attorney* [1876] (George W. Martin, Topeka, 1877), 3–11, and same for 1880, pp. 3–13.

[20] Annual Report of the Burlington and Missouri River Railroad in Nebraska, 1875, p. 16, in the Burlington Archives.

[21] See T. M. Marquett to J. M. Woolworth, Omaha, February 20, 1873, in B. & M. Misc. Legal Papers, 1873–1884, in the Burlington Archives.

[22] Summarized from the ledger titled Records, Legal, 1874–1883, in the Burlington Archives. For the cases that reached the State Supreme Court see the *Nebraska Reports*, 4:293–307 (1876); 7:33–38, 487–498 (1878); 9:449–453, 507ff. (1880); 10:211ff. (1880); 12:324–328 (1882); 13:367–370 (1882); 14:51–55 (1882); 15:251 (1883); 16:123–126, 136ff. (1884).

[23] Annual Report of the Burlington in Nebraska, 1875, pp. 16–17.

[24] These summaries are found *ibid.*, pp. 16–17; 1877, p. 24; and 1878, pp. 13–14.

ented, but between 1873 and 1877 the eighteen counties in which they lay levied a total of $460,377 in taxes against them. Meanwhile, in 1873, in a case originating in Antelope County, the railroad's right to the land was challenged. The company refused to pay taxes while the legal contest was in progress. Finally, in 1877, the United States Supreme Court decided in favor of the company.[25] Thereupon the road undertook to settle for back taxes, a bill that, with interest and penalties, amounted to $612,040.[26]

Because the growth of the counties had been seriously retarded by the controversy and because the road apparently threatened to keep the lands off the market, it succeeded in compromising the taxes in most counties almost immediately and for a tiny portion of its liability. It paid about $38,000 and deeded about 3,000 acres of land to cancel $573,762 in taxes and interest.[27] Antelope County held out. In 1879 the county sold the lands (to itself) for taxes, whereupon the railroad withdrew all lands in the county from the market. The struggle continued through offer and counteroffer until, in 1884, a settlement was reached. The company paid about $38,000 to clear 58,920 acres of back taxes. Together the tax compromises cost the Burlington only $76,000, about seventeen per cent of the original tax bill. Taxes on "outside" lands levied from 1878 onward were paid with only the usual close scrutiny of assessments, levies, and appropriations.[28]

The approach of the Union Pacific, which also included the Kansas Pacific after 1880, to problems of tax payment was very different from that of the Burlington. It litigated less[29] and apparently relied far more heavily upon influencing county officials and developing good relations with school district boards as a means of reducing tax costs. From a

[25] 98 *United States Court Reports* 334 (1877).

[26] The tabular statement of Taxes Levied in Outside Counties, in the Burlington Archives, details the assessments, interest, and totals.

[27] *Ibid.*; Annual Report of the Burlington in Nebraska, 1878, p. 14.

[28] Records, Legal, 1874–1883, pp. 84–85, and Legal Papers about Taxes, B. & M. (Neb.), L. D., both in the Burlington Archives; Roy Harold Mattison, Burlington Railroad Land Grant and the Tax Controversy in Boone County (unpublished master's thesis, University of Nebraska, 1936); Thomas Milburn Davis, George Ward Holdrege and the Burlington Lines West (unpublished doctoral thesis, University of Nebraska, 1941), 183–186; A. T. Andreas, comp., *History of the State of Nebraska, Containing a Full Account of Its Growth . . . Description of Its Counties, Cities, Towns, and Villages . . .* (Western Historical Company, Chicago, 1882), 374, 388; *Hamilton County News* (Nebraska), March 22, April 26, August 9, 1878; *Oakdale Pen and Plow* (Nebraska), June 1, June 8, November 30, 1878; *Elkhorn Pen and Plow* (Oakdale), May 8, 1879, July 1, 1880, June 14, 1883; *Pierce County Call* (Nebraska), December 12, 1884; *Beatrice Express*, August 12, 1875.

[29] Union Pacific tax levy cases reaching the Nebraska Supreme Court are in *Nebraska Reports*, 4:450–457 (1876); 7:228ff. (1878); 10:612ff. (1880); and 12:254–259 (1882). See also the "Report of the Government Directors," in the Union Pacific's *Annual Report* for 1883, p. 23, and Union Pacific, Book A, pp. 319, 321, 361.

business point of view it made at least one costly mistake, a mistake probably attributable to inexperience. Whereas the Burlington, when it contested the taxes of 1872, had deposited the sums contested with the courts, proposing to secure their return should it win the cases,[30] the Union Pacific paid the bulk of the levy, approximately $80,000, filing a written protest with each payment, and proceeded from there to litigation. When it won its case it sought to recover its money, was forced to resort to litigation, and lost. The courts decided that since no threat of seizure had been made before the taxes were paid, the payment was voluntary and not recoverable.[31] Proving the nontaxability of its unpatented lands in the long run saved the railroad large sums, but the proof had been needlessly expensive.

The Union Pacific's tax department—and the Kansas Pacific's too, so far as the limited available records show—pursued policies that are best characterized as political. The penchant for personal influence, private compromise, and public amity is clearly revealed in tax department policy. Several techniques designed for these purposes were utilized. The free pass was used both as enticement and as reward. Between September 8, 1881, and May 15, 1882, for example, tax agent T. S. McMurray wrote twenty-seven letters transmitting passes. Some went to local agents of the railroad, but many went to county treasurers, county clerks, or other locally influential people. One was sent to a state official, the treasurer of Colorado.[32] When the holder of a pass displeased the company, his privilege was in jeopardy. In one such case, for example, McMurray wrote,

It would not be good policy to revoke his pass. He said that it was given him because he was assessor and to revoke it . . . would give him the opportunity to make statements that might injure the company and put the incoming assessor in a bad position and make him feel that he might be severely criticized if he lowered Mr. Nibley's assessment . . . but he will look out that the pass is not renewed next year.[33]

Occasionally efforts may have been made to give information to or prepare materials for state officials, but for the most part this kind of "helping hand" influence was exerted on the county level or through agents. It took the form of providing arguments for the abatement of illegal taxes, suggesting assessment rates and providing lists of assessable property, and having the tax commissioner pay annual visits to each county to negotiate settlement of disagreements. The tax depart-

---

[30] Annual Report of the Burlington in Nebraska, 1875, p. 16.

[31] 98 *United States Court Reports* 541 (1877); *Beatrice Express,* April 15, 1875; *Grand Island Times* (Nebraska), May 17, 1876.

[32] Union Pacific, Book B, pp. 475, 501, 570, 625, 717, 754, 833–838, 845, 868–870, 880, 882, 933, 937, 938, 942, 944, 946, 958, 981.

[33] T. S. McMurray to George W. Thatcher, superintendent of the Utah and Northern Railway Company, November 5, 1880, in Union Pacific, Book B, pp. 232–234.

ment was particularly eager to secure abatement of taxes levied on unpatented lands in which it still had an interest and devoted much attention to achieving this end.[34] Once the land had passed to a buyer, however, as tax agent McMurray put it in a letter to one of them,

> We will resist the collection of taxes and the issuance of tax deeds upon our own lands, but we will not litigate for parties who have purchased from us. You and others similarly situated must take care of your own lands either by conducting your own litigation or paying these taxes. The lands were sold to you subject to taxes that might be levied and we did not and will not guarantee you immunity from taxation.[35]

In any event, the tax department clearly devoted much attention to the policies of accommodation and negotiation that it had adopted as its chief means of keeping taxes down.

The general tenor of Union Pacific policy toward local jurisdictions, and the tax department's strong disposition to seek as favorable treatment as possible while remaining on good terms with the localities, was best expressed in McMurray's policy of paying taxes that, because of technical errors in assessment or for other minor causes, were not legally collectable. The correspondence of the department is liberally sprinkled with observations like the following, in one of McMurray's letters to school district officials in Ogden:

> As I feel satisfied that the money is to be honestly expended and that . . . the tax is just, we do not intend to use the technicalities to defeat the tax. I think that fair dealings on both sides is the best policy both for the company and the city. And we propose to do our share and rely upon the city to act in the same way.

Or, as he wrote to a collector in another Utah county,

> The tax is a very large one comparatively, it being the extreme limit of the law and is open to technical objection arising out of your failure to comply strictly with the provisions of the law, but we have decided to pay the tax this year hoping that we will not be called upon again for a special tax in your district during the coming year.[36]

Just how far such policies were successful in keeping taxes down is not determinable. That they may have helped seems likely.

Methods of tax payment also had much to do with the translation of tax liability into tax payment. If an individual or a railroad could discharge the tax obligation at less than face value, the cash cost to the

[34] Union Pacific, Book A, pp. 18ff., 37–45, 53–55, 79–83, 153–159, 161, 181, 284–285, 324, 344, 352–353, 363–364, 367–371, 384–385, 390, 391–393, 394–395, 398, 401, 424; Book B, pp. 139–140, 156–162, 208, 328, 400–401, 737–740, 786, 788, 850–854, 898–902.

[35] T. S. McMurray to John F. G. Helmer, January 21, 1882, in Union Pacific, Book B, p. 802.

[36] T. S. McMurray to Thomas D. Dee, October 27, 1879, in Union Pacific, Book A, p. 205; McMurray to C. Dunn, Assessor and Collector, District 19, Box Elder County, Utah, January 31, 1881, in Book B, p. 345. Other examples are in Book A, pp. 193. 463–465, 473, 480–481, 490, 492–493, and in Book B, pp. 88–101, 126.

taxpayer and the cash income to the county was substantially reduced. This could be accomplished in two ways.

First, as in most rural areas, the road tax could be paid by working on the public roads. Though this provision was designed to benefit the settlers, a railroad could also benefit from it by contracting to have its tax worked off. The Union Pacific, for example, hired a number of such road-work contractors. At various times some Union Pacific road taxes (levies against branch as well as main lines) were paid in this fashion in a dozen counties in Nebraska and a half dozen in Kansas. The company usually paid seventy-five cents on the dollar for this work, but the total savings amounted to only $2,301, the sum total involved in all eighteen counties being only $9,326.[37]

Second, county warrants could be used instead of cash. Many counties—all of them in the first year of settlement and most of them for several years thereafter—were forced, because of slow tax collections, to conduct county business on credit. The floating debt thus created circulated at a discount, a discount determined by the demand for the scrip and by the anticipated tax collections of the county. Three factors made the warrants hard to obtain and difficult to use. First, there was a limited supply, especially after the first years. A comparison of Tables 25 and 26 (pages 170–171) shows that in most counties of Kansas, for example, even as early as 1874, floating debts at mid-year tended to average less than five thousand dollars. The only exceptions (those with higher debts) were Leavenworth and Saline counties, and of course their warrants could not be used to pay taxes levied by other counties. The state as a whole did have about $450,000 in warrants outstanding in mid-1874, but again each was usable only for taxes levied by the issuing jurisdiction. After 1874 the supply of warrants was reduced more and more sharply. For most of the period, then, even if the roads could have obtained all of them, warrants would have met only a part of their taxes, and as the supply dwindled so did the discount. Second, local speculation in warrants, as in tax titles, was a regular practice. On at least some occasions speculators approached the roads and tried to resell at a profit, a profit that would further reduce the discount obtained by the roads.[38] Third, by law warrants had to be redeemed in sequence. The holder could await his turn or, apparently often, the county treasurer would accept them at market value or a slight discount

[37] Union Pacific, Book B, pp. 277½, 295, 433, 478, 658, 693; Book C, p. 218; and Book 3A, pp. 136, 175. The counties involved were Jefferson, Nuckolls, Thayer, Clay, Colfax, Sarpy, Hall, Platte, Buffalo, Dawson, Douglas, and Dodge counties in Nebraska, and Marshall, Doniphan, Brown, Nemaha, Washington, and Madison counties in Kansas.

[38] A reply to such an attempt is McMurray's letter to Peter Fowlie, Hastings, Nebraska, February 7, 1881, in Union Pacific, Book B, p. 353. McMurray refused to deal with Fowlie, who was the deputy treasurer of the county, on grounds that he did not wish to subject the railroad to the charge that it encouraged county officials to speculate in county warrants.

and he or his friends would hold them until they were reached.[39] The railroad or its agents could also hold them, of course, and pay the taxes when the warrants came up for redemption, provided the taxes had not become delinquent. Exactly how much use the railroads did make of the warrant method of payment cannot be determined without reference to the records of company treasurers. Union Pacific tax department vouchers do occasionally specify the use of a warrant as part of the payment.

The multiple factors operating to determine what proportion of the tax liability was actually translated to tax payment, then, make any precise determination of the relationship impossible. Four general conclusions can be drawn, however. (1) Tax rates in any county were highest in two periods: during the first years of concentrated settlement and again in the nineties. In railroad counties this meant that the long-term tax costs of railroad property and of property purchased from the railroads was accentuated in the early years, because of the preponderance of these types of property on the tax rolls in those years. Tax costs were further accentuated in some counties during the nineties. By that time the tax liability of railroad and railroad-derived property on the one hand and of settler and settler-derived property on the other had been brought into balance in the eastern counties and was approaching a balance in the western counties. In the far western counties, however, a significant enough imbalance remained to increase still further the long-term tax costs of railroad and railroad-derived property. (2) Methods of tax payment, including substitution of labor and payment with county warrants obtained at a discount, although they probably effected some reduction of the actual cash costs of taxes for the railroads, probably did not produce important savings in the long run. Moreover, these methods were also available to the buyers of railroad land and equally available to settlers on government land. (3) Nonpayment or delayed payment of taxes by individuals was common, especially in bad crop years. Such delinquency was probably somewhat more common on taxable lands privately entered than on taxable railroad lands under contract to buyers, largely because railroads insisted upon and supervised the prompt payment of taxes as a part of the contractual arrangement. Once the contract had been fulfilled and title passed—because the railroads did not fight illegal or excessive assessments levied against buyers, only such levies against themselves—the owner of former railroad land was probably just as delinquent just as often as his neighbor on former government land. (4) Because railroads habitually opposed almost any local tax that seemed susceptible of defeat or compromise, the translation of their own tax liability into tax payment was not complete. The reductions they obtained through

[39] The Adams County Commissioners' Proceedings chronicle the defaulting and eventual trial of a county treasurer for such practices. See volume 1, pp. 418, 425, 429; volume 2, *passim*; and volume 3, pp. 5–17, 87, 121, 358.

litigation and compromise probably resulted in an average saving of fifteen to twenty per cent for the Burlington and considerably less for the other, less persistent and less successful roads. These reductions do not seem to have been sufficient, however, to invalidate the conclusion that the railroads paid an average of between eighty and ninety per cent of the taxes levied on their legally assessable property.

The ultimate effect of these tax structures and patterns of tax payment on the economic position of individual property owners and on the general growth of these areas cannot be determined on the basis of the limited data presented here. Only the possibilities can be suggested. With a tax base established earlier and broadened more rapidly than it might have been without the railroad and its lands, it seems probable that in the first years private personalty bore less than a normal burden of taxation, simply because there was some taxable real estate to bear a share. Also, the fact that there were taxable railroad lands in a county may have attracted settlers to other lands there because they could expect that the initial public improvements would be partially paid for before their own lands reached the tax rolls. These factors would have encouraged, rather than retarded, the early growth of these counties and placed the settler on non-railroad land in a position that was at least temporarily advantageous.

The position of the railroads and the buyers of their land, on the other hand, would be less favorable. The buyers of railroad lands that were already taxable or that became taxable because the road applied for patents when they were sold, would probably have been discouraged to the extent that this liability increased their financial burden. Under these conditions they would probably be willing to pay somewhat less for the land though, of course, if the area was developing rapidly (and these areas often were) the demand for railroad lands would partly, if not completely, offset the depressive tendencies produced by their liability for taxes.

It is manifestly impossible to estimate what net effect the special tax position of these lands had on the return the railroads realized from the sale of them. Only detailed study of specific land prices, sales, and tax costs would make an estimate possible. To the extent that the roads allowed the lands still unsold to become taxable (and the tax base studies show that they frequently did so, especially in the early years) the net return was probably reduced. It seems certain, however, in view of the large acreages of railroad lands that did escape taxation until 1887 and the general practice of postponing applications for patent until the lands were sold, that the tax-exemption feature did increase the ultimate return from the land grant over what it would have been had they been forced to pay taxes on them all. It is possible, even likely, that the roads could not have retained the lands had they been taxable from the start. The final answer to this question, like the others, is not provided here. It could be provided only by a close analysis of railroad financial records.

The railroad operating departments, because their share of the tax burden was reduced in direct proportion to the amount of other property on the tax rolls, probably benefited from the liability of the land departments and that of the buyers of railroad land. It is also likely that the rapid growth of these areas, increasing as it did the demand for transportation, increased operating income. Furthermore, expansion of business probably increased the opportunity to shift all or a portion of operating department taxes to shippers and passengers, though whether this shift actually took place, and if it did, to what degree, is another question that must await further analysis. If the roads were already charging all the traffic would bear, making it impossible to raise rates, taxes came from profits, that is from returns to security holders. If the roads did raise rates, the volume of business was probably reduced, and the shift was incomplete. Also, any increase in rates, because it reduced the potential net return to the settlers on products of the land shipped to market, probably reduced not only the rate of growth but also property values, including those of railroad land, thus indirectly reducing the return on the land subsidy. It is also clear that if all or part of taxes were shifted to shippers, some levies on operating property by sparsely settled, not yet agriculturally developed, counties were actually collected indirectly from customers in older areas; in other words, the more developed settlements contributed a portion of the public revenues of the newer governments.[40]

Beyond the identification of these general possibilities nothing can be said concerning the economic effects of either the taxation of railroad land and operating property in general or the tax-exemption feature in particular until a detailed study of the finances of the railroads and of the economic and social development of the locales has been made. Such a study is beyond the scope of the problem-solving approach, selective techniques, and numerical-descriptive analysis utilized here. If this volume serves merely to raise at least this aspect of mid-continent history from the political debating platform of Populist-Positivist tradition and to demonstrate the need for such knowledge, it has served the only purpose it can.

[40] This conclusion is the opposite of that reached by *Omaha Herald* editor Miller. See above, pages 27, 126. Miller thought that the effect of assessing the lands would be to shift the tax burden directly to shippers. Actually it was the nonassessment of them that produced whatever immediate shifting took place.

Eleven

An Assessment

THE story of the taxation of railroad lands touches upon aspects of national as well as Western history and on the political, social, and judicial as well as the administrative, economic, and business history of its period. Its implications are therefore many, transcending the monographic analysis in the preceding pages. The light it sheds is in many places faint and doubtless often serves to obscure as much as it serves to clarify. After all, the limited validity of the assumptions made and the methods utilized limits the validity of any general conclusions drawn from it. Yet these conclusions cannot be ignored if only because there is no effective way to fit them into the Positivist-Populist interpretation of mid-continent history.

It has long been a commonplace among historians that the Congresses of the 1860's, by the passage of a series of permissive and exploitative acts, expressly abdicated virtually all the restrictive and regulatory powers that the central government—as a proprietor of natural resources, if in no other capacity—had exercised intermittently in the first half of the century. When it did bestir itself to interfere in economic matters, it did so as a partner in exploitation, not as a policeman. Tariff schedules, diplomatic activities, money and banking legislation, and land policies were all designed to abet, not restrain, the wholesale appropriation of wealth to those strong enough or unscrupulous enough to take it. Then, over a twenty-year period, a judiciary dominated by men solicitous of the interests of expanding business, sound money, and a Darwinian theory of social change gradually took away whatever vestige of restrictive power remained and left the legislative and, to a lesser extent, the executive branch of government helpless until popular pressure and a powerful reform leadership pointed the way to regained supremacy.

This study invites an altered view. In its railroad land-grant policy Congress did not abdicate control. It first increased it, then lost it. Legislation subsidizing privately constructed internal improvements through grants of land was not new. It went back to wagon roads and canals. But the old method of supervision had used machinery created by the individual state and controlled by it. The new departure in the granting acts passed in 1862 and thereafter was the concentration of the supervisory and administrative instruments of the subsidy in the hands of the executive department of the central government. Then Congress, after taking the fatal step of committing the executive to control, failed to make two more necessary moves. It did not create the machinery to carry out its expressed intent, and it did not clarify that intent when the occasion demanded. These omissions might have been of little moment save for two additional factors over which Congress did have control and a further general development over which it had none. Within the control of Congress was the size of the grants it made. They were huge, and because they were, the administrative task created was a tremendous one. Also within its control was the nature of the land system of which the grants were a part. It was a hodgepodge of contradictory, loosely drawn legislation, ill-suited to much of the land it sought to alienate. Outside congressional control were the technological change, growth of population, and social evolution that both helped to produce and was produced by the unprecedented and dizzying national expansion of the period. The impact of this expansion on the confused system of law and inadequate and outmoded system of administration provided by Congress was first to disjoint it, then to make a farce of it.

This combination of congressional ineptitude and national growth placed before the judges a difficult task. As primary interpreter of the law the judiciary had to decide—in the face of a set of rapidly changing external circumstances—the constitutionality, intent, compatability with existing law, and function of all the statutes and parts of statutes brought before it. Confronted with an act like that of 1862 and its amendment of 1864, the judges had to identify, separate, and rank three contradictory rights in the lands granted. They also had to pass on its relation to the Preëmption Act and on the constitutionality and intent of conditions-after-the-fact added in the 1864 amendment. Hardly had that been begun when a series of new amendments, added in 1870 and 1876, demanded the same treatment. Then came a group of special laws and one general statute repealing all or parts of many of the granting acts—the forfeitures. Small wonder that the judges seemed to vacillate, to contradict themselves, to favor the one interpretation that had the sanction of centuries of Anglo-Saxon legal tradition—the inviolability of private property. There seems to be no question that many of them were influenced by a solicitous attitude toward the acquisitive champions of the new age. But it is a serious mistake to discount the pressures and complexities of the chore the legislators had set, and continued to set, before them.

If the judges' task was difficult, the administrators' was well-nigh impossible. Presented with a burden the volume of which and the implications of which were without precedent, they received neither the personnel nor the funds required for the task. Nor had they received effective instructions. The laws they administered were the same loosely drawn, ambiguous, and contradictory laws the judges interpreted. And the interpretations of the judges were slow in coming, subject to change, and germane to only a fraction of the questions that arose in the Land Office. But these administrators were usually practical men—after all, they were politicians—and, given time, a reasonable volume of business, and a reduction of legislative and judicial mind-changing, they might have worked out their problems on their own. In fact, they showed signs of doing so in the late sixties and again in the middle seventies. The eighties changed all that. The trans-Mississippi land boom robbed them of their time and the legislators sought reform. The administrators were inundated. Only when the land bubble burst and the reformers were beaten back did they begin to recover. No suggestion is here made that the fundamental differences between a William A. J. Sparks and a Lewis Groff or between a Carl Schurz and a John W. Noble did not profoundly influence land policy and land reform. What is suggested is that the conditions of their task—the incongruous land system, ambiguous laws, and mountainous arrears—as well as their attitudes toward reform and their abilities as administrators determined their roles and the role of their offices in the shaping of land policy.

The reformers, both legislative and administrative, were faced with a complex, but soluble, problem. However, because they did not recognize its true nature, they could not solve it. Blinded by the conviction that the miscarriage of a statute could be laid directly at the door of those benefited, they looked no further than that to find the villain. Their reaction in the patent-taxation controversy is an excellent example. That patents issued slowly was proven. That this saved the railroads vast sums of money was usually assumed, sometimes demonstrated. Thus, because they benefited from it, the railroads were held responsible for the delay. To end the delay it was only necessary to remove the benefit. It didn't work. It didn't work because no more complex problem than the taxation of the granted lands was ever created by the railroad land grant policy. To have solved it would have required the thorough clarification of existing conveyance law, the settlement of the railroad debt and forfeiture accounts, the overhauling and enlarging of the administrative machinery, and the adjustment of other land law (or railroad land law, or both) to make the land system internally consistent and consistent with the character of the land and the nature of the settlement on the land left in the public domain— as well as the coercion of the railroads. But there was more. Not only was the reform approach unsound, it was also self-defeating. By attacking manifestations of the problem—withdrawal, forfeiture, taxation, debt—instead of the problem, the reformers were dividing their interests and energies. They spent as much time fighting among themselves as they did doing battle with the defenders of the old, confused, confusing, and (to some) profitable system of railroad law. The diehard adherents to the status quo were few indeed. The discontented were many, but they disapproved of too many different things for too many different reasons to accomplish much. When they did get together, the product was usually too tardy and too enfeebled to work even the partial cure they sought.

The end results of the reform movement were three. (1) The remedies were partial and ineffectual: taxation came late and its application was restricted; forfeiture was relatively inconsequential; and debt settlement was tentative. (2) The land system, despite substantial changes, was still confused, fraud-ridden, and poorly adapted to the land. (3) The patenting log-jam was removed not because the reformers had repaired the administration of the land system, but because they had been defeated in the attempt. There is no doubt that the failure of railroad land reform is to be partially attributed to conservative and railroad opposition. It would be a mistake, however, to discount the contributions of the reformers to the defeat.

The subjects of all this concern, the trans-Missouri land-grant railroads, had some serious problems of their own. As recipients of a direct subsidy—land in all cases, bond as well in some—they were subject to supervision by the central government. Federal railroad regulation began in 1862, not in 1887. This liability to supervision had three direct and related effects on these companies: (1) it put them into national politics on a scale never before known, first to fight among themselves for the grants and privileges that often meant the difference between success and failure and later to fight together (at least part of the time) against those who sought to take them away; (2) it made them hyper-susceptible to political prying, criticism, and reprisal, as the promoters discovered to their sorrow when the Credit Mobilier and like scandals revealed their sharp and sometimes downright crooked practices; and (3) it gradually taught them the value of public sympathy, after they had lost it. They were among the first of the corporations to undertake the direct public defense of themselves. Political and public relations thus became standard—and necessary—parts of the regular procedure of these roads, well before business in general or even most other utilities found them essential to profitable operation.

In the last analysis, however, the political role of the roads and how they played it was a small, if highly significant, part of their business activity. Profitable operation on a month-to-month basis was possible only when operating revenue exceeded fixed and operating costs. And the land-grant railroads, partly because they were highly uncertain enterprises, carried a heavy burden of fixed costs. True, earlier roads had made a profit for both promoters and investors, but earlier roads had been built either in settled areas or on the fringes of them. The trans-Missouri roads were usually built far in advance of even prospective settlement. Large capital investment in an enterprise that would show a profit only slowly and about whose success there was much room for doubt commanded high interest and good additional bonuses, such as discounts and advantageous conversion privileges. Even without dummy construction companies and sharp promotion practices, then, the costs of capital were great. With them the costs were immense.

The land grants, viewed in these terms, functioned to reduce uncertainty and thereby cheapen capital. They supplied two means of combatting the excessive cost of the investment. First, they gave the roads the means of increasing operating revenue rapidly by promoting productive settlement on the land. Thus they reduced capital costs by making prospective operating income surer and by promising to bring it sooner. Second, they gave the roads the means of meeting a part of capital indebtedness by giving them a direct bond-retirement income from the sale of land. From this dual function there emerged a kind of corporate schizophrenia. To sell the land to actual settlers promoted transportation and increased operating revenue. But actual settlers had little money. Thus, because it was necessary to give long credit and because payments often depended on the weather, the price of wheat, and other unpredictable factors, the return for the servicing of the costs of capital and for its retirement was less sure on a sale for settlement than it was on a sale for revenue. The temptation was great, therefore, to encourage sales for cash or for the conversion of land directly into bonds for retirement, to think in short-run terms, to forget future and doubtful operating revenue, and to concentrate on the more pressing need for servicing and retiring capital indebtedness. Each element in this corporate dilemma was served, at varying and often recurrent points in the history of each road, by company policies.

In the fight over the taxation of the granted lands these political and economic peculiarities of the trans-Missouri railroads found focus. To tax the granted lands was to tax the capital fund. That is to say: taxing the land had the opposite effect from granting it. It decreased the potential return from the subsidy. It seemed logical to fight it. This is not to say that the railroadmen planned it that way from the beginning. It is conceivable. It is not very likely. However, once they had established the tax exemption in the courts, it seemed good business to take advantage of it. At one time or another every one of the long-distance roads did so. Because their individual relations with the central government and with the local governments, as well as economic need, helped determine when and how much they did so, the policies of the individual roads were very different. The Northern Pacific was perhaps the worst offender. The Kansas Pacific (with its subsidiary Denver Pacific) was a close second. The Union Pacific did it a great deal, the Central Pacific much less, and the Southern Pacific least of all. In many instances a combination of external circumstances and administrative delay forced it upon them. Only the Kansas Pacific before 1882 and the Union Pacific after 1874 were usually without such extenuating circumstances, flimsy though some of them were. In the end, what may have seemed good business turned out to have been bad politics. When the reformers attacked them they had no effective defense. That Congress, the courts, and the Land Office had helped create the situation made no difference to the critics. The railroads had not paid their share of taxes, alleged the reformers. They were, therefore, adjudged responsible and the penalty placed on their heads.

The reform estimate of the local effects of railroad land tax exemption was as superficial and myopic as its estimate of the causes. The effects were neither as completely detrimental to the settlers on government lands nor as clearly advantageous to the companies and the buyers of their lands as the critics supposed. According to the reformers, the local taxing jurisdictions suffered heavy losses from the extensive and long-continued non-taxation of granted lands. This restriction of the local tax base, they argued, produced sharp curtailment of local public expenditures and shifted the burden of local taxation to the settlers on government lands, who, they said, had no such effective loophole in federal law through which to escape assessment. Thus were the quality and quantity of local public improvements—and, consequently, the rate of growth—decreased and the burdens of the settlers increased by the operation of the exemption. Actually, however, almost everybody had available to him the means of avoiding land taxation during the first years of local development. What, in theory, seemed to give the land-grant railroads and the buyers of their lands great tax advantage over the settlers on government lands gave them, in practice, not a superior position but the possibility—rarely the actuality—of tax equality with land claimants on the public domain. For the occupants of government lands also had the benefits of tax exemption while they were perfecting title. Both groups had advantages and neither hesitated to exploit them.

Many of the advantages possessed by the settlers on public lands were shared by all residents of the locality. Not the least was the control of the county officers and, through them, of the level of local assessment and local expenditure. Within broad limits set by state legislation the residents of a county, precinct, municipality, or school district could decide for what purposes they wished to appropriate or borrow funds and how much they would spend. They could themselves supply materials and labor for county building projects, and at least some of them could collect salaries, fees, and commissions from the county government. They were close enough to the scene to profit from the use of depreciated county warrants, provided they had the means. They could supply road work to pay a part of their taxes. In short, they had the advantages endowed by their presence on the scene and their essential share in the policy decisions made there.

The occupants of government lands had one additional advantage. If their jurisdiction was possessed of a substantial quantity of taxable railroad property, either personal or real, or of taxable lands purchased from the road by neighboring settlers (or speculators)—invariably a minority—there was little to prevent them from assessing, taxing, and spending at high levels. If their own lands were not yet taxable, they could raise these levels as high as the railroad lawyers' sharp eye for the letter of the law would permit. If their own lands were taxable, they were encouraged to restrain their ambitions.

The railroads also had important advantages. Until 1887 they could keep some of their lands off the tax rolls by delaying the selection and patenting of them. They could maintain special legal departments to prosecute county officials and enjoin county expenditures whenever there was a prospect of success. They could offer passes to and otherwise solicit the allegiance of local public officials, newspapermen, and influential private citizens. They could hire local lawyers or land agents to guard their interests. They could purchase county warrants and contract for substitutes to do road work for them. They could bring pressure for compromise through their control of a key sector of the local economy—its transportation facility and part of its real estate—and of an important segment of the organized political power, at least on the state level. Finally, since their property so often comprised more than a majority of the taxable value in the county, they could, sometimes, force the inhabitants—usually desperately in need of revenues to finance their projects—to accept half a loaf, to settle for a portion of the taxes due.

In counties possessing land-grant lands or railroad personalty or both, it seems likely that the settlers on government lands were usually assessed for a lesser, often far lesser, proportion of local taxes than were the settlers on railroad lands and the railroads themselves. In the cases studied here, the roads—even though they could and often did obtain reductions in court or by compromise—and the buyers of railroad lands usually paid a greater proportion of taxes than did others in the first years, and they continued to contribute a large portion in all such counties and a predominant proportion in the western counties throughout the entire period. If the railroad-derived part of the tax base was as large as it appears to have been, then it seems legitimate to conclude that in railroad land-grant areas (1) the tax base was larger and broader in the first years of settlement than it would have been without railroad grant lands and railroad operating property; (2) public improvements came sooner and perhaps were more extensive in these areas; and (3) at least some opportunity was provided for the settlers on the public domain to benefit from these improvements and partly discharge the costs before their own lands became taxable. All this despite the tax exemptions and tax advantages given by Congress and the courts to or created for themselves by the railroads.

In this instance congressional shortsightedness and ineptitude in the provisions made in and the supervision provided for its grants of land for the encouragement of internal improvements were indeed exploitative in their results—encouraged the easy and rapid appropriation to private hands of the trans-Missouri public domain. The railroads were encouraged (perhaps enabled to survive) to the degree that non-taxation maintained (or increased) the value of the original subsidy. At the same time, to the degree that the lands were taxed in advance of neighboring property in any jurisdiction, they probably served to help the early settlers, to attract futher immigration, to hasten public improvements, and in similar ways to encourage the rapid growth of the land-grant areas.

But though both these tendencies turned out to be complementary to the original promotional intent of the grants, a serious and unforeseen problem developed—the problem of balance between the direct subsidy of the railroads on the one hand and what can legitimately be viewed as the indirect subsidy (through the early provision of taxable values) of the public revenues of the localities on the other. To maintain the exemption, especially if it was done in the face of the rapid settlement of the eighties, was to tip the balance in favor of the roads. To eliminate it was to tip the balance in favor of the localities. It was here that the crudeness of the land-grant system became most clear and the inadequate methods of amendment and control broke down. Given the original granting acts and the structure of the system of administration and legal interpretation available to them, those who attempted to change the system to benefit themselves or to abet policies they favored and those who attempted to maintain it (for the same reasons) were forced to resort to politics to gain their ends. There was no other way.

Thus it was that the conflict over the taxation of the granted lands became a conflict between political interests as well as economic; but it cannot be correctly counted as a struggle between the forces of private monopoly, exploitation, and injustice on the one side and the forces of public welfare, conservation, and fair play on the other. That railroad men and "railroad statesmen," in seeking to serve what they took to be their interests, invoked the rule of law, the sanctity of property, and the inviolability of contract surprises no one. It was the language of the day. That settlers and "agrarian crusaders," in seeking to serve what they took to be their interests, invoked human rights, popular sovereignty, and the agrarian tradition is equally unsurprising. It was the same language.

Appendix

THE diagrams reproduced on the pages that follow show the development between 1872 and 1897 of land taxability in each of the 137 townships and parts of townships studied in order to determine the relationship on the tax rolls between railroad lands and other lands. In each instance the shaded areas on the diagram represent those lands shown by the records of the county involved to have been patented, deeded, certified, or otherwise clearly taxable on the date shown. The odd-numbered sections, except in the special cases noted on the individual diagrams, represent railroad lands. The even-numbered sections represent either privately entered or state-owned lands. A map of each county showing the locations of the townships, the route of the principal railroad, and the location of the county seat is included at the beginning of the section of the Appendix dealing with that county.

For five of the six counties studied the information utilized in the preparation of these diagrams is derived from the numerical indices of the county, located in the office of the register of deeds at the county seat. Because the numerical indices of Russell County, Kansas, are kept in a form that is not usable for these purposes, the source of information for that county is Lands Entered in Russell County, a ledger showing lands reported to the county officials by the officers of the local land office as entered and therefore subject to taxation. The ledger is located in the office of the county commissioners. An extended discussion of the reliability of all these records as sources of the information presented in the diagrams, the rules of evidence followed in deciding when a given tract became taxable, and the possible distortion produced by these rules of evidence is included in the concluding section of Chapter 7 of the text.

SALINE   COUNTY,   KANSAS

T 13 — R 5	T 13 — R 4	T 13 — R 3	T 13 — R 2	
	T 14 — R 4			T 13 — R 1
T 14 — R 5		T 14 — R 3	T 14 — R 2	T 14 — R 1
T 15 — R 5	T 15 — R 4	T 15 — R 3	T 15 — R 2	T 15 — R 1
T 16 — R 5	T 16 — R 4	T 16 — R 3	T 16 — R 2	T 16 — R 1

☒ Salina   (County   Seat)

+++ Kansas   Pacific   Railroad

SALINE COUNTY, KANSAS   TOWNSHIP 13 S, RANGE 1 W

1872

1877

1882

1887

1892

1897

* Railroad lands lost to prior claimants.

SALINE COUNTY, KANSAS   TOWNSHIP 14 S, RANGE 1 W

1872

1877

1882

1887

1892

1897

* Railroad lands lost to prior claimants.

SALINE COUNTY, KANSAS   TOWNSHIP 15 S, RANGE 1 W

6	5	4	3	2	1
7	8	9	10	11	12
18	17	16	15	14	13
19	20	21	22	23	24
30	29	28	27	26	25
31	32	33	34	35	36

1872

6	5	4	3	2	1
7	8	9	10	11	12
18	17	16	15	14	13
19	20	21	22	23	24
30	29	28	27	26	25
31	32	33	34	35	36

1877

6	5	4	3	2	1
7	8	9	10	11	12
18	17	16	15	14	13
19	20	21	22	23	24
30	29	28	27	26	25
31	32	33	34	35	36

1882

6	5	4	3	2	1
7	8	9	10	11	12
18	17	16	15	14	13
19	20	21	22	23	24
30	29	28	27	26	25
31	32	33	34	35	36

1887

6	5	4	3	2	1
7	8	9	10	11	12
18	17	16	15	14	13
19	20	21	22	23	24
30	29	28	27	26	25
31	32	33	34	35	36

1892

6	5	4	3	2	1
7	8	9	10	11	12
18	17	16	15	14	13
19	20	21	22	23	24
30	29	28	27	26	25
31	32	33	34	35	36

1897

* Railroad lands lost to prior claimants.

SALINE COUNTY, KANSAS   TOWNSHIP 16 S, RANGE 1 W

1872

1877

1882

1887

1892

1897

* Railroad lands lost to prior claimants.

SALINE COUNTY, KANSAS   TOWNSHIP 13 S, RANGE 2 W

1872

1877

1882

1887

1892

1897

* Railroad lands lost to prior claimants.

SALINE COUNTY, KANSAS

TOWNSHIP 14 S, RANGE 2 W

1872

1877

1882

1887

1892

1897

* Railroad lands lost to prior claimants.

SALINE COUNTY, KANSAS   TOWNSHIP 15 S, RANGE 2 W

1872

1877

1882

1887

1892

1897

* Railroad lands lost to prior claimants.

SALINE COUNTY, KANSAS   TOWNSHIP 16 S, RANGE 2 W

1872

1877

1882

1887

1892

1897

* Railroad lands lost to prior claimants.

SALINE COUNTY, KANSAS   TOWNSHIP 13 S, RANGE 3 W

1872

1877

1882

1887

1892

1897

* Railroad lands lost to prior claimants.

SALINE COUNTY, KANSAS   TOWNSHIP 14 S, RANGE 3 W

1872

1877

1882

1887

1892

1897

* Railroad lands lost to prior claimants.

SALINE COUNTY, KANSAS   TOWNSHIP 15 S, RANGE 3 W

6	5	4	3	2	1
7	8	9	10	11	12
18	17	16	15	14	13
19	20	21	22	23	24
30	29	28	27	26	25
31	32	33	34	35	36

1872

6	5	4	3	2	1
7	8	9	10	11	12
18	17	16	15	14	13
19	20	21	22	23	24
30	29	28	27	26	25
31	32	33	34	35	36

1877

6	5	4	3	2	1
7	8	9	10	11	12
18	17	16	15	14	13
19	20	21	22	23	24
30	29	28	27	26	25
31	32	33	34	35	36

1882

6	5	4	3	2	1
7	8	9	10	11	12
18	17	16	15	14	13
19	20	21	22	23	24
30	29	28	27	26	25
31	32	33	34	35	36

1887

6	5	4	3	2	1
7	8	9	10	11	12
18	17	16	15	14	13
19	20	21	22	23	24
30	29	28	27	26	25
31	32	33	34	35	36

1892

6	5	4	3	2	1
7	8	9	10	11	12
18	17	16	15	14	13
19	20	21	22	23	24
30	29	28	27	26	25
31	32	33	34	35	36

1897

* Railroad lands lost to prior claimants.

SALINE COUNTY, KANSAS TOWNSHIP 16 S, RANGE 3 W

1872

1877

1882

1887

1892

1897

* Railroad lands lost to prior claimants.

SALINE COUNTY, KANSAS   TOWNSHIP 13 S, RANGE 4 W

1872

1877

1882

1887

1892

1897

* Railroad lands lost to prior claimants.

SALINE COUNTY, KANSAS   TOWNSHIP 14 S, RANGE 4 W

6	5	4	3	2	1
7	8	9	10	11	12
18	17	16	15	14	13
19	20	21	22	23	24
30	29	28	27	26	25
31	32	33	34	35	36

1872

1877

1882

1887

1892

1897

* Railroad lands lost to prior claimants.

SALINE COUNTY, KANSAS   TOWNSHIP 15 S, RANGE 4 W

6	5	4	3	2	1
7	8	9	10	11	12
18	17	16	15	14	13
19	20	21	22	23	24
30	29	28	27	26	25
31	32	33	34	35	36

1872

6	5	4	3	2	1
7	8	9	10	11	12
18	17	16	15	14	13
19	20	21	22	23	24
30	29	28	27	26	25
31	32	33	34	35	36

1877

6	5	4	3	2	1
7	8	9	10	11	12
18	17	16	15	14	13
19	20	21	22	23	24
30	29	28	27	26	25
31	32	33	34	35	36

1882

6	5	4	3	2	1
7	8	9	10	11	12
18	17	16	15	14	13
19	20	21	22	23	24
30	29	28	27	26	25
31	32	33	34	35	36

1887

6	5	4	3	2	1
7	8	9	10	11	12
18	17	16	15	14	13
19	20	21	22	23	24
30	29	28	27	26	25
31	32	33	34	35	36

1892

6	5	4	3	2	1
7	8	9	10	11	12
18	17	16	15	14	13
19	20	21	22	23	24
30	29	28	27	26	25
31	32	33	34	35	36

1897

SALINE COUNTY, KANSAS   TOWNSHIP 16 S, RANGE 4 W

6	5	4	3	2	1
7	8	9	10	11	12
18	17	16	15	14	13
19	20	21	22	23	24
30	29	28	27	26	25
31	32	33	34	35	36

1872

6	5	4	3	2	1
7	8	9	10	11	12
18	17	16	15	14	13
19	20	21	22	23	24
30	29	28	27	26	25
31	32	33	34	35	36

1877

6	5	4	3	2	1
7	8	9	10	11	12
18	17	16	15	14	13
19	20	21	22	23	24
30	29	28	27	26	25
31	32	33	34	35	36

1882

6	5	4	3	2	1
7	8	9	10	11	12
18	17	16	15	14	13
19	20	21	22	23	24
30	29	28	27	26	25
31	32	33	34	35	36

1887

6	5	4	3	2	1
7	8	9	10	11	12
18	17	16	15	14	13
19	20	21	22	23	24
30	29	28	27	26	25
31	32	33	34	35	36

1892

6	5	4	3	2	1
7	8	9	10	11	12
18	17	16	15	14	13
19	20	21	22	23	24
30	29	28	27	26	25
31	32	33	34	35	36

1897

SALINE COUNTY, KANSAS   TOWNSHIP 13 S, RANGE 5 W

6	5	4	3	2	1
7	8	9	10	11	12
18	17	16	15	14	13
19	20	21	22	23	24
30	29	28	27	26	25
31	32	33	34	35	36

1872

6	5	4	3	2	1
7	8	9	10	11	12
18	17	16	15	14	13
19	20	21	22	23	24
30	29	28	27	26	25
31	32	33	34	35	36

1877

6	5	4	3	2	1
7	8	9	10	11	12
18	17	16	15	14	13
19	20	21	22	23	24
30	29	28	27	26	25
31	32	33	34	35	36

1882

6	5	4	3	2	1
7	8	9	10	11	12
18	17	16	15	14	13
19	20	21	22	23	24
30	29	28	27	26	25
31	32	33	34	35	36

1887

6	5	4	3	2	1
7	8	9	10	11	12
18	17	16	15	14	13
19	20	21	22	23	24
30	29	28	27	26	25
31	32	33	34	35	36

1892

6	5	4	3	2	1
7	8	9	10	11	12
18	17	16	15	14	13
19	20	21	22	23	24
30	29	28	27	26	25
31	32	33	34	35	36

1897

* Railroad lands lost to prior claimants.

SALINE COUNTY, KANSAS   TOWNSHIP 14 S, RANGE 5 W

6	5	4	3	2	1
7	8	9	10	11	12
18	17	16	15	14	13
19	20	21	22	23	24
30	29	28	27	26	25
31	32	33	34	35	36

1872

6	5	4	3	2	1
7	8	9	10	11	12
18	17	16	15	14	13
19	20	21	22	23	24
30	29	28	27	26	25
31	32	33	34	35	36

1877

6	5	4	3	2	1
7	8	9	10	11	12
18	17	16	15	14	13
19	20	21	22	23	24
30	29	28	27	26	25
31	32	33	34	35	36

1882

6	5	4	3	2	1
7	8	9	10	11	12
18	17	16	15	14	13
19	20	21	22	23	24
30	29	28	27	26	25
31	32	33	34	35	36

1887

6	5	4	3	2	1
7	8	9	10	11	12
18	17	16	15	14	13
19	20	21	22	23	24
30	29	28	27	26	25
31	32	33	34	35	36

1892

6	5	4	3	2	1
7	8	9	10	11	12
18	17	16	15	14	13
19	20	21	22	23	24
30	29	28	27	26	25
31	32	33	34	35	36

1897

SALINE COUNTY, KANSAS   TOWNSHIP 15 S, RANGE 5 W

6	5	4	3	2	1
7	8	9	10	11	12
18	17	16	15	14	13
19	20	21	22	23	24
30	29	28	27	26	25
31	32	33	34	35	36

1872

6	5	4	3	2	1
7	8	9	10	11	12
18	17	16	15	14	13
19	20	21	22	23	24
30	29	28	27	26	25
31	32	33	34	35	36

1877

6	5	4	3	2	1
7	8	9	10	11	12
18	17	16	15	14	13
19	20	21	22	23	24
30	29	28	27	26	25
31	32	33	34	35	36

1882

6	5	4	3	2	1
7	8	9	10	11	12
18	17	16	15	14	13
19	20	21	22	23	24
30	29	28	27	26	25
31	32	33	34	35	36

1887

6	5	4	3	2	1
7	8	9	10	11	12
18	17	16	15	14	13
19	20	21	22	23	24
30	29	28	27	26	25
31	32	33	34	35	36

1892

6	5	4	3	2	1
7	8	9	10	11	12
18	17	16	15	14	13
19	20	21	22	23	24
30	29	28	27	26	25
31	32	33	34	35	36

1897

SALINE COUNTY, KANSAS TOWNSHIP 16 S, RANGE 5 W

6	5	4	3	2	1
7	8	9	10	11	12
18	17	16	15	14	13
19	20	21	22	23	24
30	29	28	27	26	25
31	32	33	34	35	36

1872

6	5	4	3	2	1
7	8	9	10	11	12
18	17	16	15	14	13
19	20	21	22	23	24
30	29	28	27	26	25
31	32	33	34	35	36

1877

6	5	4	3	2	1
7	8	9	10	11	12
18	17	16	15	14	13
19	20	21	22	23	24
30	29	28	27	26	25
31	32	33	34	35	36

1882

6	5	4	3	2	1
7	8	9	10	11	12
18	17	16	15	14	13
19	20	21	22	23	24
30	29	28	27	26	25
31	32	33	34	35	36

1887

6	5	4	3	2	1
7	8	9	10	11	12
18	17	16	15	14	13
19	20	21	22	23	24
30	29	28	27	26	25
31	32	33	34	35	36

1892

6	5	4	3	2	1
7	8	9	10	11	12
18	17	16	15	14	13
19	20	21	22	23	24
30	29	28	27	26	25
31	32	33	34	35	36

1897

RUSSELL COUNTY, KANSAS

T 11 — R 15	T 11 — R 14	T 11 — R 13	T 11 — R 12	T 11 — R 11
T 12 — R 15	T 12 — R 14	T 12 — R 13	T 12 — R 12	T 12 — R 11
T 13 — R 15	T 13 — R 14	T 13 — R 13	T 13 — R 12	T 13 — R 11
T 14 — R 15	T 14 — R 14	T 14 — R 13	T 14 — R 12	T 14 — R 11
T 15 — R 15	T 15 — R 14	T 15 — R 13	T 15 — R 12	T 15 — R 11

☒ Russell (County Seat)

+++ Kansas Pacific Railroad

RUSSELL COUNTY, KANSAS TOWNSHIP 11 S, RANGE 11 W

6	5	4	3	2	1
7	8	9 *	10	11	12
18	17	16	15	14	13
19	20	21	22	23	24
30	29	28	27	26	25
31	32	33	34	35	36

1872

6	5	4	3	2	1
7	8	9 *	10	11	12
18	17	16	15	14	13
19	20	21	22	23	24
30	29	28	27	26	25
31	32	33	34	35	36

1877

6	5	4	3	2	1
7	8	9 *	10	11	12
18	17	16	15	14	13
19	20	21	22	23	24
30	29	28	27	26	25
31	32	33	34	35	36

1882

6	5	4	3	2	1
7	8	9 *	10	11	12
18	17	16	15	14	13
19	20	21	22	23	24
30	29	28	27	26	25
31	32	33	34	35	36

1887

6	5	4	3	2	1
7	8	9 *	10	11	12
18	17	16	15	14	13
19	20	21	22	23	24
30	29	28	27	26	25
31	32	33	34	35	36

1892

6	5	4	3	2	1
7	8	9 *	10	11	12
18	17	16	15	14	13
19	20	21	22	23	24
30	29	28	27	26	25
31	32	33	34	35	36

1897

* Railroad lands lost to prior claimants.

RUSSELL COUNTY, KANSAS   TOWNSHIP 12 S, RANGE 11 W

6	5	4	3	2	1
7	8	9	10	11	12
18	17	16	15	14	13
19	20	21	22	23	24
30	29	28	27	26	25
31	32	33	34	35	36

1872

6	5	4	3	2	1
7	8	9	10	11	12
18	17	16	15	14	13
19	20	21	22	23	24
30	29	28	27	26	25
31	32	33	34	35	36

1877

6	5	4	3	2	1
7	8	9	10	11	12
18	17	16	15	14	13
19	20	21	22	23	24
30	29	28	27	26	25
31	32	33	34	35	36

1882

6	5	4	3	2	1
7	8	9	10	11	12
18	17	16	15	14	13
19	20	21	22	23	24
30	29	28	27	26	25
31	32	33	34	35	36

1887

6	5	4	3	2	1
7	8	9	10	11	12
18	17	16	15	14	13
19	20	21	22	23	24
30	29	28	27	26	25
31	32	33	34	35	36

1892

6	5	4	3	2	1
7	8	9	10	11	12
18	17	16	15	14	13
19	20	21	22	23	24
30	29	28	27	26	25
31	32	33	34	35	36

1897

RUSSELL COUNTY, KANSAS   TOWNSHIP 13 S, RANGE 11 W

6	5	4	3	2	1
7	8	9	10	11	12
18	17	16	15	14	13
19	20	21	22	23	24
30	29	28	27	26	25
31	32	33	34	35	36

1872

6	5	4	3	2	1
7	8	9	10	11	12
18	17	16	15	14	13
19	20	21	22	23	24
30	29	28	27	26	25
31	32	33	34	35	36

1877

6	5	4	3	2	1
7	8	9	10	11	12
18	17	16	15	14	13
19	20	21	22	23	24
30	29	28	27	26	25
31	32	33	34	35	36

1882

6	5	4	3	2	1
7	8	9	10	11	12
18	17	16	15	14	13
19	20	21	22	23	24
30	29	28	27	26	25
31	32	33	34	35	36

1887

6	5	4	3	2	1
7	8	9	10	11	12
18	17	16	15	14	13
19	20	21	22	23	24
30	29	28	27	26	25
31	32	33	34	35	36

1892

6	5	4	3	2	1
7	8	9	10	11	12
18	17	16	15	14	13
19	20	21	22	23	24
30	29	28	27	26	25
31	32	33	34	35	36

1897

RUSSELL COUNTY, KANSAS   TOWNSHIP 14 S, RANGE 11 W

6	5	4	3	2	1
7	8	9	10	11	12
18	17	16	15	14	13
19	20	21	22	23	24
30	29	28	27	26	25
31	32	33	34	35	36

1872

6	5	4	3	2	1
7	8	9	10	11	12
18	17	16	15	14	13
19	20	21	22	23	24
30	29	28	27	26	25
31	32	33	34	35	36

1877

6	5	4	3	2	1
7	8	9	10	11	12
18	17	16	15	14	13
19	20	21	22	23	24
30	29	28	27	26	25
31	32	33	34	35	36

1882

6	5	4	3	2	1
7	8	9	10	11	12
18	17	16	15	14	13
19	20	21	22	23	24
30	29	28	27	26	25
31	32	33	34	35	36

1887

6	5	4	3	2	1
7	8	9	10	11	12
18	17	16	15	14	13
19	20	21	22	23	24
30	29	28	27	26	25
31	32	33	34	35	36

1892

6	5	4	3	2	1
7	8	9	10	11	12
18	17	16	15	14	13
19	20	21	22	23	24
30	29	28	27	26	25
31	32	33	34	35	36

1897

RUSSELL COUNTY, KANSAS   TOWNSHIP 15 S, RANGE 11 W

6	5	4	3	2	1
7	8	9	10	11	12
18	17	16	15	14	13
19	20	21	22	23	24
30	29	28	27	26	25
31	32	33	34	35	36

1872

6	5	4	3	2	1
7	8	9	10	11	12
18	17	16	15	14	13
19	20	21	22	23	24
30	29	28	27	26	25
31	32	33	34	35	36

1877

6	5	4	3	2	1
7	8	9	10	11	12
18	17	16	15	14	13
19	20	21	22	23	24
30	29	28	27	26	25
31	32	33	34	35	36

1882

6	5	4	3	2	1
7	8	9	10	11	12
18	17	16	15	14	13
19	20	21	22	23	24
30	29	28	27	26	25
31	32	33	34	35	36

1887

6	5	4	3	2	1
7	8	9	10	11	12
18	17	16	15	14	13
19	20	21	22	23	24
30	29	28	27	26	25
31	32	33	34	35	36

1892

6	5	4	3	2	1
7	8	9	10	11	12
18	17	16	15	14	13
19	20	21	22	23	24
30	29	28	27	26	25
31	32	33	34	35	36

1897

RUSSELL COUNTY, KANSAS   TOWNSHIP 11 S, RANGE 12 W

6	5	4	3	2	1
7	8	9	10	11	12
18	17	16	15	14	13
19	20	21	22	23	24
30	29	28	27	26	25
31	32	33	34	35	36

1872

6	5	4	3	2	1
7	8	9	10	11	12
18	17	16	15	14	13
19	20	21	22	23	24
30	29	28	27	26	25
31	32	33	34	35	36

1877

6	5	4	3	2	1
7	8	9	10	11	12
18	17	16	15	14	13
19	20	21	22	23	24
30	29	28	27	26	25
31	32	33	34	35	36

1882

6	5	4	3	2	1
7	8	9	10	11	12
18	17	16	15	14	13
19	20	21	22	23	24
30	29	28	27	26	25
31	32	33	34	35	36

1887

6	5	4	3	2	1
7	8	9	10	11	12
18	17	16	15	14	13
19	20	21	22	23	24
30	29	28	27	26	25
31	32	33	34	35	36

1892

6	5	4	3	2	1
7	8	9	10	11	12
18	17	16	15	14	13
19	20	21	22	23	24
30	29	28	27	26	25
31	32	33	34	35	36

1897

RUSSELL COUNTY, KANSAS   TOWNSHIP 12 S, RANGE 12 W

6	5	4	3	2	1
7	8	9	10	11	12
18	17	16	15	14	13
19	20	21	22	23	24
30	29	28	27	26	25
31	32	33	34	35	36

1872

6	5	4	3	2	1
7	8	9	10	11	12
18	17	16	15	14	13
19	20	21	22	23	24
30	29	28	27	26	25
31	32	33	34	35	36

1877

6	5	4	3	2	1
7	8	9	10	11	12
18	17	16	15	14	13
19	20	21	22	23	24
30	29	28	27	26	25
31	32	33	34	35	36

1882

6	5	4	3	2	1
7	8	9	10	11	12
18	17	16	15	14	13
19	20	21	22	23	24
30	29	28	27	26	25
31	32	33	34	35	36

1887

6	5	4	3	2	1
7	8	9	10	11	12
18	17	16	15	14	13
19	20	21	22	23	24
30	29	28	27	26	25
31	32	33	34	35	36

1892

6	5	4	3	2	1
7	8	9	10	11	12
18	17	16	15	14	13
19	20	21	22	23	24
30	29	28	27	26	25
31	32	33	34	35	36

1897

RUSSELL COUNTY, KANSAS   TOWNSHIP 13 S, RANGE 12 W

6	5	4	3	2	1
7	8	9	10	11	12
18	17	16	15	14	13
19	20	21	22	23	24
30	29	28	27	26	25
31	32	33	34	35	36

1872

6	5	4	3	2	1
7	8	9	10	11	12
18	17	16	15	14	13
19	20	21	22	23	24
30	29	28	27	26	25
31	32	33	34	35	36

1877

6	5	4	3	2	1
7	8	9	10	11	12
18	17	16	15	14	13
19	20	21	22	23	24
30	29	28	27	26	25
31	32	33	34	35	36

1882

6	5	4	3	2	1
7	8	9	10	11	12
18	17	16	15	14	13
19	20	21	22	23	24
30	29	28	27	26	25
31	32	33	34	35	36

1887

6	5	4	3	2	1
7	8	9	10	11	12
18	17	16	15	14	13
19	20	21	22	23	24
30	29	28	27	26	25
31	32	33	34	35	36

1892

6	5	4	3	2	1
7	8	9	10	11	12
18	17	16	15	14	13
19	20	21	22	23	24
30	29	28	27	26	25
31	32	33	34	35	36

1897

RUSSELL COUNTY, KANSAS   TOWNSHIP 14 S, RANGE 12 W

6	5	4	3	2	1
7	8	9	10	11	12
18	17	16	15	14	13
19	20	21	22	23	24
30	29	28	27	26	25
31	32	33	34	35	36

1872

6	5	4	3	2	1
7	8	9	10	11	12
18	17	16	15	14	13
19	20	21	22	23	24
30	29	28	27	26	25
31	32	33	34	35	36

1877

6	5	4	3	2	1
7	8	9	10	11	12
18	17	16	15	14	13
19	20	21	22	23	24
30	29	28	27	26	25
31	32	33	34	35	36

1882

6	5	4	3	2	1
7	8	9	10	11	12
18	17	16	15	14	13
19	20	21	22	23	24
30	29	28	27	26	25
31	32	33	34	35	36

1887

6	5	4	3	2	1
7	8	9	10	11	12
18	17	16	15	14	13
19	20	21	22	23	24
30	29	28	27	26	25
31	32	33	34	35	36

1892

6	5	4	3	2	1
7	8	9	10	11	12
18	17	16	15	14	13
19	20	21	22	23	24
30	29	28	27	26	25
31	32	33	34	35	36

1897

RUSSELL COUNTY, KANSAS   TOWNSHIP 15 S, RANGE 12 W

6	5	4	3	2	1
7	8	9	10	11	12
18	17	16	15	14	13
19	20	21	22	23	24
30	29	28	27	26	25
31	32	33	34	35	36

1872

6	5	4	3	2	1
7	8	9	10	11	12
18	17	16	15	14	13
19	20	21	22	23	24
30	29	28	27	26	25
31	32	33	34	35	36

1877

6	5	4	3	2	1
7	8	9	10	11	12
18	17	16	15	14	13
19	20	21	22	23	24
30	29	28	27	26	25
31	32	33	34	35	36

1882

6	5	4	3	2	1
7	8	9	10	11	12
18	17	16	15	14	13
19	20	21	22	23	24
30	29	28	27	26	25
31	32	33	34	35	36

1887

6	5	4	3	2	1
7	8	9	10	11	12
18	17	16	15	14	13
19	20	21	22	23	24
30	29	28	27	26	25
31	32	33	34	35	36

1892

6	5	4	3	2	1
7	8	9	10	11	12
18	17	16	15	14	13
19	20	21	22	23	24
30	29	28	27	26	25
31	32	33	34	35	36

1897

RUSSELL COUNTY, KANSAS   TOWNSHIP 11 S, RANGE 13 W

6	5	4	3	2	1
7	8	9	10	11	12
18	17	16	15	14	13
19	20	21	22	23	24
30	29	28	27	26	25
31	32	33	34	35	36

1872

6	5	4	3	2	1
7	8	9	10	11	12
18	17	16	15	14	13
19	20	21	22	23	24
30	29	28	27	26	25
31	32	33	34	35	36

1877

6	5	4	3	2	1
7	8	9	10	11	12
18	17	16	15	14	13
19	20	21	22	23	24
30	29	28	27	26	25
31	32	33	34	35	36

1882

6	5	4	3	2	1
7	8	9	10	11	12
18	17	16	15	14	13
19	20	21	22	23	24
30	29	28	27	26	25
31	32	33	34	35	36

1887

6	5	4	3	2	1
7	8	9	10	11	12
18	17	16	15	14	13
19	20	21	22	23	24
30	29	28	27	26	25
31	32	33	34	35	36

1892

6	5	4	3	2	1
7	8	9	10	11	12
18	17	16	15	14	13
19	20	21	22	23	24
30	29	28	27	26	25
31	32	33	34	35	36

1897

RUSSELL COUNTY, KANSAS   TOWNSHIP 12 S, RANGE 13 W

6	5	4	3	2	1
7	8	9	10	11	12
18	17	16	15	14	13
19	20	21	22	23	24
30	29	28	27	26	25
31	32	33	34	35	36

1872

6	5	4	3	2	1
7	8	9	10	11	12
18	17	16	15	14	13
19	20	21	22	23	24
30	29	28	27	26	25
31	32	33	34	35	36

1877

6	5	4	3	2	1
7	8	9	10	11	12
18	17	16	15	14	13
19	20	21	22	23	24
30	29	28	27	26	25
31	32	33	34	35	36

1882

6	5	4	3	2	1
7	8	9	10	11	12
18	17	16	15	14	13
19	20	21	22	23	24
30	29	28	27	26	25
31	32	33	34	35	36

1887

6	5	4	3	2	1
7	8	9	10	11	12
18	17	16	15	14	13
19	20	21	22	23	24
30	29	28	27	26	25
31	32	33	34	35	36

1892

6	5	4	3	2	1
7	8	9	10	11	12
18	17	16	15	14	13
19	20	21	22	23	24
30	29	28	27	26	25
31	32	33	34	35	36

1897

RUSSELL COUNTY, KANSAS

TOWNSHIP 13 S, RANGE 13 W

6	5	4	3	2	1
7	8	9	10	11	12
18	17	16	15	14	13
19	20	21	22	23	24
30	29	28	27	26	25
31	32	33	34	35	36

1872

6	5	4	3	2	1
7	8	9	10	11	12
18	17	16	15	14	13
19	20	21	22	23	24
30	29	28	27	26	25
31	32	33	34	35	36

1877

6	5	4	3	2	1
7	8	9	10	11	12
18	17	16	15	14	13
19	20	21	22	23	24
30	29	28	27	26	25
31	32	33	34	35	36

1882

6	5	4	3	2	1
7	8	9	10	11	12
18	17	16	15	14	13
19	20	21	22	23	24
30	29	28	27	26	25
31	32	33	34	35	36

1887

6	5	4	3	2	1
7	8	9	10	11	12
18	17	16	15	14	13
19	20	21	22	23	24
30	29	28	27	26	25
31	32	33	34	35	36

1892

6	5	4	3	2	1
7	8	9	10	11	12
18	17	16	15	14	13
19	20	21	22	23	24
30	29	28	27	26	25
31	32	33	34	35	36

1897

RUSSELL COUNTY, KANSAS   TOWNSHIP 14 S, RANGE 13 W

6	5	4	3	2	1
7	8	9	10	11	12
18	17	16	15	14	13
19	20	21	22	23	24
30	29	28	27	26	25
31	32	33	34	35	36

1872

6	5	4	3	2	1
7	8	9	10	11	12
18	17	16	15	14	13
19	20	21	22	23	24
30	29	28	27	26	25
31	32	33	34	35	36

1877

6	5	4	3	2	1
7	8	9	10	11	12
18	17	16	15	14	13
19	20	21	22	23	24
30	29	28	27	26	25
31	32	33	34	35	36

1882

6	5	4	3	2	1
7	8	9	10	11	12
18	17	16	15	14	13
19	20	21	22	23	24
30	29	28	27	26	25
31	32	33	34	35	36

1887

6	5	4	3	2	1
7	8	9	10	11	12
18	17	16	15	14	13
19	20	21	22	23	24
30	29	28	27	26	25
31	32	33	34	35	36

1892

6	5	4	3	2	1
7	8	9	10	11	12
18	17	16	15	14	13
19	20	21	22	23	24
30	29	28	27	26	25
31	32	33	34	35	36

1897

RUSSELL COUNTY, KANSAS TOWNSHIP 15 S, RANGE 13 W

6	5	4	3	2	1
7	8	9	10	11	12
18	17	16	15	14	13
19	20	21	22	23	24
30	29	28	27	26	25
31	32	33	34	35	36

1872

6	5	4	3	2	1
7	8	9	10	11	12
18	17	16	15	14	13
19	20	21	22	23	24
30	29	28	27	26	25
31	32	33	34	35	36

1877

6	5	4	3	2	1
7	8	9	10	11	12
18	17	16	15	14	13
19	20	21	22	23	24
30	29	28	27	26	25
31	32	33	34	35	36

1882

6	5	4	3	2	1
7	8	9	10	11	12
18	17	16	15	14	13
19	20	21	22	23	24
30	29	28	27	26	25
31	32	33	34	35	36

1887

6	5	4	3	2	1
7	8	9	10	11	12
18	17	16	15	14	13
19	20	21	22	23	24
30	29	28	27	26	25
31	32	33	34	35	36

1892

6	5	4	3	2	1
7	8	9	10	11	12
18	17	16	15	14	13
19	20	21	22	23	24
30	29	28	27	26	25
31	32	33	34	35	36

1897

RUSSELL COUNTY, KANSAS   TOWNSHIP 11 S, RANGE 14 W

6	5	4	3	2	1
7	8	9	10	11	12
18	17	16	15	14	13
19	20	21	22	23	24
30	29	28	27	26	25
31	32	33	34	35	36

1872

6	5	4	3	2	1
7	8	9	10	11	12
18	17	16	15	14	13
19	20	21	22	23	24
30	29	28	27	26	25
31	32	33	34	35	36

1877

6	5	4	3	2	1
7	8	9	10	11	12
18	17	16	15	14	13
19	20	21	22	23	24
30	29	28	27	26	25
31	32	33	34	35	36

1882

6	5	4	3	2	1
7	8	9	10	11	12
18	17	16	15	14	13
19	20	21	22	23	24
30	29	28	27	26	25
31	32	33	34	35	36

1887

6	5	4	3	2	1
7	8	9	10	11	12
18	17	16	15	14	13
19	20	21	22	23	24
30	29	28	27	26	25
31	32	33	34	35	36

1892

6	5	4	3	2	1
7	8	9	10	11	12
18	17	16	15	14	13
19	20	21	22	23	24
30	29	28	27	26	25
31	32	33	34	35	36

1897

RUSSELL COUNTY, KANSAS   TOWNSHIP 12 S, RANGE 14 W

6	5	4	3	2	1
7	8	9	10	11	12
18	17	16	15	14	13
19	20	21	22	23	24
30	29	28	27	26	25
31	32	33	34	35	36

1872

6	5	4	3	2	1
7	8	9	10	11	12
18	17	16	15	14	13
19	20	21	22	23	24
30	29	28	27	26	25
31	32	33	34	35	36

1877

6	5	4	3	2	1
7	8	9	10	11	12
18	17	16	15	14	13
19	20	21	22	23	24
30	29	28	27	26	25
31	32	33	34	35	36

1882

6	5	4	3	2	1
7	8	9	10	11	12
18	17	16	15	14	13
19	20	21	22	23	24
30	29	28	27	26	25
31	32	33	34	35	36

1887

6	5	4	3	2	1
7	8	9	10	11	12
18	17	16	15	14	13
19	20	21	22	23	24
30	29	28	27	26	25
31	32	33	34	35	36

1892

6	5	4	3	2	1
7	8	9	10	11	12
18	17	16	15	14	13
19	20	21	22	23	24
30	29	28	27	26	25
31	32	33	34	35	36

1897

RUSSELL COUNTY, KANSAS   TOWNSHIP 13 S, RANGE 14 W

6	5	4	3	2	1
7	8	9	10	11	12
18	17	16	15	14	13
19	20	21	22	23	24
30	29	28	27	26	25
31	32	33	34	35	36

1872

6	5	4	3	2	1
7	8	9	10	11	12
18	17	16	15	14	13
19	20	21	22	23	24
30	29	28	27	26	25
31	32	33	34	35	36

1877

6	5	4	3	2	1
7	8	9	10	11	12
18	17	16	15	14	13
19	20	21	22	23	24
30	29	28	27	26	25
31	32	33	34	35	36

1882

6	5	4	3	2	1
7	8	9	10	11	12
18	17	16	15	14	13
19	20	21	22	23	24
30	29	28	27	26	25
31	32	33	34	35	36

1887

6	5	4	3	2	1
7	8	9	10	11	12
18	17	16	15	14	13
19	20	21	22	23	24
30	29	28	27	26	25
31	32	33	34	35	36

1892

6	5	4	3	2	1
7	8	9	10	11	12
18	17	16	15	14	13
19	20	21	22	23	24
30	29	28	27	26	25
31	32	33	34	35	36

1897

RUSSELL COUNTY, KANSAS   TOWNSHIP 14 S, RANGE 14 W

6	5	4	3	2	1
7	8	9	10	11	12
18	17	16	15	14	13
19	20	21	22	23	24
30	29	28	27	26	25
31	32	33	34	35	36

1872

6	5	4	3	2	1
7	8	9	10	11	12
18	17	16	15	14	13
19	20	21	22	23	24
30	29	28	27	26	25
31	32	33	34	35	36

1877

6	5	4	3	2	1
7	8	9	10	11	12
18	17	16	15	14	13
19	20	21	22	23	24
30	29	28	27	26	25
31	32	33	34	35	36

1882

6	5	4	3	2	1
7	8	9	10	11	12
18	17	16	15	14	13
19	20	21	22	23	24
30	29	28	27	26	25
31	32	33	34	35	36

1887

6	5	4	3	2	1
7	8	9	10	11	12
18	17	16	15	14	13
19	20	21	22	23	24
30	29	28	27	26	25
31	32	33	34	35	36

1892

6	5	4	3	2	1
7	8	9	10	11	12
18	17	16	15	14	13
19	20	21	22	23	24
30	29	28	27	26	25
31	32	33	34	35	36

1897

RUSSELL COUNTY, KANSAS   TOWNSHIP 15 S, RANGE 14 W

6	5	4	3	2	1
7	8	9	10	11	12
18	17	16	15	14	13
19	20	21	22	23	24
30	29	28	27	26	25
31	32	33	34	35	36

1872

6	5	4	3	2	1
7	8	9	10	11	12
18	17	16	15	14	13
19	20	21	22	23	24
30	29	28	27	26	25
31	32	33	34	35	36

1877

1882

1887

1892

1897

RUSSELL COUNTY, KANSAS   TOWNSHIP 11 S, RANGE 15 W

6	5	4	3	2	1
7	8	9	10	11	12
18	17	16	15	14	13
19	20	21	22	23	24
30	29	28	27	26	25
31	32	33	34	35	36

1872

6	5	4	3	2	1
7	8	9	10	11	12
18	17	16	15	14	13
19	20	21	22	23	24
30	29	28	27	26	25
31	32	33	34	35	36

1877

6	5	4	3	2	1
7	8	9	10	11	12
18	17	16	15	14	13
19	20	21	22	23	24
30	29	28	27	26	25
31	32	33	34	35	36

1882

6	5	4	3	2	1
7	8	9	10	11	12
18	17	16	15	14	13
19	20	21	22	23	24
30	29	28	27	26	25
31	32	33	34	35	36

1887

6	5	4	3	2	1
7	8	9	10	11	12
18	17	16	15	14	13
19	20	21	22	23	24
30	29	28	27	26	25
31	32	33	34	35	36

1892

6	5	4	3	2	1
7	8	9	10	11	12
18	17	16	15	14	13
19	20	21	22	23	24
30	29	28	27	26	25
31	32	33	34	35	36

1897

RUSSELL COUNTY, KANSAS   TOWNSHIP 12 S, RANGE 15 W

6	5	4	3	2	1
7	8	9	10	11	12
18	17	16	15	14	13
19	20	21	22	23	24
30	29	28	27	26	25
31	32	33	34	35	36

1872

6	5	4	3	2	1
7	8	9	10	11	12
18	17	16	15	14	13
19	20	21	22	23	24
30	29	28	27	26	25
31	32	33	34	35	36

1877

6	5	4	3	2	1
7	8	9	10	11	12
18	17	16	15	14	13
19	20	21	22	23	24
30	29	28	27	26	25
31	32	33	34	35	36

1882

6	5	4	3	2	1
7	8	9	10	11	12
18	17	16	15	14	13
19	20	21	22	23	24
30	29	28	27	26	25
31	32	33	34	35	36

1887

6	5	4	3	2	1
7	8	9	10	11	12
18	17	16	15	14	13
19	20	21	22	23	24
30	29	28	27	26	25
31	32	33	34	35	36

1892

6	5	4	3	2	1
7	8	9	10	11	12
18	17	16	15	14	13
19	20	21	22	23	24
30	29	28	27	26	25
31	32	33	34	35	36

1897

RUSSELL COUNTY, KANSAS

TOWNSHIP 13 S, RANGE 15 W

6	5	4	3	2	1
7	8	9	10	11	12
18	17	16	15	14	13
19	20	21	22	23	24
30	29	28	27	26	25
31	32	33	34	35	36

1872

6	5	4	3	2	1
7	8	9	10	11	12
18	17	16	15	14	13
19	20	21	22	23	24
30	29	28	27	26	25
31	32	33	34	35	36

1877

6	5	4	3	2	1
7	8	9	10	11	12
18	17	16	15	14	13
19	20	21	22	23	24
30	29	28	27	26	25
31	32	33	34	35	36

1882

6	5	4	3	2	1
7	8	9	10	11	12
18	17	16	15	14	13
19	20	21	22	23	24
30	29	28	27	26	25
31	32	33	34	35	36

1887

6	5	4	3	2	1
7	8	9	10	11	12
18	17	16	15	14	13
19	20	21	22	23	24
30	29	28	27	26	25
31	32	33	34	35	36

1892

6	5	4	3	2	1
7	8	9	10	11	12
18	17	16	15	14	13
19	20	21	22	23	24
30	29	28	27	26	25
31	32	33	34	35	36

1897

RUSSELL COUNTY, KANSAS   TOWNSHIP 14 S, RANGE 15 W

6	5	4	3	2	1
7	8	9	10	11	12
18	17	16	15	14	13
19	20	21	22	23	24
30	29	28	27	26	25
31	32	33	34	35	36

1872

6	5	4	3	2	1
7	8	9	10	11	12
18	17	16	15	14	13
19	20	21	22	23	24
30	29	28	27	26	25
31	32	33	34	35	36

1877

6	5	4	3	2	1
7	8	9	10	11	12
18	17	16	15	14	13
19	20	21	22	23	24
30	29	28	27	26	25
31	32	33	34	35	36

1882

6	5	4	3	2	1
7	8	9	10	11	12
18	17	16	15	14	13
19	20	21	22	23	24
30	29	28	27	26	25
31	32	33	34	35	36

1887

6	5	4	3	2	1
7	8	9	10	11	12
18	17	16	15	14	13
19	20	21	22	23	24
30	29	28	27	26	25
31	32	33	34	35	36

1892

6	5	4	3	2	1
7	8	9	10	11	12
18	17	16	15	14	13
19	20	21	22	23	24
30	29	28	27	26	25
31	32	33	34	35	36

1897

RUSSELL COUNTY, KANSAS TOWNSHIP 15 S, RANGE 15 W

6	5	4	3	2	1
7	8	9	10	11	12
18	17	16	15	14	13
19	20	21	22	23	24
30	29	28	27	26	25
31	32	33	34	35	36

1872

6	5	4	3	2	1
7	8	9	10	11	12
18	17	16	15	14	13
19	20	21	22	23	24
30	29	28	27	26	25
31	32	33	34	35	36

1877

6	5	4	3	2	1
7	8	9	10	11	12
18	17	16	15	14	13
19	20	21	22	23	24
30	29	28	27	26	25
31	32	33	34	35	36

1882

6	5	4	3	2	1
7	8	9	10	11	12
18	17	16	15	14	13
19	20	21	22	23	24
30	29	28	27	26	25
31	32	33	34	35	36

1887

6	5	4	3	2	1
7	8	9	10	11	12
18	17	16	15	14	13
19	20	21	22	23	24
30	29	28	27	26	25
31	32	33	34	35	36

1892

6	5	4	3	2	1
7	8	9	10	11	12
18	17	16	15	14	13
19	20	21	22	23	24
30	29	28	27	26	25
31	32	33	34	35	36

1897

TREGO COUNTY, KANSAS

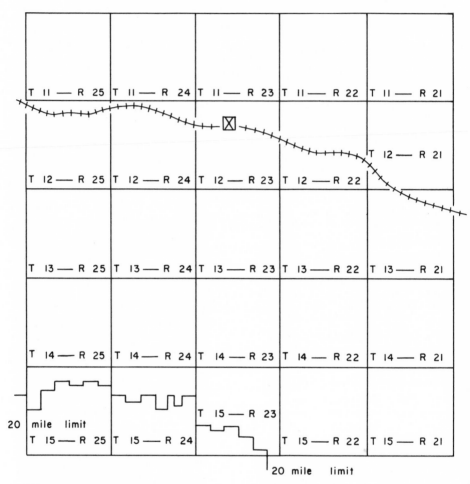

T 11 — R 25	T 11 — R 24	T 11 — R 23	T 11 — R 22	T 11 — R 21
				T 12 — R 21
T 12 — R 25	T 12 — R 24	T 12 — R 23	T 12 —R 22	
T 13 — R 25	T 13 — R 24	T 13 — R 23	T 13 — R 22	T 13 — R 21
T 14 — R 25	T 14 — R 24	T 14 — R 23	T 14 — R 22	T 14 — R 21
20 mile limit T 15 — R 25	T 15 — R 24	T 15 — R 23	T 15 — R 22	T 15 — R 21

20 mile limit

⊠ Wakeeney (County Seat)

+++ Kansas Pacific Railroad

TREGO COUNTY, KANSAS   TOWNSHIP 11 S, RANGE 21 W

6	5	4	3	2	1
7	8	9	10	11	12
18	17	16	15	14	13
19	20	21	22	23	24
30	29	28	27	26	25
31	32	33	34	35	36

1872

6	5	4	3	2	1
7	8	9	10	11	12
18	17	16	15	14	13
19	20	21	22	23	24
30	29	28	27	26	25
31	32	33	34	35	36

1877

6	5	4	3	2	1
7	8	9	10	11	12
18	17	16	15	14	13
19	20	21	22	23	24
30	29	28	27	26	25
31	32	33	34	35	36

1882

6	5	4	3	2	1
7	8	9	10	11	12
18	17	16	15	14	13
19	20	21	22	23	24
30	29	28	27	26	25
31	32	33	34	35	36

1887

6	5	4	3	2	1
7	8	9	10	11	12
18	17	16	15	14	13
19	20	21	22	23	24
30	29	28	27	26	25
31	32	33	34	35	36

1892

6	5	4	3	2	1
7	8	9	10	11	12
18	17	16	15	14	13
19	20	21	22	23	24
30	29	28	27	26	25
31	32	33	34	35	36

1897

TREGO COUNTY, KANSAS   TOWNSHIP 12 S, RANGE 21 W

6	5	4	3	2	1
7	8	9	10	11	12
18	17	16	15	14	13
19	20	21	22	23	24
30	29	28	27	26	25
31	32	33	34	35	36

1872

6	5	4	3	2	1
7	8	9	10	11	12
18	17	16	15	14	13
19	20	21	22	23	24
30	29	28	27	26	25
31	32	33	34	35	36

1877

6	5	4	3	2	1
7	8	9	10	11	12
18	17	16	15	14	13
19	20	21	22	23	24
30	29	28	27	26	25
31	32	33	34	35	36

1882

6	5	4	3	2	1
7	8	9	10	11	12
18	17	16	15	14	13
19	20	21	22	23	24
30	29	28	27	26	25
31	32	33	34	35	36

1887

6	5	4	3	2	1
7	8	9	10	11	12
18	17	16	15	14	13
19	20	21	22	23	24
30	29	28	27	26	25
31	32	33	34	35	36

1892

6	5	4	3	2	1
7	8	9	10	11	12
18	17	16	15	14	13
19	20	21	22	23	24
30	29	28	27	26	25
31	32	33	34	35	36

1897

TREGO COUNTY, KANSAS   TOWNSHIP 13 S, RANGE 21 W

6	5	4	3	2	1
7	8	9	10	11	12
18	17	16	15	14	13
19	20	21	22	23	24
30	29	28	27	26	25
31	32	33	34	35	36

1872

6	5	4	3	2	1
7	8	9	10	11	12
18	17	16	15	14	13
19	20	21	22	23	24
30	29	28	27	26	25
31	32	33	34	35	36

1877

6	5	4	3	2	1
7	8	9	10	11	12
18	17	16	15	14	13
19	20	21	22	23	24
30	29	28	27	26	25
31	32	33	34	35	36

1882

6	5	4	3	2	1
7	8	9	10	11	12
18	17	16	15	14	13
19	20	21	22	23	24
30	29	28	27	26	25
31	32	33	34	35	36

1887

6	5	4	3	2	1
7	8	9	10	11	12
18	17	16	15	14	13
19	20	21	22	23	24
30	29	28	27	26	25
31	32	33	34	35	36

1892

6	5	4	3	2	1
7	8	9	10	11	12
18	17	16	15	14	13
19	20	21	22	23	24
30	29	28	27	26	25
31	32	33	34	35	36

1897

TREGO COUNTY, KANSAS   TOWNSHIP 14 S, RANGE 21 W

1872

1877

1882

1887

1892

1897

TREGO COUNTY, KANSAS   TOWNSHIP 15 S, RANGE 21 W

6	5	4	3	2	1
7	8	9	10	11	12
18	17	16	15	14	13
19	20	21	22	23	24
30	29	28	27	26	25
31	32	33	34	35	36

1872

6	5	4	3	2	1
7	8	9	10	11	12
18	17	16	15	14	13
19	20	21	22	23	24
30	29	28	27	26	25
31	32	33	34	35	36

1877

6	5	4	3	2	1
7	8	9	10	11	12
18	17	16	15	14	13
19	20	21	22	23	24
30	29	28	27	26	25
31	32	33	34	35	36

1882

6	5	4	3	2	1
7	8	9	10	11	12
18	17	16	15	14	13
19	20	21	22	23	24
30	29	28	27	26	25
31	32	33	34	35	36

1887

6	5	4	3	2	1
7	8	9	10	11	12
18	17	16	15	14	13
19	20	21	22	23	24
30	29	28	27	26	25
31	32	33	34	35	36

1892

6	5	4	3	2	1
7	8	9	10	11	12
18	17	16	15	14	13
19	20	21	22	23	24
30	29	28	27	26	25
31	32	33	34	35	36

1897

TREGO COUNTY, KANSAS   TOWNSHIP 11 S, RANGE 22 W

6	5	4	3	2	1
7	8	9	10	11	12
18	17	16	15	14	13
19	20	21	22	23	24
30	29	28	27	26	25
31	32	33	34	35	36

1872

6	5	4	3	2	1
7	8	9	10	11	12
18	17	16	15	14	13
19	20	21	22	23	24
30	29	28	27	26	25
31	32	33	34	35	36

1877

6	5	4	3	2	1
7	8	9	10	11	12
18	17	16	15	14	13
19	20	21	22	23	24
30	29	28	27	26	25
31	32	33	34	35	36

1882

6	5	4	3	2	1
7	8	9	10	11	12
18	17	16	15	14	13
19	20	21	22	23	24
30	29	28	27	26	25
31	32	33	34	35	36

1887

6	5	4	3	2	1
7	8	9	10	11	12
18	17	16	15	14	13
19	20	21	22	23	24
30	29	28	27	26	25
31	32	33	34	35	36

1892

6	5	4	3	2	1
7	8	9	10	11	12
18	17	16	15	14	13
19	20	21	22	23	24
30	29	28	27	26	25
31	32	33	34	35	36

1897

TREGO COUNTY, KANSAS TOWNSHIP 12 S, RANGE 22 W

6	5	4	3	2	1
7	8	9	10	11	12
18	17	16	15	14	13
19	20	21	22	23	24
30	29	28	27	26	25
31	32	33	34	35	36

1872

6	5	4	3	2	1
7	8	9	10	11	12
18	17	16	15	14	13
19	20	21	22	23	24
30	29	28	27	26	25
31	32	33	34	35	36

1877

6	5	4	3	2	1
7	8	9	10	11	12
18	17	16	15	14	13
19	20	21	22	23	24
30	29	28	27	26	25
31	32	33	34	35	36

1882

6	5	4	3	2	1
7	8	9	10	11	12
18	17	16	15	14	13
19	20	21	22	23	24
30	29	28	27	26	25
31	32	33	34	35	36

1887

6	5	4	3	2	1
7	8	9	10	11	12
18	17	16	15	14	13
19	20	21	22	23	24
30	29	28	27	26	25
31	32	33	34	35	36

1892

6	5	4	3	2	1
7	8	9	10	11	12
18	17	16	15	14	13
19	20	21	22	23	24
30	29	28	27	26	25
31	32	33	34	35	36

1897

TREGO COUNTY, KANSAS TOWNSHIP 13 S, RANGE 22 W

6	5	4	3	2	1
7	8	9	10	11	12
18	17	16	15	14	13
19	20	21	22	23	24
30	29	28	27	26	25
31	32	33	34	35	36

1872

6	5	4	3	2	1
7	8	9	10	11	12
18	17	16	15	14	13
19	20	21	22	23	24
30	29	28	27	26	25
31	32	33	34	35	36

1877

6	5	4	3	2	1
7	8	9	10	11	12
18	17	16	15	14	13
19	20	21	22	23	24
30	29	28	27	26	25
31	32	33	34	35	36

1882

6	5	4	3	2	1
7	8	9	10	11	12
18	17	16	15	14	13
19	20	21	22	23	24
30	29	28	27	26	25
31	32	33	34	35	36

1887

6	5	4	3	2	1
7	8	9	10	11	12
18	17	16	15	14	13
19	20	21	22	23	24
30	29	28	27	26	25
31	32	33	34	35	36

1892

6	5	4	3	2	1
7	8	9	10	11	12
18	17	16	15	14	13
19	20	21	22	23	24
30	29	28	27	26	25
31	32	33	34	35	36

1897

TREGO COUNTY, KANSAS TOWNSHIP 14 S, RANGE 22 W

6	5	4	3	2	1
7	8	9	10	11	12
18	17	16	15	14	13
19	20	21	22	23	24
30	29	28	27	26	25
31	32	33	34	35	36

1872

6	5	4	3	2	1
7	8	9	10	11	12
18	17	16	15	14	13
19	20	21	22	23	24
30	29	28	27	26	25
31	32	33	34	35	36

1877

6	5	4	3	2	1
7	8	9	10	11	12
18	17	16	15	14	13
19	20	21	22	23	24
30	29	28	27	26	25
31	32	33	34	35	36

1882

6	5	4	3	2	1
7	8	9	10	11	12
18	17	16	15	14	13
19	20	21	22	23	24
30	29	28	27	26	25
31	32	33	34	35	36

1887

6	5	4	3	2	1
7	8	9	10	11	12
18	17	16	15	14	13
19	20	21	22	23	24
30	29	28	27	26	25
31	32	33	34	35	36

1892

6	5	4	3	2	1
7	8	9	10	11	12
18	17	16	15	14	13
19	20	21	22	23	24
30	29	28	27	26	25
31	32	33	34	35	36

1897

TREGO COUNTY, KANSAS   TOWNSHIP 15 S, RANGE 22 W

6	5	4	3	2	1
7	8	9	10	11	12
18	17	16	15	14	13
19	20	21	22	23	24
30	29	28	27	26	25
31	32	33	34	35	36

1872

6	5	4	3	2	1
7	8	9	10	11	12
18	17	16	15	14	13
19	20	21	22	23	24
30	29	28	27	26	25
31	32	33	34	35	36

1877

6	5	4	3	2	1
7	8	9	10	11	12
18	17	16	15	14	13
19	20	21	22	23	24
30	29	28	27	26	25
31	32	33	34	35	36

1882

6	5	4	3	2	1
7	8	9	10	11	12
18	17	16	15	14	13
19	20	21	22	23	24
30	29	28	27	26	25
31	32	33	34	35	36

1887

6	5	4	3	2	1
7	8	9	10	11	12
18	17	16	15	14	13
19	20	21	22	23	24
30	29	28	27	26	25
31	32	33	34	35	36

1892

6	5	4	3	2	1
7	8	9	10	11	12
18	17	16	15	14	13
19	20	21	22	23	24
30	29	28	27	26	25
31	32	33	34	35	36

1897

TREGO COUNTY, KANSAS   TOWNSHIP 11 S, RANGE 23 W

6	5	4	3	2	1
7	8	9	10	11	12
18	17	16	15	14	13
19	20	21	22	23	24
30	29	28	27	26	25
31	32	33	34	35	36

1872

6	5	4	3	2	1
7	8	9	10	11	12
18	17	16	15	14	13
19	20	21	22	23	24
30	29	28	27	26	25
31	32	33	34	35	36

1877

6	5	4	3	2	1
7	8	9	10	11	12
18	17	16	15	14	13
19	20	21	22	23	24
30	29	28	27	26	25
31	32	33	34	35	36

1882

6	5	4	3	2	1
7	8	9	10	11	12
18	17	16	15	14	13
19	20	21	22	23	24
30	29	28	27	26	25
31	32	33	34	35	36

1887

6	5	4	3	2	1
7	8	9	10	11	12
18	17	16	15	14	13
19	20	21	22	23	24
30	29	28	27	26	25
31	32	33	34	35	36

1892

6	5	4	3	2	1
7	8	9	10	11	12
18	17	16	15	14	13
19	20	21	22	23	24
30	29	28	27	26	25
31	32	33	34	35	36

1897

TREGO COUNTY, KANSAS   TOWNSHIP 12 S, RANGE 23 W

6	5	4	3	2	1
7	8	9	10	11	12
18	17	16	15	14	13
19	20	21	22	23	24
30	29	28	27	26	25
31	32	33	34	35	36

1872

6	5	4	3	2	1
7	8	9	10	11	12
18	17	16	15	14	13
19	20	21	22	23	24
30	29	28	27	26	25
31	32	33	34	35	36

1877

6	5	4	3	2	1
7	8	9	10	11	12
18	17	16	15	14	13
19	20	21	22	23	24
30	29	28	27	26	25
31	32	33	34	35	36

1882

6	5	4	3	2	1
7	8	9	10	11	12
18	17	16	15	14	13
19	20	21	22	23	24
30	29	28	27	26	25
31	32	33	34	35	36

1887

6	5	4	3	2	1
7	8	9	10	11	12
18	17	16	15	14	13
19	20	21	22	23	24
30	29	28	27	26	25
31	32	33	34	35	36

1892

6	5	4	3	2	1
7	8	9	10	11	12
18	17	16	15	14	13
19	20	21	22	23	24
30	29	28	27	26	25
31	32	33	34	35	36

1897

TREGO COUNTY, KANSAS   TOWNSHIP 13 S, RANGE 23 W

6	5	4	3	2	1
7	8	9	10	11	12
18	17	16	15	14	13
19	20	21	22	23	24
30	29	28	27	26	25
31	32	33	34	35	36

1872

6	5	4	3	2	1
7	8	9	10	11	12
18	17	16	15	14	13
19	20	21	22	23	24
30	29	28	27	26	25
31	32	33	34	35	36

1877

6	5	4	3	2	1
7	8	9	10	11	12
18	17	16	15	14	13
19	20	21	22	23	24
30	29	28	27	26	25
31	32	33	34	35	36

1882

6	5	4	3	2	1
7	8	9	10	11	12
18	17	16	15	14	13
19	20	21	22	23	24
30	29	28	27	26	25
31	32	33	34	35	36

1887

6	5	4	3	2	1
7	8	9	10	11	12
18	17	16	15	14	13
19	20	21	22	23	24
30	29	28	27	26	25
31	32	33	34	35	36

1892

6	5	4	3	2	1
7	8	9	10	11	12
18	17	16	15	14	13
19	20	21	22	23	24
30	29	28	27	26	25
31	32	33	34	35	36

1897

TREGO COUNTY, KANSAS   TOWNSHIP 14 S, RANGE 23 W

6	5	4	3	2	1
7	8	9	10	11	12
18	17	16	15	14	13
19	20	21	22	23	24
30	29	28	27	26	25
31	32	33	34	35	36

1872

6	5	4	3	2	1
7	8	9	10	11	12
18	17	16	15	14	13
19	20	21	22	23	24
30	29	28	27	26	25
31	32	33	34	35	36

1877

6	5	4	3	2	1
7	8	9	10	11	12
18	17	16	15	14	13
19	20	21	22	23	24
30	29	28	27	26	25
31	32	33	34	35	36

1882

6	5	4	3	2	1
7	8	9	10	11	12
18	17	16	15	14	13
19	20	21	22	23	24
30	29	28	27	26	25
31	32	33	34	35	36

1887

6	5	4	3	2	1
7	8	9	10	11	12
18	17	16	15	14	13
19	20	21	22	23	24
30	29	28	27	26	25
31	32	33	34	35	36

1892

6	5	4	3	2	1
7	8	9	10	11	12
18	17	16	15	14	13
19	20	21	22	23	24
30	29	28	27	26	25
31	32	33	34	35	36

1897

TREGO COUNTY, KANSAS TOWNSHIP 15 S, RANGE 23 W

6	5	4	3	2	1
7	8	9	10	11	12
18	17	16	15	14	13
19	20	21	22	23	24
30	29	28	27	26	25
31	32	33	34	35	36

1872

6	5	4	3	2	1
7	8	9	10	11	12
18	17	16	15	14	13
19	20	21	22	23	24
30	29	28	27	26	25
31	32	33	34	35	36

1877

6	5	4	3	2	1
7	8	9	10	11	12
18	17	16	15	14	13
19	20	21	22	23	24
30	29	28	27	26	25
31	32	33	34	35	36

1882

6	5	4	3	2	1
7	8	9	10	11	12
18	17	16	15	14	13
19	20	21	22	23	24
30	29	28	27	26	25
31	32	33	34	35	36

1887

6	5	4	3	2	1
7	8	9	10	11	12
18	17	16	15	14	13
19	20	21	22	23	24
30	29	28	27	26	25
31	32	33	34	35	36

1892

6	5	4	3	2	1
7	8	9	10	11	12
18	17	16	15	14	13
19	20	21	22	23	24
30	29	28	27	26	25
31	32	33	34	35	36

1897

* Outside the limits of the land grant.

TREGO COUNTY, KANSAS   TOWNSHIP 11 S, RANGE 24 W

6	5	4	3	2	1
7	8	9	10	11	12
18	17	16	15	14	13
19	20	21	22	23	24
30	29	28	27	26	25
31	32	33	34	35	36

1872

6	5	4	3	2	1
7	8	9	10	11	12
18	17	16	15	14	13
19	20	21	22	23	24
30	29	28	27	26	25
31	32	33	34	35	36

1877

6	5	4	3	2	1
7	8	9	10	11	12
18	17	16	15	14	13
19	20	21	22	23	24
30	29	28	27	26	25
31	32	33	34	35	36

1882

6	5	4	3	2	1
7	8	9	10	11	12
18	17	16	15	14	13
19	20	21	22	23	24
30	29	28	27	26	25
31	32	33	34	35	36

1887

6	5	4	3	2	1
7	8	9	10	11	12
18	17	16	15	14	13
19	20	21	22	23	24
30	29	28	27	26	25
31	32	33	34	35	36

1892

6	5	4	3	2	1
7	8	9	10	11	12
18	17	16	15	14	13
19	20	21	22	23	24
30	29	28	27	26	25
31	32	33	34	35	36

1897

TREGO COUNTY, KANSAS   TOWNSHIP 12 S, RANGE 24 W

6	5	4	3	2	1
7	8	9	10	11	12
18	17	16	15	14	13
19	20	21	22	23	24
30	29	28	27	26	25
31	32	33	34	35	36

1872

6	5	4	3	2	1
7	8	9	10	11	12
18	17	16	15	14	13
19	20	21	22	23	24
30	29	28	27	26	25
31	32	33	34	35	36

1877

6	5	4	3	2	1
7	8	9	10	11	12
18	17	16	15	14	13
19	20	21	22	23	24
30	29	28	27	26	25
31	32	33	34	35	36

1882

6	5	4	3	2	1
7	8	9	10	11	12
18	17	16	15	14	13
19	20	21	22	23	24
30	29	28	27	26	25
31	32	33	34	35	36

1887

6	5	4	3	2	1
7	8	9	10	11	12
18	17	16	15	14	13
19	20	21	22	23	24
30	29	28	27	26	25
31	32	33	34	35	36

1892

6	5	4	3	2	1
7	8	9	10	11	12
18	17	16	15	14	13
19	20	21	22	23	24
30	29	28	27	26	25
31	32	33	34	35	36

1897

TREGO COUNTY, KANSAS   TOWNSHIP 13 S, RANGE 24 W

6	5	4	3	2	1
7	8	9	10	11	12
18	17	16	15	14	13
19	20	21	22	23	24
30	29	28	27	26	25
31	32	33	34	35	36

1872

6	5	4	3	2	1
7	8	9	10	11	12
18	17	16	15	14	13
19	20	21	22	23	24
30	29	28	27	26	25
31	32	33	34	35	36

1877

6	5	4	3	2	1
7	8	9	10	11	12
18	17	16	15	14	13
19	20	21	22	23	24
30	29	28	27	26	25
31	32	33	34	35	36

1882

6	5	4	3	2	1
7	8	9	10	11	12
18	17	16	15	14	13
19	20	21	22	23	24
30	29	28	27	26	25
31	32	33	34	35	36

1887

6	5	4	3	2	1
7	8	9	10	11	12
18	17	16	15	14	13
19	20	21	22	23	24
30	29	28	27	26	25
31	32	33	34	35	36

1892

6	5	4	3	2	1
7	8	9	10	11	12
18	17	16	15	14	13
19	20	21	22	23	24
30	29	28	27	26	25
31	32	33	34	35	36

1897

TREGO COUNTY, KANSAS   TOWNSHIP 14 S, RANGE 24 W

6	5	4	3	2	1
7	8	9	10	11	12
18	17	16	15	14	13
19	20	21	22	23	24
30	29	28	27	26	25
31	32	33	34	35	36

1872

6	5	4	3	2	1
7	8	9	10	11	12
18	17	16	15	14	13
19	20	21	22	23	24
30	29	28	27	26	25
31	32	33	34	35	36

1877

6	5	4	3	2	1
7	8	9	10	11	12
18	17	16	15	14	13
19	20	21	22	23	24
30	29	28	27	26	25
31	32	33	34	35	36

1882

6	5	4	3	2	1
7	8	9	10	11	12
18	17	16	15	14	13
19	20	21	22	23	24
30	29	28	27	26	25
31	32	33	34	35	36

1887

6	5	4	3	2	1
7	8	9	10	11	12
18	17	16	15	14	13
19	20	21	22	23	24
30	29	28	27	26	25
31	32	33	34	35	36

1892

6	5	4	3	2	1
7	8	9	10	11	12
18	17	16	15	14	13
19	20	21	22	23	24
30	29	28	27	26	25
31	32	33	34	35	36

1897

TREGO COUNTY, KANSAS   TOWNSHIP 15 S, RANGE 24 W

1872

1877

1882

1887

1892

1897

* Outside the limits of the land grant.

TREGO COUNTY, KANSAS TOWNSHIP 11 S, RANGE 25 W

6	5	4	3	2	1
7	8	9	10	11	12
18	17	16	15	14	13
19	20	21	22	23	24
30	29	28	27	26	25
31	32	33	34	35	36

1872

6	5	4	3	2	1
7	8	9	10	11	12
18	17	16	15	14	13
19	20	21	22	23	24
30	29	28	27	26	25
31	32	33	34	35	36

1877

6	5	4	3	2	1
7	8	9	10	11	12
18	17	16	15	14	13
19	20	21	22	23	24
30	29	28	27	26	25
31	32	33	34	35	36

1882

6	5	4	3	2	1
7	8	9	10	11	12
18	17	16	15	14	13
19	20	21	22	23	24
30	29	28	27	26	25
31	32	33	34	35	36

1887

6	5	4	3	2	1
7	8	9	10	11	12
18	17	16	15	14	13
19	20	21	22	23	24
30	29	28	27	26	25
31	32	33	34	35	36

1892

6	5	4	3	2	1
7	8	9	10	11	12
18	17	16	15	14	13
19	20	21	22	23	24
30	29	28	27	26	25
31	32	33	34	35	36

1897

TREGO COUNTY, KANSAS TOWNSHIP 12 S, RANGE 25 W

6	5	4	3	2	1
7	8	9	10	11	12
18	17	16	15	14	13
19	20	21	22	23	24
30	29	28	27	26	25
31	32	33	34	35	36

1872

6	5	4	3	2	1
7	8	9	10	11	12
18	17	16	15	14	13
19	20	21	22	23	24
30	29	28	27	26	25
31	32	33	34	35	36

1877

6	5	4	3	2	1
7	8	9	10	11	12
18	17	16	15	14	13
19	20	21	22	23	24
30	29	28	27	26	25
31	32	33	34	35	36

1882

6	5	4	3	2	1
7	8	9	10	11	12
18	17	16	15	14	13
19	20	21	22	23	24
30	29	28	27	26	25
31	32	33	34	35	36

1887

6	5	4	3	2	1
7	8	9	10	11	12
18	17	16	15	14	13
19	20	21	22	23	24
30	29	28	27	26	25
31	32	33	34	35	36

1892

6	5	4	3	2	1
7	8	9	10	11	12
18	17	16	15	14	13
19	20	21	22	23	24
30	29	28	27	26	25
31	32	33	34	35	36

1897

TREGO COUNTY, KANSAS TOWNSHIP 13 S, RANGE 25 W

1872

6	5	4	3	2	1
7	8	9	10	11	12
18	17	16	15	14	13
19	20	21	22	23	24
30	29	28	27	26	25
31	32	33	34	35	36

1877

6	5	4	3	2	1
7	8	9	10	11	12
18	17	16	15	14	13
19	20	21	22	23	24
30	29	28	27	26	25
31	32	33	34	35	36

1882

6	5	4	3	2	1
7	8	9	10	11	12
18	17	16	15	14	13
19	20	21	22	23	24
30	29	28	27	26	25
31	32	33	34	35	36

1887

6	5	4	3	2	1
7	8	9	10	11	12
18	17	16	15	14	13
19	20	21	22	23	24
30	29	28	27	26	25
31	32	33	34	35	36

1892

6	5	4	3	2	1
7	8	9	10	11	12
18	17	16	15	14	13
19	20	21	22	23	24
30	29	28	27	26	25
31	32	33	34	35	36

1897

6	5	4	3	2	1
7	8	9	10	11	12
18	17	16	15	14	13
19	20	21	22	23	24
30	29	28	27	26	25
31	32	33	34	35	36

TREGO COUNTY, KANSAS   TOWNSHIP 14 S, RANGE 25 W

1872

1877

1882

1887

1892

1897

TREGO COUNTY, KANSAS TOWNSHIP 15 S, RANGE 25 W

1872

6	5	4	3	2	1
7	8	9	10	11	12
18	17	16	15	14	13
19	20	21	22	23	24
30	29	28	27	26	25
31	32	33	34	35	36

1877

6	5	4	3	2	1
7	8	9	10	11	12
18	17	16	15	14	13
19	20	21	22	23	24
30	29	28	27	26	25
31	32	33	34	35	36

1882

6	5	4	3	2	1
7	8	9	10	11	12
18	17	16	15	14	13
19	20	21	22	23	24
30	29	28	27	26	25
31	32	33	34	35	36

1887

6	5	4	3	2	1
7	8	9	10	11	12
18	17	16	15	14	13
19	20	21	22	23	24
30	29	28	27	26	25
31	32	33	34	35	36

1892

6	5	4	3	2	1
7	8	9	10	11	12
18	17	16	15	14	13
19	20	21	22	23	24
30	29	28	27	26	25
31	32	33	34	35	36

1897

6	5	4	3	2	1
7	8	9	10	11	12
18	17	16	15	14	13
19	20	21	22	23	24
30	29	28	27	26	25
31	32	33	34	35	36

* Outside the limits of the land grant.

ADAMS COUNTY, NEBRASKA

Platte River

T 8 — R 12

B&MN

T 8 — R 11   T 8 — R 10   T 8 — R 9

B&MN   B&MN

STJ&DC

T 7 — R 12   T 7 — R 11   T 7 — R 10   T 7 — R 9

T 6 — R 12   T 6 — R 11   T 6 — R 10   T 6 — R 9

T 5 — R 12   T 5 — R 11   T 5 — R 10   T 5 — R 9

☒ Hastings   (County Seat)

+++ Original land grant railroads

ADAMS COUNTY, NEBRASKA   TOWNSHIP 8 N, RANGE 9 W

1872

1877

1882

1887

1892

1897

ADAMS COUNTY, NEBRASKA   TOWNSHIP 7 N, RANGE 9 W

1872

1877

1882

1887

1892

1897

ADAMS COUNTY, NEBRASKA   TOWNSHIP 6 N, RANGE 9 W

6	5	4	3	2	1
7	8	9	10	11	12
18	17	16	15	14	13
19	20	21	22	23	24
30	29	28	27	26	25
31	32	33	34	35	36

1872

6	5	4	3	2	1
7	8	9	10	11	12
18	17	16	15	14	13
19	20	21	22	23	24
30	29	28	27	26	25
31	32	33	34	35	36

1877

6	5	4	3	2	1
7	8	9	10	11	12
18	17	16	15	14	13
19	20	21	22	23	24
30	29	28	27	26	25
31	32	33	34	35	36

1882

6	5	4	3	2	1
7	8	9	10	11	12
18	17	16	15	14	13
19	20	21	22	23	24
30	29	28	27	26	25
31	32	33	34	35	36

1887

6	5	4	3	2	1
7	8	9	10	11	12
18	17	16	15	14	13
19	20	21	22	23	24
30	29	28	27	26	25
31	32	33	34	35	36

1892

6	5	4	3	2	1
7	8	9	10	11	12
18	17	16	15	14	13
19	20	21	22	23	24
30	29	28	27	26	25
31	32	33	34	35	36

1897

* Railroad lands lost to prior claimants.

ADAMS COUNTY, NEBRASKA   TOWNSHIP 5 N, RANGE 9 W

1872

1877

1882

1887

1892

1897

* Railroad lands lost to prior claimants.

ADAMS COUNTY, NEBRASKA   TOWNSHIP 8 N, RANGE 10 W

6	5	4	3	2	1
7	8	9	10	11	12
18	17	16	15	14	13
19	20	21	22	23	24
30	29	28	27	26	25
31	32	33	34	35	36

1872

6	5	4	3	2	1
7	8	9	10	11	12
18	17	16	15	14	13
19	20	21	22	23	24
30	29	28	27	26	25
31	32	33	34	35	36

1877

6	5	4	3	2	1
7	8	9	10	11	12
18	17	16	15	14	13
19	20	21	22	23	24
30	29	28	27	26	25
31	32	33	34	35	36

1882

6	5	4	3	2	1
7	8	9	10	11	12
18	17	16	15	14	13
19	20	21	22	23	24
30	29	28	27	26	25
31	32	33	34	35	36

1887

6	5	4	3	2	1
7	8	9	10	11	12
18	17	16	15	14	13
19	20	21	22	23	24
30	29	28	27	26	25
31	32	33	34	35	36

1892

6	5	4	3	2	1
7	8	9	10	11	12
18	17	16	15	14	13
19	20	21	22	23	24
30	29	28	27	26	25
31	32	33	34	35	36

1897

ADAMS COUNTY, NEBRASKA   TOWNSHIP 7 N, RANGE 10 W

6	5	4	3	2	1
7	8	9	10	11	12
18	17	16	15	14	13
19	20	21	22	23	24
30	29	28	27	26	25
31	32	33	34	35	36

1872

1877

1882

1887

1892

1897

ADAMS COUNTY, NEBRASKA　　TOWNSHIP 6 N, RANGE 10 W

6	5	4	3	2	1
7	8	9	10	11	12
18	17	16	15	14	13
19	20	21	22	23	24
30	29	28	27	26	25
31	32	33	34	35	36

1872

6	5	4	3	2	1
7	8	9	10	11	12
18	17	16	15	14	13
19	20	21	22	23	24
30	29	28	27	26	25
31	32	33	34	35	36

1877

6	5	4	3	2	1
7	8	9	10	11	12
18	17	16	15	14	13
19	20	21	22	23	24
30	29	28	27	26	25
31	32	33	34	35	36

1882

6	5	4	3	2	1
7	8	9	10	11	12
18	17	16	15	14	13
19	20	21	22	23	24
30	29	28	27	26	25
31	32	33	34	35	36

1887

6	5	4	3	2	1
7	8	9	10	11	12
18	17	16	15	14	13
19	20	21	22	23	24
30	29	28	27	26	25
31	32	33	34	35	36

1892

6	5	4	3	2	1
7	8	9	10	11	12
18	17	16	15	14	13
19	20	21	22	23	24
30	29	28	27	26	25
31	32	33	34	35	36

1897

ADAMS COUNTY, NEBRASKA TOWNSHIP 5 N, RANGE 10 W

6	5	4	3	2	1
7	8	9	10	11	12
18	17	16	15	14	13
19	20	21	22	23	24
30	29	28	27	26	25
31	32	33	34	35	36

1872

6	5	4	3	2	1
7	8	9	10	11	12
18	17	16	15	14	13
19	20	21	22	23	24
30	29	28	27	26	25
31	32	33	34	35	36

1877

6	5	4	3	2	1
7	8	9	10	11	12
18	17	16	15	14	13
19	20	21	22	23	24
30	29	28	27	26	25
31	32	33	34	35	36

1882

6	5	4	3	2	1
7	8	9	10	11	12
18	17	16	15	14	13
19	20	21	22	23	24
30	29	28	27	26	25
31	32	33	34	35	36

1887

6	5	4	3	2	1
7	8	9	10	11	12
18	17	16	15	14	13
19	20	21	22	23	24
30	29	28	27	26	25
31	32	33	34	35	36

1892

6	5	4	3	2	1
7	8	9	10	11	12
18	17	16	15	14	13
19	20	21	22	23	24
30	29	28	27	26	25
31	32	33	34	35	36

1897

ADAMS COUNTY, NEBRASKA   TOWNSHIP 8 N, RANGE 11 W

6	5	4	3	2	1
7	8	9	10	11	12
18	17	16	15	14	13
19	20	21	22	23	24
30	29	28	27	26	25
31	32	33	34	35	36

1872

6	5	4	3	2	1
7	8	9	10	11	12
18	17	16	15	14	13
19	20	21	22	23	24
30	29	28	27	26	25
31	32	33	34	35	36

1877

6	5	4	3	2	1
7	8	9	10	11	12
18	17	16	15	14	13
19	20	21	22	23	24
30	29	28	27	26	25
31	32	33	34	35	36

1882

6	5	4	3	2	1
7	8	9	10	11	12
18	17	16	15	14	13
19	20	21	22	23	24
30	29	28	27	26	25
31	32	33	34	35	36

1887

6	5	4	3	2	1
7	8	9	10	11	12
18	17	16	15	14	13
19	20	21	22	23	24
30	29	28	27	26	25
31	32	33	34	35	36

1892

6	5	4	3	2	1
7	8	9	10	11	12
18	17	16	15	14	13
19	20	21	22	23	24
30	29	28	27	26	25
31	32	33	34	35	36

1897

ADAMS COUNTY, NEBRASKA   TOWNSHIP 7 N, RANGE 11 W

6	5	4	3	2	1
7	8	9	10	11	12
18	17	16	15	14	13
19	20	21	22	23	24
30	29	28	27	26	25
31	32	33	34	35	36

1872

6	5	4	3	2	1
7	8	9	10	11	12
18	17	16	15	14	13
19	20	21	22	23	24
30	29	28	27	26	25
31	32	33	34	35	36

1877

6	5	4	3	2	1
7	8	9	10	11	12
18	17	16	15	14	13
19	20	21	22	23	24
30	29	28	27	26	25
31	32	33	34	35	36

1882

6	5	4	3	2	1
7	8	9	10	11	12
18	17	16	15	14	13
19	20	21	22	23	24
30	29	28	27	26	25
31	32	33	34	35	36

1887

6	5	4	3	2	1
7	8	9	10	11	12
18	17	16	15	14	13
19	20	21	22	23	24
30	29	28	27	26	25
31	32	33	34	35	36

1892

6	5	4	3	2	1
7	8	9	10	11	12
18	17	16	15	14	13
19	20	21	22	23	24
30	29	28	27	26	25
31	32	33	34	35	36

1897

ADAMS COUNTY, NEBRASKA TOWNSHIP 6 N, RANGE 11 W

6	5	4	3	2	1
7	8	9	10	11	12
18	17	16	15	14	13
19	20	21	22	23	24
30	29	28	27	26	25
31	32	33	34	35	36

1872

6	5	4	3	2	1
7	8	9	10	11	12
18	17	16	15	14	13
19	20	21	22	23	24
30	29	28	27	26	25
31	32	33	34	35	36

1877

6	5	4	3	2	1
7	8	9	10	11	12
18	17	16	15	14	13
19	20	21	22	23	24
30	29	28	27	26	25
31	32	33	34	35	36

1882

6	5	4	3	2	1
7	8	9	10	11	12
18	17	16	15	14	13
19	20	21	22	23	24
30	29	28	27	26	25
31	32	33	34	35	36

1887

6	5	4	3	2	1
7	8	9	10	11	12
18	17	16	15	14	13
19	20	21	22	23	24
30	29	28	27	26	25
31	32	33	34	35	36

1892

6	5	4	3	2	1
7	8	9	10	11	12
18	17	16	15	14	13
19	20	21	22	23	24
30	29	28	27	26	25
31	32	33	34	35	36

1897

ADAMS COUNTY, NEBRASKA   TOWNSHIP 5 N, RANGE 11 W

6	5	4	3	2	1
7	8	9	10	11	12
18	17	16	15	14	13
19	20	21	22	23	24
30	29	28	27	26	25
31	32	33	34	35	36

1872

6	5	4	3	2	1
7	8	9	10	11	12
18	17	16	15	14	13
19	20	21	22	23	24
30	29	28	27	26	25
31	32	33	34	35	36

1877

6	5	4	3	2	1
7	8	9	10	11	12
18	17	16	15	14	13
19	20	21	22	23	24
30	29	28	27	26	25
31	32	33	34	35	36

1882

6	5	4	3	2	1
7	8	9	10	11	12
18	17	16	15	14	13
19	20	21	22	23	24
30	29	28	27	26	25
31	32	33	34	35	36

1887

6	5	4	3	2	1
7	8	9	10	11	12
18	17	16	15	14	13
19	20	21	22	23	24
30	29	28	27	26	25
31	32	33	34	35	36

1892

6	5	4	3	2	1
7	8	9	10	11	12
18	17	16	15	14	13
19	20	21	22	23	24
30	29	28	27	26	25
31	32	33	34	35	36

1897

ADAMS COUNTY, NEBRASKA   TOWNSHIP 8 N, RANGE 12 W

1872

1877

1882

1887

1892

1897

ADAMS COUNTY, NEBRASKA   TOWNSHIP 7 N, RANGE 12 W

6	5	4	3	2	1
7	8	9	10	11	12
18	17	16	15	14	13
19	20	21	22	23	24
30	29	28	27	26	25
31	32	33	34	35	36

1872

6	5	4	3	2	1
7	8	9	10	11	12
18	17	16	15	14	13
19	20	21	22	23	24
30	29	28	27	26	25
31	32	33	34	35	36

1877

6	5	4	3	2	1
7	8	9	10	11	12
18	17	16	15	14	13
19	20	21	22	23	24
30	29	28	27	26	25
31	32	33	34	35	36

1882

6	5	4	3	2	1
7	8	9	10	11	12
18	17	16	15	14	13
19	20	21	22	23	24
30	29	28	27	26	25
31	32	33	34	35	36

1887

6	5	4	3	2	1
7	8	9	10	11	12
18	17	16	15	14	13
19	20	21	22	23	24
30	29	28	27	26	25
31	32	33	34	35	36

1892

6	5	4	3	2	1
7	8	9	10	11	12
18	17	16	15	14	13
19	20	21	22	23	24
30	29	28	27	26	25
31	32	33	34	35	36

1897

ADAMS COUNTY, NEBRASKA   TOWNSHIP 6 N, RANGE 12 W

6	5	4	3	2	1
7	8	9	10	11	12
18	17	16	15	14	13
19	20	21	22	23	24
30	29	28	27	26	25
31	32	33	34	35	36

1872

6	5	4	3	2	1
7	8	9	10	11	12
18	17	16	15	14	13
19	20	21	22	23	24
30	29	28	27	26	25
31	32	33	34	35	36

1877

6	5	4	3	2	1
7	8	9	10	11	12
18	17	16	15	14	13
19	20	21	22	23	24
30	29	28	27	26	25
31	32	33	34	35	36

1882

6	5	4	3	2	1
7	8	9	10	11	12
18	17	16	15	14	13
19	20	21	22	23	24
30	29	28	27	26	25
31	32	33	34	35	36

1887

6	5	4	3	2	1
7	8	9	10	11	12
18	17	16	15	14	13
19	20	21	22	23	24
30	29	28	27	26	25
31	32	33	34	35	36

1892

6	5	4	3	2	1
7	8	9	10	11	12
18	17	16	15	14	13
19	20	21	22	23	24
30	29	28	27	26	25
31	32	33	34	35	36

1897

ADAMS COUNTY, NEBRASKA   TOWNSHIP 5 N, RANGE 12 W

1872

1877

1882

1887

1892

1897

PHELPS COUNTY, NEBRASKA

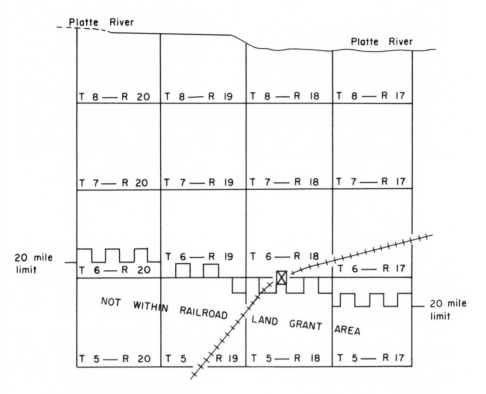

⊠   Holdrege   (County   Seat)

+++   Burlington's   Denver   Extension,   "Holdrege   Cutoff"

PHELPS COUNTY, NEBRASKA   TOWNSHIP 8 N, RANGE 17 W

S u	6	5	4	3	2	1
r v	7	Buffalo County		10	11	12
e y	18	Platte River 17 18 19 14				13
e d	19	20	21	22	23	24
o	30	29	28	27	26	25
u t	31	32	33	34	35	36

1872

S u	6	5	4	3	2	1
r v	7	Buffalo County		10	11	12
e y	18	Platte River 17 18 19 14				13
e d	19	20	21	22	23	24
o	30	29	28	27	26	25
u t	31	32	33	34	35	36

1877

S u	6	5	4	3	2	1
r v	7	Buffalo County		10	11	12
e y	18	Platte River 17 18 19 14				13
e d	19	20	21	22	23	24
o	30	29	28	27	26	25
u t	31	32	33	34	35	36

1882

S u	6	5	4	3	2	1
r v	7	Buffalo County		10	11	12
e y	18	Platte River 17 18 19 14				13
e d	19	20	21	22	23	24
o	30	29	28	27	26	25
u t	31	32	33	34	35	36

1887

S u	6	5	4	3	2	1
r v	7	Buffalo County		10	11	12
e y	18	Platte River 17 18 19 14				13
e d	19	20	21	22	23	24
o	30	29	28	27	26	25
u t	31	32	33	34	35	36

1892

S u	6	5	4	3	2	1
r v	7	Buffalo County		10	11	12
e y	18	Platte River 17 18 19 14				13
e d	19	20	21	22	23	24
o	30	29	28	27	26	25
u t	31	32	33	34	35	36

1897

PHELPS COUNTY, NEBRASKA TOWNSHIP 7 N, RANGE 17 W

6	5	4	3	2	1
7	8	9	10	11	12
18	17	16	15	14	13
19	20	21	22	23	24
30	29	28	27	26	25
31	32	33	34	35	36

1872

6	5	4	3	2	1
7	8	9	10	11	12
18	17	16	15	14	13
19	20	21	22	23	24
30	29	28	27	26	25
31	32	33	34	35	36

1877

6	5	4	3	2	1
7	8	9	10	11	12
18	17	16	15	14	13
19	20	21	22	23	24
30	29	28	27	26	25
31	32	33	34	35	36

1882

6	5	4	3	2	1
7	8	9	10	11	12
18	17	16	15	14	13
19	20	21	22	23	24
30	29	28	27	26	25
31	32	33	34	35	36

1887

6	5	4	3	2	1
7	8	9	10	11	12
18	17	16	15	14	13
19	20	21	22	23	24
30	29	28	27	26	25
31	32	33	34	35	36

1892

6	5	4	3	2	1
7	8	9	10	11	12
18	17	16	15	14	13
19	20	21	22	23	24
30	29	28	27	26	25
31	32	33	34	35	36

1897

PHELPS COUNTY, NEBRASKA   TOWNSHIP 6 N, RANGE 17 W

6	5	4	3	2	1
7	8	9	10	11	12
18	17	16	15	14	13
19	20	21	22	23	24
30	29	28	27	26	25
31	32	33	34	35	36

1872

6	5	4	3	2	1
7	8	9	10	11	12
18	17	16	15	14	13
19	20	21	22	23	24
30	29	28	27	26	25
31	32	33	34	35	36

1877

6	5	4	3	2	1
7	8	9	10	11	12
18	17	16	15	14	13
19	20	21	22	23	24
30	29	28	27	26	25
31	32	33	34	35	36

1882

6	5	4	3	2	1
7	8	9	10	11	12
18	17	16	15	14	13
19	20	21	22	23	24
30	29	28	27	26	25
31	32	33	34	35	36

1887

6	5	4	3	2	1
7	8	9	10	11	12
18	17	16	15	14	13
19	20	21	22	23	24
30	29	28	27	26	25
31	32	33	34	35	36

1892

6	5	4	3	2	1
7	8	9	10	11	12
18	17	16	15	14	13
19	20	21	22	23	24
30	29	28	27	26	25
31	32	33	34	35	36

1897

PHELPS COUNTY, NEBRASKA   TOWNSHIP 5 N, RANGE 17 W

S u r v e y e d o u t					
6	5	4	3	2	1
7	8	9	10	11	12
18	17	16	15	14	13
19	20	21	22	23	24
30	29	28	27	26	25
31	32	33	34	35	36

1872

S u r v e y e d o u t					
6	5	4	3	2	1
7	8	9	10	11	12
18	17	16	15	14	13
19	20	21	22	23	24
30	29	28	27	26	25
31	32	33	34	35	36

1877

S u r v e y e d o u t					
6	5	4	3	2	1
7	8	9	10	11	12
18	17	16	15	14	13
19	20	21	22	23	24
30	29	28	27	26	25
31	32	33	34	35	36

1882

S u r v e y e d o u t					
6	5	4	3	2	1
7	8	9	10	11	12
18	17	16	15	14	13
19	20	21	22	23	24
30	29	28	27	26	25
31	32	33	34	35	36

1887

S u r v e y e d o u t					
6	5	4	3	2	1
7	8	9	10	11	12
18	17	16	15	14	13
19	20	21	22	23	24
30	29	28	27	26	25
31	32	33	34	35	36

1892

S u r v e y e d o u t					
6	5	4	3	2	1
7	8	9	10	11	12
18	17	16	15	14	13
19	20	21	22	23	24
30	29	28	27	26	25
31	32	33	34	35	36

1897

* Outside the limits of the land grant.

PHELPS COUNTY, NEBRASKA   TOWNSHIP 8 N, RANGE 18 W

6	5	4	3	2	1
7	8	9	10	11	12
18	17	16	15	14	13
19	20	21	22	23	24
30	29	28	27	26	25
31	32	33	34	35	36

1872

6	5	4	3	2	1
7	8	9	10	11	12
18	17	16	15	14	13
19	20	21	22	23	24
30	29	28	27	26	25
31	32	33	34	35	36

1877

6	5	4	3	2	1
7	8	9	10	11	12
18	17	16	15	14	13
19	20	21	22	23	24
30	29	28	27	26	25
31	32	33	34	35	36

1882

6	5	4	3	2	1
7	8	9	10	11	12
18	17	16	15	14	13
19	20	21	22	23	24
30	29	28	27	26	25
31	32	33	34	35	36

1887

6	5	4	3	2	1
7	8	9	10	11	12
18	17	16	15	14	13
19	20	21	22	23	24
30	29	28	27	26	25
31	32	33	34	35	36

1892

6	5	4	3	2	1
7	8	9	10	11	12
18	17	16	15	14	13
19	20	21	22	23	24
30	29	28	27	26	25
31	32	33	34	35	36

1897

PHELPS COUNTY, NEBRASKA

TOWNSHIP 7 N, RANGE 18 W

6	5	4	3	2	1
7	8	9	10	11	12
18	17	16	15	14	13
19	20	21	22	23	24
30	29	28	27	26	25
31	32	33	34	35	36

1872

6	5	4	3	2	1
7	8	9	10	11	12
18	17	16	15	14	13
19	20	21	22	23	24
30	29	28	27	26	25
31	32	33	34	35	36

1877

6	5	4	3	2	1
7	8	9	10	11	12
18	17	16	15	14	13
19	20	21	22	23	24
30	29	28	27	26	25
31	32	33	34	35	36

1882

6	5	4	3	2	1
7	8	9	10	11	12
18	17	16	15	14	13
19	20	21	22	23	24
30	29	28	27	26	25
31	32	33	34	35	36

1887

6	5	4	3	2	1
7	8	9	10	11	12
18	17	16	15	14	13
19	20	21	22	23	24
30	29	28	27	26	25
31	32	33	34	35	36

1892

6	5	4	3	2	1
7	8	9	10	11	12
18	17	16	15	14	13
19	20	21	22	23	24
30	29	28	27	26	25
31	32	33	34	35	36

1897

PHELPS COUNTY, NEBRASKA   TOWNSHIP 6 N, RANGE 18 W

6	5	4	3	2	1
7	8	9	10	11	12
18	17	16	15	14	13
19	20	21	22	23	24
30	29	28	27	26	25
31	32	33	34	35	36

1872

6	5	4	3	2	1
7	8	9	10	11	12
18	17	16	15	14	13
19	20	21	22	23	24
30	29	28	27	26	25
31	32	33	34	35	36

1877

6	5	4	3	2	1
7	8	9	10	11	12
18	17	16	15	14	13
19	20	21	22	23	24
30	29	28	27	26	25
31	32	33	34	35	36

1882

6	5	4	3	2	1
7	8	9	10	11	12
18	17	16	15	14	13
19	20	21	22	23	24
30	29	28	27	26	25
31	32	33	34	35	36

1887

6	5	4	3	2	1
7	8	9	10	11	12
18	17	16	15	14	13
19	20	21	22	23	24
30	29	28	27	26	25
31	32	33	34	35	36

1892

6	5	4	3	2	1
7	8	9	10	11	12
18	17	16	15	14	13
19	20	21	22	23	24
30	29	28	27	26	25
31	32	33	34	35	36

1897

PHELPS COUNTY, NEBRASKA   TOWNSHIP 5 N, RANGE 18 W

6	5	4	3	2	1
7*	8	9*	10	11*	12
18	17*	16	15*	14	13
19*	20	21*	22	23*	24
30	29*	28	27*	26	25*
31*	32	33*	34	35*	36

1872

6	5	4	3	2	1
7*	8	9*	10	11*	12
18	17	16	15*	14	13
19*	20	21*	22	23*	24
30	29*	28	27*	26	25*
31*	32	33*	34	35*	36

1877

6	5	4	3	2	1
7*	8	9*	10	11*	12
18	17*	16	15*	14	13*
19*	20	21*	22	23*	24
30	29*	28	27*	26	25*
31*	32	33*	34	35*	36

1882

6	5	4	3	2	1
7*	8	9*	10	11*	12
18	17*	16	15*	14	13*
19*	20	21*	22	23*	24
30	29*	28	27*	26	25*
31*	32	33*	34	35*	36

1887

6	5	4	3	2	1
7*	8	9*	10	11*	12
18	17*	16	15*	14	13*
19*	20	21*	22	23*	24
30	29*	28	27*	26	25*
31*	32	33*	34	35*	36

1892

6	5	4	3	2	1
7*	8	9*	10	11*	12
18	17*	16	15*	14	13*
19*	20	21*	22	23*	24
30	29*	28	27*	26	25*
31*	32	33*	34	35*	36

1897

* Outside the limits of the land grant.

PHELPS COUNTY, NEBRASKA   TOWNSHIP 8 N, RANGE 19 W

6	Dawson County 2				1
7	Platte River 8	9	10	11	12
18	17	16	15	14	13
19	20	21	22	23	24
30	29	28	27	26	25
31	32	33	34	35	36

1872

6	Dawson County 2				1
7	Platte River 8	9	10	11	12
18	17	16	15	14	13
19	20	21	22	23	24
30	29	28	27	26	25
31	32	33	34	35	36

1877

6	Dawson County 2				1
7	Platte River 8	9	10	11	12
18	17	16	15	14	13
19	20	21	22	23	24
30	29	28	27	26	25
31	32	33	34	35	36

1882

6	Dawson County 2				1
7	Platte River 8	9	10	11	12
18	17	16	15	14	13
19	20	21	22	23	24
30	29	28	27	26	25
31	32	33	34	35	36

1887

6	Dawson County 2				1
7	Platte River 8	9	10	11	12
18	17	16	15	14	13
19	20	21	22	23	24
30	29	28	27	26	25
31	32	33	34	35	36

1892

6	Dawson County 2				1
7	Platte River 8	9	10	11	12
18	17	16	15	14	13
19	20	21	22	23	24
30	29	28	27	26	25
31	32	33	34	35	36

1897

PHELPS COUNTY, NEBRASKA   TOWNSHIP 7 N, RANGE 19 W

6	5	4	3	2	1
7	8	9*	10	11	12
18	17	16	15	14	13
19	20	21	22	23	24
30	29	28	27	26	25
31	32	33	34	35	36

1872

6	5	4	3	2	1
7	8	9*	10	11	12
18	17	16	15	14	13
19	20	21	22	23	24
30	29	28	27	26	25
31	32	33	34	35	36

1877

6	5	4	3	2	1
7	8	9*	10	11	12
18	17	16	15	14	13
19	20	21	22	23	24
30	29	28	27	26	25
31	32	33	34	35	36

1882

6	5	4	3	2	1
7	8	9*	10	11	12
18	17	16	15	14	13
19	20	21	22	23	24
30	29	28	27	26	25
31	32	33	34	35	36

1887

6	5	4	3	2	1
7	8	9*	10	11	12
18	17	16	15	14	13
19	20	21	22	23	24
30	29	28	27	26	25
31	32	33	34	35	36

1892

6	5	4	3	2	1
7	8	9*	10	11	12
18	17	16	15	14	13
19	20	21	22	23	24
30	29	28	27	26	25
31	32	33	34	35	36

1897

* Railroad lands lost to prior claimants.

PHELPS COUNTY, NEBRASKA

TOWNSHIP 6 N, RANGE 19 W

1872

1877

1882

1887

1892

1897

PHELPS COUNTY, NEBRASKA

TOWNSHIP 5 N, RANGE 19 W

6	5	4	3	2	1
7	8	9	10	11	12
18	17	16	15	14	13
19	20	21	22	23	24
30	29	28	27	26	25
31	32	33	34	35	36

1872

6	5	4	3	2	1
7	8	9	10	11	12
18	17	16	15	14	13
19	20	21	22	23	24
30	29	28	27	26	25
31	32	33	34	35	36

1877

6	5	4	3	2	1
7	8	9	10	11	12
18	17	16	15	14	13
19	20	21	22	23	24
30	29	28	27	26	25
31	32	33	34	35	36

1882

6	5	4	3	2	1
7	8	9	10	11	12
18	17	16	15	14	13
19	20	21	22	23	24
30	29	28	27	26	25
31	32	33	34	35	36

1887

6	5	4	3	2	1
7	8	9	10	11	12
18	17	16	15	14	13
19	20	21	22	23	24
30	29	28	27	26	25
31	32	33	34	35	36

1892

6	5	4	3	2	1
7	8	9	10	11	12
18	17	16	15	14	13
19	20	21	22	23	24
30	29	28	27	26	25
31	32	33	34	35	36

1897

* Outside the limits of the land grant.

PHELPS COUNTY, NEBRASKA   TOWNSHIP 8 N, RANGE 20 W

Dawson County				2	1
6	5	4	3		
7	8	9	10	11	12
18	17	16	15	14	13
19	20	21	22	23	24
30	29	28	27	26	25
31	32	33	34	35	36

Platte River

1872

Dawson County				2	1
6	5	4	3		
7	8	9	10	11	12
18	17	16	15	14	13
19	20	21	22	23	24
30	29	28	27	26	25
31	32	33	34	35	36

Platte River

1877

Dawson County				2	1
6	5	4	3		
7	8	9	10	11	12
18	17	16	15	14	13
19	20	21	22	23	24
30	29	28	27	26	25
31	32	33	34	35	36

Platte River

1882

Dawson County				2	1
6	5	4	3		
7	8	9	10	11	12
18	17	16	15	14	13
19	20	21	22	23	24
30	29	28	27	26	25
31	32	33	34	35	36

Platte River

1887

Dawson County				2	1
6	5	4	3		
7	8	9	10	11	12
18	17	16	15	14	13
19	20	21	22	23	24
30	29	28	27	26	25
31	32	33	34	35	36

Platte River

1892

Dawson County				2	1
6	5	4	3		
7	8	9	10	11	12
18	17	16	15	14	13
19	20	21	22	23	24
30	29	28	27	26	25
31	32	33	34	35	36

Platte River

1897

PHELPS COUNTY, NEBRASKA   TOWNSHIP 7 N, RANGE 20 W

6	5	4	3	2	1
7	8	9	10	11	12
18	17	16	15	14	13
19	20	21	22	23	24
30	29	28	27	26	25
31	32	33	34	35	36

1872

6	5	4	3	2	1
7	8	9	10	11	12
18	17	16	15	14	13
19	20	21	22	23	24
30	29	28	27	26	25
31	32	33	34	35	36

1877

6	5	4	3	2	1
7	8	9	10	11	12
18	17	16	15	14	13
19	20	21	22	23	24
30	29	28	27	26	25
31	32	33	34	35	36

1882

6	5	4	3	2	1
7	8	9	10	11	12
18	17	16	15	14	13
19	20	21	22	23	24
30	29	28	27	26	25
31	32	33	34	35	36

1887

6	5	4	3	2	1
7	8	9	10	11	12
18	17	16	15	14	13
19	20	21	22	23	24
30	29	28	27	26	25
31	32	33	34	35	36

1892

6	5	4	3	2	1
7	8	9	10	11	12
18	17	16	15	14	13
19	20	21	22	23	24
30	29	28	27	26	25
31	32	33	34	35	36

1897

PHELPS COUNTY, NEBRASKA   TOWNSHIP 6 N, RANGE 20 W

6	5	4	3	2	1
7	8	9	10	11	12
18	17	16	15	14	13
19	20	21	22	23	24
30	29	28	27	26	25
31	32	33	34	35	36

1872

6	5	4	3	2	1
7	8	9	10	11	12
18	17	16	15	14	13
19	20	21	22	23	24
30	29	28	27	26	25
31	32	33	34	35	36

1877

6	5	4	3	2	1
7	8	9	10	11	12
18	17	16	15	14	13
19	20	21	22	23	24
30	29	28	27	26	25
31	32	33	34	35	36

1882

6	5	4	3	2	1
7	8	9	10	11	12
18	17	16	15	14	13
19	20	21	22	23	24
30	29	28	27	26	25
31	32	33	34	35	36

1887

6	5	4	3	2	1
7	8	9	10	11	12
18	17	16	15	14	13
19	20	21	22	23	24
30	29	28	27	26	25
31	32	33	34	35	36

1892

6	5	4	3	2	1
7	8	9	10	11	12
18	17	16	15	14	13
19	20	21	22	23	24
30	29	28	27	26	25
31	32	33	34	35	36

1897

* Outside the limits of the land grant.

PHELPS COUNTY, NEBRASKA   TOWNSHIP 5 N, RANGE 20 W

6	5	4	3	2	1
7	8	9	10	11	12
18	17	16	15	14	13
19	20	21	22	23	24
30	29	28	27	26	25
31	32	33	34	35	36

1872

6	5	4	3	2	1
7	8	9	10	11	12
18	17	16	15	14	13
19	20	21	22	23	24
30	29	28	27	26	25
31	32	33	34	35	36

1877

6	5	4	3	2	1
7	8	9	10	11	12
18	17	16	15	14	13
19	20	21	22	23	24
30	29	28	27	26	25
31	32	33	34	35	36

1882

6	5	4	3	2	1
7	8	9	10	11	12
18	17	16	15	14	13
19	20	21	22	23	24
30	29	28	27	26	25
31	32	33	34	35	36

1887

6	5	4	3	2	1
7	8	9	10	11	12
18	17	16	15	14	13
19	20	21	22	23	24
30	29	28	27	26	25
31	32	33	34	35	36

1892

6	5	4	3	2	1
7	8	9	10	11	12
18	17	16	15	14	13
19	20	21	22	23	24
30	29	28	27	26	25
31	32	33	34	35	36

1897

The entire township is outside the limits of the land grant.

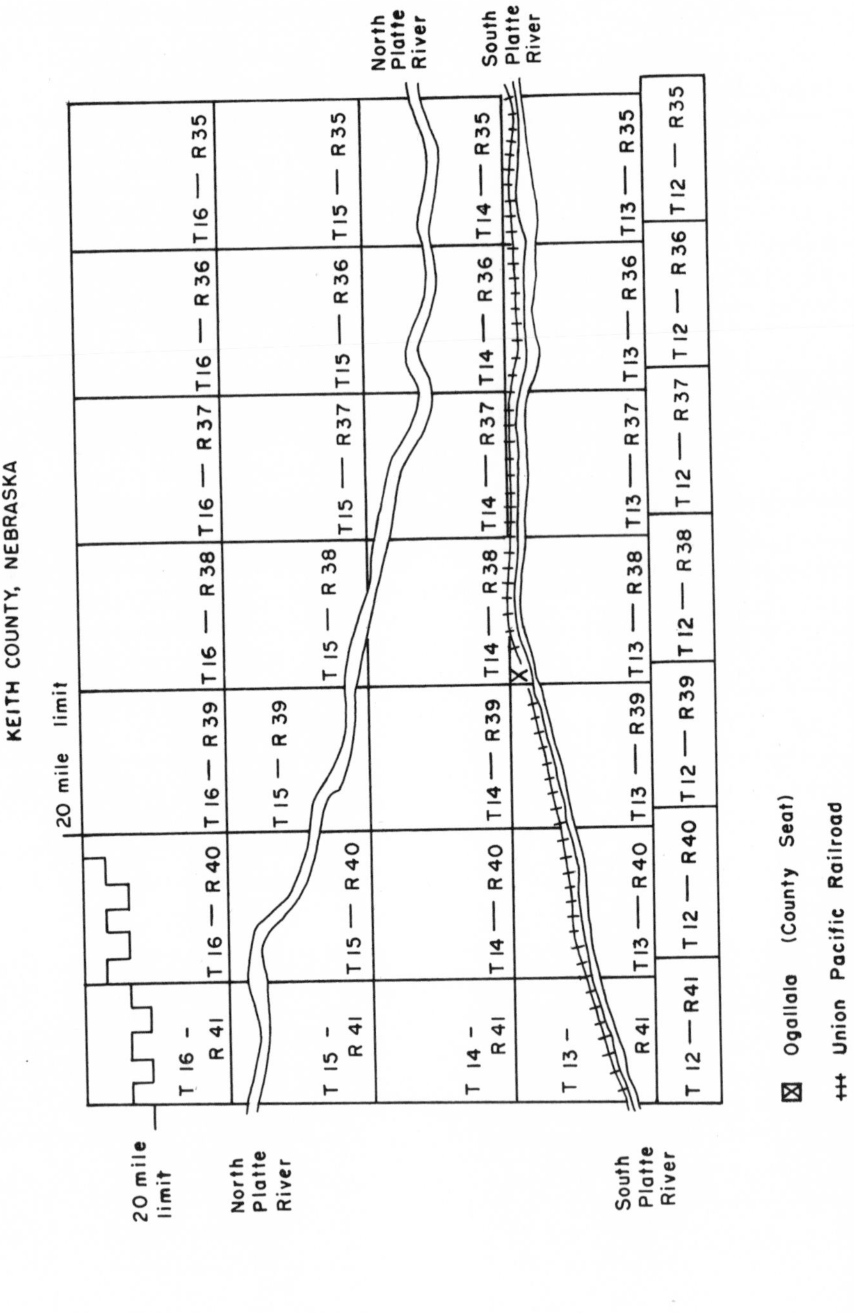
KEITH COUNTY, NEBRASKA
20 mile limit
North Platte River
South Platte River
T 16 — R 35
T 16 — R 36
T 16 — R 37
T 16 — R 38
T 16 — R 39
T 16 — R 40
T 16 - R 41
T 15 — R 35
T 15 — R 36
T 15 — R 37
T 15 — R 38
T 15 — R 39
T 15 — R 40
T 15 - R 41
T 14 — R 35
T 14 — R 36
T 14 — R 37
T 14 — R 38
T 14 — R 39
T 14 — R 40
T 14 - R 41
T 13 — R 35
T 13 — R 36
T 13 — R 37
T 13 — R 38
T 13 — R 39
T 13 — R 40
T 13 - R 41
T 12 — R 35
T 12 — R 36
T 12 — R 37
T 12 — R 38
T 12 — R 39
T 12 — R 40
T 12 — R 41
Ogallala (County Seat)
Union Pacific Railroad

KEITH COUNTY, NEBRASKA   TOWNSHIP 16 N, RANGE 35 W

6	5	4	3	2	1
7	8	9	10	11	12
18	17	16	15	14	13
19	20	21	22	23	24
30	29	28	27	26	25
31	32	33	34	35	36

1872

6	5	4	3	2	1
7	8	9	10	11	12
18	17	16	15	14	13
19	20	21	22	23	24
30	29	28	27	26	25
31	32	33	34	35	36

1877

6	5	4	3	2	1
7	8	9	10	11	12
18	17	16	15	14	13
19	20	21	22	23	24
30	29	28	27	26	25
31	32	33	34	35	36

1882

6	5	4	3	2	1
7	8	9	10	11	12
18	17	16	15	14	13
19	20	21	22	23	24
30	29	28	27	26	25
31	32	33	34	35	36

1887

6	5	4	3	2	1
7	8	9	10	11	12
18	17	16	15	14	13
19	20	21	22	23	24
30	29	28	27	26	25
31	32	33	34	35	36

1892

6	5	4	3	2	1
7	8	9	10	11	12
18	17	16	15	14	13
19	20	21	22	23	24
30	29	28	27	26	25
31	32	33	34	35	36

1897

KEITH COUNTY, NEBRASKA   TOWNSHIP 15 N, RANGE 35 W

6	5	4	3	2	1
7	8	9	10	11	12
18	17	16	15	14	13
19	20	21	22	23	24
30	29	28	27	26	25
31	32	33	34	35	36

1872

6	5	4	3	2	1
7	8	9	10	11	12
18	17	16	15	14	13
19	20	21	22	23	24
30	29	28	27	26	25
31	32	33	34	35	36

1877

6	5	4	3	2	1
7	8	9	10	11	12
18	17	16	15	14	13
19	20	21	22	23	24
30	29	28	27	26	25
31	32	33	34	35	36

1882

6	5	4	3	2	1
7	8	9	10	11	12
18	17	16	15	14	13
19	20	21	22	23	24
30	29	28	27	26	25
31	32	33	34	35	36

1887

6	5	4	3	2	1
7	8	9	10	11	12
18	17	16	15	14	13
19	20	21	22	23	24
30	29	28	27	26	25
31	32	33	34	35	36

1892

6	5	4	3	2	1
7	8	9	10	11	12
18	17	16	15	14	13
19	20	21	22	23	24
30	29	28	27	26	25
31	32	33	34	35	36

1897

KEITH COUNTY, NEBRASKA   TOWNSHIP 14 N, RANGE 35 W

1872

1877

1882

1887

1892

1897

Tracts eliminated by the North Platte River.

KEITH COUNTY, NEBRASKA   TOWNSHIP 13 N, RANGE 35 W

6	5	4	3	2	1
7	8	9	10	11	12
18	17	16	15	14	13
19	20	21	22	23	24
30	29	28	27	26	25
31	32	33	34	35	36

1872

6	5	4	3	2	1
7	8	9	10	11	12
18	17	16	15	14	13
19	20	21	22	23	24
30	29	28	27	26	25
31	32	33	34	35	36

1877

6	5	4	3	2	1
7	8	9	10	11	12
18	17	16	15	14	13
19	20	21	22	23	24
30	29	28	27	26	25
31	32	33	34	35	36

1882

6	5	4	3	2	1
7	8	9	10	11	12
18	17	16	15	14	13
19	20	21	22	23	24
30	29	28	27	26	25
31	32	33	34	35	36

1887

6	5	4	3	2	1
7	8	9	10	11	12
18	17	16	15	14	13
19	20	21	22	23	24
30	29	28	27	26	25
31	32	33	34	35	36

1892

6	5	4	3	2	1
7	8	9	10	11	12
18	17	16	15	14	13
19	20	21	22	23	24
30	29	28	27	26	25
31	32	33	34	35	36

1897

 Tracts eliminated by the South Platte River.

KEITH COUNTY, NEBRASKA   TOWNSHIP 12 N, RANGE 35 W

6	5	4	3	2	1
7	8	9	10	11	12
18	17	16	15	14	13
19	20	21	22	23	24
30	Perkins County 29 28 27 26				25
31	32	33	34	35	36

1872

6	5	4	3	2	1
7	8	9	10	11	12
18	17	16	15	14	13
19	20	21	22	23	24
30	Perkins County 29 28 27 26				25
31	32	33	34	35	36

1877

6	5	4	3	2	1
7	8	9	10	11	12
18	17	16	15	14	13
19	20	21	22	23	24
30	Perkins County 29 28 27 26				25
31	32	33	34	35	36

1882

6	5	4	3	2	1
7	8	9	10	11	12
18	17	16	15	14	13
19	20	21	22	23	24
30	Perkins County 29 28 27 26				25
31	32	33	34	35	36

1887

6	5	4	3	2	1
7	8	9	10	11	12
18	17	16	15	14	13
19	20	21	22	23	24
30	Perkins County 29 28 27 26				25
31	32	33	34	35	36

1892

6	5	4	3	2	1
7	8	9	10	11	12
18	17	16	15	14	13
19	20	21	22	23	24
30	Perkins County 29 28 27 26				25
31	32	33	34	35	36

1897

KEITH COUNTY, NEBRASKA　　　TOWNSHIP 16 N, RANGE 36 W

6	5	4	3	2	1
7	8	9	10	11	12
18	17	16	15	14	13
19	20	21	22	23	24
30	29	28	27	26	25
31	32	33	34	35	36

1872

6	5	4	3	2	1
7	8	9	10	11	12
18	17	16	15	14	13
19	20	21	22	23	24
30	29	28	27	26	25
31	32	33	34	35	36

1877

6	5	4	3	2	1
7	8	9	10	11	12
18	17	16	15	14	13
19	20	21	22	23	24
30	29	28	27	26	25
31	32	33	34	35	36

1882

6	5	4	3	2	1
7	8	9	10	11	12
18	17	16	15	14	13
19	20	21	22	23	24
30	29	28	27	26	25
31	32	33	34	35	36

1887

6	5	4	3	2	1
7	8	9	10	11	12
18	17	16	15	14	13
19	20	21	22	23	24
30	29	28	27	26	25
31	32	33	34	35	36

1892

6	5	4	3	2	1
7	8	9	10	11	12
18	17	16	15	14	13
19	20	21	22	23	24
30	29	28	27	26	25
31	32	33	34	35	36

1897

KEITH COUNTY, NEBRASKA · TOWNSHIP 15 N, RANGE 36 W

1872

6	5	4	3	2	1
7	8	9	10	11	12
18	17	16	15	14	13
19	20	21	22	23	24
30	29	28	27	26	25
31	32	33	34	35	36

1877

6	5	4	3	2	1
7	8	9	10	11	12
18	17	16	15	14	13
19	20	21	22	23	24
30	29	28	27	26	25
31	32	33	34	35	36

1882

6	5	4	3	2	1
7	8	9	10	11	12
18	17	16	15	14	13
19	20	21	22	23	24
30	29	28	27	26	25
31	32	33	34	35	36

1887

6	5	4	3	2	1
7	8	9	10	11	12
18	17	16	15	14	13
19	20	21	22	23	24
30	29	28	27	26	25
31	32	33	34	35	36

1892

6	5	4	3	2	1
7	8	9	10	11	12
18	17	16	15	14	13
19	20	21	22	23	24
30	29	28	27	26	25
31	32	33	34	35	36

1897

6	5	4	3	2	1
7	8	9	10	11	12
18	17	16	15	14	13
19	20	21	22	23	24
30	29	28	27	26	25
31	32	33	34	35	36

KEITH COUNTY, NEBRASKA   TOWNSHIP 14 N, RANGE 36 W

6	5	4	3	2	1
7	8	9	10	11	12
18	17	16	15	14	13
19	20	21	22	23	24
30	29	28	27	26	25
31	32	33	34	35	36

1872

6	5	4	3	2	1
7	8	9	10	11	12
18	17	16	15	14	13
19	20	21	22	23	24
30	29	28	27	26	25
31	32	33	34	35	36

1877

6	5	4	3	2	1
7	8	9	10	11	12
18	17	16	15	14	13
19	20	21	22	23	24
30	29	28	27	26	25
31	32	33	34	35	36

1882

6	5	4	3	2	1
7	8	9	10	11	12
18	17	16	15	14	13
19	20	21	22	23	24
30	29	28	27	26	25
31	32	33	34	35	36

1887

6	5	4	3	2	1
7	8	9	10	11	12
18	17	16	15	14	13
19	20	21	22	23	24
30	29	28	27	26	25
31	32	33	34	35	36

1892

6	5	4	3	2	1
7	8	9	10	11	12
18	17	16	15	14	13
19	20	21	22	23	24
30	29	28	27	26	25
31	32	33	34	35	36

1897

 Tracts eliminated by the North Platte River.

KEITH COUNTY, NEBRASKA   TOWNSHIP 13 N, RANGE 36 W

6	5	4	3	2	1
7	8	9	10	11	12
18	17	16	15	14	13
19	20	21	22	23	24
30	29	28	27	26	25
31	32	33	34	35	36

1872

6	5	4	3	2	1
7	8	9	10	11	12
18	17	16	15	14	13
19	20	21	22	23	24
30	29	28	27	26	25
31	32	33	34	35	36

1877

6	5	4	3	2	1
7	8	9	10	11	12
18	17	16	15	14	13
19	20	21	22	23	24
30	29	28	27	26	25
31	32	33	34	35	36

1882

6	5	4	3	2	1
7	8	9	10	11	12
18	17	16	15	14	13
19	20	21	22	23	24
30	29	28	27	26	25
31	32	33	34	35	36

1887

6	5	4	3	2	1
7	8	9	10	11	12
18	17	16	15	14	13
19	20	21	22	23	24
30	29	28	27	26	25
31	32	33	34	35	36

1892

6	5	4	3	2	1
7	8	9	10	11	12
18	17	16	15	14	13
19	20	21	22	23	24
30	29	28	27	26	25
31	32	33	34	35	36

1897

Tracts eliminated by the South Platte River.

KEITH COUNTY, NEBRASKA   TOWNSHIP 12 N, RANGE 36 W

1872

1877

1882

1887

1892

1897

KEITH COUNTY, NEBRASKA   TOWNSHIP 16 N, RANGE 37 W

6	5	4	3	2	1
7	8	9	10	11	12
18	17	16	15	14	13
19	20	21	22	23	24
30	29	28	27	26	25
31	32	33	34	35	36

1872

6	5	4	3	2	1
7	8	9	10	11	12
18	17	16	15	14	13
19	20	21	22	23	24
30	29	28	27	26	25
31	32	33	34	35	36

1877

6	5	4	3	2	1
7	8	9	10	11	12
18	17	16	15	14	13
19	20	21	22	23	24
30	29	28	27	26	25
31	32	33	34	35	36

1882

6	5	4	3	2	1
7	8	9	10	11	12
18	17	16	15	14	13
19	20	21	22	23	24
30	29	28	27	26	25
31	32	33	34	35	36

1887

6	5	4	3	2	1
7	8	9	10	11	12
18	17	16	15	14	13
19	20	21	22	23	24
30	29	28	27	26	25
31	32	33	34	35	36

1892

6	5	4	3	2	1
7	8	9	10	11	12
18	17	16	15	14	13
19	20	21	22	23	24
30	29	28	27	26	25
31	32	33	34	35	36

1897

KEITH COUNTY, NEBRASKA   TOWNSHIP 15 N, RANGE 37 W

6	5	4	3	2	1
7	8	9	10	11	12
18	17	16	15	14	13
19	20	21	22	23	24
30	29	28	27	26	25
31	32	33	34	35	36

1872

6	5	4	3	2	1
7	8	9	10	11	12
18	17	16	15	14	13
19	20	21	22	23	24
30	29	28	27	26	25
31	32	33	34	35	36

1877

6	5	4	3	2	1
7	8	9	10	11	12
18	17	16	15	14	13
19	20	21	22	23	24
30	29	28	27	26	25
31	32	33	34	35	36

1882

6	5	4	3	2	1
7	8	9	10	11	12
18	17	16	15	14	13
19	20	21	22	23	24
30	29	28	27	26	25
31	32	33	34	35	36

1887

6	5	4	3	2	1
7	8	9	10	11	12
18	17	16	15	14	13
19	20	21	22	23	24
30	29	28	27	26	25
31	32	33	34	35	36

1892

6	5	4	3	2	1
7	8	9	10	11	12
18	17	16	15	14	13
19	20	21	22	23	24
30	29	28	27	26	25
31	32	33	34	35	36

1897

KEITH COUNTY, NEBRASKA TOWNSHIP 14 N, RANGE 37 W

1872

1877

1882

1887

1892

1897

Tracts eliminated by the North Platte River.

KEITH COUNTY, NEBRASKA   TOWNSHIP 13 N, RANGE 37 W

6	5	4	3	2	1
7	8	9	10	11	12
18	17	16	15	14	13
19	20	21	22	23	24
30	29	28	27	26	25
31	32	33	34	35	36

1872

6	5	4	3	2	1
7	8	9	10	11	12
18	17	16	15	14	13
19	20	21	22	23	24
30	29	28	27	26	25
31	32	33	34	35	36

1877

6	5	4	3	2	1
7	8	9	10	11	12
18	17	16	15	14	13
19	20	21	22	23	24
30	29	28	27	26	25
31	32	33	34	35	36

1882

6	5	4	3	2	1
7	8	9	10	11	12
18	17	16	15	14	13
19	20	21	22	23	24
30	29	28	27	26	25
31	32	33	34	35	36

1887

6	5	4	3	2	1
7	8	9	10	11	12
18	17	16	15	14	13
19	20	21	22	23	24
30	29	28	27	26	25
31	32	33	34	35	36

1892

6	5	4	3	2	1
7	8	9	10	11	12
18	17	16	15	14	13
19	20	21	22	23	24
30	29	28	27	26	25
31	32	33	34	35	36

1897

 Tracts eliminated by the South Platte River.

KEITH COUNTY, NEBRASKA   TOWNSHIP 12 N, RANGE 37 W

6	5	4	3	2	1
7	8	9	10	11	12
18	17	16	15	14	13
19	20	21	22	23	24
30	29 28	27 26			25
31	32	33	34	35	36

Perkins County

1872

6	5	4	3	2	1
7	8	9	10	11	12
18	17	16	15	14	13
19	20	21	22	23	24
30	29 28	27 26			25
31	32	33	34	35	36

Perkins County

1877

6	5	4	3	2	1
7	8	9	10	11	12
18	17	16	15	14	13
19	20	21	22	23	24
30	29 28	27 26			25
31	32	33	34	35	36

Perkins County

1882

6	5	4	3	2	1
7	8	9	10	11	12
18	17	16	15	14	13
19	20	21	22	23	24
30	29 28	27 26			25
31	32	33	34	35	36

Perkins County

1887

6	5	4	3	2	1
7	8	9	10	11	12
18	17	16	15	14	13
19	20	21	22	23	24
30	29 28	27 26			25
31	32	33	34	35	36

Perkins County

1892

6	5	4	3	2	1
7	8	9	10	11	12
18	17	16	15	14	13
19	20	21	22	23	24
30	29 28	27 26			25
31	32	33	34	35	36

Perkins County

1897

KEITH COUNTY, NEBRASKA   TOWNSHIP 16 N, RANGE 38 W

6	5	4	3	2	1
7	8	9	10	11	12
18	17	16	15	14	13
19	20	21	22	23	24
30	29	28	27	26	25
31	32	33	34	35	36

1872

6	5	4	3	2	1
7	8	9	10	11	12
18	17	16	15	14	13
19	20	21	22	23	24
30	29	28	27	26	25
31	32	33	34	35	36

1877

6	5	4	3	2	1
7	8	9	10	11	12
18	17	16	15	14	13
19	20	21	22	23	24
30	29	28	27	26	25
31	32	33	34	35	36

1882

6	5	4	3	2	1
7	8	9	10	11	12
18	17	16	15	14	13
19	20	21	22	23	24
30	29	28	27	26	25
31	32	33	34	35	36

1887

6	5	4	3	2	1
7	8	9	10	11	12
18	17	16	15	14	13
19	20	21	22	23	24
30	29	28	27	26	25
31	32	33	34	35	36

1892

6	5	4	3	2	1
7	8	9	10	11	12
18	17	16	15	14	13
19	20	21	22	23	24
30	29	28	27	26	25
31	32	33	34	35	36

1897

KEITH COUNTY, NEBRASKA   TOWNSHIP 15 N, RANGE 38 W

1872

1877

1882

1887

1892

1897

Tracts eliminated by the North Platte River.

KEITH COUNTY, NEBRASKA   TOWNSHIP 14 N, RANGE 38 W

6	5	4	3	2	1
7	8	9	10	11	12
18	17	16	15	14	13
19	20	21	22	23	24
30	29	28	27	26	25
31	32	33	34	35	36

1872

6	5	4	3	2	1
7	8	9	10	11	12
18	17	16	15	14	13
19	20	21	22	23	24
30	29	28	27	26	25
31	32	33	34	35	36

1877

6	5	4	3	2	1
7	8	9	10	11	12
18	17	16	15	14	13
19	20	21	22	23	24
30	29	28	27	26	25
31	32	33	34	35	36

1882

6	5	4	3	2	1
7	8	9	10	11	12
18	17	16	15	14	13
19	20	21	22	23	24
30	29	28	27	26	25
31	32	33	34	35	36

1887

6	5	4	3	2	1
7	8	9	10	11	12
18	17	16	15	14	13
19	20	21	22	23	24
30	29	28	27	26	25
31	32	33	34	35	36

1892

6	5	4	3	2	1
7	8	9	10	11	12
18	17	16	15	14	13
19	20	21	22	23	24
30	29	28	27	26	25
31	32	33	34	35	36

1897

 Tracts eliminated by the North Platte River.

KEITH COUNTY, NEBRASKA   TOWNSHIP 13 N, RANGE 38 W

1872

1877

1882

1887

1892

1897

Tracts eliminated by the South Platte River.

KEITH COUNTY, NEBRASKA   TOWNSHIP 12 N, RANGE 38 W

6	5	4	3	2	1
7	8	9	10	11	12
18	17	16	15	14	13
19	20	21	22	23	24
30	Perkins County				25
31	32	33	34	35	36

1872

6	5	4	3	2	1
7	8	9	10	11	12
18	17	16	15	14	13
19	20	21	22	23	24
30	Perkins County				25
31	32	33	34	35	36

1877

6	5	4	3	2	1
7	8	9	10	11	12
18	17	16	15	14	13
19	20	21	22	23	24
30	Perkins County				25
31	32	33	34	35	36

1882

6	5	4	3	2	1
7	8	9	10	11	12
18	17	16	15	14	13
19	20	21	22	23	24
30	Perkins County				25
31	32	33	34	35	36

1887

6	5	4	3	2	1
7	8	9	10	11	12
18	17	16	15	14	13
19	20	21	22	23	24
30	Perkins County				25
31	32	33	34	35	36

1892

6	5	4	3	2	1
7	8	9	10	11	12
18	17	16	15	14	13
19	20	21	22	23	24
30	Perkins County				25
31	32	33	34	35	36

1897

KEITH COUNTY, NEBRASKA TOWNSHIP 16 N, RANGE 39 W

6	5	4	3	2	1
7	8	9	10	11	12
18	17	16	15	14	13
19	20	21	22	23	24
30	29	28	27	26	25
31	32	33	34	35	36

1872

6	5	4	3	2	1
7	8	9	10	11	12
18	17	16	15	14	13
19	20	21	22	23	24
30	29	28	27	26	25
31	32	33	34	35	36

1877

6	5	4	3	2	1
7	8	9	10	11	12
18	17	16	15	14	13
19	20	21	22	23	24
30	29	28	27	26	25
31	32	33	34	35	36

1882

6	5	4	3	2	1
7	8	9	10	11	12
18	17	16	15	14	13
19	20	21	22	23	24
30	29	28	27	26	25
31	32	33	34	35	36

1887

6	5	4	3	2	1
7	8	9	10	11	12
18	17	16	15	14	13
19	20	21	22	23	24
30	29	28	27	26	25
31	32	33	34	35	36

1892

6	5	4	3	2	1
7	8	9	10	11	12
18	17	16	15	14	13
19	20	21	22	23	24
30	29	28	27	26	25
31	32	33	34	35	36

1897

KEITH COUNTY, NEBRASKA   TOWNSHIP 15 N, RANGE 39 W

6	5	4	3	2	1
7	8	9	10	11	12
18	17	16	15	14	13
19	20	21	22	23	24
30	29	28	27	26	25
31	32	33	34	35	36

1872

6	5	4	3	2	1
7	8	9	10	11	12
18	17	16	15	14	13
19	20	21	22	23	24
30	29	28	27	26	25
31	32	33	34	35	36

1877

6	5	4	3	2	1
7	8	9	10	11	12
18	17	16	15	14	13
19	20	21	22	23	24
30	29	28	27	26	25
31	32	33	34	35	36

1882

6	5	4	3	2	1
7	8	9	10	11	12
18	17	16	15	14	13
19	20	21	22	23	24
30	29	28	27	26	25
31	32	33	34	35	36

1887

6	5	4	3	2	1
7	8	9	10	11	12
18	17	16	15	14	13
19	20	21	22	23	24
30	29	28	27	26	25
31	32	33	34	35	36

1892

6	5	4	3	2	1
7	8	9	10	11	12
18	17	16	15	14	13
19	20	21	22	23	24
30	29	28	27	26	25
31	32	33	34	35	36

1897

 Tracts eliminated by the North Platte River.

KEITH COUNTY, NEBRASKA TOWNSHIP 14 N, RANGE 39 W

6	5	4	3	2	1
7	8	9	10	11	12
18	17	16	15	14	13
19	20	21	22	23	24
30	29	28	27	26	25
31	32	33	34	35	36

1872

6	5	4	3	2	1
7	8	9	10	11	12
18	17	16	15	14	13
19	20	21	22	23	24
30	29	28	27	26	25
31	32	33	34	35	36

1877

6	5	4	3	2	1
7	8	9	10	11	12
18	17	16	15	14	13
19	20	21	22	23	24
30	29	28	27	26	25
31	32	33	34	35	36

1882

6	5	4	3	2	1
7	8	9	10	11	12
18	17	16	15	14	13
19	20	21	22	23	24
30	29	28	27	26	25
31	32	33	34	35	36

1887

6	5	4	3	2	1
7	8	9	10	11	12
18	17	16	15	14	13
19	20	21	22	23	24
30	29	28	27	26	25
31	32	33	34	35	36

1892

6	5	4	3	2	1
7	8	9	10	11	12
18	17	16	15	14	13
19	20	21	22	23	24
30	29	28	27	26	25
31	32	33	34	35	36

1897

KEITH COUNTY, NEBRASKA TOWNSHIP 13 N, RANGE 39 W

6	5	4	3	2	1
7	8	9	10	11	12
18	17	16	15	14	13
19	20	21	22	23	24
30	29	28	27	26	25
31	32	33	34	35	36

1872

6	5	4	3	2	1
7	8	9	10	11	12
18	17	16	15	14	13
19	20	21	22	23	24
30	29	28	27	26	25
31	32	33	34	35	36

1877

6	5	4	3	2	1
7	8	9	10	11	12
18	17	16	15	14	13
19	20	21	22	23	24
30	29	28	27	26	25
31	32	33	34	35	36

1882

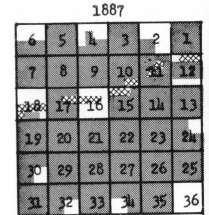

1887

6	5	4	3	2	1
7	8	9	10	11	12
18	17	16	15	14	13
19	20	21	22	23	24
30	29	28	27	26	25
31	32	33	34	35	36

1892

1897

 Tracts eliminated by the South Platte River.

KEITH COUNTY, NEBRASKA   TOWNSHIP 12 N, RANGE 39 W

6	5	4	3	2	1
7	8	9	10	11	12
18	17	16	15	14	13
19	20	21	22	23	24
30	Perkins 29	County 28	27	26	25
31	32	33	34	35	36

1872

6	5	4	3	2	1
7	8	9	10	11	12
18	17	16	15	14	13
19	20	21	22	23	24
30	Perkins 29	County 28	27	26	25
31	32	33	34	35	36

1877

6	5	4	3	2	1
7	8	9	10	11	12
18	17	16	15	14	13
19	20	21	22	23	24
30	Perkins 29	County 28	27	26	25
31	32	33	34	35	36

1882

6	5	4	3	2	1
7	8	9	10	11	12
18	17	16	15	14	13
19	20	21	22	23	24
30	Perkins 29	County 28	27	26	25
31	32	33	34	35	36

1887

6	5	4	3	2	1
7	8	9	10	11	12
18	17	16	15	14	13
19	20	21	22	23	24
30	Perkins 29	County 28	27	26	25
31	32	33	34	35	36

1892

6	5	4	3	2	1
7	8	9	10	11	12
18	17	16	15	14	13
19	20	21	22	23	24
30	Perkins 29	County 28	27	26	25
31	32	33	34	35	36

1897

KEITH COUNTY, NEBRASKA   TOWNSHIP 16 N, RANGE 40 W

6	5*	4	3*	2	1
7	8	9	10	11	12
18	17	16	15	14	13
19	20	21	22	23	24
30	29	28	27	26	25
31	32	33	34	35	36

1872

6	5*	4	3*	2	1
7	8	9	10	11	12
18	17	16	15	14	13
19	20	21	22	23	24
30	29	28	27	26	25
31	32	33	34	35	36

1877

6	5*	4	3*	2	1
7	8	9	10	11	12
18	17	16	15	14	13
19	20	21	22	23	24
30	29	28	27	26	25
31	32	33	34	35	36

1882

6	5*	4	3*	2	1
7	8	9	10	11	12
18	17	16	15	14	13
19	20	21	22	23	24
30	29	28	27	26	25
31	32	33	34	35	36

1887

6	5*	4	3*	2	1
7	8	9	10	11	12
18	17	16	15	14	13
19	20	21	22	23	24
30	29	28	27	26	25
31	32	33	34	35	36

1892

6	5*	4	3*	2	1
7	8	9	10	11	12
18	17	16	15	14	13
19	20	21	22	23	24
30	29	28	27	26	25
31	32	33	34	35	36

1897

* Outside the limits of the land grant.

KEITH COUNTY, NEBRASKA   TOWNSHIP 15 N, RANGE 40 W

1872

1877

1882

1887

1892

1897

Tracts eliminated by the North Platte River.

KEITH COUNTY, NEBRASKA   TOWNSHIP 14 N, RANGE 40 W

6	5	4	3	2	1
7	8	9	10	11	12
18	17	16	15	14	13
19	20	21	22	23	24
30	29	28	27	26	25
31	32	33	34	35	36

1872

6	5	4	3	2	1
7	8	9	10	11	12
18	17	16	15	14	13
19	20	21	22	23	24
30	29	28	27	26	25
31	32	33	34	35	36

1877

6	5	4	3	2	1
7	8	9	10	11	12
18	17	16	15	14	13
19	20	21	22	23	24
30	29	28	27	26	25
31	32	33	34	35	36

1882

6	5	4	3	2	1
7	8	9	10	11	12
18	17	16	15	14	13
19	20	21	22	23	24
30	29	28	27	26	25
31	32	33	34	35	36

1887

6	5	4	3	2	1
7	8	9	10	11	12
18	17	16	15	14	13
19	20	21	22	23	24
30	29	28	27	26	25
31	32	33	34	35	36

1892

6	5	4	3	2	1
7	8	9	10	11	12
18	17	16	15	14	13
19	20	21	22	23	24
30	29	28	27	26	25
31	32	33	34	35	36

1897

KEITH COUNTY, NEBRASKA TOWNSHIP 13 N, RANGE 40 W

6	5	4	3	2	1
7	8	9	10	11	12
18	17	16	15	14	13
19	20	21	22	23	24
30	29	28	27	26	25
31	32	33	34	35	36

1872

6	5	4	3	2	1
7	8	9	10	11	12
18	17	16	15	14	13
19	20	21	22	23	24
30	29	28	27	26	25
31	32	33	34	35	36

1877

6	5	4	3	2	1
7	8	9	10	11	12
18	17	16	15	14	13
19	20	21	22	23	24
30	29	28	27	26	25
31	32	33	34	35	36

1882

6	5	4	3	2	1
7	8	9	10	11	12
18	17	16	15	14	13
19	20	21	22	23	24
30	29	28	27	26	25
31	32	33	34	35	36

1887

6	5	4	3	2	1
7	8	9	10	11	12
18	17	16	15	14	13
19	20	21	22	23	24
30	29	28	27	26	25
31	32	33	34	35	36

1892

6	5	4	3	2	1
7	8	9	10	11	12
18	17	16	15	14	13
19	20	21	22	23	24
30	29	28	27	26	25
31	32	33	34	35	36

1897

Tracts eliminated by the South Platte River.

KEITH COUNTY, NEBRASKA

TOWNSHIP 12 N, RANGE 40 W

6	5	4	3	2	1
7	8	9	10	11	12
18	17	16	15	14	13
19	20	21	22	23	24
30	29	28	27	26	25
31	32	33	34	35	36

Perkins County

1872

6	5	4	3	2	1
7	8	9	10	11	12
18	17	16	15	14	13
19	20	21	22	23	24
30	29	28	27	26	25
31	32	33	34	35	36

Perkins County

1877

6	5	4	3	2	1
7	8	9	10	11	12
18	17	16	15	14	13
19	20	21	22	23	24
30	29	28	27	26	25
31	32	33	34	35	36

Perkins County

1882

6	5	4	3	2	1
7	8	9	10	11	12
18	17	16	15	14	13
19	20	21	22	23	24
30	29	28	27	26	25
31	32	33	34	35	36

Perkins County

1887

6	5	4	3	2	1
7	8	9	10	11	12
18	17	16	15	14	13
19	20	21	22	23	24
30	29	28	27	26	25
31	32	33	34	35	36

Perkins County

1892

6	5	4	3	2	1
7	8	9	10	11	12
18	17	16	15	14	13
19	20	21	22	23	24
30	29	28	27	26	25
31	32	33	34	35	36

Perkins County

1897

KEITH COUNTY, NEBRASKA TOWNSHIP 16 N, RANGE 41 W

1872

6	5	4	3	2	1
7	8	9	10	11	12
18	17	16	15	14	13
19	20	21	22	23	24
30	29	28	27	26	25
31	32	33	34	35	36

1877

6	5	4	3	2	1
7	8	9	10	11	12
18	17	16	15	14	13
19	20	21	22	23	24
30	29	28	27	26	25
31	32	33	34	35	36

1882

6	5	4	3	2	1
7	8	9	10	11	12
18	17	16	15	14	13
19	20	21	22	23	24
30	29	28	27	26	25
31	32	33	34	35	36

1887

6	5	4	3	2	1
7	8	9	10	11	12
18	17	16	15	14	13
19	20	21	22	23	24
30	29	28	27	26	25
31	32	33	34	35	36

1892

6	5	4	3	2	1
7	8	9	10	11	12
18	17	16	15	14	13
19	20	21	22	23	24
30	29	28	27	26	25
31	32	33	34	35	36

1897

6	5	4	3	2	1
7	8	9	10	11	12
18	17	16	15	14	13
19	20	21	22	23	24
30	29	28	27	26	25
31	32	33	34	35	36

Along the left edge of each grid the letters read vertically: G-r-e-e-n-o-o-n-y (Greenwood / County).

* Outside the limits of the land grant.

KEITH COUNTY, NEBRASKA   TOWNSHIP 15 N, RANGE 41 W

1872

1877

1882

1887

1892

1897

Tracts eliminated by the North Platte River.

KEITH COUNTY, NEBRASKA TOWNSHIP 14 N, RANGE 41 W

1872

De 6	5	4	3	2	1
ue 7	8	9	10	11	12
l 18	17	16	15	14	13
Cd 19	20	21	22	23	24
un 30	29	28	27	26	25
ty 31	32	33	34	35	36

1877

De 6	5	4	3	2	1
ue 7	8	9	10	11	12
l 18	17	16	15	14	13
Co 19	20	21	22	23	24
un 30	29	28	27	26	25
ty 31	32	33	34	35	36

1882

De 6	5	4	3	2	1
ue 7	8	9	10	11	12
l 18	17	16	15	14	13
Cd 19	20	21	22	23	24
un 30	29	28	27	26	25
ty 31	32	33	34	35	36

1887

De 6	5	4	3	2	1
ue 7	8	9	10	11	12
l 18	17	16	15	14	13
Cd 19	20	21	22	23	24
un 30	29	28	27	26	25
ty 31	32	33	34	35	36

1892

De 6	5	4	3	2	1
ue 7	8	9	10	11	12
l 18	17	16	15	14	13
Cd 19	20	21	22	23	24
un 30	29	28	27	26	25
ty 31	32	33	34	35	36

1897

D6	5	4	3	2	1
ue 7	8	9	10	11	12
l 18	17	16	15	14	13
Cd 19	20	21	22	23	24
un 30	29	28	27	26	25
ty 31	32	33	34	35	36

KEITH COUNTY, NEBRASKA TOWNSHIP 13 N, RANGE 41 W

1872

1877

1882

1887

1892

1897

Tracts eliminated by the South Platte River.

KEITH COUNTY, NEBRASKA   TOWNSHIP 12 N, RANGE 41 W

6	5	4	3	2	1
7	8	9	10	11	12
18	17	16	15	14	13
19	20	21	22	23	24
30	Perkins 29 28	County 27 26			25
31	32	33	34	35	36

1872

6	5	4	3	2	1
7	8	9	10	11	12
18	17	16	15	14	13
19	20	21	22	23	24
30	Perkins 29 28	County 27 26			25
31	32	33	34	35	36

1877

6	5	4	3	2	1
7	8	9	10	11	12
18	17	16	15	14	13
19	20	21	22	23	24
30	Perkins 29 28	County 27 26			25
31	32	33	34	35	36

1882

6	5	4	3	2	1
7	8	9	10	11	12
18	17	16	15	14	13
19	20	21	22	23	24
30	Perkins 29 28	County 27 26			25
31	32	33	34	35	36

1887

6	5	4	3	2	1
7	8	9	10	11	12
18	17	16	15	14	13
19	20	21	22	23	24
30	Perkins 29 28	County 27 26			25
31	32	33	34	35	36

1892

6	5	4	3	2	1
7	8	9	10	11	12
18	17	16	15	14	13
19	20	21	22	23	24
30	Perkins 29 28	County 27 26			25
31	32	33	34	35	36

1897

Bibliography

MATERIALS consulted in the preparation of this study are voluminous, too voluminous to list and hold the bibliography within reasonable bounds. Of those utilized only two general types are included here: (1) items used directly in the text and cited in the footnotes and (2) items whose applications are not direct enough to require footnote references (or which simply duplicate or buttress materials cited there) but which have contributed substantially, albeit often indirectly, to the work. The long list of materials consulted and found useless for either purpose—the "nix file"—is omitted.

1. AIDS, PUBLISHED COLLECTIONS, AND BIBLIOGRAPHIES

Most of the standard general guides to government documents and general bibliographies are necessary starting points, and those found most useful are listed in category A below. Newspaper and periodical guides are also essential. Both Winifred Gregory, comp., *Union List of Serials in Libraries of the United States and Canada* (2d ed., H. W. Wilson, New York, 1943), and same compiler, *American Newspapers, 1821–1936: A Union List of Files Available in the United States and Canada* (H. W. Wilson, New York, 1937), though the listings of local holders are often outdated by the activities of hyperefficient newspaper officials, janitors, or librarians, are indispensable, and *Poole's Index to Periodical Literature, 1802–81* [with supplements to 1907] (Houghton Mifflin, Boston, 1887–1908), provides, in supplementary volumes 2 through 4, an index to the contemporary periodical literature. *The New York Times Index*, consulted for the pertinent years, besides serving to locate items in that paper's pages, identifies important dates and thereby aids in locating material in other general coverage newspapers.

Kansas local newspapers are preserved to a remarkable degree of completeness in the Kansas State Historical Society and a guide to them is William E. Connelley, ed., *History of Kansas Newspapers* (Kansas State Historical Society and Department of Archives, Topeka, 1916). Nebraska newspapers are less completely preserved and more widely scattered. Some guidance is provided, however, by "Nebraska Newspapers," in *Nebraska History*, 15:67–75 (April-June, 1934). Local newspapers consulted in substantial runs are listed in section 4 of this bibliography.

Many specialized bibliographies are of importance but of especial value is Association of American Railroads, Bureau of Railway Economics, Railroad Land Grants—Transcript of Cards in Library, Bureau of Railway Economics (Mimeographed, Washington, November 1, 1951), which provides a guide to one of the best collections of railroad materials. Also very useful is the excellent bibliography of materials published before 1909 in Frederick A. Cleveland and Fred Wilbur Powell, *Railroad Promotion and Capitalization in the United States* (Longmans, Green, New York, 1909), 295–342. The Jackson and Mohr guides to the Burlington and Illinois Central manuscript collections at the Newberry Library in Chicago immeasurably expedite the use of those materials. United States Interstate Commerce Commission, *Recent Accessions: A Selected List* (Government Printing Office, Washington, 1931 to date), and Everett E. Edwards, *A Bibliography of the History of Agriculture in the United States* (United States Department of Agriculture, Miscellaneous Publication 84, Government Printing Office, Washington, 1934), are the most massive and generally useful compilations on railroads and agriculture respectively. Because much material is drawn from state documents, Adelaide R. Hasse, *Index of Economic Material in Documents of the States of the United States* (13 vols., Carnegie Institution, Washington, 1907–1922) is an important tool. Other bibliographies of and guides to special and local materials are listed in categories B and C below.

Also indispensable for this study, both as guides and bibliographical aids and as repositories of much published material on Kansas and Nebraska history, are the serials and journals of the state historical societies. Even though these publications are overly concerned with "first things," with Indians, and (especially in Kansas) with "territorial days," they are fruitful sources of information and, in the past twenty years or more, the journals have been the medium for publication of much of the scholarly work done on the two states. For example, many of the most valuable of the writings of the outstanding student of grasslands history, James C. Malin, have appeared in the Kansas journal. The Kansas society's series publications include *Transactions* (1876–1908), *Collections* (1910–1928), and the *Kansas Historical Quarterly* (1931 to date). The Nebraska society's monograph series includes *Transactions and Reports* (1885–1893), *Proceedings and Collections* (1894–1902), *Nebraska Constitutional Conventions* (1906–1907), *Collections* (1911–1913), and *Publications* (1917–1936). There are twenty-two volumes. The society's periodical, now called *Nebraska History*, was begun in 1918. Articles or monographs of special significance for this study are individually listed in section 6 of this bibliography.

A. General

Ames, J. G., ed. *Comprehensive Index to the Publications of the United States Government, 1881–1893*. Washington: Government Printing Office, 1905.

Beers, Henry P. *Bibliographies in American History: Guide to Materials for Research*. New York: H. W. Wilson Company, 1942.

Channing, Edward, Albert B. Hart, and Frederick Jackson Turner. *Guide to the Study and Reading of American History*. Revised edition. Boston: Ginn and Company, 1912.

Griffin, Grace Gardner. *Writings on American History*. Variously printed, 1909–1940.

Guide to Records in the National Archives. Washington: Government Printing Office, 1948.

Handlin, Oscar, Arthur Meier Schlesinger, Samuel Eliot Morison, Frederick Merk, Arthur Meier Schlesinger, Jr., and Paul Herman Buck. *Harvard Guide to American History*. Cambridge: The Belknap Press of Harvard University, 1954.

Hartwell, M. A., ed. *Checklist of United States Public Documents, 1789–1909. Congressional to the Close of the Sixtieth Congress; Departmental to End of Calendar Year 1909*. 3d edition. Washington: Government Printing Office, 1911.

Larson, Henrietta M. *Guide to Business History: Materials for the Study of American Business History and Suggestions for Their Use*. Cambridge: Harvard University Press, 1948.

Poore, Benjamin Perley, ed. *Descriptive Catalog of the Government Publications of the United States, 1774–1881*. 49 Congress, 2 session, *Senate Miscellaneous Document 67* (1885).

United States Superintendent of Public Documents. *Tables of and Annotated Index to the Congressional Series of United States Public Documents* (1817–1893). Washington: Government Printing Office, 1902.

B. Lands and Railroads

Association of American Railroads, Bureau of Railway Economics. Bibliography of the Northern Pacific Railway. Mimeographed. Washington, December 7, 1921.

———. List of References to Literature Relating to the Union Pacific System. Mimeographed. Washington, 1922.

———. Railroad Histories and Sources of Historical Information about Railroads. Mimeographed. Washington, April 25, 1940.

Bercaw, Louise O., and A. M. Hannay. *Bibliography on Land Utilization, 1918–1936*. United States Department of Agriculture, Miscellaneous Publication 294. Washington: Government Printing Office, 1938.

——, and Esther M. Colvin. *Bibliography of Land Settlement with Particular Reference to Small Holdings and Subsistence Homesteads*. United States Department of Agriculture, Miscellaneous Publication 172. Washington: Government Printing Office, 1934.

Cordz, Marian. "Bibliography of Railroads in the Pacific Northwest," in the *Washington Historical Quarterly*, 11:91–114 (April, 1921).

Cullen, Elizabeth. "Source Material on Railroad History," in *Special Libraries*, 16:44–48 (February, 1925).

Jackson, Elizabeth Coleman, and Carolyn Curtis, comps. *Guide to the Burlington Archives in the Newberry Library, 1851–1901*. Chicago: Newberry Library, 1949.

Mohr, Carolyn Curtis, comp. *Guide to the Illinois Central Archives in the Newberry Library, 1851–1906*. Chicago: Newberry Library, 1951.

Ripley, William Z. "Railroads: Recent Books and Neglected Problems," in the *Quarterly Journal of Economics*, 40:152–166 (November, 1925).

United States Library of Congress, Division of Bibliography. *List of Works on Railroads in Their Relation to the Government and the Public, with Appendix. . . .* Washington: Government Printing Office, 1907.

Wagner, W. H. "Bibliography of Bibliographies Applicable to Transportation," in the *I. C. C. Practitioners Journal*, 4:308–320 (March, 1937).

C. State and Local

Anderson, Lorene, and Alan W. Farley. "A Bibliography of Town and County Histories of Kansas," in the *Kansas Historical Quarterly*, 21:513–551 (Autumn, 1955).

Berry, Myrtle D., comp. "Local Nebraska History—A Bibliography," in *Nebraska History*, 26:104–115 (April-June, 1945).

"Catalogue of Publications of the Nebraska Historical Society, 1885–1942," in *Nebraska History*, 22:319–391 (December, 1941).

Child, Sargent B., and D. P. Holmes. *Bibliography of Research Projects Reports: Check List of Historical Records Survey Publications*. Works Projects Administration. Technical Series, Research and Records Bibliography 7. Washington: Government Printing Office, 1943.

"Important Works on Nebraska History," in *Nebraska History*, 22:392–402 (December, 1941).

Malin, James C. "Notes on the Writing of General Histories of Kansas. Part Four: The Kansas State Historical Society; Repository of the Material of History," in the *Kansas Historical Quarterly*, 21:407–444 (Summer, 1955).

Nebraska Historical Records Survey Project. *Preliminary Edition of Guide to Depositories of Manuscripts Collections in the United States—Nebraska*. Mimeographed. June, 1940.

Socolofsky, Homer E., ed. *Kansas History in Graduate Study*. Manhattan, Kansas: Kansas State University, 1959.

2. PUBLIC RECORDS AND DOCUMENTS

The most valuable single source for land and railroad-land history, both as policy and as practice, is the public record—federal, state, and local. That record is immense in volume, broad in scope, and often deeply significant; and it has hardly been touched by the practicing historian. For this compilation the mass of public materials consulted is divided into three broad groupings.

A. The United States

A number of the published federal studies of and compilations on lands, railroads, population, and personalities are important. Thomas Donaldson, *The Pub-*

lic Domain: Its History, with Statistics (47 Congress, 2 session, *House Miscellaneous Document 1*, Washington, 1883), is the classic, but often overrated, presentation of the materials collected and published in "Report of the Public Lands Commission of 1880" (46 Congress, 2 session, *House Executive Document 46*, Washington, 1886). Donaldson contributes editorial comment. Two other commission reports, that of the Pacific Railway Commission of 1887 (50 Congress, 1 session, *Senate Executive Document 51*, Washington, 1888) and that of the Public Lands Commission of 1905 (58 Congress, 3 session, *Senate Document 189*, Washington, 1905), are valuable collections of data, and the volumes of testimony on the practices and policies of land-grant railroads collected by the Pacific Railway Commission are indispensable. Volume two of Federal Coordinator of Transportation, *Public Aids to Transportation* (4 vols., Government Printing Office, Washington, 1938–1940) is an attempt to assess the value of those aids to the railroads and presents many valuable tabulations of legislation and of total and average receipts for lands sold. United States Interstate Commerce Commission, *Statistics of Railways in the United States* (Government Printing Office, Washington, 1889 to date) is an annual compilation of mileage, operating expenses, taxes, and other important data. United States General Land Office, *Circulars and Regulations of the General Land Office, with Reference Tables and Index* (Government Printing Office, Washington, 1930), provides a convenient reference to those important documents. The individual circulars are also filed in the National Archives. *Biographical Directory of the American Congress 1774–1949* (Government Printing Office, Washington, 1950) is a basic reference. Finally, the publications of the United States Census Bureau are important. Especially useful for this study is Part I of *Compendium of the Eleventh Census* (Government Printing Office, Washington, 1890), which provides an effectively organized comparison of population structures in the period 1870–1890.

Of the federal reporting and records series, the pertinent volumes and entries in *United States Statutes at Large, United States Supreme Court Reports* (by reporter before 1876), *Federal Cases* (to 1879), and *Federal Reporter* (after 1879) are referred to in the footnotes. So too are the applicable materials on congressional debates, as printed in *Congressional Globe* (to 1873), *Congressional Record*, and the Senate and House journals, identified in footnote citations. Important congressional reports, even though most are also cited in footnotes, because they are so numerous and because they are nowhere reliably indexed, are identified in the list that follows:

40 Congress, 3 session, *House Executive Document 15* (1868). "Report of Commission Investigating the Condition of the Union Pacific Railroad."

40 Congress, 3 session, *House Executive Document 25* (1869). "Report of Commissioners Investigating the Condition of the Union Pacific, Eastern Division, and the Sioux City and Pacific."

40 Congress, 3 session, *Senate Executive Document 54* (1869). "Report of Special Commission Investigating the Condition of the Central Pacific Railroad."

41 Congress, 2 session, *Senate Executive Document 20* (1870). "Report on the Final Completion of the Pacific Railroad."

42 Congress, 2 session, *House Miscellaneous Document 228* (1872). "Northern Pacific Railroad—Present Condition."

42 Congress, 3 session, *House Report 78* (1873). "Affairs of the Union Pacific Railroad Company."

42 Congress, 3 session, *House Report 77* (1873). "Credit Mobilier Investigation."

43 Congress, 1 session, *House Report 474* (1874). "Taxation of Railroad Lands, to Accompany HR 3026."

44 Congress, 1 session, *House Miscellaneous Document 107* (1876). "State Senate of California—Resolution, Passed February 7, 1876." A resolution against the Dillingham decision, which gave lands already settled upon to the railroad grantee.

44 Congress, 1 session, *Senate Executive Document 20* (1876). "Taxation of Lands Granted to States and Corporations."

45 Congress, 2 session, *House Report 709* (1878). "Taxation of Railroad Lands, to Accompany HR 747."

47 Congress, 1 session, *House Report 1312* (1882). "Survey of Pacific Railroad Lands, to Acompany HR 6397." A taxation report and bill.

47 Congress, 2 session, *Senate Report 990* (1883). "Donating Lands to Railroad Companies, to Accompany S 1306." A taxation report and bill.

48 Congress, 1 session, *House Report 478* (1884). "Telegraph Line from Missouri River to the Pacific Ocean, to Accompany HR 5442." A taxation report and bill.

48 Congress, 1 session, *Senate Report 88* (1884). "Lands Subject to Taxation, to Accompany S 60."

49 Congress, 1 session, *House Report 607* (1886). "Telegraph Line from Missouri River to the Pacific Ocean, to Accompany HR 574." A taxation report and bill.

49 Congress, 1 session, *House Report 1002* (1886). "Northern Pacific Railroad Company, to Accompany HR 6667." To apply the tax law to the Northern Pacific.

49 Congress, 1 session, *Senate Executive Document 126* (1886). "Northern Pacific Railroad Company." The correspondence of the Interior Department and the Northern Pacific in the controversy over patenting.

49 Congress, 1 session, *Senate Executive Document 135* (1886). "Survey of Lands of Land-Grant Railroads in Nebraska."

49 Congress, 1 session, *Senate Report 199* (1886). "Taxation of Railroad Lands, to Accompany S 1812."

51 Congress, 1 session, *House Executive Document 453* (1890). "Land Patents to the Union Pacific Railway Company."

51 Congress, 1 session, *House Miscellaneous Document 252* (1890). "Resolutions in Reference to the Lands of the Union Pacific Railroad."

51 Congress, 1 session, *Senate Executive Document 169* (1890). "Withholding Patents for Public Lands."

53 Congress, 3 session, *House Executive Document 315* (1895). "Land Patented to the Land Grant Railroad Companies since May 26, 1894."

53 Congress, 3 session, *Senate Executive Document 93* (1895). "Lands owned by the Union and Central Pacific Railroads."

The annual reports of the secretaries of the interior and the commissioners of the General Land Office are important sources of general data on land surveys, patents, clerk shortages, and administrative policy and have been carefully gleaned, but the manuscript records of those offices are, of course, much more valuable. In fact, they shed more light on land-grant policy and administration than any other source. They are especially valuable for the study of the roles of administrative officers in the making of land policy. These materials are deposited in the National Archives in two groups: Record Group 48 (Records of the Office of the Secretary of the Interior) and Record Group 49 (Records of the General Land Office). In Record Group 48 the subdivisions of documents important to this study include Pacific Railroads, Letters Sent; Lands and Railroads, Letters Sent; Lands and Railroads, Letters Received; and Selection Docket, a ledger supposedly listing all railroad-land selections made up to December 31, 1897. In Record Group 49 the important subdivisions are Railroad Land Grant Records, boxes of letters received, dockets filed, and drafts of tabulations and similar items prepared in the Land Office; the general letters sent and letters received files; and Division F, Letters Sent. Besides the letters and ledgers of the government officers these collections yield large quantities of correspondence, legal briefs, and printed pamphlets and reports by railroadmen, political figures, legal firms, and private parties.

B. Kansas and Nebraska

Several special studies and reports of Kansas and Nebraska state commissions and agencies are very useful. Nebraska State Planning Board, *Water Resources of Nebraska: Preliminary Report* (Lincoln, December, 1936), is an invaluable compilation of material not only on water but also on geologic history, types of soil, and areas of potential land use. Kansas Water Resources Fact-Finding and Research Committee, *Water in Kansas, 1955. A Report to the Kansas State Legislature* (Topeka, 1954), is confined to information on water. *Assessment and Collection of Property Taxes in Nebraska* (Nebraska Legislative Council, Research Department, Report No. 16, August, 1941) discusses the abuses and weaknesses in the system, seemingly little changed from those of the 1880's, and provides valuable material on the continuing problems of the tax assessor and tax collector.

Among the reports of contemporary agencies Nebraska State Board of Transportation [Board of Railway Commissioners in 1885 and 1886], *Annual Report* (Journal Company, Lincoln, 1885–1896), presents data on rates but is of more importance because it also records complaints received. The most valuable of these agency reports are those of the Kansas State Board of Agriculture, made annually 1872–1876 and biennially thereafter. There are also special reports, issued during booms, especially that of the eighties, and designed to attract settlers. Because this agency was designed to advertise the state, the reports sometimes wax a bit eloquent. Nonetheless, they have many uses and their data can often be cross-checked with other reports or with United States Census reports. They do provide listings of lands for sale in the various counties of the state, the only comprehensive source of such information.

Most twentieth century research and study agencies of both states report through various state university or college monograph series and those directly applicable to the subjects of this volume are listed in their proper place, part 6 of this bibliography. One group of these publications requires additional mention —the studies of ground water and soil types, often conducted in cooperation with the United States Department of Agriculture Soil Conservation Service, and producing invaluable maps and short monographs. As a group this material provides the knowledge of physical characteristics and potentials basic to selecting the counties to be studied. Without it there would be slight possibility of reducing the physical variant in the selection to manageable proportions.

The regular and special messages of the governors and the annual or biennial reports of the lesser executive officers are the most useful of published state materials. Governors' messages were published as pamphlets and variously printed, but compilations exist in both states. The Kansas State Historical Society has those for the period 1857–1895 bound into four volumes and cited collectively as *Messages of the Governors of Kansas*. The Nebraska society also has many of the individual pamphlets—nearly all for the period covered by the study—but the messages have also been compiled in *Messages and Proclamations of the Governors of Nebraska, 1854–1941* (4 vols., Works Projects Administration Project 165-1-81-317, Lincoln, 1941). These messages are sometimes valuable for data on tax levels and state lands not published elsewhere, but their chief importance is in their inclusion of comments by the governors on needed revisions of the land laws, on the controversy over railroad land patents, and on tax assessments and tax levies.

Reports of lesser executive officers provide much of the data tabulated in the comparisons of counties made in chapters 8 and 9. They reveal the attitudes and problems of state officials dealing with local officers. They also provide information on the disposition of state lands, tax delinquency, and like matters. Of all such reports those of the auditor of public accounts (who was also the register of the State Land Office in Kansas) in both states and of Nebraska's commissioner of public lands and buildings are the most valuable. The auditor compiled and published a census of population, valuations before equalization, tax structure, acres cultivated, crop yields, railroad mileage, and other such data by year and by county. The receipt and disposition of state lands is also chronicled in these reports. Other important reports include those of the secretary of state, for supplemental data on population, data on equalization, names of county officers, results of elections, and registries of bonded indebtedness; the superintendent of public instruction, for numbers of school-age children and for reports and complaints from county superintendents; and the state treasurer, for supplementary data on county finances and tax delinquency and for state financial reports.

State legislative and judicial series are also valuable sources. The session laws and legislative journals are chiefly useful in this volume for the study of the evolution of the tax systems, but they also show the process of enactment and the texts of memorials to Congress on further aid to railroads, on special land problems, and on the tax issue. The supreme court reports are chronicles of the development through interpretation of state tax law, record railroad-county tax litigation if appeal was made, and report the first steps in the railroad-tax cases that eventually reached the United States Supreme Court. Specific laws and cases utilized here are referred to in the footnotes.

The county records, especially the land title records, of six counties are the major source for the analysis of the tax base included in chapters 8 and 9. Important guides to these materials, especially useful in the process of narrowing the selection to the six counties finally chosen, are the manuscript records of the Works Projects Administration's Historical Records Survey, filed in the state historical societies. Though incomplete, these files give some indication of the quantity, quality, and nature of local holdings, and their study is a necessary preliminary step to any selection of counties for intensive study, for whatever purpose. A few of these surveys were finished, three for counties studied here. See the Inventory of the County Archives of Kansas, No. 89. Shawnee County (Mimeographed, Topeka, 1940) ; the Inventory of the County Archives of Nebraska— Merrick County (Mimeographed, Lincoln, 1942) ; and the Inventory of the County Archives of Nebraska—Howard County (Mimeographed, Lincoln, 1941).

Of the county records themselves, the basic source in five of the six counties is the numerical index, a calendar by date of instrument, date of registry, type of instrument, property description, and the parties to the transaction of every real estate patent, sale, or mortgage in the county. In Russell County, Kansas, because the numerical index does not include the date of the transaction, another and less reliable source—Lands Entered in Russell County, a ledger of entries reported to the county clerk by the local land office—is used instead. The date of alienation, as recorded within the ken of local public officials, for every acre of land in each of these counties comes from these sources and this information is the basis of the 137 diagrams presented in the appendix—the authority for most of the conclusions about comparative taxability. Additional title and deed records provide more detailed information on specific transactions, such as the Warren and Keeney promotion in Trego County, Kansas. Other valuable local records utilized include the files of county court cases, for tax cases brought in the county; the assessment rolls, useful as checks on the accuracy of the title records, as indicators of taxability, and as indicators of rates of assessment and tax levels and the share borne by non-real property—but usually too incomplete to provide adequate information on taxability by themselves; and county commissioner's or supervisor's proceedings, which include hearings on equalization and give important clues to the objectives of and are the records of the activities of county governments. The findings reported in this volume are principally based on the numerical indices and related data, drawing only incidentally on other local records.

C. Miscellaneous Additional Public Documents

Some governmental sources for other states than Kansas and Nebraska are occasionally drawn upon here, chiefly in the general survey of state tax exemption and litigation included in chapter 2. Besides the state session laws and supreme court reports cited there, two special items, both produced by Oregon, are valuable to the general study of state taxation and tax exemption. *Report of the Board of Commissioners to Examine the Matter of Assessment and Taxation in the State of Oregon, Together with a Bill Submitted by Said Commission* (W. H. Byais, Salem, 1886), a compilation of data on valuations and assessments, much of it by county, shows the nature, character, and what seemingly was the near universality of the problems of tax administration described in this volume. No modern historical study of these difficulties has been published, though the earlier works of Hsien-Ju Haung, J. H. Hollander and others (including Elbert J. Benton's study of Kansas), and James E. Boyle, listed in section 6 of this bibliography, pioneered in the contemporary study of them. *Tabular Statement, Compiled by the State Tax Commission of Oregon, Showing the Effect of the Reversion of the Grant Lands of the Oregon and California Railroad Company Upon the Apportionment of State Taxes to the Several Counties* (State Printing Department, Salem, 1927) provides an example of the effects on the local tax base and the resources of local government of the halving of the amount of taxable land in several counties.

3. RAILROAD RECORDS, PERSONAL PAPERS, AND SPECIAL COLLECTIONS

A. Railroad Records

Files of the annual reports of railroad companies are a major source of data for taxes paid and lands sold and for statements of general tax, land, and sales policy—for some railroads they are the principal source and for others second only to the results of governmental investigations, the federal coordinator's study, and, after 1888, statistics published by the Interstate Commerce Commission. Most of the important annual reports are preserved in the Bureau of Railway Economics Library in Washington but the collections of the Cornell University Library contain important supplements. The reports of the Burlington in Nebraska are available in manuscript at the Newberry Library in Chicago. The reports utilized include: Atchison, Topeka and Santa Fe (1873–1893); Atlantic and Pacific (1874, 1882)—later reports of the Santa Fe include material on the lands of the Atlantic and Pacific and on the Frisco; Burlington and Missouri River, in Iowa (1858, 1860–1866), in Nebraska (1872–1896); Central Pacific (1872–1886)—included in the Southern Pacific System after 1888; Chicago, Burlington and Quincy (1855–1893); Kansas Pacific (1868–1880)—include the Denver Pacific and both are in the reports of the Union Pacific after 1880; Leavenworth, Lawrence and Galveston (1871, 1872); Missouri, Kansas and Texas (1874, 1876–1879); Missouri Pacific (1882–1892)—include reports on the Katy and the Texas Pacific while they were leased to it; Northern Pacific (1876–1893); Southern Pacific of California (1876–1884); Southern Pacific System (1888–1895); Texas and Pacific (1872–1894); and Union Pacific (1870–1890).

Two types of materials were made available at the Omaha office of the Union Pacific. One, a compilation of general company history, is all but useless, but the other, miscellaneous records of the Properties Division, is of tremendous value. This group of records includes eighteen volumes of tax vouchers, covering all or part (depending on the year) of taxes paid from 1877 through the middle of 1892 and numerous scattered earlier tax payments; one voucher index; one ledger of county taxes, 1878–1888; and two volumes of tax vouchers interleaved with correspondence of the tax department, 1877–1882. The vouchers show levels of taxes, total railroad taxes, delinquencies, and methods of payment in every county where the road held property. After 1880 they also include some Kansas Pacific taxes and after 1888, seemingly all of them. These inclusions are of special importance because no other collection of Kansas Pacific records was located. The correspondence of the tax department is an invaluable source of information on policies of payment, methods of supervising payment, and efforts to obtain reductions or abatements of taxes. Materials used in this volume are cited in chapter 10.

The collection of company records deposited at the Newberry Library is also of extreme value. These records consist of extensive files on two companies, the Illinois Central Railroad and the Burlington System. A guide has been published for each of these record groups (see the entries under Mohr and Jackson in category B of section 1). These guides provide detailed summaries of the documents and are indispensable aids. Of these materials, because its tax problems were of a different order than those of the areas subjected to close study in this volume, but incidental use is made of Illinois Central materials. A great deal is drawn from the Burlington collections. The record of land taxes on the Burlington's original grant as well as the chronicle of the development of tax policy and the levels paid in each county is conveniently organized in decimal classification 768. These materials include forty-six volumes of lists of taxes by county, 1872–1901; thirty-five volumes of tax receipts, 1872–1916; four volumes of land tax statements, 1874–1882; ledger volumes of county warrants, tax certificates, tax sales, errors and corrections, and delinquents; and several bundles of legal papers on land tax litigation. Other legal records include statements of cases prosecuted and of their results. Records of land sales (classification 764) chronicle the disposal of the grant and town lot properties of the company. Included in the executive files (classification 63) are miscellaneous summaries of taxes and sales, some of great value; extensive files on the Hunnewell tax case; and correspondence with other railroadmen about taxes. The manuscript annual reports are also of great value. Of Chicago, Burlington and Quincy System materials two groups are generally useful, though neither shows concern with exemption questions. These are three boxes of legal opinions, 1874–1903 (classification 33 1890 4.6) and thirty-eight volumes of president's memoranda, 1872–1918, with an index (classification 32.7).

These railroad collections are surprisingly barren of direct comment by railroad officials on the larger questions of the propriety and justice of tax exemption for railroad land. Those files of such commentary included in Department of the Interior and General Land Office records, described above and cited extensively in the footnotes of chapters 4 and 5, remain the principal source of such information.

B. Personal Papers and Special Collections

Non-railroad private papers have contributed but slightly to the findings reported here. No collection bearing directly on questions of tax exemption was found. Of the papers consulted four used at the Collection of Regional History and Cornell University Archives in Ithaca, New York—Cornell University, Western Land Papers, 1873–1913; the Davenport Collection; the Carter Kingsley Papers; and the Reuben Robie Papers—shed some light on tax levels on the frontier and methods of tax payment, but the last-named three of these collections are concerned mostly with the loaning of money by Bath, New York, investors in western mortgages. The Davenport and Kingsley collections, along with the Jabez B. Watkins Papers at the University of Kansas Library in Lawrence (also consulted) provide the chief sources for Allan G. Bogue's excellent *Money at Interest: The Farm Mortgage on the Middle Border* (Cornell University Press, Ithaca, 1955), and Professor Bogue has already reported all important references to tax problems. Another collection at the University of Kansas—the Charles H. Van Wyck Papers, seven boxes of miscellaneous papers of one of the prime movers in the drive to remove the exemption feature in the 1880's— does yield some information on this reformer's land speculations and include a number of letters from land reformers and favor-seekers. There is no direct reference to tax matters. Two of the manuscript collections of the Kansas State Historical Society—the George Martin Papers and the Anderson Family Papers—shed considerable light on the politics of reform and of the chief tax reformer. Five of the collections consulted at the Nebraska State Historical Society in Lincoln—the papers of Samuel Chapman, Robert W. Furnas, T. J. Majors, Samuel Maxwell, and J. Sterling Morton—are valuable for local and state politics but not directly concerned with tax reform or tax problems. There are some references in the Morton Papers for August of 1872 bearing on the questions raised by the Prescott and McShane decisions.

Three special collections are important as introductions to the land, railroad, political, and governmental history of Kansas and Nebraska. They supply some excellent directly valuable material and also function as suppliers of leads. The most extensive of these is the clippings file of the Kansas State Historical Society. This file covers a broad list of categories and locales. Those found useful here include five volumes of Atchison, Topeka and Santa Fe newspaper clippings; the Huling Collection on strikes on Gould lines in Missouri and the Southwest which, despite its title, includes several items on the move to tax Kansas Pacific lands; one partial volume on the Kansas Pacific; one volume each on local government of cities and counties; one volume on public lands; one on Russell County; three and a partial fourth on Saline County; three and a partial fourth on taxation; one volume on Trego County; and one and a partial second on the Union Pacific. A second valuable collection also at the Kansas Historical Society is a four-volume collection of Kansas Pacific Railroad pamphlets and a single volume of Santa Fe descriptive pamphlets on Kansas. The third of these special collections is the fourteen-volume file of Burlington scrapbooks and a one-volume scrapbook (not otherwise identified) on the activities of the Burlington and counties traversed by the Burlington held by the Nebraska State Historical Society.

4. LOCAL NEWSPAPERS

In addition to the runs of local newspapers used extensively and listed below a number of individual issues and short files yield some information. These items are too scattered and too numerous to list here. Where they contribute directly to this volume they are cited in the footnotes. Scattered items in general coverage newspapers—notably the *St. Louis Post-Dispatch* and the *Washington Post*—are of some value. The general coverage paper read most extensively for the period is the file of the *New York Evening Post* in the Cornell University Library.

The Kansas newspapers are in the Kansas State Historical Society's Collections, though a file of the *Atchison Champion* was also read in the Cornell University Library.

Nebraska newspapers utilized, unless otherwise identified, are found in the Nebraska State Historical Society's collections. Because Nebraska newspaper collections is the fourteen-volume file of Burlington scrapbooks and a one-volume it is necessary to use more, more scattered, and necessarily shorter runs of papers to obtain coverage.

A. Kansas

Abilene Chronicle, 1888–1890. Successor to the paper next listed.
Abilene, *Dickinson County Chronicle*, 1875–1888.
Atchison Champion, 1870–1890.
Bunker Hill News, 1887–1888.
Dodge City Times, 1883–1890.
Dorrance Nuggett, 1886–1889.
Enterprise, *Anti-Monopolist*, 1883–1887. Published in Topeka until April 16, 1884.
Hayes City, *Ellis County Star*, 1876–1882.
Junction City Tribune, 1878–1890.
Junction City Union, 1869–1890.
Leavenworth, *Democratic Standard*, 1881–1886.
Leavenworth, *Kansas Commoner*, 1884–1885.

Leavenworth Times, 1870–1882.
Lyons, *Central Kansas Democrat*, 1879–1881, 1884–1887, 1890.
Lyons Democrat, 1889–1890.
Manhattan Nationalist, 1870–1890.
Mankato, *Jewell County Monitor*, 1876–1890.
Russell Independent, 1879–1881.
Russell Review, 1886–1888.
Russell, *Russell County Record*, 1874–1890, January 29, 1914.
Russell, *Saturday Record*, 1888. Successor to the *Review*.
Salina, *Farmer's Advocate*, 1876–1879.
Salina, *Saline County Journal*, 1880–1888.
Scott, *Western Times*, 1886–1891.
Topeka Commonwealth, 1874–1888.
WaKeeney World, 1879–1885. Predecessor of the paper next listed.
Wakeeney, *Western Kansas World*, 1885–1890.

B. Nebraska

Arapahoe Pioneer, 1879–1882.
Aurora, *Hamilton County News*, 1877–1880.
Beatrice Express, 1871–1875.
Beemer Times, 1886–1890.
Brownville, *Nemaha County Granger*, 1876–1886, 1887–1890.
Central City, *Merrick County Item*, 1880–1881.
Fremont Herald, 1878–1885.
Grand Island, *Anti-monopolist*, 1883.
Grand Island Independent, 1884–1887. Successor to the paper next listed.
Grand Island, *Platte Valley Independent*, 1876–1880.
Grand Island Times, 1873–1882, 1887.
Harvard Courier, 1885.
Hastings Gazette Journal, weekly 1880–1883, daily 1884, weekly late 1884, 1885 missing, weekly 1886–1888. The file consulted is located at the office of the *Hastings Tribune*.
Hastings Journal, 1878–1880. One of the predecessors of the *Gazette Journal*. The file consulted is located at the office of the *Hastings Tribune*.
Hastings Nebraskan, 1883–1884. The file consulted is located at the Hastings Museum.
Juniata, *Adams County Gazette*, 1872–1880. One of the predecessors of the *Hastings Gazette Journal*.
Juniata Herald, 1876–1890. The file at the Hastings Museum was also consulted.
Lincoln, *Farmers Alliance*, 1889–1891.
Lincoln, *Nebraska State Journal*, 1874–1888. The file consulted is located at the office of the *State Journal*.
Lowell Register, 1876–1877. The file consulted is located at the Jensen Memorial Library, Minden.
Minden, *Kearney County Bee*, 1878–1882. The file consulted is located at the Jensen Memorial Library.
Minden, *Kearney County Democrat*, 1886–1890. The file consulted is located at the Jensen Memorial Library.
Minden, *Kearney County Gazette*, 1882–1889. Successor to the *Bee*. The file consulted is located at the Jensen Memorial Library.
Nebraska City News, 1882–1885, 1888–1890.
Newark Herald, 1881–1882. The file consulted is located at the Jensen Memorial Library.
Norfolk Journal, 1883–1886.
Norfolk Times, 1880–1881.
North Platte, *Lincoln County Tribune*, 1885–1889.
Oakdale Pen and Plow, 1877–1887. There are numerous short gaps.

Ogallala, *Keith County News*, 1885–1889.
Omaha Bee, 1869–1892. Daily or weekly after 1878. Footnote citations differentiate the weekly after 1878. The file at the Omaha Public Library was also consulted.
Omaha Weekly Herald, 1873–1882.
Omaha Weekly Republican, 1873–1883.
Pierce, *Pierce County Call*, 1884–1889.
Plattsmouth, *Nebraska Herald*, 1870–1872, 1873–1882. The file at the Omaha Public Library was also consulted.
West Point Republican, 1871–1892. There are numerous short gaps.

5. PAMPHLETS AND BROADSIDES

Two groups of pamphlet materials are useful. One group, listed in category A below, is that produced on the local level with reference to local history, local attractions, or local problems or produced by state and local organizations only indirectly concerned with the taxation of the granted lands. These materials are valuable sources—sometimes they are the only ones—for local history, local political controversy, and local efforts to attract settlers. The second group of materials, listed in category B, is composed of materials either produced by or written about railroads. The greater number of those listed are concerned either with efforts on the part of railroad land departments to sell lands or with the arguments of railroad attorneys and railroad officials against the taxation of their lands, their operating property, or both. Another large number are political attacks on the roads or miscellaneous publications having to do with such peripheral matters as the proper standards of construction to be applied to the transcontinentals. All those listed in one way or another shed light on the taxation of the railroad lands.

A. General

Ames, John H. *The Taxation of Personal Property.* Des Moines, Iowa: Mills and Company, 1877.
Arizona Tax Conference. *Report of the Proceedings of the Arizona Tax Conference. Sixth Annual Session. El Tovar Hotel, Grand Canyon, Arizona. July Twenty-Second to July Twenty-Sixth, 1918.* No imprint.
Bodine, L. T. *Kansas Illustrated: An Accurate and Reliable Description of This Marvelous State.* Kansas City, Missouri: Ramsey, Millet and Hudson, 1879.
Bronson, Henry. *Farmers Unions and Tax Reform.* Jackson, Tennessee: Advocate Publishing Company, 1873.
The Centennial Sketch of Clay County, Nebraska: Compiled by the Historical Committee and Read by Dr. M. Clark, Chairman, at the Centennial Celebration of American Independence at Smith, the County Seat, July Fourth, 1876. Sutton, Nebraska: E. H. White, 1876. Reprinted, Clay Center: *Clay County Sun*, 1933.
A Descriptive Review of Adams County, Neb., Showing the Resources, Climate, Water, Timber, Grasses, Grains, Towns, and People: A General Letter of Information for Parties Seeking Homes in the West. Omaha: Pagett and Stinchcomb, Immigration Agents, 1879.
Directory of Dickinson County, Kansas. Salina: Kansas Directory Company, 1887.
Directory of Saline County, Kansas. Salina: J. M. Davis and Warren Knaus, 1885.
Giles, F. W. *Review of the Tax System of the State of Kansas.* Topeka: Commonwealth Printing House, 1872.
Handbook of Ford County, Kansas. Published for the Ford County Immigration Society. Chicago: C. S. Burch Publishing Company, 1887.
Handbook of Pottawatomie and Riley Counties, Kansas. N.p.: published by the Modern Argo, [1883].
Hastings, Nebraska. Hastings: Democratic Press, 1921. Two others, one undated and another dated 1952, were published by this company.

Jelinek, George. *Ellsworth, Kansas, 1867–1947.* Salina: Consolidated, 1947.

The Leading Cities of Southeastern Nebraska: A Review of the Mercantile, Banking, Real Estate, Manufacturing, Railroad and Other Material Interests of the Garden of the West, Together with Its Resources and Prospects, and Advantages for the Investment of Capital, and Inducements Offered to Settlers. Chicago: H. S. Reed and Company, 1883.

The Leading Industries of the West. Lincoln: H. S. Reed and Company, 1886.

Loomis, N. H., comp. *Directory of Saline County, Kansas.* Lawrence: J. S. Boughton, 1882.

McKeith, G. R., comp. *Pioneer Stories of the Pioneers of Fillmore and Adjoining Counties.* Exeter, Nebraska: *Fillmore County News,* 1915.

Nance, Albinus. *Centennial History of Polk County.* Osceola, Nebraska: *Osceola Record,* 1876.

Olney, C. C., and Company. *Handbook of Ottawa County, Kansas.* [Minneapolis, Kansas: *Solomon Valley Mirror,* n.d.].

Pioneer Story of Harvard. Reprinted from a pamphlet published in Harvard in 1894. Clay Center: *Clay County Sun,* 1933.

Resources of Russell County, Kansas! Cheap Farms! Healthy Climate! Mild Winters! Best Soil in the World! (Broadside). Russell: Russell County Immigration Association [1889].

Smith, Henry G., comp. *The Book of Hastings: A Sketch of the Town, with Illustrations.* Hastings: *The Tribune,* 1906.

Sterling, Kansas: The Actual Advantages and Resources of a Grand Young Town Candidly Discussed. Published by the Sterling Land and Investment Company. No imprint [1887].

Tawney, Mrs. Norah Yette, and Mrs. Hattie Ridgeway Clark. *In Remembrance: Early Pioneer Settlers of Ogallah and Community, 1877–1881.* No imprint.

Tibbles, T. H. *Nebraska Redeemed.* Lincoln: Independent Publishing Company, 1897.

Warren, Keeney and Company. *Trego County, Kansas: Its Soil and Climate.* . . . Chicago: J. J. Spalding and Company, 1878.

Winsor, M., and James A. Scarbrough. *History of Jewell County, Kansas, with a Full Account of Its Early Settlements and the Indian Atrocities Committed within Its Borders.* . . . Jewell City: Diamond Printing Office, 1878.

B. Railroads

Adams, Charles Francis, Jr. *The Case of the Union Pacific Railway Company: Statement Made by Charles Francis Adams, before the Committee on Pacific Railroads, March 17, 1890.* Boston: Rand Avery Supply Company, 1890.

———, W. B. Williams, and J. H. Oberly. *Taxation of Railroads and Railroad Securities.* New York: The Railway Gazette, 1880.

Atchison, Topeka and Santa Fe Railroad. *Memorial of the Atchison, Topeka and Santa Fe Railway Company to the Legislature of the State of Kansas.* No imprint [1897?]. An appeal for the reduction of taxes.

———. *Report of Ross Burns, Attorney.* Topeka: George W. Martin, 1877. A second report, dated 1880, was produced by the same printer.

Atkinson, Edwin. *The Railroad and the Farmer.* No imprint [1881].

Atlantic & Pacific R. R. Co. and Atchison, Topeka & Santa Fe R. R. Co.: Contracts, Deeds, Votes, and Other Documents as between the Two Companies, Together with the Charter of the Atlantic & Pacific R. R. Co. and Legislation Subsequent Thereto. Boston: Alfred Mudge and Son, 1887.

Baldwin, W. W. *Railroad Land Grants: A Statement of Their History, Their Value, and Their Cost.* No imprint [1927].

Beard, Henry. *Before the Honorable Secretary of the Interior: The Listing and Patenting of Lands Granted to the Central Pacific Railroad Co.: The "Mineral Lands" Excepted from the Grant.* Washington: Judd and Detweiler, 1890.

――――. *Motion Relating to Patenting Lands Granted to the Central Pacific Railroad Company.* Washington: Judd and Detweiler, 1890.

――――. *Printed Letter to J. A. Williamson, Commissioner of the General Land Office.* No imprint [April 30, 1880].

――――. *Protest of the Central Pacific Railroad Company against Interruptions in the Administration of Its Land Grant by Executive Action or Decisions Tending to Disturb the Limits of Its Grant as Heretofore Adjusted.* Washington: Judd and Detweiler, 1886.

Blair, Henry W., and J. T. Morgan. *Atlantic and Pacific Railroad Land Grant: Remarks in the Senate, June 28 and July 3, 1884.* No imprint.

Blair, John S. *Before the Secretary of the Interior in the Matter of the Application of the Union Pacific Railway Company for Patents for Lands Along the Line of the Kansas Pacific Railway and the Proposed Readjustment of the Grant.* Washington: Gibson Brothers, 1886.

Bledsoe, S. T. *Kansas and the Santa Fe: An Address Before the Santa Fe Dinner Club, Topeka, April 18, 1927.* No imprint.

Burlington and Missouri River Railroad Company in Nebraska. Sectional Map of Land Sold to February 1, 1873 (Broadside). No imprint.

Central Pacific Railroad Company. *Railroad Lands in California and Nevada.* Sacramento: Record Printing House, 1872.

――――. *Relations Between the Central Pacific Railroad Company and the United States Government: Summary of Facts.* San Francisco: H. S. Crocker and Company, 1889.

Circular to the Stock and Bond Holders of the Leavenworth, Lawrence and Galveston Railroad Company. Boston: Thomas W. Ripley, 1873.

Clarke, Sidney. *The Kansas Pacific Railroad: Speech in the House, January 22, 1869.* No imprint.

――――. *The Taxation of Railroads in Kansas: Speech of the Hon. Sidney Clarke, Delivered before the Anti-Monopoly Clubs of Lawrence, December 12, 1873. A Startling Array of Facts and Figures.* Published by the Anti-Monopoly Clubs and Tax Reform Association of Lawrence, Kansas. Lawrence: The Standard Book and Job Office, 1873.

Copley, Josiah. *Kansas and the Country Beyond on the Line of the Union Pacific Railway, Eastern Division, from the Missouri to the Pacific Ocean.* . . . Philadelphia: J. B. Lippincott and Company, 1867.

Corliss, Carlton J. *Land Grants to Railroads.* Chicago: Office of the Assistant to the Vice President, Illinois Central System, June 29, 1926.

Crawford, Samuel J. *Before the Committee on Public Lands, House of Representatives—48th Congress. Adjustment of Land Grants to Aid in the Construction of Railroads in Kansas. Brief and Argument for the State.* Topeka: Kansas Publishing House, 1884.

――――. *Before the Committee on Public Lands, House of Representatives. Argument in Support of H. R. No. 3076, Relative to Public Lands Wrongfully Certified to Railroads in Kansas.* Washington: W. H. Moore, 1886.

――――. *Before the Hon. L. Q. C. Lamar, Secretary of the Interior. In the Matter of Adjustment of the Kansas Pacific Land Grant. Supplemental Argument.* Washington: W. H. Moore, 1885.

――――. *Before the Hon. W. A. J. Sparks, Commissioner of the General Land Office: Adjustment of the Atchison, Topeka and Santa Fe Land Grant in the State of Kansas. Brief and Argument for the State.* Washington: W. H. Moore, 1885.

――――. *Before the Judiciary Committee, House of Representatives. Argument in Opposition to H. R. 3392 Relative to Public Lands Unlawfully Certified to Railroad Companies within the State of Kansas.* No imprint, 1886.

Dennis, Edgar W. *Tabulated Statement Relating to Taxation of Railroads, 1873.* Topeka: Kansas State Record Office, 1873.

Elliott, R. S., Kansas Pacific Industrial Agent. *Report on the Industrial Resources of Western Kansas and Eastern Colorado.* St. Louis: Levison and Blyth, 1871.

Evarts, William M. *Opinion of Hon. Wm. M. Evarts, Atty. General, Upon the Duties of the Executive Relative to the Pacific Railroad, the Acceptance of the Same, and the Issue of United States Subsidies Thereon.* No imprint, September 5, 1868.

Gage, Norris L. *The Relations of Kansas Railroads to the State of Kansas.* Topeka: Kansas Publishing House, 1884.

Garber, W. S., Secretary of the Nebraska State Board of Transportation. *Land Grants and Bond Subsidies and Their Bearing on Maximum Rates for Railroad Transportation.* No imprint.

Gray, George. *Northern Pacific Railroad Company: Summary of Arguments Made Before the Respective Committees on Public Lands, Senate and House of Representatives, on the Legal Question of Forfeiture, Feb. 6, 1884.* No imprint.

————. *Before the Secretary of the Interior—Application of the Commissioner of the General Land Office for Instructions Relative to the Indemnity Lands of the Atchison, Topeka & Santa Fe R. R. Co.* Washington: Gibson Brothers Printers, 1883.

————, and J. Lewis Stackpole. *In the Matter of the Northern Pacific Railroad Land Grant.* Boston: Alfred Mudge and Son, 1886.

Handbook & Guide to 1,200,000 Acres of Iowa Land in the Middle Region of Western Iowa and 35,000 Acres in Eastern Nebraska. For Sale by the Iowa Railroad Land Company, in Farms to Suit Purchasers. Cedar Rapids: Times Steam Printing House, 1876.

Handbook for the Kansas Pacific Railway, Containing a Description of the Country, Towns, etc., Lying Along the Line of the Road and Its Branches: Extracted from "Tracy's Guide to the Great West." St. Louis: Wiebusch and Son, 1870.

Kelly, N. D. *The New Northwest: An Address on the Northern Pacific Railway in Its Relations to the Northwestern Section of the United States.* No imprint, 1871.

Land Grant Railroads [in Kansas]. No imprint [1892?]. A Populist Party pamphlet.

McAllaster, Benjamin, Land Commissioner. *Kansas: The Golden Belt Lands Along the Line of the Union Pacific R. R.* No imprint.

————. *List of Lands of the Union Pacific R'y in Kansas Still for Sale, March 1, 1886.* Kansas City, Missouri: Ramsey, Millet and Hudson, 1886.

Mills, William H., Land Agent of the Central Pacific Railroad Company. *Payment of Survey Fees Upon and Taxation of Granted Lands: Review of House Bill No. 5874: Letter Addressed to the Chairman of the Senate Committee on Public Lands.* San Francisco: N.p., March 2, 1886.

Mitchell, John H. *Brief and Synopsis of An Oral Argument before the Committee on Public Lands of the Senate and House of the First Session of the Forty-Eighth Congress. The Oregon and California Railroad Co. Grants of July 25, 1866, and May 4, 1870, in Aid of the Construction of Railroads in Oregon (January 15 & 22, 1884).* Washington: Thomas McGill and Company, 1834.

Northern Pacific Railroad Company. *Facts and Argument in Support of Senate Bill No. ——. "To Amend An Act in Relation to the Survey of Certain Lands Granted to the Northern Pacific Railroad Company."* No imprint.

————. *Guide to the Northern Pacific Railroad Lands in Minnesota.* No imprint [1872?].

————. *The Northern Pacific Railroad: Its Route, Resources, Program and Business.* Issued by Jay Cooke and Company. No imprint, October 25, 1871.

————. *The Northern Pacific Railroad's Land Grant and the Future Business of the Road.* Issued by Jay Cooke and Company. No imprint [1872?].

Peters, E. T. *The Policy of Railroad Land Grants: A Lecture Delivered Before the Pre-emptors' Union in Metzevott Hall, Washington, D.C., on Wednesday Evening, April 27, 1870.* No imprint.

Railroads of Nebraska. *Railroad Taxation in Nebraska.* No imprint [1902].

Report of Board Convened to Determine on a Standard of Construction of the Pacific Railroad Made to Honorable James Harlan, Secretary of the Interior, February 24, 1866, with Accompanying Documents. Washington: Government Printing Office, 1866.

Report of Lieut. Col. James H. Simpson, Corps of Engineers, U.S.A., on the Change of the Route West from Omaha, Nebraska Territory, Proposed By the Union Pacific Railroad Company Made to Honorable James Harlan, Secretary of the Interior, September 18, 1865, with the President's Decision Thereon. Washington: Government Printing Office, 1865.

Smart, Stephen F. *Colorado Tourist and Illustrated Guide via the Golden Belt Route . . . to the Rocky Mountain Resorts.* Published by the Kansas Pacific Railway. Kansas City, Missouri: Ramsey, Millet and Hudson, 1879.

"Spec." *Line Etchings: A Trip from the Missouri River to the Rocky Mountains via the Kansas Pacific Railway.* St. Louis: Woodward, Tiermont and Hale, 1875.

Storrs, James H. *Argument of James H. Storrs, Counsel for Central Pacific Railroad Company, before the Committee on Public Lands, United States Senate . . . in Relation to the Taxation of Lands Granted to Railroad Companies, March 8, 1876.* Washington: John L. Ginck, 1876.

————. *The Southern Pacific Railroad Comp'y: In the Matter of Sundry Bills and Resolutions Introduced in the Senate and House of Representatives Affecting the Rights and Interests of the Southern Pacific Railroad Company.* Washington: Joseph L. Pearson, 1876.

Talbott, E. H. *Railway Land Grants in the United States: Their History, Economy and Influence Upon the Development and Prosperity of the Country.* Prepared for the Association of Land Commissioners. Chicago: The Railway Age Publishing Company, 1880.

Tweed, G. H. *In the Matter of the Payment for Surveys and the Taxation of Granted Lands of the Central Pacific Railroad.* No imprint.

Union Pacific Railroad. *The Union Pacific Railroad Company, Chartered by the United States. Progress of Their Road West from Omaha, Across the Continent. Five Hundred and Forty Miles Completed December, 1867.* New York: Union Pacific, 1868.

————. *Central and Western Nebraska and the Experiences of Its Stock Growers.* Omaha: Union Pacific Land Department, 1883.

————. *Creameries and Dairying in Nebraska: What Has Been Done and What May Be Done.* Compiled by J. T. Allan. Omaha: Union Pacific Land Department, 1883.

————. *Guide to the Lands of the Union Pacific Ry. Co. in Nebraska.* Omaha: Union Pacific Land Department [1883?].

————. *Guide to the Union Pacific Railroad Lands: 12,000,000 Acres Best Farming, Grazing, and Mineral Lands in America. . . .* Omaha: Union Pacific Land Department, 1871.

————. *Kansas: Its Resources and Attractions.* 9th edition. Omaha: Union Pacific, 1903.

————. *Lands in Kansas.* Omaha: Union Pacific, 1893.

————. *Monarch of the West: Corn is King and How It Rules in Nebraska.* Omaha: Union Pacific Land Department, n.d.

————. *Nebraska and Its Settlers: What They Have Done and How They Do it: Its Crops and People.* Compiled by J. T. Allan. Omaha: Union Pacific Land Department, 1883.

———. *Pacific Railroad Legislation, 1862–1885.* Boston: Rand, Avery and Company, n.d.

———. *The Resources and Attractions of Nebraska: Facts on Farming, Stock Raising, and Other Industries, and Notes on Climate.* Omaha: Union Pacific Passenger Department, 1893. This pamphlet went through three more editions— 1894, 1897, 1899.

Western Pacific Railroad. *Laws and Documents showing the Organization, Powers, and Rights of the Western Pacific Railroad Co. of California.* San Francisco: Towne and Bacon, 1865.

Weston's Guide to the Kansas Pacific Railway. . . . Kansas City, Missouri: Bulletin Steam Printing and Engraving, 1872.

6. ARTICLES, BOOKS, AND MONOGRAPHS

The body of historical literature on western railroads, on the public lands, and on western politics in the eighties and nineties is vast. The body of historical literature on locales, on individuals, and on specific episodes is almost equally vast. And contemporary descriptions, memoirs, and political tracts in book and article form are only slightly less numerous. Because this monograph is directly concerned with all these subjects, perhaps its bibliography should include an exhaustive list of all these works. The physical limitations of the volume preclude this. Yet, the easy alternative of listing only those works that appear in the footnotes is also precluded. The plethora of writings on the "Populist mind," on "western radicalism," on land policy and the study of land policy, on the "business mind," on theories of public finance, and on numerous related subjects are part of the grist on which the fledgling's mind perforce grinds. And they contribute: a language for one thing, a basis of historiographical comparison and evaluation for another.

Thus—besides including the important works bearing directly on aspects of the taxation of the railroad lands—the lists that follow include a substantial number of those works that form the literature of general western, railroad, land, and political history. Only a few, perhaps a quarter, of those works worthy of inclusion in any exhaustive list are actually listed. Those included are only those that made a significant contribution to this monograph. More particularly, they are those that form part of the basis for the propositions made in chapters 1 and 6 and for the conclusions drawn in chapter 11.

A. Articles

Aandahl, Andrew R., William G. Murray, and Wayne Scholtes. "Economic Rating of Soils for Tax Assessment," in the *Journal of Farm Economics,* 36: 483–499 (August, 1954).

Abel, Annie H. "Indian Reservations in Kansas and the Extinguishment of Their Title," in the *Transactions of the Kansas State Historical Society,* 8:72–109 (1903–1904).

[Adams, Charles Francis]. "Railroad Subsidies," in *The Nation,* 11:219–220 (October, 1870).

Adams, Henry C. "The Farmer and Railway Legislation," in the *Century Magazine,* 21:780–783 (March, 1892).

Aeschbacher, William D. "Development of Cattle Raising in the Sandhills," in *Nebraska History,* 28:41–64 (January-March, 1947).

———. "Development of the Sandhill Lake Country," in *Nebraska History,* 27:205–221 (July-September, 1946).

Ager, John H. "Nebraska Politics and Nebraska Railroads," in the *Proceedings and Collections of the Nebraska State Historical Society,* 10:35–42 (1907).

Alexis, Joseph. "Swedes in Nebraska," in the *Publications of the Nebraska State Historical Society,* 19:78–85 (1919).

"Along the Line of the Kansas Pacific Railway in Western Kansas in 1870," in the *Kansas Historical Quarterly,* 19:207–211 (May, 1951).

Anderson, George L. "The Administration of Federal Land Laws in Western Kansas, 1880–1890: A Factor in Adjustment to a New Environment," in the *Kansas Historical Quarterly*, 20:233–251 (November, 1952).

———. "The Board of Equitable Adjudication, 1846–1930," in *Agricultural History*, 29:65–72 (April, 1955).

Anderson, John A. "Sketch of Kansas Agriculture," pp. 72–101 in the *Annual Report of the Kansas State Board of Agriculture*, 1875.

Barnhart, John D. "Rainfall and the Populist Party in Nebraska," in the *American Political Science Review*, 19:527–540 (August, 1925).

Barr, Elizabeth N. "The Populist Uprising," pp. 1137–1204 in William E. Connelley, comp., *History of Kansas, State and People*. 3d edition. 5 vols. Chicago: American Historical Society, 1928.

Beard, Earl S. "Local Aid to Railroads in Iowa," in the *Iowa Journal of History and Politics*, 50:1–34 (January, 1952).

Beard, Henry. "The Railways and the United States Land Office," in the *Agricultural Review*, 3:423–443 (April, 1883).

Blackmar, Frank W. "Taxation in Kansas," in the *Kansas University Quarterly*, 7:171–180 (October, 1897).

Blake, Henry Taylor. 'The Pacific Railroads and the Government," in the *New Englander*, 37:490–513, 642–669 (1878).

Blake, James J. "The Brownville, Fort Kearney and Pacific Railroad," in *Nebraska History*, 29:238–272 (September, 1948).

"The Bonanza Farms of the West," in the *Atlantic Monthly*, 45:33–44 (January, 1880).

Briggs, Harold E. "Early Bonanza Farming in the Red River Valley of the North," in *Agricultural History*, 6:26–37 (January, 1932).

Buchanan, John R. "The Great Railroad Migration into Northern Nebraska," in the *Proceedings and Collections of the Nebraska State Historical Society*, 10:25–34 (1907).

Burr, George. "Judge Gaslin Stories," in *Nebraska History*, 4:44–45 (July-September, 1921).

Carman, Henry J., and Charles H. Mueller. "The Contract and Finance Company and the Central Pacific Railroad," in the *Mississippi Valley Historical Review*, 14:326–341 (December, 1927).

Carruth, William H. "Foreign Settlements in Kansas," in the *Kansas University Quarterly*, 1:71–84 (October, 1892) ; 3:159–163 (October, 1894).

Cochran, Thomas C. "The Executive Mind: The Role of Railroad Leaders, 1845–1890," in the *Bulletin of the Business Historical Society*, 25:230-241 (December, 1951).

———. "Land Grants and Railroad Entrepreneurship," in the *Journal of Economic History*, 10:53–67 (March, 1950).

———. "The Legend of the Robber Barons," in the *Pennsylvania Magazine of History and Biography*, 74:307–321 (July, 1950).

Colburn, R. T. "United States Land Grants," in the *International Review*, 3:351–367 (May-June, 1876).

Connolly, C. P. "Raiding the People's Land: Control of the General Land Office by the Railroads," in *Colliers*, 44:18–19 (January 8, 1910).

Cook, James H. "Early Days in Ogallala," in *Nebraska History*, 14:86–99 (April-June, 1933).

Cushman, George L. "Abilene, First of the Kansas Cow Towns," in the *Kansas Historical Quarterly*, 9:240–258 (August, 1940).

Danker, Donald F. "Columbus, a Territorial Town in the Platte Valley," in *Nebraska History*, 34:275–288 (December, 1953).

Davis, C. Wood. "The Farmer, the Investor, and the Railway," in the *Arena*, 3:291–313 (February, 1891).

Davis, Thomas M. "Building the Burlington Through Nebraska—A Summary View," in *Nebraska History*, 30:317–347 (December, 1949).

———. "Lines West—The Story of George W. Holdrege," in *Nebraska History*, 31:25–47, 107–125, 204–225 (March-September, 1950).

Decker, Leslie E. "The Railroads and the Land Office: Administrative Policy and the Land Patent Controversy, 1864–1896," in the *Mississippi Valley Historical Review*, 46:679–699 (March, 1960).

Destler, Chester McArthur. "Agricultural Readjustment and Agrarian Unrest in Illinois," in *Agricultural History*, 21:104–116 (April, 1947).

———. "The Opposition of American Businessmen to Social Control during the Gilded Age," in the *Mississippi Valley Historical Review*, 39:641–672 (March, 1953.

———. "Western Radicalism, 1865–1901: Concepts and Origins," in the *Mississippi Valley Historical Review*, 31:335–368 (December, 1944).

Dick, Everett N. "Problems of the Post-Frontier Prairie City as Portrayed by Lincoln, Nebraska, 1880–1890," in *Nebraska History*, 27:132–143 (April-June, 1947).

Dillon, Sidney. "The West and the Railroads," in the *North American Review*, 152:443–452 (April, 1891).

Dixon, Frank H. "Railroad Control in Nebraska," in the *Political Science Quarterly*, 13:617–647 (December, 1898).

Donald, W. J. "Land Grants for Internal Improvements in the United States," in the *Journal of Political Economy*, 19:404–410 (May, 1911).

Drummond, Willis, Jr. "Land Grants in Aid of Internal Improvements," chapter 10 in J. W. Powell, *Report on the Arid Region of the United States*. Washington: Government Printing Office, 1878.

Dunham, Harold Hathaway. "Some Crucial Years of the General Land Office," in *Agricultural History*, 11:227–240 (April, 1937).

Ellis, David M. "The Forfeiture of Railroad Land Grants, 1867–1894," in the *Mississippi Valley Historical Review*, 33:27–60 (June, 1946).

Ernst, C. J. "The Railroad as Creator of Wealth," in *Nebraska History and Record of Pioneer Days*, 7:18–22 (January-March, 1924).

Farley, Alan W. "Samuel Hallett and the Union Pacific Railway Company in Kansas," in the *Kansas Historical Quarterly*, 25:1–16 (Spring, 1959).

Farmer, Hallie. "The Economic Background of Frontier Populism," in the *Mississippi Valley Historical Review*, 10:406–427 (March, 1924).

———. "The Railroads and Frontier Populism," in the *Mississippi Valley Historical Review*, 13:387–397 (December, 1926).

Fowke, Vernon W. "National Policy and Western Development in North America," in the *Journal of Economic History*, 16:461–479 (December, 1956).

Ganoe, J. T. "The Beginnings of Irrigation in the United States," in the *Mississippi Valley Historical Review*, 25:59–78 (June, 1938).

Gates, Paul W. "The Homestead Law in an Incongruous Land System," in the *American Historical Review*, 41:652–681 (July, 1936).

———. "The Railroad Land Grant Legend," in the *Journal of Economic History*, 14:143–146 (March, 1954).

———. "The Railroads of Missouri, 1850–1870," in the *Missouri Historical Review*, 26:126–141 (January, 1932).

———. "Research in the History of American Land Tenure," in *Agricultural History*, 28:121–126 (July, 1954).

———. "The Role of the Land Speculator in Western Development," in the *Pennsylvania Magazine of History and Biography*, 66:314–333 (July, 1942).

Geist, Ralph. "Early Days in Russell County," in *The Aesend, A Kansas Quarterly* (Kansas State College, Hays), 10:51–53 (Winter, 1939).

Glynn, Herbert L. "The Urban Real Estate Boom in Nebraska during the Eighties," in the *Nebraska Law Bulletin*, 6:455–481 (May, 1928); 7:228–254 (November, 1928).

Goodrich, Carter. "American Development Policy: The Case of Internal Improvements," in the *Journal of Economic History*, 16:449–460 (December, 1956).

Green, Fletcher M. "Origins of the Credit Mobilier of America," in the *Mississippi Valley Historical Review*, 46:238–251 (September, 1959).

Harmer, Marie U., and James L. Sellers. "Charles H. VanWyck—Soldier and Statesman," in *Nebraska History*, 12:81–128, 190–246, 322–373 (March-December, 1931) ; 13:3–36 (March, 1932).

Harrington, W. P. "The Populist Party in Kansas," in the *Collections of the Kansas State Historical Society*, 16:402–450 (1923-1924).

Harrison, Robert W. "Public Land Records of the Federal Government," in the *Mississippi Valley Historical Review*, 41:277–288 (September, 1954).

Hart, Albert Bushnell. "The Disposition of Our Public Lands," in the *Quarterly Journal of Economics*, 1:169–183, 252–254 (January, 1887).

Hedges, James Blaine. "The Colonization Work of the Northern Pacific Railroad," in the *Mississippi Valley Historical Review*, 13:311–342 (December, 1926).

———. "Promotion of Immigration to the Pacific Northwest by the Railroads," in the *Mississippi Valley Historical Review*, 15:183–203 (September, 1928).

Henderson, Harold J. "The Building of the First Kansas Railroad South of the Kaw River," in the *Kansas Historical Quarterly*, 15:225–239 (August, 1947).

Henry, Robert S. "The Railroad Land Grant Legend in American History Texts," in the *Mississippi Valley Historical Review*, 32:171–194 (September, 1945). "Comments" on this article appear *ibid.*, 557–576 (March, 1946).

Hicks, John D. "The People's Party in Minnesota," in the *Minnesota History Bulletin*, 5:531–560 (November, 1924).

———. "The Third Party Tradition in American Politics," in the *Mississippi Valley Historical Review*, 20:3–28 (June, 1933).

Hodgskin, J. B. "The Truth About Land Grants," in *The Nation*, 11:417–418 (December, 1870).

Horton, Agnes. "Nebraska's Agricultural-College Land," in *Nebraska History*, 30:50–76 (March, 1949).

Hrbkora, Sarka B. "Bohemians in Nebraska," in the *Publications of the Nebraska State Historical Society*, 19:141–147 (1919).

Hull, O. C. "Railroads in Kansas," in the *Collections of the Kansas State Historical Society*, 12:37–46 (1911-1912).

Ingalls, John James. "Kansas, 1541–1891," in *Harpers Magazine*, 86:697–713 (April, 1893).

Jackson, W. Turrentine. "Materials for Western History in the Department of the Interior Archives," in the *Mississippi Valley Historical Review*, 35:61–76 (June, 1948).

Jeffrey, Mary Louise. "Young Radicals of the Nineties," in *Nebraska History*, 38:25–41 (March, 1957).

Johnston, John Warfield. "Railway Land-Grants," in the *North American Review*, 140:280–289 (March, 1885).

Jones, C. Clyde. "A Survey of the Agricultural Development Program of the Chicago, Burlington and Quincy Railroad," in *Nebraska History*, 30:226–256 (September, 1949).

Julian, George W. "Our Land Grant Railways in Congress," in the *International Review*, 14:198–212 (1883).

———. "Railway Influence in the Land Office," in the *North American Review*, 136:237–256 (March, 1883).

"Land Grants to Pacific Railroad Companies Aided by Lands and Bonds under the Act of 1862," in the *Railway World*, 4:752 (August 3, 1878).

LeDuc, Thomas. "The Disposal of the Public Domain on the Trans-Mississippi Plains: Some Opportunities for Investigation," in *Agricultural History*, 24:199–204 (October, 1950).

———. "State Administration of the Land Grant to Kansas for Internal Improvements," in the *Kansas Historical Quarterly*, 20:545–552 (November, 1953).

——. "State Disposal of Agricultural College Scrip," in *Agricultural History,* 28:99–107 (July, 1954).

Lomax, E. L. "The Work of the U P in Nebraska," in the *Proceedings and Collections of the Nebraska State Historical Society,* 10:181–188 (1907).

McCrea, Roswell. "Taxation of Transportation Companies," chapter 9 in the *Report of the Industrial Commission.* Washington: Government Printing Office, 1901.

Mahnken, Norbert R. "Early Nebraska Markets for Texas Cattle," in *Nebraska History,* 26:3–25 (January-March, 1945); 91–103 (April-June, 1945).

——. "Ogallala—Nebraska's Cowboy Capital," in *Nebraska History,* 28:85–109 (April-June, 1947).

Malin, James C. "Adaptation of the Agricultural System to Sub-Humid Environment, Illustrated by the Wayne County Farmers' Club of Edwards County, Kansas," in *Agricultural History,* 10:118–141 (July, 1936).

——. "The Agricultural Regionalism of the Trans-Mississippi West as Delineated by Cyrus Thomas," in *Agricultural History,* 21:208–217 (October, 1947).

——. "An Introduction to the History of the Bluestem Pastures," in the *Kansas Historical Quarterly,* 11:3–28 (February, 1942).

——. "Beginnings of Winter Wheat Production in the Upper Kansas and Lower Smoky Hill River Valleys," in the *Kansas Historical Quarterly,* 10:227–259 (August, 1941).

——. "Ecology and History," in the *Scientific Monthly,* 60:295–298 (May, 1950).

——. "The Farmers' Alliance Subtreasury Plan and European Precedents," in the *Mississippi Valley Historical Review,* 31:255–260 (September, 1944).

——. "The Grassland of North America: Its Occupance and the Challenge of Continuous Reappraisals." Background Paper No. 19, prepared for the Werner-Gren Foundation International Symposium, "Man's Role in Changing the Face of the Earth," Princeton Inn, Princeton, New Jersey, June 16–22, 1955.

——. "The Kingsley Boom of the Late Eighties," in the *Kansas Historical Quarterly,* 4:23–49, 164–187 (February, May, 1935).

——. "Man, the State of Nature, and Climax: As Illustrated by Some Problems of the North American Grassland," in the *Scientific Monthly,* 74:1–8 (January, 1952).

——. "Notes on the Literature of Populism," in the *Kansas Historical Quarterly,* 1:160–164 (February, 1932).

——. "Soil, Animal, and Plant Relations of the Grassland, Historically Reconsidered," in the *Scientific Monthly,* 76:207–220 (April, 1953).

——. "The Turnover of Farm Population in Kansas," in the *Kansas Historical Quarterly,* 4:339–372 (November, 1935).

——, ed. "J. A. Walker's Early History of Edwards County," in the *Kansas Historical Quarterly,* 9:259–284 (August, 1940).

Martin, George W. "John Anderson—A Character Sketch," in the *Transactions of the Kansas State Historical Society,* 8:315–323 (1903-1904).

Martin, John A. "The Progress of Kansas," in the *North American Review,* 142:348–355 (April, 1886).

Mason, Henry F. "County Seat Controversies in Southwestern Kansas," in the *Kansas Historical Quarterly,* 2:45–65 (February, 1933).

Mattison, Ray H. "The Burlington Tax Controversy in Nebraska Over the Federal Land Grants," in *Nebraska History,* 28:110–131 (April-June, 1947).

Medbery, J. K. "Our Pacific Railroads," in the *Atlantic Monthly,* 20:704–715 (December, 1867).

Meyer, Balthasar H. "A History of Early Railroad Legislation in Wisconsin," in the *Collections of the State Historical Society of Wisconsin,* 14:206–300 (1918).

Millbrook, Minnie Dubbs. "Dr. Samuel Grant Rodgers, Gentleman from Ness," in the *Kansas Historical Quarterly,* 20:305–349 (February, 1953).

Miller, George H. "Origins of the Iowa Granger Law," in the *Mississippi Valley Historical Review*, 40:657–680 (March, 1954).

Miller, Raymond C. "The Economic Background of Populism in Kansas," in the *Mississippi Valley Historical Review*, 11:469–489 (March, 1925).

Million, John Wilson. "State Aid to Railways in Missouri," in the *Journal of Political Economy*, 3:73–97 (1895).

Montgomery, Mrs. Frank C. "Fort Wallace and Its Relation to the Frontier," in the *Collections of the Kansas State Historical Society*, 17:1–95 (1926-1928).

Morgan, Appleton. "Are Railroads Public Enemies?" in *Popular Science Monthly*, 30:576–590 (March, 1887).

Murray, Stanley N. "Railroads and the Agricultural Development of the Red River Valley of the North, 1870–1890," in *Agricultural History*, 31:57–66 (October, 1957).

Nelson, Henry L. "Schurz's Administration of the Interior Department," in the *International Review*, 10:380–396 (1881).

Nixon, Herman Clarence. "The Populist Movement in Iowa," in the *Iowa Journal of History and Politics*, 24:3–107 (January, 1926).

Ottoson, Howard W., Andrew R. Aandahl, and L. Burbank Kristjanson. "A Method of Farm Real Estate Valuation for Tax Assessment," in the *Journal of Farm Economics*, 37:471–483 (August, 1955).

Palmer, Edgar Z. "The Correctness of the 1890 Census of Population for Nebraska Cities," in *Nebraska History*, 32:259–267 (December, 1951).

Parker, Edna M. "The Southern Pacific Railroad and the Settlement of Southern California," in the *Pacific Historical Review*, 6:103–119 (June, 1937).

Paxson, Frederic L. "The Pacific Railroads and the Disappearance of the Frontier in America," in the *Annual Report of the American Historical Association, 1907*, 1:105–118.

Peffer, William A. "The Farmer's Defensive Movement," in the *Forum*, 8:464–473 (December, 1889).

———. "The Mission of the Populist Party," in the *North American Review*, 157:665–678 (December, 1893).

Pendergast, F. E. "Transcontinental Railways," in *Harper's Magazine*, 67:936–944 (November, 1883).

Peterson, Harold. "Early Minnesota Railroads and the Quest for Settlers," in *Minnesota History*, 13:25–44 (March, 1932).

———. "Some Colonizing Efforts of the Northern Pacific Railroad," in *Minnesota History*, 10:127–144 (June, 1929).

Pollack, Norman. "Hofstadter on Populism: A Critique of 'The Age of Reform,'" in the *Journal of Southern History*, 26:478–500 (November, 1960).

Poor, Henry Varnum. "The Pacific Railroad," in the *North American Review*, 128:664–680 (June, 1879).

Rae, John B. "Commissioner Sparks and the Railroad Land Grants," in the *Mississippi Valley Historical Review*, 25:211–230 (September, 1933).

———. "The Great Northern's Land Grant," in the *Journal of Economic History*, 12:140–145 (Spring, 1952).

"Railway Land Grants in Kansas," in the *Railway World*, 5:772 (August 16, 1879).

Raney, William F. "The Timber Culture Acts," in the *Proceedings of the Mississippi Valley Historical Association*, 10:219–229 (1919-1920).

Reynolds, Arthur R. "The Kinkaid Act and Its Effects on Western Nebraska," in *Agricultural History*, 23:20–29 (January, 1949).

Riegel, Robert E. "The Missouri Pacific Railroad to 1879," in the *Missouri Historical Review*, 18:3–26 (October, 1923).

"Right of Railway Companies to Their Land Grants," in the *Railway World*, 5:388–389 (April 26, 1879).

Rightmire, W. F. "The Alliance Movement in Kansas—Origin of the People's Party," in the *Transactions of the Kansas State Historical Society*, 9:1–8 (1906).

Robbins, Roy M. "The Federal Land System in an Embryo State: Washington Territory, 1853–1890," in the *Pacific Historical Review*, 4:356–375 (November, 1935).

———. "The Public Domain in the Era of Exploitation, 1862–1901," in *Agricultural History*, 13:97–108 (April, 1939).

Ross, Earle D. "Squandering Our Public Land," in the *American Scholar*, 2:77–86 (January, 1933).

Ruppenthal, J. C. "The German Element in Central Kansas," in the *Collections of the Kansas State Historical Society*, 13:513–534 (1913-1914).

Saloutos, Theodore. "The Agricultural Problem and Nineteenth-Century Industrialism," in *Agricultural History*, 22:156–174 (July, 1948).

———. "The Spring Wheat Farmer in a Maturing Economy, 1870–1920." in the *Journal of Economic History*, 6:173–190 (November, 1946).

Schoewe, Walter H. "The Geography of Kansas," in the *Transactions of the Kansas Academy of Science*, 51:253–288 (September, 1948); 52:261–333 (September, 1949); 54:263–329 (September, 1951); 56:131–190 (June, 1953); 61:359–468 (Winter, 1958).

Scott, Roy V. "Milton George and the Farmers' Alliance Movement," in the *Mississippi Valley Historical Review*, 45:90–109 (June, 1958).

Shannon, Fred A. "The Homestead Act and the Labor Surplus," in the *American Historical Review*, 41:637–651 (July, 1936).

Sheldon, Addison E. "Early Railroad Development of Nebraska," in *Nebraska History and Record of Pioneer Days*, 7:16–17 (January-March, 1924).

"Some Lost Towns of Kansas," in the *Collections of the Kansas State Historical Society*, 12:426–490 (1911-1912).

Stolley, William. "History of the First Settlement of Hall County, Nebraska," in *Nebraska History*, special edition, April, 1946.

Streeter, F. B. "Ellsworth as a Texas Cattle Market," in the *Kansas Historical Quarterly*, 4:388–398 (November, 1935).

Taft, Robert. "Kansas and the Nation's Salt," in the *Transactions of the Kansas Academy of Science*, 49:223–272 (December, 1946).

Thompson, J. M. "The Farmers' Alliance in Nebraska: Something of Its Origin, Growth, and Influence," in the *Proceedings and Collections of the Nebraska State Historical Society*, 10:199–206 (1902).

Tingley, C. E. "Bond Subsidies to Railroads in Nebraska," in the *Quarterly Journal of Economics*, 6:346–352 (April, 1892).

Traxler, Ralph N., Jr. "The Texas and Pacific Railroad Land Grants," in the *Southwestern Historical Quarterly*, 51:359–369 (January, 1958).

Warner, Amos G. "Railroad Problems in a Western State [Nebraska]," in the *Political Science Quarterly*, 6:66–89 (March, 1891).

Wilcox, Benton H. "An Historical Definition of Northwestern Radicalism," in the *Mississippi Valley Historical Review*, 26:377–394 (December, 1939).

Woodburn, James A. "Western Radicalism in American Politics," in the *Mississippi Valley Historical Review*, 13:143–168 (September, 1926).

Woodward, C. Vann. "The Populist Heritage and the Intellectual," in the *American Scholar*, 29:55–72 (Winter, 1959-1960).

Wyman, Walker D. "Omaha: Frontier Depot and Prodigy of Council Bluffs," in *Nebraska History*, 17:143–155 (September, 1936).

B. Books and Monographs

Abbott, Othman A. *Recollections of a Pioneer Lawyer.* Lincoln: Nebraska State Historical Society, 1929.

Ackerman, William K. *Early Illinois Railroads.* Chicago: Fergus Printing Company, 1884.

Adams, Thomas Henry. A Study of Nebraska School Lands. Unpublished master's thesis, University of Nebraska, 1936.

Albrecht, Abraham. Mennonite Settlements in Kansas. Unpublished master's thesis, University of Kansas, 1925.

Anderson, Helen. The Influence of Railway Advertising on the Settlement of Nebraska. Unpublished master's thesis, University of Nebraska, 1926.

Andreas, Alfred T. *History of the State of Kansas, Containing a Full Account of Its Growth from an Uninhabited Territory to a Wealthy and Important State.* 2 vols. Chicago: A. T. Andreas, 1883.

————, comp. *History of the State of Nebraska, Containing a Full Account of Its Growth . . . Description of its Counties, Cities, Towns, and Villages. . . .* Chicago: Western Historical Company, 1882.

Arrington, Leonard J. *Great Basin Kingdom: An Economic History of the Latter-Day Saints, 1830–1900.* Cambridge: Harvard University Press, 1958.

Aylsworth, L. E., and John G. W. Lewis, eds. *Nebraska Party Platforms.* Published as a report on Works Projects Administration Official Project No. 665-81-3-19. Sponsored by the University of Nebraska, March, 1940.

Bade, Gustav Adolph. A History of the Dutch Settlement in Lancaster County, Nebraska. Unpublished master's thesis, University of Nebraska, 1938.

Baker, Oliver E., comp. *Atlas of American Agriculture.* Washington: Government Printing Office, 1936.

Baldwin, W. W., comp. *Chicago, Burlington and Quincy Railroad Company—Documentary History.* 3 vols. Chicago: Chicago, Burlington and Quincy, 1929.

Barr, Elizabeth N. *A Souvenir History of Lincoln County, Kansas.* [Topeka: *Kansas Farmer* Job Office], 1908.

Barrett, Jay Amos. *The History and Government of Nebraska.* Lincoln: J. H. Miller, 1892.

Barrows, Leland J. An Outline of County Government in Kansas. Unpublished master's thesis, University of Kansas, 1932.

Beezley, Edyth Louise. A History of Webster County, Nebraska. Unpublished master's thesis, University of Nebraska, 1937.

Bell, W. L. *Bell's Kansas Portfolio.* Kansas City, Missouri: W. L. Bell and Company, 1897.

Bentley, Arthur F. *The Condition of the Western Farmer as Illustrated by the Economic History of a Nebraska Township. Johns Hopkins Studies in Historical and Political Science.* Eleventh series, nos. 7 and 8. Baltimore, 1893.

Benton, Elbert J. *Taxation in Kansas. Johns Hopkins University Studies in Historical and Political Science.* Vol. 18. Baltimore, 1900.

Bidwell, O. W. *Major Soils of Kansas. Circular of the Kansas Agricultural Experiment Station.* No. 336. Contribution No. 551, Department of Agronomy, Manhattan, July, 1956.

Biographical and Genealogical History of Southeastern Nebraska. Chicago: Lewis Publishing Company, 1904.

Biographical and Historical Memoirs of Adams, Clay, Hall and Hamilton Counties, Nebraska. Chicago: Goodspeed Publishing Company, 1890.

Biographical Souvenir of Buffalo, Kearney and Phelps Counties. Chicago: P. A. Battey Company, 1890.

Blackmar, Frank W. *The Life of Charles Robinson, the First State Governor of Kansas.* Topeka: Crane and Company Printers, 1902.

————, ed. *Kansas: A Cyclopedia of State History. . . .* 2 vols. Chicago: Standard Publishing Company, 1912.

Blanchard, Leola Howard. *Conquest of Southwest Kansas.* Wichita: *Wichita Eagle* Press, 1931.

Bogue, Allan G. *Money at Interest: The Farm Mortgage on the Middle Border.* Ithaca: Cornell University Press, 1955.

Boyle, James E. *Financial History of Kansas. University of Wisconsin Bulletin in Economics and Political Science.* Vol. 5, no. 1. Madison, 1909.

Bradford, H. E., and G. A. Spidel, *Nebraska: Its Geography and Agriculture*. New York: Macmillan Company, 1931.

Bradley, Glenn D. *The Story of the Santa Fe*. Boston: Gorham Press, 1920.

Brayer, Herbert O. *William Blackmore: Early Financing of the Denver and Rio Grande Railway and Ancillary Land Companies*. Denver: Bradford-Robinson, 1949.

Brindley, John E. *History of Taxation in Iowa*. 2 vols. Iowa City: State Historical Society of Iowa, 1911.

Brown, Harry Gunnison. *The Economics of Taxation*. New York: Henry Holt and Company, 1924.

Brownson, Howard Gray. *History of the Illinois Central Railroad to 1870*. *University of Illinois Studies in the Social Sciences*. Vol. 1, nos. 3 and 4, in the *Bulletin of the University of Illinois*, vol. 13, no. 10. Urbana, November 8, 1915.

Buck, Solon Justus. *The Agrarian Crusade: A Chronicle of the Farmer in Politics*. New Haven: Yale University Press, 1920.

————. *The Granger Movement: A Study of Agricultural Organization and Its Political, Economic, and Social Manifestations, 1870–1880*. Cambridge: Harvard University Press, 1913.

Bunting, Anna Maury. *Our People and Ourselves*. Lincoln: N.p., 1909.

Burleigh, David Robert. Range Cattle Industry in Nebraska to 1890. Unpublished master's thesis, University of Nebraska, 1937.

Burr, George L., and O. O. Buck, eds. *History of Hamilton and Clay Counties, Nebraska*. 2 vols. Chicago: S. J. Clarke, 1921.

Burton, William R., and David J. Lewis, eds. *Past and Present of Adams County, Nebraska*. 2 vols. Chicago: S. J. Clarke, 1916.

Buss, William H., and Thomas T. Osterman. *History of Dodge and Washington Counties, Nebraska, and Their People*. 2 vols. Chicago: American Historical Society, 1921.

Canfield, James Hulme. *History and Government of Kansas*. Philadelphia: E. H. Butler and Company, 1894.

Cary, John W. *The Organization and History of the Chicago, Milwaukee and St. Paul*. Milwaukee: Cramer, Aikens and Cramer, 1892.

Caylor, John Arnett. The Disposition of the Public Domain in Pierce County, Nebraska. Unpublished master's thesis, University of Nebraska, 1951.

Chaney, C. R. *Nebraska Citations*. Hastings: Gazette Journal Company, 1888.

Clarke, George T. *Leland Stanford*. Stanford: Stanford University Press, 1931.

Cochran, Thomas C. *Railroad Leaders, 1845–1890: The Business Mind in Action*. Cambridge: Harvard University Press, 1953.

Coffey, George N., and others. *Reconnaissance Soil Survey of Western Kansas*. Washington: Government Printing Office, 1912.

Compendium of History, Reminiscence, and Biography of Nebraska, Containing a History of the State of Nebraska. . . . Chicago: Alden Publishing Company, 1912.

Connelley, William E. *Ingalls of Kansas: A Character Study*. Topeka: The Author, 1909.

————. *The Life of Preston B. Plumb, 1837–1891*. Chicago: Browne and Howard Company, 1913.

————, comp. *History of Kansas, State and People*. 3d edition. 5 vols. Chicago: American Historical Society, 1928.

————, ed. *The Writings of John James Ingalls*. Kansas City, Missouri: Hudson Kimberly Publishing Company, 1902.

Corliss, Carlton J. *Main Line of Mid-America: The Story of the Illinois Central*. New York: Creative Age Press, 1950.

Craik, Elmer LeRoy. *A History of the Church of the Brethren in Kansas*. McPherson, Kansas: The Author, 1922.

Crippen, Waldo. The Kansas Pacific Railroad: A Cross Section of an Age of Railroad Building. Unpublished master's thesis, University of Chicago, 1932.

Curti, Merle, with Robert Daniel, Shaw Livermore, Jr., Joseph Van Hise, and Margaret W. Curti. The Making of an American Community: A Case Study of Democracy in a Frontier County. Stanford: Stanford University Press, 1959.

Daggett, Stuart. Chapters in the History of the Southern Pacific. New York: Ronald Press, 1922.

Dale, Edward Everett. The Range Cattle Industry. Norman: University of Oklahoma Press, 1930.

Dassler, C. F. W. Digest of Decisions of the Supreme Court of Kansas. 2 vols. Topeka: Crane and Company, 1889–1894.

Davis, John Patterson. The Union Pacific Railway: A Study in Railway Politics, History, and Economics. Chicago: S. C. Griggs and Company, 1894.

Destler, Chester McArthur. American Radicalism, 1865–1901: Essays and Documents. New London: Connecticut College, 1946.

Dockeray, James Carlton. Public Utility Taxation in Ohio. Columbus: Ohio State University Press, 1938.

Dunham, Harold Hathaway. Government Handout: A Study in the Administration of the Public Lands, 1875–1891. New York: The Author, 1941.

Edwards' Atlas of Saline County, Kansas. Philadelphia: John P. Edwards, 1884.

Ellis, David Maldwyn. The Forfeiture of Railroad Land Grants. Unpublished master's thesis, Cornell University, 1939.

Epp, Abram W. An Economic History of Agriculture in Gage County, Nebraska. Unpublished master's thesis, University of Nebraska, 1937.

Evans, Evan E. An Analytical Study of Land Transfer to Private Ownership in Johnson County, Nebraska. Unpublished master's thesis, University of Nebraska, 1950.

Fankhauser, William C. A Financial History of California: Public Revenues, Debts, and Expenditures. University of California Publications in Economics. Vol. 3, no. 2. Berkeley, 1913.

Farmer, Floyd Merle. Land Boom of Southwest Nebraska, 1880–1890. Unpublished master's thesis, University of Nebraska, 1936.

Federal Writers Project. A Guide to Salina, Kansas. Salina: Advertiser-Sun, n.d.

———. Nebraska: A Guide to the Cornhusker State. New York: Viking Press, 1939.

Fine, Nathan. Labor and Farmer Parties in the United States, 1828–1928. New York: Rand School of Social Science, 1928.

Flint, Henry M. The Railroads of the United States: Their History and Statistics. Philadelphia: John E. Potter and Company, 1868.

Flora, S. D. Climate of Kansas. Report of the Kansas State Board of Agriculture, 57:1–320. Topeka, 1948.

Fogel, Robert William. The Union Pacific Railroad: A Case in Premature Enterprise. Baltimore: Johns Hopkins University Press, 1960.

Foulton, Robert Lardin. Epic of the Overland: An Account of the Building of the Central and Union Pacific Railroad. Los Angeles: N. A. Kovach, 1954.

Friday, David. Railway Land Valuation. Unpublished manuscript, Bureau of Railway Economics Library. Dated August 19, 1924.

Frye, John C., and James J. Brazil. Ground Water in the Oil-Field Areas of Ellis and Russell Counties, Kansas. Bulletin of the Kansas State Geological Survey. No. 50. University of Kansas, Lawrence, 1943.

Frye, John C., and A. Byron Leonard. Pleistocene Geology of Kansas. Bulletin of the Kansas State Geological Survey. No. 99. University of Kansas, Lawrence, 1952.

Gaines, John Franklin. Geographic Study of the Nebraska Loess Plain. Unpublished doctor's dissertation, University of Nebraska, 1951.

Galloway, John Debo. The First Transcontinental Railroad: Central Pacific, Union Pacific. New York: Simmons-Boardman, 1950.

Garey, L. F. *Factors Determining Type-of-Farming Areas in Nebraska. Bulletin of the Nebraska Agricultural Experiment Station.* No. 299. University of Nebraska, Lincoln, 1936.

———. *Systems of Farming and Possible Alternates in Nebraska. Bulletin of the Nebraska Agricultural Experiment Station.* No. 309. University of Nebraska, Lincoln, 1937.

Garrett, Hubert. A History of Brownville, Nebraska. Unpublished master's thesis, University of Nebraska, 1927.

Gates, Paul W. *Fifty Million Acres: Conflicts over Kansas Land Policy, 1854–1890.* Ithaca: Cornell University Press, 1954.

———. *Frontier Landlords and Pioneer Tenants.* Ithaca: Cornell University Press, 1945.

———. *The Illinois Central Railroad and Its Colonization Work.* Cambridge: Harvard University Press, 1934.

———. *The Wisconsin Pine Lands of Cornell University: A Study in Land Policy and Absentee Ownership.* Ithaca: Cornell University Press, 1943.

George, Henry. *Our Land and Land Policy: Speeches, Lectures, and Miscellaneous Writings.* Garden City, New York: Doubleday, Page and Company, 1912.

Greever, William S. *Arid Domain: The Santa Fe Railway and Its Western Land Grant.* Stanford: Stanford University Press, 1954.

Goodrich, Carter. *Government Promotion of American Canals and Railroads, 1800–1890.* New York: Columbia University Press, 1960.

Haig, Robert M. *A History of the General Property Tax in Illinois. University of Illnois Studies in the Social Sciences.* Vol. 3, nos. 1 and 2. Urbana, 1914.

Hall, Jesse A., and LeRoy T. Hand. *History of Leavenworth County, Kansas.* Topeka: Historical Publishing Company, 1921.

Hamilton, James M. *From Wilderness to Statehood: A History of Montana, 1805–1900.* Edited by Merrill G. Burlingame. Portland, Oregon: Binfords and Mort, 1957.

Haney, Lewis. *A Congressional History of Railways in the United States, 1850–1887. University of Wisconsin Bulletin in Economics and Political Science.* Vol. 6, no. 1. Madison, 1910.

Hayes, Jennie L. Kansas Cow Towns, 1865–1885. Unpublished master's thesis, University of Oklahoma, 1938.

Haynes, Frederick Emory. *Third Party Movements since the Civil War, with Special Reference to Iowa: A Study in Social Politics.* Iowa City: State Historical Society of Iowa, 1916.

Hedges, James Blaine. *Henry Villard and the Railways of the Northwest.* New Haven: Yale University Press, 1930.

Hennessey, W. B., comp. *History of North Dakota.* Bismarck: *Bismarck Tribune,* 1910.

Henry, Stuart. *Conquering Our Great American Plains: A Historical Development.* New York: E. P. Dutton, 1930.

Herschen, Juliette. Early Third Party Movements in Nebraska. Unpublished master's thesis, University of Nebraska, 1931.

Hibbard, Benjamin Horace. *A History of the Public Land Policies.* New York: Peter Smith, 1939.

Hicks, John D. *The Populist Revolt: A History of the Farmers' Alliance and the People's Party.* Minneapolis: University of Minnesota Press, 1931.

Hinman, Eleanor. *History of Farm Land Prices in Eleven Nebraska Counties, 1873–1933. Bulletin of the Nebraska Agricultural Experiment Station.* No. 72. University of Nebraska, Lincoln, 1934.

Historical Records Survey, Kansas. History of Pottawatomie County. Mimeographed. No Imprint.

Hofstadter, Richard. *The Age of Reform: From Bryan to F. D. R.* New York: Alfred A. Knopf, 1956.

Hollander, J. H., ed. *Studies in State Taxation. Johns Hopkins University Studies in Historical and Political Science.* Vol. 18. Baltimore, 1900.

Hollingshead, A. DeB. Trends in Community Development: A Study of Ecological and Institutional Processes in Thirty-Four Southeastern Nebraska Counties. Unpublished doctor's dissertation, University of Nebraska, 1935.

Huang, Hsien-Ju. *State Taxation of Railroads in The United States.* New York: Columbia University Press, 1928.

Hudson, James F. *The Railways and the Republic.* 3d edition. New York: Harper and Brothers, 1889.

Humphrey, Seth K. *Following the Prairie Frontier.* Minneapolis: University of Minnesota Press, 1931.

Ise, John. *Sod and Stubble: The Story of a Kansas Homestead.* New York: Wilson and Erickson, 1936.

————. *United States Forest Policy.* New Haven: Yale University Press, 1920.

Jarchow, Merrill E. *The Earth Brought Forth: A History of Minnesota Agriculture to 1885.* St. Paul: Minnesota Historical Society, 1949.

Joel, Arthur H. *Soil Conservation Reconnaissance Survey of the Southern Great Plains Erosion Area.* Washington: Government Printing Office, 1937.

Johnson, Harrison, *Johnson's History of Nebraska.* Omaha: Henry Gibson, 1880.

Jones, Horace. *The Story of Early Rice County* [Kansas]. [Wichita: *Wichita Eagle* Press], 1928.

Jones, Virginia Bowen. The Influence of the Railroads of Nebraska on Nebraska State Politics. Unpublished master's thesis, University of Nebraska, 1927.

Judson, Frederick N. *A Treatise Upon the Law and Practice of Taxation in Missouri.* Columbia, Missouri: E. W. Stephens, 1900.

Keefer, Ellen Eloise. The Chicago, Burlington and Quincy in the Early History of Nebraska. Unpublished master's thesis, University of Nebraska, 1929.

Kendrick, M. Slade. *Public Finance: Principles and Problems.* Boston: Houghton-Mifflin Company, 1951.

King, James L., ed. and comp. *History of Shawnee County, Kansas and Representative Citizens.* Chicago: Richmond and Arnold, 1905.

Kraenzel, Carl Frederick. *The Great Plains in Transition.* Norman: University of Oklahoma Press, 1955.

Kramer, Dale. *The Wild Jackasses: The American Farmer in Revolt.* New York: Hastings House, 1956.

Kuester, Frieda C. The Farmers' Alliance in Nebraska. Unpublished master's thesis, University of Nebraska, 1927.

Lacey, Wesley A. The Development of Agriculture in the Great Plains as Typified by Its Growth in Kansas. Unpublished master's thesis, University of Kansas, 1911.

Lamar, Howard R. *Dakota Territory, 1861–1889: A Study of Frontier Politics.* New Haven: Yale University Press, 1956.

Larrabee, William. *The Railroad Question: A Historical and Practical Treatise on Railroads and Remedies for Their Abuses.* Chicago: Schulte Publishing Company, 1893.

Larson, Henrietta M. *Jay Cooke, Private Banker.* Cambridge: Harvard University Press, 1936.

Latta, Bruce F. *Ground-Water Conditions in the Smoky Hill Valley in Saline, Dickinson, and Geary Counties, Kansas. Bulletin of the Kansas State Geological Survey.* No. 84. University of Kansas, Lawrence, 1949.

————. *Ground-Water Supplies at Hays, Victoria, Walker, Gorham, and Russell, Kansas with Special Reference to Future Needs. Bulletin of the Kansas State Geological Survey.* No. 76, part 6. University of Kansas, Lawrence, 1948.

Lewis, Oscar. *The Big Four: The Story of Huntington, Stanford, Hopkins, and Crocker, and the Building of the Central Pacific.* New York: Alfred A. Knopf, 1938.

Lindsay, Charles. The Political Antecedents of the Progressive Movement. Unpublished master's thesis, University of Nebraska, 1925.

Lokken, Roscoe L. *Iowa Public Land Disposal.* Iowa City: Iowa State Historical Society, 1942.

Lopata, Edwin L. *Local Aid to Railroads in Missouri.* New York: Parnassus Press, 1937.

Lutz, Harley Leist. *The State Tax Commission: A Study of the Development and Results of State Control over the Assessment of Property for Taxation.* Cambridge: Harvard University Press, 1918.

McKay, Jack F. *Property Assessment in Kansas. Bulletin of the University of Kansas, Governmental Research Series,* no. 7. Lawrence, 1950.

———. Property Tax Assessment in Kansas: An Administrative Study. Unpublished master's thesis, University of Kansas, 1950.

McNeal, Tom A. *When Kansas Was Young.* New York: Macmillan Company, 1922.

McVey, Frank L. *The Populist Movement.* New York: Macmillan Company, 1896.

Malin, James C. *Grassland Historical Studies: Natural Resources Utilization in a Background of Science and Technology:* Volume One, *Geology and Geography.* Lawrence: The Author, 1950.

———. *The Grassland of North America: Prolegomena to Its History.* Lawrence: The Author, 1947.

———. *Winter Wheat in the Golden Belt of Kansas: A Study in Adaption to Subhumid Geographical Environment.* Lawrence: University of Kansas Press, 1944.

Mangum, A. W., and J. A. Drake. *Soil Survey of the Russell Area, Kansas.* Washington: Government Printing Office, 1904.

Marshall, James. *Santa Fe: The Railroad that Built an Empire.* New York: Random House, 1945.

Masterson, V. V. *The Katy Railroad and the Last Frontier.* Norman: University of Oklahoma Press, 1952.

Mattison, Roy Harold. Burlington Railroad Land Grant and the Tax Controversy in Boone County. Unpublished master's thesis, University of Nebraska, 1936.

Maxwell, James A. *Federal Subsidies to the Provincial Governments in Canada.* Cambridge: Harvard University Press, 1937.

Mering, Otto von. *The Shifting and Incidence of Taxation.* Philadelphia: Blakiston Company, 1942.

Merrill, Horace S. *Bourbon Democracy of the Middle West, 1865–1896.* Baton Rouge: Louisiana State University Press, 1953.

Meyer, Balthasar Henry. *Railway Legislation in the United States.* New York: Macmillan Company, 1903.

Miller, Glenn H. Financing the Boom in Kansas, with Special Reference to Municipal Indebtedness and the Real Estate Mortgages. Unpublished master's thesis, University of Kansas, 1954.

Miller, Raymond C. The Populist Party in Kansas. Unpublished doctor's dissertation, University of Chicago, 1928.

Million, John W. *State Aid to Railways in Missouri.* Chicago: University of Chicago Press, 1896.

Mitchell, Joseph Clark. Early History of Phelps County, Nebraska. Unpublished master's thesis, University of Nebraska, 1927.

Morton, J. Sterling. *Illustrated History of Nebraska.* 3 vols. Lincoln: Jacob North and Company, 1905–1913.

———, and Albert Watkins. *History of Nebraska From the Earliest Explorations of the Transmississippi Region.* Revised edition. Lincoln: Western Publishing and Engraving Company, 1918.

Nebraska Daughters of the American Revolution. *Collection of Nebraska Pioneer Reminiscences.* Cedar Rapids, Iowa: The Torch Press, 1916.

Nims, Fred A., and Hal E. McNeil. *Compilation of the General Railroad Legislation of the State of Michigan.* Detroit: Times Steam Printing and Binding Company, 1870.

Noble, F. H. *Taxation in Iowa: Historical Sketch, Present Status and Suggested Reforms.* New York: Columbia University Press, 1897.

Nye, Russel Blaine. *Midwestern Progressive Politics: A Historical Study of Its Origins and Development, 1870-1950.* East Lansing: Michigan State College Press, 1951.

Oberholtzer, Ellis Paxson. *Jay Cooke, Financier of the Civil War.* 2 vols. Philadelphia: G. W. Jacobs and Company, 1907.

Official State Atlas of Nebraska. Philadelphia: Evarts and Kirk, 1885.

Olson, James C. *History of Nebraska.* Lincoln: University of Nebraska Press, 1955.

———. *J. Sterling Morton.* Lincoln: University of Nebraska Press, 1942.

Orfield, Matthias N. *Federal Land Grants to the States with Special Reference to Minnesota. University of Minnesota Studies in the Social Sciences.* No. 2. Minneapolis, 1915.

Ottoson, Howard W., Andrew R. Aandahl, and L. Burbank Kristjanson. *Valuation of Farm Land for Tax Assessment. Bulletin of the Nebraska Agricultural Experiment Station.* No. 27. University of Nebraska, Lincoln, December, 1954.

Overton, Richard C. *Burlington West: A Colonization History of the Burlington Railroad.* Cambridge: Harvard University Press, 1941.

Peffer, E. Louise. *The Closing of the Public Domain: Disposal and Reservation Policies, 1900-1950.* Stanford: Stanford University Press, 1951.

Peffer, William A. *The Farmer's Side: His Troubles and Their Remedy.* New York: D. Appleton and Company, 1892.

Perkins, Jacob R. *Trails, Rails and War: The Life of General G. M. Dodge.* Indianapolis: Bobbs-Merrill, 1929.

Peterson, Harold J. *Federal Payment in Place of Taxes in Harlan County.* Unpublished master's thesis, University of Nebraska, 1953.

Pierce, Harry H. *Railroads of New York: A Study of Government Aid, 1826-1875.* Cambridge: Harvard University Press, 1953.

The Pioneer Record. 4 vols. Verdun, Nebraska: Richardson County Pioneer Society, 1893-1897.

Poppleton, Andrew J. *Reminiscences.* [Omaha: Union Pacific Railroad Company, 1915].

Ratner, Sidney. *American Taxation: Its History as a Social Force in Democracy.* New York: W. W. Norton and Company, 1942.

Ream, Virginia B. *The Kansas Pacific.* Unpublished master's thesis, University of Kansas, 1920.

Reed, St. Clair Griffin. *A History of the Texas Railroads.* Houston, Texas: St. Clair Publishing Company, 1941.

Reeves, Harry Elton. *Application of Frontier Safety Valve Theory to Nebraska Pioneers.* Unpublished master's thesis, University of Nebraska, 1938.

Richardson, Elmo R., and Alan W. Farley. *John Palmer Usher, Lincoln's Secretary of the Interior.* Lawrence: University of Kansas Press, 1960.

Riegel, Robert E. *The Story of the Western Railroads.* New York: Macmillan Company, 1926.

Robbins, Roy M. *Our Landed Heritage: The Public Domain, 1776-1936.* Princeton: Princeton University Press, 1942.

Rochester, Anna. *The Populist Movement in the United States.* New York: International Publishers Company, 1944.

Rosewater, Victor. *The Life and Times of Edward Rosewater.* Typewritten, n.d. Donated to the Nebraska State Historical Society by the Edward Rosewater Family.

Ross, Harry E. *What Price White Rock? A Chronicle of Northwestern Jewell County.* Burr Oak, Kansas: *Burr Oak Herald,* 1937.

Russell, Robert R. *Improvement of Communication with the Pacific Coast as an Issue in American Politics.* Cedar Rapids, Iowa: The Torch Press, 1948.

Sabin, Edwin L. *Building the Pacific Railway.* Philadelphia: J. B. Lippincott Company, 1919.

Sakolski, Aaron M. *The Great American Land Bubble.* New York: Harper and Brothers, 1932.

Sanborn, John B. *Congressional Grants of Land in Aid of Railways. University of Wisconsin Bulletin in Economics, Political Science, and History.* Vol. 2, no. 3. Madison, 1899.

Sawyer, Andrew J. *History of Lincoln and Lancaster County.* 2 vols. Chicago: S. J. Clarke, 1916.

Schmidt, E. B. *An Appraisal of the Nebraska Tax System.* Lincoln: University of Nebraska Press, 1941.

Schmidt, Nicholas J., Jr. Evolving Geographic Concepts of the Kansas Area with Emphasis on the Land Literature of the Santa Fe Railroad. Unpublished master's thesis, University of Kansas, 1949.

Schoville, C. H., comp. *History of the Elkhorn Valley of Nebraska: An Album of History and Biography.* Chicago: National Publishing Company, 1892.

Seligman, Edwin R. A. *Essays in Taxation.* 8th edition. New York: Macmillan Company, 1915.

———. *The Shifting and Incidence of Taxation.* 3d edition, revised. New York: Columbia University Press, 1910.

Sellin, Lloyd Bernard. The Settlement of Nebraska to 1880. Unpublished master's thesis, University of California at Los Angeles, 1940.

Shallcross, William J. *Romance of a Village* [Bellevue]. Omaha: The Author, 1954.

Shannon, Fred A. *The Farmer's Last Frontier: Agriculture, 1860–1897.* New York: Farrar and Rinehart, 1945.

Sharp, Paul F. *Agrarian Revolt in Western Canada: A Survey Showing American Parallels.* Minneapolis: University of Minnesota Press, 1948.

Sheldon, Addison E. *Land Systems and Land Policies in Nebraska. Publications of the Nebraska State Historical Society.* Vol. 22. Lincoln, 1936.

———. *Nebraska: The Land and the People.* 3 vols. Chicago: Lewis Publishing Company, 1931.

Shumway, Grant Lee. *History of Western Nebraska and Its People.* 2 vols. Lincoln: Western Publishing and Engraving Company, 1921.

Skeen, Lydia A. The History of the Cattle Industry in the Flint Hills of Kansas. Unpublished master's thesis, Kansas State College, 1938.

Smalley, Eugene V. *History of the Northern Pacific Railroad.* New York: G. P. Putnam's Sons, 1883.

Smith, C. Henry. *Mennonites: A Brief History of Their Origin and Later Development in Both Europe and America.* Bern, Indiana: Mennonite Book Concern, 1923.

Smith, Henry Nash. *Virgin Land: The American West as Symbol and Myth.* Cambridge: Harvard University Press, 1950.

Smith, Hilda. The Advance and Recession of the Agricultural Frontier in Kansas, 1865–1900. Unpublished master's thesis, University of Minnesota, 1931.

Smith, J. Harold. History of the Grange in Kansas, 1883–1897. Unpublished master's thesis, University of Kansas, 1940.

Sorenson, Alfred. *The Story of Omaha.* Omaha: National Printing Company, 1923.

Spencer, Morris Nelson. The Union Pacific's Utilization of Its Land Grant, with Emphasis on Its Colonization Program. Unpublished doctor's dissertation, University of Nebraska, 1950.

Stough, Dale P. *History of Hamilton and Clay Counties* [Nebraska]. 2 vols. Chicago: S. J. Clarke, 1921.

Taylor, Carl Cleveland. *The Farmers' Movement, 1620–1920.* New York: American Book Company, 1953.

Taylor, George Rogers, and Irene D. Neu. *The American Railroad Network, 1861–1890.* Cambridge: Harvard University Press, 1956.

Thompson, Leonard W. The History of Railway Development in Kansas. Unpublished doctor's dissertation, University of Iowa, 1942.

Tipton, Thomas Weston. *Forty Years of Nebraska at Home and in Congress. Proceedings and Collections of the Nebraska State Historical Society.* Vol. 4. Lincoln, 1902.

Trottman, Nelson. *History of the Union Pacific: A Financial and Economic Survey.* New York: Ronald Press, 1923.

U. S. Department of Agriculture, Soil Conservation Service and the Kansas Agricultural Experiment Station, cooperating. *Physical Land Conditions Affecting Use, Conservation, and Management of Land Resources, Russell County, Kansas.* Manhattan: Kansas State University, 1954.

Vance, Amos Milton. Nebraska Local Government. Unpublished master's thesis, University of Nebraska, 1915.

Villard, Henry. *Memoirs of Henry Villard, Journalist and Financier.* 2 vols. Boston: Houghton, Mifflin and Company, 1904.

Wakeley, Arthur C. *Omaha and Douglas County.* 2 vols. Chicago: S. J. Clarke, 1917.

Waldron, Nell B. Colonization of Kansas from 1861 to 1890. Unpublished doctor's dissertation, Northwestern University, 1923.

Washington Tax Conference. *Taxation in Washington: Papers and Discussions of the State Tax Conference at the University of Washington, May 27, 28, and 29, 1914.* Seattle: University of Washington Press, 1914.

Waters, L. L. *Steel Trails to Santa Fe.* Lawrence: University of Kansas Press, 1950.

Weaver, James Baird. *A Call to Action. An Interpretation of the Great Uprising. Its Source and Causes.* Des Moines: Iowa Printing Company, 1892.

Webb, Walter Prescott. *The Great Plains.* New York: Ginn and Company, 1931.

Wheeler, Mabel R. The Germanic Element in the Settlement and Development of Kansas. Unpublished master's thesis, University of Kansas, 1920.

Wilder, D. W. *The Annals of Kansas, 1541–1885.* Topeka: State Printer, 1886.

Wildes, Bessie E. *Governmental Agencies of the State of Kansas, 1861–1946. Bulletin of the University of Kansas, Governmental Research Series,* no. 4, Lawrence, 1946.

Williamson, H. A. The Effect of Railroads on the Development of Kansas to 1870. Unpublished master's thesis, Kansas State College, 1930.

Wilson, Neill C., and Frank J. Taylor. *Southern Pacific: The Roaring Story of a Fighting Railroad.* New York: McGraw-Hill, 1952.

Woodward, C. Vann. *Origins of the New South, 1877–1913.* Baton Rouge: Louisiana State University Press, 1960.

———. *Reunion and Reaction: The Compromise of 1877 and the End of Reconstruction.* Boston: Little, Brown and Company, 1951.

Wolf, Frank E. Railway Development of Kansas. Unpublished master's thesis, University of Kansas, 1917.

Wright, Robert M. *Dodge City, the Cowboy Capital, and the Great Southwest in the Days of the Wild Indian, the Buffalo, and Cowboy, Dance Halls, Gambling Halls and Bad Men.* Wichita: *Wichita Eagle* Press, 1913.

Zornow, William Frank. *Kansas: A History of the Jayhawk State.* Norman: University of Oklahoma Press, 1957.

Index

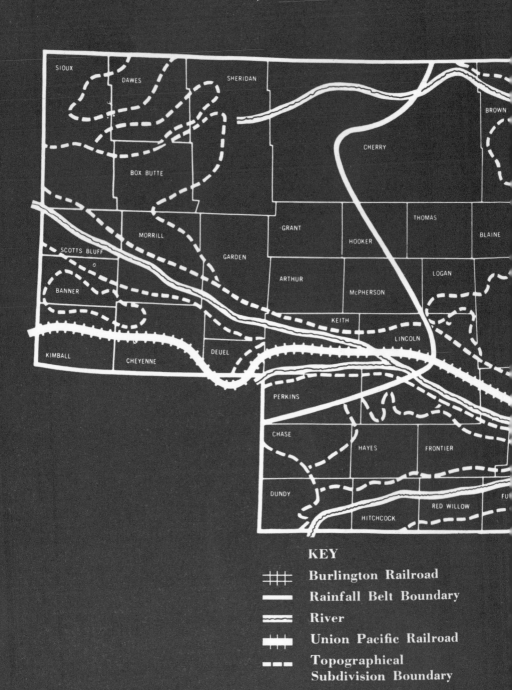

The State of Nebraska

KEY

┼┼┼	**Burlington Railroad**
▬▬▬	**Rainfall Belt Boundary**
～～～	**River**
┼┼┼	**Union Pacific Railroad**
▬ ▬ ▬	**Topographical Subdivision Boundary**